Writing for the Government

THE ALLYN AND BACON SERIES
IN TECHNICAL COMMUNICATION
Series Editor: Sam Dragga, Texas Tech University

Thomas T. Barker
*Writing Software Documentation:
A Task-Oriented Approach, Second Edition*

Carol M. Barnum
Usability Testing and Research

Deborah S. Bosley
*Global Contexts: Case Studies in International
Technical Communication*

Melody Bowdon and Blake Scott
*Service-Learning in Technical and
Professional Communication*

R. Stanley Dicks
*Management Principles and Practices
for Technical Communicators*

Paul M. Dombrowski
Ethics in Technical Communication

David K. Farkas
Principles of Web Design

Laura Gurak
Oral Presentations for Technical Communication

Sandra Harner and Tom Zimmerman
Technical Marketing Communication

Barbara A. Heifferon
Writing in the Health Professions

TyAnna K. Herrington
A Legal Primer for the Digital Age

Richard Johnson-Sheehan
Writing Proposals

Dan Jones
Technical Writing Style

Charles Kostelnick and David D. Roberts
*Designing Visual Strategies for
Professional Communicators*

**Victoria Mikelonis, Signe T. Betsinger,
and Constance Kampf**
Grant-Seeking in an Electronic Age

Ann M. Penrose and Steven B. Katz
*Writing in the Sciences: Exploring
Conventions of Scientific Discourse,
Second Edition*

Gerald J. Savage and Dale L. Sullivan
*Writing a Professional Life: Stories
of Technical Communicators On
and Off the Job*

Writing for the Government

Libby Allison
Miriam F. Williams

PEARSON
Longman

New York Boston San Francisco
London Toronto Sydney Tokyo Singapore Madrid
Mexico City Munich Paris Cape Town Hong Kong Montreal

Acquisitions Editor: Lauren A. Finn
Executive Marketing Manager: Sandra McGuire
Production Manager: Stacey Kulig
Project Coordination, Text Design, and Electronic Page Makeup: Pre-Press PMG
Cover Designer/Manager: Nancy Danahy
Manufacturing Buyer: Lucy Hebard
Printer and Binder: R.R. Donnelley and Sons/Crawfordsville
Cover Printer: R.R. Donnelley and Sons/Crawfordsville

Library of Congress Cataloging-in-Publication Data
Allison, Libby.
Writing for the government / Libby Allison, Miriam F. Williams.
p. cm.
Includes bibliographical references and indexes.
ISBN 978-0-321-42701-4
1. Government report writing—Handbooks, manuals, etc. 2. Government report writing—United States. 3.
Authorship—Handbooks, manuals, etc. I.
Williams, Miriam F. II. Title.
JF1525.R46.A55 2008
808'.06635173—dc22
2007019019

Copyright © 2008 by Pearson Education, Inc.

Please visit us at http://www.ablongman.com

ISBN 13: 978-0-321-42701-4
ISBN 10: 0-321-42701-7

1 2 3 4 5 6 7 8 9 10—DOC—10 09 08 07

DEDICATION

Libby dedicates this book to her husband, Joe West, to her brother and sister-in-law Jack and Betty Allison, and to her parents, John A. Allison, Jr. and Anne Rigler Allison. Miriam dedicates this book to her parents, Eddie W. Williams, Sr. and Nora J. Williams.

CONTENTS

PART 3   Writing to Communicate Policy Issues to Agencies and the Public   107

6   Public Policy Reports   109

7   Government Grants and Proposals   130

FOREWORD
by the Series Editor

The Allyn and Bacon Series in Technical Communication is designed to meet the continuing education needs of professional technical communicators, both those who desire to upgrade or update their own communication abilities as well as those who train or supervise writers, editors, and artists within their organization. This series also serves the growing number of students enrolled in undergraduate and graduate programs in technical communication. Such programs offer a wide variety of courses beyond the introductory technical writing course—advanced courses for which fully satisfactory and appropriately focused textbooks have often been impossible to locate.

The chief characteristic of the books in this series is their consistent effort to integrate theory and practice. The books offer both research-based and experience-based instruction, describing not only what to do and how to do it but explaining why. The instructors who teach advanced courses and the students who enroll in these courses are looking for more than rigid rules and ad hoc guidelines. They want books that demonstrate theoretical sophistication and a solid foundation in the research of the field as well as pragmatic advice and perceptive applications. Instructors and students will also find these books filled with activities and assignments adaptable to the classroom and to the self-guided learning processes of professional technical communicators.

To operate effectively in the field of technical communication, today's technical communicators require extensive training in the creation, analysis, and design of information for both domestic and international audiences, for both paper and electronic environments. The books in the Allyn and Bacon Series address those subjects that are most frequently taught at the undergraduate and graduate levels as a direct response to both the educational needs of students and the practical demands of business and industry. Additional books will be developed for the series in order to satisfy or anticipate changes in writing technologies, academic curricula, and the profession of technical communication.

Sam Dragga
Texas Tech University

PREFACE

From the Declaration of Independence in 1776 to a city hall website today, government writers have penned the words that have shaped and continue to shape our lives as Americans. *Writing for the Government* introduces students to the large, diverse, and interesting world of government writing by presenting and discussing a wide range of government documents and webpages from varied agencies and organizations. The book underscores the importance of the long-standing, time-tested rhetorical principles and approaches of knowing an audience, having a clear purpose, and understanding the cultural context of a writing environment as fundamental to effective communication. In the spirit of the Allyn and Bacon series in Technical Communication, *Writing for the Government* ties together rhetorical theory and writing practice.

Audience for *Writing for the Government*

The student audience for *Writing for the Government* includes undergraduate and graduate students in technical communication, rhetoric and composition, public administration, political science, social work, and any other class in any discipline that involves writing and interpreting government documents. This textbook is also useful to anyone beginning a career in government or government employees who have writing responsibilities.

In addition, the book serves the needs of new as well as seasoned faculty who teach courses about writing for the government. With this textbook, we want to give new teachers of government writing confidence that they can teach these classes; yet, at the same time, we offer seasoned teachers fresh ideas, materials, information, and resources to inspire their students.

Purpose for *Writing for the Government*

Ultimately, the purpose of the textbook is to prepare and develop better government writers. We want to help students develop the analytical, writing, and communicating skills necessary to write and communicate well at any level of government. Furthermore, the textbook is designed to prepare students to become "adaptable" writers no matter what position or title they may hold in a government job, or the writing tasks involved, or the agency or organization where they go to work. We believe that by knowing their audience or audiences, the purposes for which they write, and the cultural context of a document or webpage, they can more easily slide into the role of the writer—and communicate more effectively.

Cultural Context for *Writing for the Government*

From excerpts of large-scale investigative reports to brief emails, *Writing for the Government* includes "real" government documents from "real" government writers, not hypothetical documents or situations. We believe "real" documents garner respect and appreciation from students because they can see the application of their learning experience. Writing matters related to agencies and organizations as dissimilar as the Federal Aviation Administration (FAA) and the Food and Drug Administration (FDA) and from state governments as far apart as Georgia, New York, and Oregon are presented in this textbook. We devote an entire chapter to writing government websites. Many examples are annotated with explanations for students to compare the documents and or websites with the lessons presented in the chapters. We want readers to understand not only the purposes and contexts of some types of government documents but also how and whether the documents were effectively used historically and in present-day government organizations. In addition, throughout the textbook chapters include a working vocabulary for government writers.

Teaching Strategies

Rationale for the Organization of this Textbook

Writing for the Government is divided into four parts: Part 1 (Chapters 1 and 2) is an introduction to the rhetorical principles and approaches that underpin successful government communication.

Part 2 (Chapters 3–5) is about documents written to develop public policy, which is how public officials address ways for citizens to solve problems, make decisions, and complete tasks. Those ways appear in rules and regulations, handbooks, and policy memorandums.

Part 3 (Chapters 6–8) is about reports, grant proposals, and websites used to implement public policy. Because many of the documents that develop policy have been around much longer than documents that implement policy, the organization of this textbook represents the developmental phases of policy writing as well as a chronological ordering of how these writing conventions have emerged. With this organization, we walk teachers and students through the policy development and implementation phases by introducing them to the documents used in various stages of these processes. However, we should add that because Chapters 3–8 focus on specific types of documents and/or webpages, teachers may also choose which chapters they want to emphasize and/or the way the chapters are scheduled for study during a semester.

Part 4 of the textbook are three case studies. The case studies are about Hurricane Katrina, the Southwest Florida Water Management District (SWFWMD), and the National Multiple Sclerosis Society. These case studies are opportunities for students to read, think about, discuss, and write to further apply the lessons within the textbook as the details of the cases add contexts for which the documents are set.

Special Features of *Writing for the Government*

- Activities and assignments. The end of each chapter has activities and as-signments with questions, so that students can engage in thoughtful dis-cussion and practice writing. There are in-class and out-of-class activities and assignments, which students can do as individuals or in groups. All of the activities and assignments are to bring home to students the relevancy of the chapter's information and lessons to their lives, no matter where in the country they live.
- Copies of the Declaration of Independence, the U.S. Constitution, and the Bill of Rights in Appendix B.
- Detailed Index at the end of the book.
- Glossary. The glossary has definitions for any words or terms we believe might be helpful to readers.
- List of federal agencies. This is a list of federal agencies from the U.S. De-partment of Justice website.
- Vignettes. Each chapter begins with a vignette to peak students' interest and underscore the lessons within each chapter.

Chapter Summaries

- Part 1: Government Writing: Theory, Principles, and Ethics. Chapter 1: Introduction to *Writing for the Government*

  The aim of Chapter 1 is to introduce the important rhetorical principles and approaches of knowing an audience, having a clear purpose, and un-derstanding the cultural context—for the audience, writer, or communica-tor, and for the government document or website. Chapter 1 focuses on how government writers get to know their audiences, while Chapter 2 addresses purpose and cultural context.

- Chapter 2: Purpose and Cultural Context

  While Chapter 1 focuses on knowing an audience, Chapter 2 emphasizes having a purpose and understanding the cultural context of a government writing situation. The chapter discusses how deciding what you want to ac-complish is the *purpose* of a document or website and that sometimes the best means for shaping effective communication of a document or website is by *genre*, the writing and design conventions of an agency or organization.

  The cultural context comprises the historical, political, social, economic, ethical, and technological circumstances and constraints of the time. It is the confluence of the social exchange of people within a particular time and place. In the case of government writers, the cultural context encom-passes their interactions with their audiences, with each other within their own agencies, with other agencies, and with the documents they read, study, and create.

  A large part of the chapter is directed toward ethical issues in govern-ment writing. We discuss how a text creates a professional *ethos*, and the importance of that *ethos* for effective writing that demonstrates rhetorical skill in accommodating public input and ethical consensus building among potentially adversarial stakeholders.

- Part 2: Writing to Make Public Policy
- Chapter 3: Rules and Regulations

    Chapter 3 describes the processes and procedures involved in the development of rules and regulations, preambles, public comments, and other documents that government writers use in the development of regulations. We introduce the *Federal Register,* examples of regulatory documents, and discuss the audiences for these documents. We discuss the rhetorical and political challenges that policy writers encounter when trying to negotiate the wants and needs of competing constituencies as well as the rhetorical strategies government agencies currently use to improve communication with the public.

- Chapter 4: Policy Handbooks, Manuals, and Guides

    The invention and maintenance of internal government agency handbooks, which explain the specific steps involved in enforcing and implementing policy, are extremely important for internal government agency staff. We discuss the specific stakeholders, internal and external to government agencies, addressed by writers of government handbooks and the various project management issues and technologies used to keep handbooks current and accessible.

- Chapter 5: Policy Memorandums

    In government agencies, policy memorandums are written before, during, and after the implementation of public policies. In this chapter, we present various types of policy memorandums and the various contexts in which these documents are created. We also present guidelines for writing persuasive policy memorandums. There are numerous public documents that illustrate the unique considerations that government writers must address when drafting internal memorandums—as well as the rhetorical strategies that government writers use to communicate within government agencies and across jurisdictions. We also discuss the difference between public documents and confidential government documents and how these documents are obtained by constituents.

- Part 3: Writing to Communicate Policy Issues to Agencies and the Public
- Chapter 6: Government Reports

    In this chapter, we present formal reports written by investigators for public review, such as *The 9-11 Commission Report* and Surgeon General reports. We discuss studies that explain the various purposes for government reports. Specifically, we discuss reports used to investigate policy issues, describe past events, make recommendations for policy change and prescribe steps for implementation of policy changes.

- Chapter 7: Government Proposals and Grants

    In Chapter 3, we introduced students to the *Federal Register*, which is the federal publication that announces proposed and adopted federal regulations. The *Federal Register* is also responsible for publishing federal requests for proposals (RFPs) and requests for applications (RFAs) that make public announcements of new grant opportunities, contracting opportunities, and grant awards. In this chapter we describe the various purposes for government grants and the grant proposal development process.

- Chapter 8: Government Websites

A large study by the Pew Internet & Life Project done in July 2003 found that 77% of Internet users, or 97 million Americans, went online to search for information from government agencies or to communicate with them. This was a 50% increase from the same time in 2002 (Horrigan). Undoubtedly, the number of Americans getting online to search government websites has risen substantially from 2003, and as more Americans go online, government information online becomes increasingly important. This chapter is an introduction to writing and designing government websites for the lone webmaster for a small town community website or for someone starting as part of a team for a large federal government agency website. Because the writing and designing of websites are so closely related, the chapter presents introductory information about website designing too. Regardless of where they work, knowledgeable government website writers, designers, and developers understand that these websites are more than information portals; they are a means for Americans to be closer to and more involved with their government.

- Part 4: Case Studies
- Case Study 1 is about Hurricane Katrina. We chose a case study on Hurricane Katrina not only because it is arguably the worst natural disaster in American history, which played out on Americans' television screens, but also because all levels of government from local, state, regional, and federal were involved. In December 2005 when Louisiana Governor Kathleen Blanco's office handed over documents to Congressional committees investigating the government's failure in preparing for and responding to Hurricane Katrina, among the 100,000 pages of documents were emails, police reports, weather reports, logs of calls to be rescued, public statements, and many others (Simpson). This case study includes a sample of these documents and others from a variety of governmental agencies.
- Case Study 2 is about the Southwest Florida Water Management District (SWFWMD). Every day Americans across the country turn on faucets without worrying whether clean and sanitary water will come out. We take for granted one of the most important resources to sustain life. Florida is a state blessed by great water resources; yet, because of its phenomenal growth and the growth's affect on water resources, there are ongoing large conflicts about the resources, as is the case in many parts of the country. With an increasingly environmentally aware student population, this case study offers students a look into the different documents in the vital role of a regional agency concerned with environmental issues from water resources to wetlands and into the function of interagency cooperation.
- Case Study 3 is about the National Multiple Sclerosis Society. You may wonder why we chose a nonprofit organization because it is not a governmental agency per se. However, the nonprofit sector is the third largest economic sector of the country aside from the government and private sector (*Encyclopedia of Small Business*). Many college graduates, especially

students from humanities and social sciences begin their careers at non-profits, where they build on the civic consciousness inspired by their college courses, and nonprofit employees contribute to the writing of many government documents, and sometimes nonprofits' life blood is government grants. This chapter about a nonprofit health-related organization focuses on advocacy writing. Multiple Sclerosis is the most common neurological disease leading to disability in young adults in the United States.

WORKS CITED

Horrigan, John. B. "How Americans Get in Touch with Government: Internet Users Benefit from the Efficiency of E-government, but Multiple Channels are still Needed for Citizens to Reach Agencies and Solve Problems." Pew Internet & American Life Project. 24 May 2004. 31 Oct. 2006 <http://www.pewinternet.org>.

"Nonprofit." *Encyclopedia of Small Business*. 15 Feb. 2007 <http://www.answers.com/topic/nonprofit>.

Simpson, Doug. "Blanco's Katrina Correspondence Reveals Extent of Chaos." Associated Press. 4 Dec. 2005. AOL news. 4 Dec. 2005 <http://aolsvc.news.aol.com/>.

ACKNOWLEDGMENTS

We wish to thank Thereisa Coleman, Maureen M. Hourigan, and Jennifer Ramirez Johnson for proofreading and editing help with this book. We wish to thank the following colleagues who reviewed our manuscript and offered valuable suggestions for revision: Anthony Di Renzo, Ithaca College; Huey Crisp, The University of Arkansas at Little Rock; James M. Dubinsky, Virginia Tech; Janice R Walker, Georgia Southern University; Robert McEachern, Southern Conneticut State University. We also want to thank our editors: Technical Communication Series Editor Sam Dragga of Texas Tech University; Lauren Finn, Acquisitions Editor of Pearson Longman; and Carmen O'Donnell, Editorial Assistant of Pearson Longman. In addition we thank our family and friends, many of whom are public servants, who helped us understand the complexities of government writing, and all government employees, including those who worked on the important documents in this book, who write to make our democracy work for us.

Libby Allison
Miriam F. Williams

PART 1

Government Writing: Theory, Principles, and Ethics

Introduction to Writing for the Government

About 10 A.M. Sunday, August 28, 2005, meteorologist Robert Ricks, Lead Forecaster, sat in front of his computer in the National Weather Service office in Slidell, Louisiana, and chose what has become some of the strongest and most prophetic words in the history of weather forecasting. Trying to warn citizens of his beloved New Orleans of the impending disaster from Hurricane Katrina, an approaching Category 5 hurricane of the highest magnitude, heading straight for the delta areas, Ricks knew that the typical NOAA (National Oceanic & Atmospheric Administration) weather bulletin language just wouldn't do. Backed by his co-workers, computer technology, and historical experience, Ricks issued an Urgent Weather Message (see Figure 1.1) to radio, TV, newspapers, and every available outlet for mass communication.

In the days that followed, Americans watched their TVs in horror as citizens in New Orleans and surrounding communities begged to get rescued from the rooftops of their homes, which were being submerged in toxic water because of breaks in the city's levees, as people handed off their babies to strangers on buses (so if the parents couldn't make it out because of the crowds, their children wouldn't die from dehydration), as elderly sat in wheelchairs in blazing sunshine without food or water, and as people abandoned their much-loved pets to evacuate. It was one of the most destructive natural disasters in American history, if not the most destructive. It was an event many never imagined happening in our country.

Ricks said he had chosen a **template** with impact statements—blocks of wording that describe certain consequences of a weather event—for a Category 4 landfall hurricane. He had never used a template with as many impact statements describing such potentially disastrous consequences (Ricks, Interview). The language was strong and vivid. Barry Goldsmith and Walter Zaleski of the Tampa office of the National Weather Service had developed the templates in 1999 as part of a project to provide real-world information so users could know "what would actually happen" (Goldsmith) in weather-related events. However, according to Ricks, it is up to the individual forecaster to determine which impact statements will go out to the media and public.

```
000
WWUS74 KLIX 281550
NPWLIX

URGENT - WEATHER MESSAGE
NATIONAL WEATHER SERVICE NEW ORLEANS LA
1011 AM CDT SUN AUG 28 2005

...DEVASTATING DAMAGE EXPECTED...

.HURRICANE KATRINA...A MOST POWERFUL HURRICANE WITH UNPRECEDENTED
STRENGTH...RIVALING THE INTENSITY OF HURRICANE CAMILLE OF 1969.

MOST OF THE AREA WILL BE UNINHABITABLE FOR WEEKS...PERHAPS LONGER.
AT LEAST ONE HALF OF WELL CONSTRUCTED HOMES WILL HAVE ROOF AND WALL
FAILURE. ALL GABLED ROOFS WILL FAIL...LEAVING THOSE HOMES SEVERELY
DAMAGED OR DESTROYED.

THE MAJORITY OF INDUSTRIAL BUILDINGS WILL BECOME NON FUNCTIONAL.
PARTIAL TO COMPLETE WALL AND ROOF FAILURE IS EXPECTED. ALL WOOD
FRAMED LOW RISING APARTMENT BUILDINGS WILL BE DESTROYED. CONCRETE
BLOCK LOW RISE APARTMENTS WILL SUSTAIN MAJOR DAMAGE...INCLUDING SOME
WALL AND ROOF FAILURE.

HIGH RISE OFFICE AND APARTMENT BUILDINGS WILL SWAY DANGEROUSLY...
A FEW TO THE POINT OF TOTAL COLLAPSE. ALL WINDOWS WILL BLOW OUT.

AIRBORNE DEBRIS WILL BE WIDESPREAD...AND MAY INCLUDE HEAVY ITEMS SUCH
AS HOUSEHOLD APPLIANCES AND EVEN LIGHT VEHICLES. SPORT UTILITY
VEHICLES AND LIGHT TRUCKS WILL BE MOVED. THE BLOWN DEBRIS WILL CREATE
ADDITIONAL DESTRUCTION. PERSONS...PETS...AND LIVESTOCK EXPOSED TO THE
WINDS WILL FACE CERTAIN DEATH IF STRUCK.

POWER OUTAGES WILL LAST FOR WEEKS...AS MOST POWER POLES WILL BE DOWN
AND TRANSFORMERS DESTROYED. WATER SHORTAGES WILL MAKE HUMAN SUFFERING
INCREDIBLE BY MODERN STANDARDS.

THE VAST MAJORITY OF NATIVE TREES WILL BE SNAPPED OR UPROOTED. ONLY
THE HEARTIEST WILL REMAIN STANDING...BUT BE TOTALLY DEFOLIATED. FEW
CROPS WILL REMAIN. LIVESTOCK LEFT EXPOSED TO THE WINDS WILL BE
KILLED.

AN INLAND HURRICANE WIND WARNING IS ISSUED WHEN SUSTAINED WINDS NEAR
HURRICANE FORCE...OR FREQUENT GUSTS AT OR ABOVE HURRICANE FORCE...
ARE CERTAIN WITHIN THE NEXT 12 TO 24 HOURS.

ONCE TROPICAL STORM AND HURRICANE FORCE WINDS ONSET...DO NOT VENTURE
OUTSIDE!
```

FIGURE 1.1 Excerpt from "Inland Hurricane Warning." Source: National Oceanic & Atmospheric Administration. http://www.srh.noaa.gov/

Ricks went through the weather bulletin template, point by point, validating each statement. He was trying to eliminate anything he thought did not seem legitimate (Ricks, Interview). However, he knew the statements were valid from his experience going through hurricanes Betsy and Camille in the Lower Ninth Ward, the section of New Orleans hardest hit by the levee flooding.

Even though every day forecasters make careful educated guesses in their weather bulletins, Ricks understood that this particular one was very risky. Before it was sent out, the message was scrutinized as much as possible in the time allowed; Ricks's co-workers met to confer about it, and in the "Area Forecast Discussion" summary of their discussion that day, it said, "Southeast Louisiana seems poised for a date with destiny as Category 5 Hurricane Katrina continues [toward]. . . the greater New Orleans area. . . . The worst can be anticipated and urgency is being stressed in all products [bulletins] as a worst case hurricane scenario for this very fragile and vulnerable stretch of U.S. coastline. . . . Things will be deteriorating steadily from this point forward for the next 24 hours. . . . Good luck and Godspeed to all in the path of this storm" (Ricks, Email). Even Ricks's regional director, who rarely does, phoned to question the validity of the bulletin. Ricks said, "I did it at the time because of a sense of duty. It was a calculated risk of the event coming to fruition" (Ricks, Interview).

On one hand, some say the warning message contributed to saving many lives (Kirst); others say that few, including the media, heeded the severity of the warning (Brian Williams). However, in a 2006 report a U.S. House of Representatives Select Bipartisan Committee found that the forecasts by the National Weather Service were not only timely and accurate but moreover responsible for saving lives (70). Also an Executive Report from the White House on the Federal Response to Hurricane Katrina praised the Weather Service for developing warning language ahead of time so that they did not have to waste time creating the impact statements; they could be issued immediately. Today, Ricks's historic Urgent Weather Message is among the items in the Smithsonian National Museum of American History, Hurricane Katrina collection (National Museum).

Unlike employees of many government agencies, National Weather Service personnel write and issue different communication with the public daily, and although Ricks's writing responsibilities during the days of Hurricane Katrina do not represent typical types of writing done by government writers, they do demonstrate how critical governmental writing can be for Americans. The investigative reports after the 9/11 terrorist attacks and the space shuttles *Challenger* and *Columbia* disasters are other examples of the importance of governmental writing. However, these documents—unlike the weather bulletins, which are done "on the fly" as Ricks calls it (Interview)—are written, developed, edited, and reviewed by large numbers of people over a long time period before being finalized and released. Ricks's co-workers and supervisors, who are also weather experts, did review Ricks's message, but the message had to be relayed to the public very quickly.

This textbook is about the world of technical writing and communicating for the government. *Writing for the Government* covers a wide spectrum of writing and communicating activities in local, state, federal agencies, and nonprofit organizations. Our purpose is to help you develop the analytical, writing, and communication skills necessary to write and communicate well for any level of government. The aim of Chapter 1 and Chapter 2 of *Writing for the Government* is to provide some important principles and approaches to analyzing, writing, editing, designing, and distributing government documents. These principles and approaches are knowing an audience, having a clear purpose, and understanding the **cultural context** for the audience, for the writer or communicator, and for the document or website. Chapter 3 through Chapter 7 focus on regulations, handbooks, memorandums, reports, and proposals and Chapter 8 is about writing government websites.

Included also are case studies with numerous types of government documents and websites from the Hurricane Katrina tragedy, the Southwest Florida Water Management District, and the National Multiple Sclerosis Society, a nonprofit organization, to assist you in learning to apply the principles, approaches, and information in the earlier chapters.

Regardless of whether the final product is a paper document or website, the keys to writing, editing, and designing documents and websites as effective communication are the same: knowing your audience, having a clear purpose, and understanding the cultural context—the historical, political, social, economic, and ethical aspects—as well as technological possibilities and constraints of the time. Research-based and time-proven, these principles and approaches underpin each of the chapters, whether the subject is conventional paper documents or online documents or websites.

Today, *audience* can mean a reader, a viewer of a media presentation, or a user of a website—or all three. We use the terms *reader*, *viewer*, and *user* interchangeably throughout this textbook. Whatever they are called, readers, viewers, and users all need government information to solve problems, make decisions, and complete tasks. In a similar vein, we use *writer* at times to refer to not only writing but also editing, designing, and sometimes distributing messages—all aspects of being a government communicator. Although this textbook focuses on the writing of government documents and websites, we will also introduce various design concepts and formatting techniques of documents and websites because today's government communicator will likely be involved in all of these areas as text, visuals, and the Internet have begun to merge together.

Even though government writers may not have job titles such as technical writer or communicator or policy writer, almost every government job requires writing. There are literally hundreds of government agencies and hundreds of thousands of government employees. Excluding the U.S. Postal Service, security agencies, and military service men and women, the Federal Government, with nearly 2 million civilian employees, is the largest employer in the United States (U.S. Department of Labor "Fed Gov" 272), and the "analytical and technical nature of many government duties translates into a much higher proportion of professional, management, business, and financial occupations in the Federal Government, compared with most industries" (U.S. Department of Labor "Fed Gov" 274). Additionally, state and local governments together are also one of the "largest employers in the economy" (U.S. Department of Labor "State and Local" 279). A National Commission on Writing study by the College Board said: "Writing is a universal responsibility for professional employees in state government. All 49 respondents reported that two-thirds or more of professional employees have some responsibility for writing, either explicit or implicit" (9).

Government documents are a wide variety of types. To mention a few, they are international treaties, urban and regional plans, environmental protection permits, probation and parole forms, nonprofit grants, area water supply plans, disaster relief policy and procedures, computer system documentation for national security agencies, drug research protocols, distribution and storage records for museum artifacts, rules and regulations for child care centers, and brochures and magazines for national, state, and local parks. These documents can affect entire countries, a community, or a relatively small number of individuals.

Government writers have penned some of the most important documents in America's history, which testify to significant benchmarks. *Our Documents: 100 Milestone Documents from the National Archives* demonstrates the critical importance of documents in the development of the United States from the Declaration of Independence in 1776 to the Federal Judiciary Act in 1789 to the patent for the cotton gin in 1794 to the Louisiana Purchase Treaty of 1803 to the Treaty of Fort Laramie in 1868 to the Social Security Act of 1935 to the Executive Order 8802 Prohibiting Discrimination in the Defense Industry in 1941 to the Tonkin Gulf Resolution in 1964 to the Voting Rights Act of 1965 (Compston and Seidman).

These crucial documents required the rhetorical skill needed to make knowledge, shape public opinion, codify public policy, and construct a vision for the future. Effective government writers have problem-solving skills and political savvy with a capacity to negotiate between many disparate groups to create text that is acceptable to many, if not all, involved in an issue. They understand how to meet the needs of an audience.

Rhetorical Principles and Approaches

Audience, Purpose, and Cultural Context

In writing and communicating any information, you can count on three rhetorical principles to help ensure that your message will get across well. The word *rhetoric* is commonly thought to mean a comment that has no substance—"It is just rhetoric," is how we often express it. However, according to one of the most influential thinkers in the history of Western philosophy, Aristotle, rhetoric is the art of discovering a possible means of persuasion (15). Effective writers are able to persuade their readers because they make a careful determination of the following:

- The audience or audiences
- The purpose of the document or website
- The cultural context—the historical, political, social, economic, and ethical aspects as well as technological possibilities and constraints of a time for a document or website, the writer and reader.

Knowing an audience, having a clear purpose, and understanding the cultural context are all part of the "rhetorical situation" of a document or website (see Figure 1.2). The rhetorical situation entails the cultural context for the reader, the writer, and the document. The historical, political, social, economic, ethical, and technological factors under which the writer works impact the communicative act. For example, if a writer is working for a governmental agency or an organization that fosters technological change, then that writer's working environment within the agency can make a difference in whether information is communicated via the Internet or paper or both.

Knowing an Audience or Audiences

The audience for a particular government document or website can be the general public and/or diverse groups of people. The document or website will then have

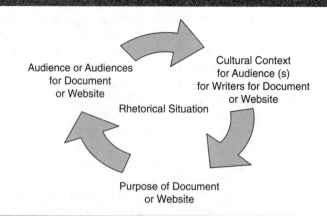

FIGURE 1.2   The rhetorical situation

more than one audience; there will be *audiences* for them. For instance, an audience, or audiences, can be activists, artists, attorneys, business owners, educators, fund-raisers, grandparents, hobby enthusiasts, industrialists, judges, lobbyists, musicians, parents, physicians, politicians, scientists, students, taxpayers, technical experts, teenagers, and/or any constituency of **stakeholders**—individuals and/or groups affected by a government communication, who thus have a "stake" or vested interest in what happens. A case in point is Ricks's "Urgent Weather Message" at the beginning of this chapter. The message was issued for the media and general public, but, as you will see in the following chapters and case studies, different government documents can be targeted for different audiences at different times; yet, they are all government writing.

Effective government writers have formal and informal opportunities to determine who the audience is for a particular document or website. One common informal approach is to ask other government writers the journalism questions of *who, what, when, where, why,* and *how.* You could ask:

Who are the readers of this document or viewers or users of this website?

What topics and information in this document or webpage might the audiences need?

When do they need this information?

Where will they need to find this information?

Why do they need this information?

How will the audiences use this information?

Demographics of an Audience

These journalistic types of questions are a beginning point for knowing an audience, but another useful way to know an audience or audiences is to consider

FIGURE 1.3 "Kids' Only" website feature. Source: EPA. http://www.epa.gov

the demographics—the characteristics or traits of individuals in a group. Typical demographic characteristics are age, income, sex, race, ethnicity, educational status, and national origin. How might understanding demographics help you in analyzing, writing, and communicating government information? Imagine the difference in how you might approach creating a website for nonnative speakers as opposed to native English speakers. What about the difference in writing and communicating to teenagers than retirees? Might vocabulary be a consideration? The Environmental Protection Agency (EPA) has a feature called "For Kids" on its website (see Figure 1.3). This is an introductory webpage to the feature; the figures are illustrated in childlike cartoons, the text is short words, and there are bright colors in it. This would appeal to children more than adults who would be looking for the more "serious" side of environmental matters. Creating a webpage like this for children, however, invites them to learn about the agency's workings.

Level of Knowledge and Expertise of an Audience

Another approach to knowing an audience or audiences is to have an understanding of the level of knowledge and/or expertise of the readers. A document may need to be written to laypeople, who are unfamiliar with an issue and need a great deal of background, facts, and definitions of key terms. Or a document may need to be directed to experts in a field, who have a great deal of technical knowledge, are familiar with technical jargon, and have professional experience in a field. Sometimes a document or website needs to address one of those audiences as well as people in the "middle," who have some knowledge but are not experts.

Expert audiences consist of people are who experienced with the subject matters and language used by specific governmental agencies and professions. These audiences require less explanatory information than **nonexpert audiences** do. Sometimes federal and state agencies will employ **subject matter experts** to write documents because of their specialized knowledge. Chapter 3 discusses subject matter experts for writing rules and regulations.

Professional and Personal Needs of an Audience

A third approach to understanding a reader is to consider his or her professional and personal needs for reading the document or viewing the website. One of the best ways to understand individuals' needs is to try to imagine their daily concerns—to walk in their shoes. Most often government documents are meant to help readers solve problems, make decisions, and/or complete a task. Knowing your audience's professional needs goes a long way to effective communicating. Appreciating the political realities of your audience's professional and personal needs helps you to fashion documents and create websites that go to the heart of what needs to be addressed and not waste your readers' time. It helps you anticipate the kinds of questions the reader will have about the information.

How Government Writers Get to Know Their Audience(s)

Knowing the audience for a government document or website is essential to the message's effectiveness. Depending on the agency or problem, stakeholders may or may not be easily ascertained. For instance, if a newly incorporated town begins permitting local businesses, then the audience for those permits would be the individuals who want to conduct business within the town limits. Yet, at times, government writers represent the voice and views of those stakeholders who cannot speak for themselves. For example, if you write rules and regulations for day care, you may need to speak for the children who are stakeholders as well as their parents and child care workers. After all, the children's safety and welfare are at stake within a day care environment. In the case of a government communication that is directed to an industry or organization, the stakeholders can be an even more diverse group. In the distribution of AIDS drugs worldwide, for example, stakeholders include scientists, stockholders in pharmaceutical companies, and national governments, while future stakeholders are the IGOs (international governmental organizations) and NGOs (nongovernmental organizations that do service/advocacy) (Kennedy 130–35), and, of course, pharmaceutical companies and individuals with AIDS.

Regardless of whether you are writing day care rules for children who will depend on them for their safety or writing rules for the worldwide distribution of AIDS drugs, you need to know your audiences and their needs to communicate effectively. Because government writing comprises so many kinds of writing activities, documents, and most recently websites, government writers interact with audiences in scores of formal and informal ways to get to know them. Public hearings and notices for comments on rules and regulations are formal routes for public input, while informal routes consist of new government writers within agencies learning about audiences by talking with seasoned writers.

In future chapters, we will discuss getting to know specific audiences in more detail. Chapter 8, "Government Websites", for example, discusses how some agency website writers and developers now fashion fictionalized personas with real names, professional backgrounds, expertise, and jobs from well-informed audience research that encapsulates audience demographics and characteristics of an individual audience member or members. The writers and developers then use these personas as points of reference from which to write, edit, and design websites. Some informal and formal means by which government writers get to know their audiences are these:

- Community and government partnerships
- Community workshops and training
- Email
- Focus groups
- Letters
- Market research
- Other government writers' experience and knowledge
- Personal contacts
- Phone calls
- Public hearings
- Public notices
- Requests for input
- Surveys
- Workgroups

No matter how structured or unstructured the procedures that an agency or organization has for a writer to get to know an audience, the principle of knowing an audience in order to communicate effectively remains the same. From highly formal Congressional hearings for stakeholders about an issue to impromptu phone calls from constituents about a local concern, government writers have numerous formal settings and informal chances to get to know their audiences.

Summary and Looking Forward

Government writers have penned some of the most important documents in American history. These crucial documents required the rhetorical skill needed to make knowledge, shape public opinion, codify public policy, and construct a vision for the future. Effective government writers have problem-solving skills and political savvy with a capacity to negotiate between many disparate groups to create text that is acceptable to many, if not all, involved in an issue. Government documents are a wide variety of types. These documents can affect entire countries, a community, or a relatively small number of individuals.

Chapter 1 introduces key principles and approaches to writing effective communication. Effective writers are able to persuade their readers because they make a careful determination of the following:

- The audience or audiences
- The purpose of the document or website
- The cultural context—the historical, political, social, economic, and ethical aspects, as well as technological possibilities and constraints of a time for the document or website, the writer, and reader or user.

Chapter 1 focuses on how to understand an audience or audiences. The ways include determining demographics, the level of knowledge and background of the audience, and ascertaining the personal and professional needs of an audience has for the government information. Chapter 2 focuses on having a clear purpose and understanding the cultural context for an audience, for writers, and for the paper documents and websites.

Activities and Assignments

1. **Individual Activity:** Suppose you are responsible for writing some kinds of government documents for your classmates, such as student loan application forms, jury exemption forms, or income tax forms. Create a list of demographic characteristics that you imagine of your classmates such as age, income, sex, race, ethnicity, educational status, and national origin. Discuss with your classmates how these characteristics might affect the language and/or format and/or technological aspects of these government documents. For instance, consider the difference in how the Internet would affect the distribution of these documents today compared to say 20 years ago before the Internet became available to most everyone.

2. **Individual Activity:** Contact your local government or state government officials to find someone to interview who writes government documents or manages a government website. Find out the various methods this person or his or her agency uses to determine the audience or audiences for the documents or website. Ask about what demographics, expertise-level, and/or professional needs, or anything else the writer will provide about the characteristics of the audiences and/or how they go about learning about their audiences. Find a template for memorandums on a software word-processing program, and then use it to write a memo to your class about what you found.

3. **Individual Activity:** Find a government document written for a specific audience and rewrite it for another audience.

4. **Individual Activity:** Find a document or website for a local government agency and compare what you can glean about its audience with a document or website from a state-level and/or federal-level agency. Write about what you found.

5. **Individual Activity:** Review several paper documents or online documents for a website for a nonprofit organization similar to the Multiple Sclerosis

Society case study at the end of the textbook. Find out who is the audience or audiences for the documents, and describe what you could tell about the characteristics of the audience or audiences.

6. **Individual Activity:** Peruse from the Hurricane Katrina Case Study at the end of the textbook documents and any others related to Hurricane Katrina or its aftermath. Describe who the primary audience is for each document, and what you think the characteristics are of this audience. What other audience(s) might the documents be targeted toward? Compare the documents and their audiences.

7. **Individual Activity:** Check out the documents from the Southwest Florida Water Management District, a case study at the end of the textbook, and/or go to its website. Find documents that are directed to audiences with different characteristics—age, ethnicity, level of expertise, and personal or professional needs. Write a report on what you found.

8. **Group Activity:** Break into groups with each group choosing a particular agency or a few agencies and go to a library that has a collection of government documents. Each student should choose two or three different documents to analyze the characteristics of the audience or audiences. Then group members can make a presentation to the class about what they found.

9. **Group Activity:** Break into groups and have different groups look at documents for different levels of government, local, state, and federal. Analyze what the audience characteristics might be for each document at each level. Then report to your classmates what you found.

Works Cited

Aristotle. *"Art" of Rhetoric.* Trans. John Henry Freese. 1926. Cambridge: Harvard UP, 1982. 15.

College Board. "Writing: A Powerful Message from State Government." *Report of the National Commission on Writing for America's Families, Schools, and Colleges.* July 2005. 19 May 2007 <http://www.writingcommission.org/report.html>.

Compston, Christine and Rachel Filene Seidman, eds. *Our Documents: 100 Milestone Documents from the National Archives.* New York: Oxford UP, 2003.

Environmental Protection Agency "For Kids". *Environmental Kids Club* 19 May 2007 <http://www.epa.gov/kids>.

Goldsmith, Barry S. "How NWS Impact Statements Were Used to Communicate Imminent Danger from Severe Hurricanes." NOAA/National Weather Service Forecast Office, Tampa Bay Area, Ruskin, FL. 19 May 2007 <http://ams.confex.com/ams/pdfpapers/107735.pdf>.

Kennedy, Charles R., Frederick H.deB. Harris, and Michael Lord. "Integrating Public Policy and Public Affairs in a Pharmaceutical Marketing Program: The AIDS Pandemic." *Journal of Public Policy & Marketing* 23.2 (fall 2004): 128–39.

Kirst, Sean. "Ominous Words Foretold Catastrophic Suffering, Saved Lives." 7 Sept. 2005. *The Post-Standard.* 9 Sept 2006 <http://www.syracuse.com>.

National Museum of American History. "NOAA Donates Hurricane Katrina Materials to Smithsonian Collection." 14 June 2006. Press Release. 19 May 2007 <http://americanhistory.si.edu/news/pressrelease.cfm?key=29&newskey=366>.

National Oceanic and Atmospheric Administration (NOAA). "Inland Hurricane Warning." 28 August 2005. 19 May 2007 <http://www.srh.noaa.gov/data/warn_archive/ LIX/NPW/ 0828_155101.tx>.

National Oceanic and Atmospheric Association (NOAA), National Weather Service, National Hurricane Center, Tropic Prediction Center. 28 August 2005. <http://www.nhc.noaa.gov/index.shtml>.

Ricks, Robert. "Area Forecast Discussion." National Weather Service, New Orleans, LA. 349 PM CDT Sun Aug 28 2005. Email to Libby Allison. 5 Oct. 2006.

—. Telephone interview. 4 Oct. 2006.

U.S. Department of Labor, Bureau of Labor Statistics. "Federal Government, Excluding the Postal Service." 272–78. 22 May 2007 <http://www.bls.gov/oco/cgs041.pdf>.

U.S. Department of Labor, Bureau of Labor Statistics. "State and Local Government, Excluding Education and Hospitals." 279-83. 22 May 2007 <http://www.bls.gov/ oco/cg/pdf/cgs042.pdf>.

U.S. House of Representatives Select Bipartisan Committee to Investigate the Preparation for and Response to Hurricane Katrina. *A Failure of Initiative: Final Report of the Select Bipartisan Committee to Investigate the Preparation for and Response to Hurricane Katrina.* Washington, D.C.: U.S. Government Printing Office. 15 Feb. 2006.

White House, The. *The Federal Response to Hurricane Katrina: Lessons Learned.* Appendix B: What Went Right: 138. February 2006. 19 May 2007 <http://www.whitehouse.gov/ reports/katrina-lessons-learned/>.

Williams, Brian. "The Weatherman Nobody Heard." 15 Sept. 2005. 19 May 2007 <http://www.msnbc.msn.com/id/9358447/>.

Purpose and Cultural Contexts in Government Writing

The 2000 U.S. presidential election was one of the closest in our country's history, having been decided by only 527 votes in Florida. Republican George W. Bush won the state's 25 electoral votes by a very small margin of popular votes in the state and defeated incumbent vice-president Democrat Al Gore for the presidency. Only four times in U.S. history has a candidate won the presidency while losing the nationwide popular vote.

One of the outcomes of the close election was an investigation into the use of the butterfly ballot voting form in Palm Beach County, Florida, where there was an unexpected amount of votes for third-party candidate Patrick Buchanan. Some contend that voters in Palm Beach, many of whom are elderly, were confused by the format of the ballot, which listed Al Gore as second on the left-hand column but the punch hole for the second choice on the card was for Buchanan. Specialists in human-computer interaction and document **usability testing**, the study of how documents are used, made these observations about the butterfly ballot:

- The layout of double pages with punch holes in between was new and unfamiliar because ballots in previous elections had a single column with punch holes on the right (Miller-Jacobs).
- Text in the left column was left-aligned while text in the right column was right-aligned (Miller-Jacobs).
- The right column was slightly lower than the left column (Miller-Jacobs).
- The arrows were very small (Miller-Jacobs).
- A font size of 12 points rather than 10 points would have been more appropriate because 12 points is larger and easier to read (Bailey).
- The level of light illumination at the polling places could have been too low (Bailey).

The butterfly ballot and related controversies about the election led to the Help America Vote Act, authorizing the federal government to provide funding to states to replace mechanical voting equipment with electronic equipment.

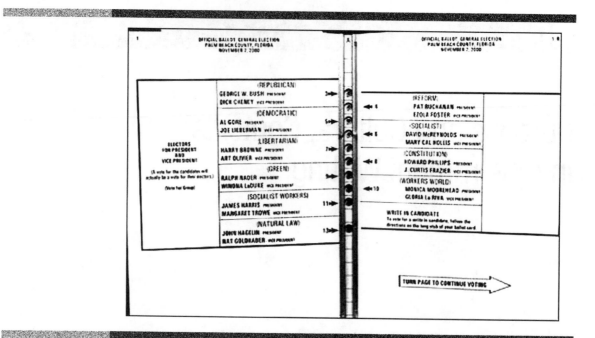

FIGURE 2.1   The butterfly ballot format was the focus of controversy in the 2000 presidential election. Pictured here is the official ballot, general election, Palm Beach County, Florida, November 7, 2000

Writing and communicating is never done in a vacuum. It is done within a cultural context for the reader, for the writer, and for the document or website. "The text never exists in isolation from people, places, values, and needs" (Rude *Technical Editing* 20). As we noted in Chapter 1 the cultural context comprises the historical, political, social, economic, ethical, and technological, circumstances and conditions of the time. Cultural context is the confluence of the social exchange of people within a particular time and place. In the case of government writers, the cultural context encompasses their interactions with their audiences, with each other in their own agency and with other agencies, and with the documents they read, study, and create.

The butterfly ballot controversy in the 2000 election brings to light political, social, and technological cultural conditions of that time: the newness of the ballot design for voters, the age of the voters, and even the low lighting within the voting locations could have all been factors in the effectiveness of the ballot, for which there were political consequences. Researchers argue that usability testing of the ballot with the appropriate age group under the exact voting conditions would have provided feedback about ballot design that could have corrected any design flaws.

Effective governmental documentation brings together ideas, voices, and values of many people, which is indicative of the social nature of writing and communicating. The social interchange among writers, readers, and text brings together the political, historical, social, economic, ethical, and technological, dimensions of the writing endeavor. Effective government writing is a shared social endeavor. In fact, government writing often comprises procedures, even legal mandates, for socially constructed documents.

To see how government writing is a shared activity consider the historical documents mentioned earlier. For example, the Declaration of Independence in 1776, the document that declared the 13 colonies free from Britain, and a unified country, was the result of the work of many writers, not just the skillful Thomas Jefferson, or John Hancock, whose bold signature is so associated with the document (Compston and Seidman 10). While the Social Security Act of 1935, following the devastating Depression in which the elderly were particularly vulnerable, "encountered opposition from Americans who considered social security a governmental invasion of the private sphere and employers who sought exemption from payroll taxes for having adopted government-approved private pension plans. Eventually, compromise legislation passed, and President Roosevelt signed it into law in August 1935" (Compston and Seidman 164). Think about who the audience was for these documents, the purpose of them, how they were printed and distributed, and who signed them. Both documents, underpinning the history of our country, were written, edited, and distributed among many writers for many readers. Both were created during a specific historical time, under specific circumstances, with specific consequences.

Process Writing, Social Interchange, and Cultural Contexts

Research shows that writers, whether they are beginners or professionals, go through a mental "process" of stages as they write—brainstorming, drafting, organizing, editing, and polishing (see Figure 2.2). This process is an ongoing selection of words, sentences, paragraphs, graphics, images, etc., and sometimes what writers choose to leave out is as important as what they decide to incorporate. Writers are constantly weighing and balancing what to include in a document and what to exclude, and just when they think a document is finished, they may find they need to brainstorm about something they left out, and/or reorganize, and/or revise text; it can be much more than the polishing stage of "fixing" the punctuation and the like; it can be a major overhaul. Even writers who work under tight deadlines have to rethink word usage, change words and sentences, reorganize, and reedit as time ticks away. For government writers, this "process" also encompasses social interchange with others.

For government writers, the "process" of writing that goes from a draft to the polished written product does not just occur within the mind of the individual writer as he or she creates text for documents; many government documents are indeed *mandated* to be drafted, redrafted, rewritten, reedited, redesigned, and republished, with input from other government experts, the general public, and stakeholders, a process that goes on over and over. For instance, the course of

The Writing Process

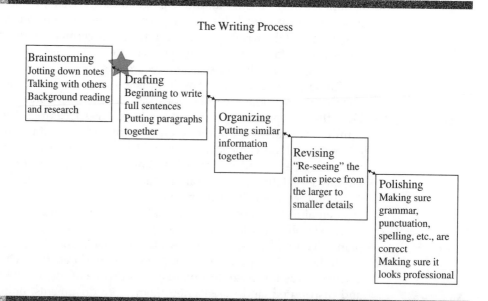

FIGURE 2.2   The Writing Process. These steps are not always linear; sometimes they are recursive, falling back to the steps before or sometimes to the beginning

action by which rules and regulations become part of the *Federal Register*, a publication of the federal government that notifies the public of proposed and adopted rules, grant and contract announcements and awards, and other notices, is a series of legally sanctioned brainstorming, drafting, organizing, editing, and polishing writing activities that require *public* input all along the way. The route of gathering public input, of incorporating public comments, of interagency editing, of agency responses to the comments, and of post-publication response that leads to it starting all over again is a lengthy individual and social interaction writing approach. Figure 2.3 depicts the process by which rules and regulations are written with public input for National Priority Hazardous Waste Sites, and how these rules and regulations make their way into the *Federal Register* for the National Priorities List, a group of known releases or threatened releases of major concern of hazardous substances, pollutants, or contaminants throughout the United States and its territories.

The Environmental Protection Agency uses this list as a guide to determine which sites need further investigation (http://www.epa.gov/superfund/sites/npl/index.htm). When a potential hazardous waste site is discovered, a preliminary assessments site investigation begins, then it is proposed that the site be placed on the National Priorities List—in which public comment is required and response to the comments—and if it is warranted, the site is listed. A cleanup begins, and there is public input into the cleanup procedures as well, and finally, if the cleanup is deemed successful, the site is taken off the National Priorities List.

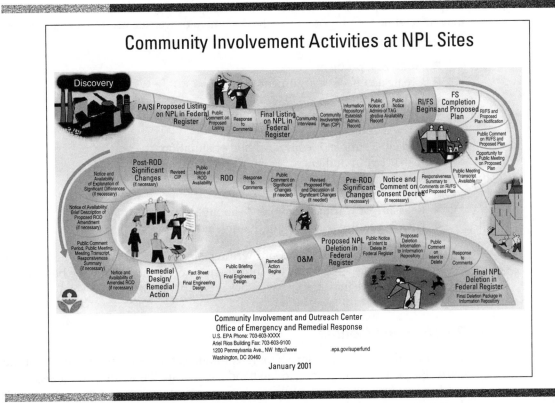

FIGURE 2.3 The Process of Public Input for NPL. Source: EPA. http://www.epa.gov

Throughout this lengthy process, public input is required, and the written information about the site undergoes revision and modification repeatedly.

The cultural context for these EPA rules and regulations for the National Priorities List comprise today's political climate that requires potentially hazardous waste sites to be investigated, the public's and stakeholders' ideas to be heeded and incorporated in the written documents, and the writers at the EPA to follow legally mandated steps to get input. Within this shared writing experience will be information about the social and economic issues for the communities and the industries involved, as well as ethical and technological decisions to be made, including ones by the writers about how, when, and where to distribute certain kinds of information.

Purpose in Writing

Deciding what you want to accomplish is the *purpose* of a document or website. A successful government writer carefully analyzes the purpose for writing a particular document or a specific website. Most people seek government information to help solve problems, make decisions, and/or complete tasks. However, to delve deeper into the persuasive goal of your writing, editing, or designing, the following may help refine the purpose. Does the document or website need to do one or more of the following?

- Analyze a problem
- Create an effective argument
- Define a matter
- Discover a reason and find a solution for a problem
- Draw an analogy
- Explain a simple or complex issue or situation
- Instruct your audience
- Introduce new information
- Make a comparison
- Reassure or warn your audience about a situation
- Uncover faulty reasoning or debunk a myth

The purpose for which you are writing, designing, or editing should arise from your audience's needs for the information and should shape the best means to communicate the information, whether it is paper or online.

Purpose and Genres

Sometimes the best means for shaping communication is a document or website **genre**. Purpose and genre go hand in hand. Genres are the writing and design conventions of documents and websites. Genres are categories or forms into which documents and websites are grouped together based on written and visual characteristics they have in common, and which readers associate with them. Genres are valuable because their predictable forms and consistency aid in reading comprehension and efficiency. Genres help readers grasp information quickly and effectively.

For a start, you may already be familiar with some genres because you've internalized them during your lifetime. You may for instance recognize a business card genre **layout** or **format,** which is a 3 × 2-inch card with an individual's agency, organization, or company name, office phone number, office address, and email address. The purpose of this genre is to introduce new information to the reader; in this case, to introduce someone and his or her professional information to another. Readers, viewers, and users begin to recognize genres of documents and websites over time, particularly when they interact frequently with a business, an agency, organization, or institution; however, genres are organic; they change and grow over time. Perhaps one of the best examples of the change within genres is the format of a résumé. Résumés traditionally have been one-page documents with an applicant's name, address, and phone number on the top, and employment experience listed in chronological order with the most recent job first in line. Technological advances and the Internet have revolutionized the format of this genre. Résumés that are digitally scanned into databases have keywords to describe the candidate's skills and experience, and when posted on the web may only have an email address and not a home address to protect an applicant's privacy.

Government writers learn the written and visual conventions of documents and websites through training and education (such as this textbook), on-the-job experience, trial and error, and membership in professional associations. As in the résumé example, genres, layout, and format conventions in government documents and websites change because audiences' needs change over time and technology changes. A savvy government communicator can study the established genres of any workplace setting to determine how to write in them. An even more sophisticated communicator can adapt quickly to writing in an established genre as well as critiquing the genre to determine how to make it better.

Upcoming chapters in this textbook cover key genres in government writing: rules and regulations, policy handbooks, manuals, guides, policy memorandums, public policy reports, and government grants and proposals, and Chapter 8 discusses website genres. Design features of documents and websites also entail genres with conventional layout and format. Throughout the chapters are examples of design features for documents, and Chapter 8, "Government Websites" has examples of various design conventions like pie charts, bar graphs, line graphs, and illustrations, which are found in documents and websites to help visually explain information.

Discourse Conventions in Government Writing

Genres and Discourse Conventions

Effective government communicators also recognize the **discourse conventions** within a **discourse community**—the verbal and written language interchange of members of groups: agency employees, stakeholders, and interested people interact with each other, which creates and emphasizes the usage of certain words, acronyms, terms, and language. The discourse conventions in a community can include the structure of arguments, specific vocabulary, how sentences are structured, use of images, figures of speech, and so forth.

To demonstrate, let's look at a document from the year 1606 to show the dramatic contrast with today's discourse conventions. The brief excerpt in Figure 2.4 is from a set of instructions for the ships' crews of the Virginia Company of Britain on what to do when their ships land on what would become the Virginia Colony. Historians believe Richard Hakluyt, the younger, probably contributed to the writing of them because Hakluyt had written earlier about the possibilities of western colonization.

For his day Hakluyt's writing style would have been considered straight forward (Osselton); however, can you envision official instructions today that use words like *runneth*, *bendeth*, and *soonest*? How about the difference in punctuation from then and today? What about ". . . to observe the ordinances set down by the King's Majestie"? Clearly the politics of the times are different from today. And what about the phrase, "When it shall please God to send you . . . "? As you can imagine, the navigation of ships then depended on what we would consider rudimentary instruments and the expertise of the ship's crew, so the timetable for landing was very tenuous and rested primarily with the weather and the seas, controlled by God. Also, the phrase, "and, if you happen to Discover Divers portable Rivers . . . " is vague to us today. The word *divers* then meant "diverse" or "various" (OED). Now reread the passage substituting the word *diverse* in place of divers and see if it makes more sense.

As We Doubt not but you will have especial Care to Observe the Ordinances set Down by the Kings Majestie and Delivered unto you under the privy Seal So for your better Directions upon your first Landing we have thought Good to recommend unto your Care these Instructions and articles following. When it Shall please God to Send you on the Coast of Virginia you shall Do your best Endeavor to find out a Safe port in the Entrance of Some navigable River making Choise of Such a one as runneth furthest into the Land and if you happen to Discover Divers portable Rivers and amongst them any one that hath two main branches if the Difference be not Great make Choise of that which bendeth most towards the Northwest for that way You soonest find the Other Sea. [In 1606, "Other Sea" was the Pacific Ocean, and some believed it lay just beyond the Appalachian Mountains.] (Barbour).

FIGURE 2.4   Excerpt from Instructions in 1606 for the Virginia Company. Source: *The Jamestown Voyages Under the First Charter, 1606–1609* Vol. 1, The Hakluyt Society: 49

The point is that a careful study of language usage can help writers understand the discourse conventions within the cultural context for the writers, readers, and documents. Discourse conventions can become standard practice within an agency's or organization's verbal and written communication. A familiar discourse convention in government today is the use of acronyms and abbreviations. Take the example of the Community Involvement Activities at NPL Sites in Figure 2.3. Among the abbreviations are NPL (National Priorities List), ROD (Records of Decision), and O&M (Operation and Maintenance). When a writer is learning about the discourse conventions of a government agency or organization, the type of language usage may not be as evident as in the example from 1606, but there are methods to discern discourse conventions as well as the genres useful for an agency or organization. For instance, researching the history of an agency or organization, its mission, how it has been funded, what other agencies and organizations it is affiliated with, its major accomplishments, and its leaders and their backgrounds (Bowdon and Scott 153–54) can help to understand discourse conventions. In addition, studying the kinds of argument in its documents and websites, the way information is presented by headings, lists, paragraphs, the terms that are frequently used, the patterns in use of personal pronouns in sentences, the pattern of active or passive voice in sentences, and how the agency depicts its constituency (Bowdon and Scott 154) can all provide insights into the agency or organization's discourse conventions and community.

As a more current case, take the Ricks example at the beginning of Chapter 1. Ricks described how he chose a template—a predetermined pattern—of language usage for the Category 4 hurricane. Ricks's overall message could be considered within the National Weather Service Urgent Message genre, divided into sections with storm location, movement, and wind and barometric pressure. Many sentences in Ricks's message are **passive voice**, meaning that the "doer of the action" is not mentioned in them because the wind, water, and and/or flying debris could all or some at any time cause or contribute to any of these disaster scenarios; the paragraphs are short for quick reading; the words are capitalized because the convention of broadcasting is to have text in all capitalized lettering so broadcasters can see the words easily as they read them out loud; and the heading gives the type of message it is and when it was posted. Ricks's message does show the discourse conventions of the National Weather Service Urgent Message advisories genre. Please keep in mind, however, that the genre and discourse conventions for the Weather Service are unique to it. Most government writing calls for full and complete active **voice** sentences, with proper upper and lower case letters, and appropriate headings and subheadings to set off sections of information, which will be discussed in upcoming chapters.

What Ricks's message does present is clear, uncomplicated vocabulary. Technical weather terms are deliberately left out for the public. Because a great deal of government writing and communicating is directed toward a general audience—readers, viewers, or users who have an interest in an agency, project, or problem but are not technical experts—government writers in all agencies and departments are encouraged to write in "plain language" for paper documents and websites.

The "**Plain Language**" movement for government writing focuses on language that is clear, straightforward writing that avoids unnecessarily complicated and legal language and keep readers interested in the message. Plain language is a deliberate effort to write for the reader rather than expecting the reader to figure out the jargon and details. Even a government letter with unclear language can have large-scale consequences.

A report in 2002 from Cynthia A. Bascetta, Director of the Education, Workforce, and Income Security Issues of the Department of Veterans Affairs office describes a research study of letters sent to veterans and their families about VA compensation claims. Ms. Bascetta points out that in 1995 the VA launched an ongoing initiative called "Reader-Focused Writing" (see Flower) to improve its written communication; yet, a random sample of about 1.2 million letters found that

> [a]bout half of VBA's [Veterans Benefits Administration] compensation letters did not clearly explain pertinent financial information concerning the claimants' benefit. Similarly, nearly 30 percent of compensation letters did not explain the reason for the VBA's decision whether or not to award benefits ... [and] about 43 percent did not clearly explain the actions that claimants were to take to support their claims. (3)

The negative consequences of such writing range from client frustration with the agency, to additional work for VA employees, to delay or denial of benefits for eligible claimants because of inadequate evidence. Writing in plain language is especially vital for government websites. More about the use of plain language in government writing will be discussed in upcoming chapters.

Ethical Issues in Cultural Contexts

An essential component of the cultural context for any text is the ethical choices—the value judgments made by writers, communicators, editors, designers, and distributors—and the personal and professional consequences of those choices for readers as well as writers. According to the website for the Markkula Center for Applied Ethics, "[E]thics refers to well based standards of right and wrong that prescribe what humans ought to do, usually in terms of rights, obligations, benefits to society, fairness, or specific virtues."

In a research survey of technical communicators, Sam Dragga found that the most frequent reason for ethical choices in communication decisions was the consequences of a choice on readers ("Is it Ethical?"). Effective government writers try to consider the ethical consequences of any writing endeavor. Some would think that government documents simply do not have as large of consequences as other types of writing, such as a newspaper article that can make or break careers, but nothing is further from reality. Investigations into the *Challenger* and *Columbia* space shuttle disasters demonstrate how critically important the choices about language use and format of documents (Tufte) can be even in the most sophisticated technological organizations such as the National Aeronautics and Space Administration (NASA).

An individual writer's ethical choices, an agency and organization's cultural workplace setting, and the larger arena of societal ethics all factor into the effectiveness of a government document or website. Effective government writers try to foresee as much as possible the large and small consequences of their words, documents, and websites. Ethical choices for writing can range from relatively simple situations such as where to post notices about public meetings, so all affected by a potential policy decision will have an opportunity to see the notice, to complex decisions about what information could positively or negatively affect international relations or national security or an individual's personal safety or privacy. Ethical issues arise in every writing and communicating situation. The following news story dramatically demonstrates the consequences of ethical choices in the writing and distribution of procedures:

On October 15, 2003, a 310-foot Staten Island ferry, which typically carries about 1,500 passengers, slammed into a concrete maintenance pier near the St. George terminal in New York harbor, which then ripped through the ferry's steel and windows, killing 11 passengers and injuring many more. In "A Cautionary Tale," Shelia C. Jones said the Director of Operations for the ferries, Patrick Ryan, pleaded guilty in April 2005 to negligent manslaughter, even though he was not on the vessel at the time. Ryan had drafted a series of standard operating procedures confirming that two employees capable of navigating the ferry must be in the wheelhouse at the same time, but Ryan admitted that he had not distributed the procedures or trained his staff about the two-pilot rule. When the accident happened, only the assistant captain was at the controls, and he had lost consciousness. "According to the lead prosecutor, Ryan's executive and managerial failings made him just as blameworthy of the incident as anyone on the ferry"; it was a cause of the crash (9).

Social and Cultural Ethics

Richard Johnson-Sheehan offers the work of Manual Velasquez, an ethics scholar, as an approach to analyzing ethical issues in documents and writing and communicating. There are four categories to analyze the ethical situations of a document.

> *Rights*—human rights such as life, liberty, and the pursuit of happiness, and Constitutional rights such as freedom of speech, freedom of religion, the right to bear arms, and the right to a speedy trial
>
> *Justice*—a sense of fairness to all

Utility—the greatest good for the greatest number

Care—the notion of kindness, understanding, and compassion should take precedence over inflexible and absolute rules.

Johnson-Sheehan adds another category: *Conservation ethics*—how documents and information not only affect humans and their communities but also the ecosystems around them (76–80).

Conservation ethics are becoming increasingly important to all government writers because of the interconnection between incidents, activities, laws, and the ecosystem. The Environmental Protection Agency (EPA) has one of the most user-friendly websites, which not only educates readers about federal regulations but also prompts them to find out when and how to report environmental problems and emergencies such as chemical and oil spills.

Hurricane Katrina's effects and aftermath is an example of how much government writing and communicating today touches on a myriad of environmental issues. In early December 2005, Louisiana's Governor Kathleen Blanco sent some 100,000 pages of documents to congressional committees investigating the failures of preparing and responding to Katrina. There were emails, police reports, logs of people asking to be rescued, press releases, public statements, requests for interviews, and much more (Simpson). Of course, the EPA has been significantly involved in the recovery of oil spilled and other kinds of environmental damage as a result of the hurricane.

Plagiarism, Copyright, and Other Ethical Matters

Just as is the situation with other kinds of writing activities, government writers must be always careful not to plagiarize the work of someone else. **Plagiarism** is using or incorporating the work of someone else in your work as if your wrote it or designed it on you own. It is better to err on the side of over-citing sources than plagiarizing at the expense of the creator's work and your professional good word.

In the United States, unlike some countries, people own their written words and visual and musical performances in much the same fashion that they own their homes and property. The laws that govern **copyright** for these matters are complex and dependent on the situation in which a work is being created, used, produced, performed, and distributed. The emerging digital world has added to the complexity of matters in issues of "**intellectual property**." Intellectual Property is defined as

> tangible products of the human mind and intelligence entitled to the legal status of personal property, especially works protected by copyright, inventions that have been patented, and registered trademarks. An idea is considered the intellectual property of its creator only after it has been recorded or made manifest in specific form. (Reitz)

The topic of copyright cannot be entirely covered in this textbook, but this section will cover some general principles to keep in mind when writing government documents or creating websites. Government writers should seek expert advice when they have questions about copyright as well as for trademarks and patents. When considering copyright restrictions, it is helpful to think of it from two perspectives: from the creator of a work and/or the copyright holder's, and on the other hand, from the user's, who is wanting to apply the work.

Copyright protects 'original works of authorship,' "including literary, dramatic, musical, artistic, and certain other intellectual works" that are "fixed in a tangible form of expression" ("Copyright Basics" 1–2). These categories are broad, though. For example, computer programs can be registered as "literary works"; while, maps and architectural plans can be registered as "pictorial, graphic, and sculptural works" ("Copyright Basics" 3). Published and unpublished works can be copyrighted, and a work does not have to have a copyright notice on it for it to be copyrighted.

The copyright owner has the right to do and authorize others to do the following:

- To reproduce the work in copies or phonorecords;
- To prepare derivative works based upon the work;
- To distribute copies or phonorecords of the work to the public by sale or other transfer of ownership, or by rental, lease, or lending;
- To perform the work publicly, in the case of literary, musical, dramatic, and choreographic works, pantomimes, and motion pictures and other audiovisual works;
- To display the work publicly, in the case of literary, musical, dramatic, and choreographic works, pantomimes, and pictorial, graphic, or sculptural works, including the individual images of a motion picture or other audiovisual work; and
- In the case of sound recordings, to perform the work publicly by means of a digital audio transmission. ("Copyright Basics" 1).

From the perspective of someone wanting to use or apply the work but does not hold copyright, there are some exceptions to copyright ownership, when permission may not be required. For instance, the **fair use** of a copyrighted work can be the reproduction for purposes such as criticism comment, news reporting, teaching (including multiple copies for classroom use), scholarship, or research (CENDI "FAQ" 11). There are four factors in determining fair use:

1. Purpose and character of the use, including whether such use is of a commercial nature or is for nonprofit educational purposes;
2. Nature of the copyrighted work;
3. Amount and substantiality of the portion used in relation to the copyrighted work as a whole; and
4. Effect of the use upon the potential market for or value of the copyrighted work. (CENDI "FAQ" 11).

Generally most work produced by government employees are not eligible for copyright protection. "Most government publications and commonplace information, such as height and weight charts or a table of diacritical marks, are considered to be in the public domain" (Addison 29). Government works are supported by tax dollars and therefore most fall within the public domain, which means the work can be used by anyone anywhere without permission. However there are exceptions.

A work is not in the public domain simply because it does not have a copyright notice. Additionally, the fact that a privately created work is, with permission, included in a U.S. Government work does not place the private work into the public domain. The user is responsible for determining whether a work is in the public domain.

It is important to read the permissions and copyright notices on U.S. Government publications and websites. Many Government agencies follow the practice of providing notice for material that is copyrighted and not for those that are in the public domain (CENDI "FAQ" 12).

In addition, there are restrictions of access for government information because of national security, export control, and patent applications, for example (CENDI "FAQ" 17). Government contractors' and grantees' work, for instance, "who work with the government are not considered government employees for purposes of copyright" (CENDI "FAQ" 15), and therefore their work may be eligible for copyright protection (CENDI "FAQ" 15) rather the work is in paper form, embedded in other public domain work, and/or on websites. For websites, Chapter 8 discusses this matter in more detail.

It would seem unnecessary to say, but government writers need to be careful about presenting untruths, misinformation, data misinformation, and any other types of content or graphic displays that could mislead readers or negatively reflect on the agency's mission or organization. As we will see in the following real accounts, poor ethical choices can also mean the end of a writer's career. In this case, writers are working for nonprofit organizations.

Scientists depend on grants from the governments and private foundations to fund their research. To obtain these funds, scientists, many of whom are employed by educational institutions that cannot afford to fund scientific projects costing millions of dollars, apply to government-funded foundations. Applications for these funds are highly competitive and require the submittal of grant proposals.

Unfortunately, in writing and submitting grant proposals, some scientists use false and/or plagiarized information in their proposals to increase their chances of winning grants. Today, the United States Office of Research Integrity (ORI) within the Office of Public Health and Science (OPHS) is responsible for investigating plagiarism and misconduct in research funded by OPHS (Price 1). While the United States Public Health Service "provided at least $30 billion for health research and development" in 2004, ORI uncovered 162 cases of scientific misconduct from 1992 to 2005 (Price 1). Alan R. Price, Associate Director for Investigature Over-sight in the Office of Research Integrity, gives these cases:

In 1993 a biochemistry professor at a small Midwest medical school submitted a grant proposal to the National Institutes of Health (NIH) to obtain funding for his research project. While writing the proposal, the professor, who also served as the chairman of his department, copied "method designs on membrane-transport of the anti-cancer drug methotrexate" (4) from a grant proposal that he read while serving as a proposal reviewer for a researcher at another college. Once the professor submitted the proposal for consideration for funding, he learned that the NIH reviewer for his grant proposal was none other than the researcher whose proposal he plagiarized. After the biochemistry professor learned that the NIH reviewer had discovered his indiscretion and accused him of plagiarism, the professor claimed that the ideas in the proposal were indeed his own ideas—but government investigations into the matter revealed otherwise (4).

In 2000 a research scientist employed by a small business submitted a grant proposal to the NIH that included "images from Internet sources without attribution for his NIH small business innovation research grant, including two images that he claimed were the output of his new imaging technology" (4). As in the previous case, this researcher's plagiarism was discovered by an NIH reviewer who recalled seeing one of the images years earlier on the cover of *Science* magazine. In both of these cases, the scientists were debarred from participation in NIH funding and service and the university professor was forced to resign.

Also in a recent survey of thousands of NIH-funded scientists, "more than one-third of them admitted research wrongdoings between 2002 and 2005" (Levin). Aside from the negative ramifications for the writers who get caught, what about the consequences for readers? What is the significance of plagiarism or false information or misleading data in grant proposals? Suppose false or misleading data wind up in medical journals that your physician uses to treat your illness. Now, the ethical ramifications of those choices mean something to the readers and you.

Style Guides

When we refer to "style" here we are not talking about an author's personal "voice" or **style** of writing, personal choice of vocabulary, or the **tone** of his or her prose but rather the decisions that are made in writing a document (or website) that pertain to grammar, syntax, the mechanics of punctuation, and the like. That is to say, a style guide dictates basic language usage and the mechanics of punctuation, spelling, abbreviations, and so forth that appear multiple times in a document. In agencies, organizations, and businesses these choices will be collected in what may be called a "style guide" or "style manual" or "style handbook" or a similar type of title. For many professional writers, *The Chicago Manual of Style* has served as the bible for answers on how to do everything from basic punctuation to how to appropriately write a military title, to how to do citations, to how to make proofreader's marks, to how typographical decisions matter in the printing process. What may seem as insignificant choices such as whether website is one word or two becomes very important because readers need consistency in these mechanical matters to easily comprehend messages. Consistency is vital to comprehension.

Some of the other well-known style guides are *The Associated Press Stylebook* (Goldstein) for newspapers and magazines, the *Microsoft Manual of Style for Technical Publications,* and the *MLA Style Manual and Guide to Scholarly Publishing* (Gibaldi) and the *MLA Handbook for Writers of Research Papers* (Gibaldi) of the Modern Language Association for academic endeavors in the Humanities. The *Publication Manual of the American Psychological Association* (*APA*) primarily is for Psychology and Social Sciences; the *Scientific Style and Format*: The *CSE Manual for Authors, Editors, and Publishers* is for the biological, agricultural, and other sciences. The style guide for some scientific and technical reports is *Scientific and Technical Reports: Preparation, Presentation and Preservation* by the National Information Standards Organization. Because many technical communication, technical writing, and professional writing courses are in English Departments, *Writing for the Government* is in MLA documentation style. There are commercial software programs available that can convert a documentation style to another.

Every professional publication and government website needs to adhere to a style guide or to have style guidelines created for it. Moreover, because of the interrelationship between text and visuals—between writing and design—style guides for publications today usually incorporate information about graphics as well. Consistency in written content and design features help readers comprehend messages easily, efficiently, and effectively. However, government writers should be aware that a site's URL (Universal Resource Locator) and/or content likely change as the site is updated.

The government style guide is the *U.S. Government Printing Office Manual.* Useful style guides for agencies and organizations also contain information on ethical and legal issues that government writers need to know. These books are resources for government employees to turn to for advice about a myriad of topics. Chapter 4 goes into more detail about paper document style guides and Chapter 8 discusses style guides for websites.

Technological Factors

Some want to believe that technology is value-neutral; however, just because technologies such as computers and cell phones are not human beings does not mean that they were and continue to be devoid of human-value judgments in their development. They have been and continue to be created and developed by people, and, as a result, they work within cultural contexts, as does text, which is also created by people. Writers need to consider not only the content of the message but also how it is delivered (Rude, "Toward" 274).

Technology today offers government communicators many opportunities to prepare documents that are well written, edited, published, and disseminated. Computers and software technology help writers build and store information as well as research, while allowing individuals to reach across the globe in ways never before imagined; yet, technology can in and of itself pose political, social, economical and even ethical questions and problems. As we saw in the beginning of the chapter, the technology of voting raises political, social, economical, and ethical issues.

Let's take the difference between a billboard about a public meeting posted in a community's U.S. Post Office and one posted on the same community's website. Citizens within a community who may not have access to a computer can see the postings at the Post Office while they will miss a notice online. On the other hand, someone who lives in a community but is temporarily out of town may see the notice on the community website but would have missed it in the Post Office. To be ethical and fair as much as possible to every citizen, government writers need to consider how the venue for the delivery of a message might privilege one person or group over another and prevent that from happening.

Organizational Culture and Ethics

All workplace settings have their own cultures that affect how documents are written, communicated, edited, designed, and distributed. No individual is free from the political and social realities of the organization in which he or she works. An organization can be unusually hierarchical—where writers have little autonomy and all their work has to be approved by people up the chain of command—or it can be a place where writers have a great deal of autonomy; it can be a situation where there are lots of writers working, or a single writer doing all the communicating to various audiences. Writers with savoir faire can go into different work environments and immediately assess the organizational culture—not only the document genres but also other things like the lines of authority, the flexibility of the organization toward change, and the level of respect for the writer's job. Agencies and organizations have their own constraints on the writing, editing, designing, and distributing of documents. For instance, there are deadlines to meet, budgetary restrictions, legal issues to deal with, personality differences, and so forth, all of which contribute to the cultural context of the writing circumstances within agencies and organizations and to their own ethical environments and dilemmas.

If you are in a position in which you ethically disagree with your agency or even your boss, Dragga ("A Question") suggests approaches to resolving ethical dilemmas: Are there laws or rules governing a decision? Are there historical records to learn from? Do any corporate or professional codes of ethics offer guidance? What will co-workers think about this action? What would our moral leaders do in this situation? (Johnson-Sheehan 84–86).

One of the best ways to change the course of a decision is to "do your homework"—meaning research the facts related to the decision, especially the cost-benefit of any situation. Demonstrating that the decision you are opposed to can be costly in terms of money, prestige, and/or community goodwill for your employer in the short or long run can go a long way towards swaying the decision maker (Johnson-Sheehan 86). If that does not sway him or her, ask for legal advice, write a memo to the workplace files to demonstrate your doubts, and keep copies of your memos to yourself on your own private computer, not the agency's, about what has happened. Email and other information is not considered private on an agency's computer and can be accessed by supervisors.

Finally, there may be a time when the corporate or individual decision you are faced with is simply something you feel you ethically cannot carry out, and you will have to either be a whistleblower, which in itself can affect your career, or resign (Johnson-Sheehan 86–87). People get tangled in unethical situations because they feel that their boss or agency has given them no choice because they need the money from their work. Some would say that having enough money saved makes you less vulnerable so that you can leave if you feel forced to do something you consider unethical.

Professional groups and organizations have codes or guidelines for ethical conduct and these help guide writers as well. Professional organizations include the American Society of Public Administration (ASPA), Association of Computing Machinery (ACM), the Association for Educational Communications and Technology (AECT), the Association of Fund Raising Professionals (AFP), the Institute of Electrical and Electronic Engineers (IEEE), the National Association of Science Writers (NASW), and the Society for Technical Communication (STC). You can also seek help through websites such as Onlineethics.org for Engineering and Science (Johnson-Sheehan 87).

Personal Ethics and Government Writer Ethos

Ethics is also the development of one's own ethical standards (Markkula). Individuals hold values—principles and rules of thought, belief, and behavior—that have been internalized during a lifetime by family, education, religion, social organizations, and other groups. These values underpin ethical choices. One of the first places to begin thinking about ethical issues in documents is to consider how text creates the professional *ethos* of the writer—the ethical personae of its writer. One thing to keep in mind is that you are not writing to a close family member or friend; you are communicating to many people whom you do not know personally, although what you write will be read one person at a time. You are "conversing" with an individual.

Two other important rhetorical principles that affect *ethos* are *tone* and *style*. The tone of any document is critical to its impact. It conveys an attitude to a reader and to the document.

How does the reader feel about the writer? Does the writer seem to care about the individual?

Does the writer have credibility to the reader?

Does the writer seem to care whether he or she is communicating effectively with the individual? Are the people who depend on you, as a government writer, able to decipher the information you are providing because you have written for them, or is it nearly impossible for them to understand because it is full of jargon, legalese, or missing key information?

Your writing can seem flippant, disrespectful, serious, and/or dismissive. Sometimes the individuals for whom you write will be people who fundamentally distrust the government. How will the words you craft represent the agency or organization? How will they engender trust? Effective writers and communicators want their messages to engender credibility and trust. This is one of the challenges of writing and communicating for the government.

No matter what agency or organization a writer works for, the *ethos*—the persuasive persona of the writer—is especially important for government writers who are seeking public input and especially when they are trying to build consensus among potentially adversarial stakeholders. An approach for communicating with stakeholders is to think of them as partners who **collaborate** with you rather than with opponents, an argument strategy that can be attributed to psychologist Carl Rogers, whose work centered on effective communication (Shiyab). According to Rogers, communication works better when parties:

- Begin with reducing tension rather than being confrontational
- Find common ground instead of what divides
- Listen to each other and avoid the natural tendency to pass judgment
- Understand the other's position

By approaching a potential confrontational situation in this manner, Rogerians contend that a writer/communicator can eliminate the threat that opponents feel and move toward solving a problem together (Shiyab). When working with adversarial stakeholders, government writers will find approaching their constituency with these strategies will help diffuse tensions and foster better communication.

The U.S. Government Office of Ethics, which focuses on general ethical behavior of all federal government employees, has advice that is useful for government writers. The website says there are two ethical core concepts:

- Employees shall not use public office for private gain
- Employees shall act impartially and not give preferential treatment to any private organization or individual

In addition, employees must strive to avoid any action that would create the appearance that they are violating the law or ethical standards.

By observing these general principles, and specific ethics standards, employees help to ensure that citizens have confidence in the integrity of Government operations and programs (<http://www.usoge.gov/pages/index.html>).

To summarize ethical considerations and consequences, Dragga's quote is to the point:

[I]t is all too often easy for each of us to get caught up in the immediate needs of the organizations for which we work, to feel the pressures of personal ambition, to do that which is convenient, to want whatever it takes to satisfy the boss or client while completing the job on time and within budget, and to rationalize the dubious practices we momentarily adopt. Periodic self-examination is thus important as a way of orienting ourselves again as professionals and reaffirming the principles of ethical communication ("Is It Ethical?" 264).

Summary and Looking Forward

Writing and communicating is never done in a vacuum. It is done within a cultural context for the reader, writer, and for the document or website. Cultural context is the confluence of the social exchange of people within a particular time and place. Deciding what you want to accomplish is the purpose of a document or website. The purpose for which you are writing, designing, or editing should arise from your audience's needs for the information and should shape the best means to communicate the information, whether it is paper or online. In like manner having a clear purpose in writing emerges from understanding the cultural context of a document or website.

In the case of government writers, the cultural context encompasses their interactions with their audiences, each other within their own agency and with other agencies, and with the documents they read, study, and create. The cultural context involves the discourse conventions of agency employees, stakeholders, and interested people. This interchange of groups creates and emphasizes certain kinds of language usage and often shapes genres for documents and websites. An essential component of the cultural context for any text is the ethical choices—the value judgments made by writers, communicators, editors, designers, and distributors—and the personal and professional consequences of those choices for readers as well as those involved with the creation, editing, and distribution of a work. Finally, a key component of the cultural context is the technological possibilities and constraints of the time in which text and documents are written and developed for paper or for the digital world. Chapter 3 focuses on one specific kind of government writing, rules and regulations. Although we may not realize it, government rules and regulations surround our entire daily professional and personal activities, as the chapter will show.

Activities and Assignments

1. **Individual Activity:** Electronic voting has its own possibilities and problems. Research electronic voting, and write a research paper about your findings. Share your findings with your classmates.
2. **Individual Activity:** Find a political issue that you are interested in, find documents related to it, and write about the list of ethical matters related to the issue and/or any of the documents about the issue.
3. **Individual Activity:** Review the various documents in Case Study 1 about Hurricane Katrina and consider the ethical circumstances and consequences of the documents. Write a research paper about what you found.
4. **Individual Activity:** Chapters 1 and 2 list important documents in America's history: the Declaration of Independence, Federal Judiciary Act in 1789, the Louisiana Purchase Treaty of 1803, Treaty of Fort Laramie in 1868, the Social Security Act of 1935, Executive Order 8802 Prohibiting Discrimination in the Defense Industry in 1941, the Tonkin Gulf Resolution in 1964, and the Voting Rights Act of 1965. Find copies of two of these documents and compare the language in them. (See Appendix B for copies of the Declaration of Independence, the U.S. Constitution, and the Bill of Rights.) Research the history of the documents. Write a report about the cultural context of the documents, and share it with your classmates.
5. **Group Internet Activity:** Go to your campus website or to various offices on campus or their websites and collect a variety of documents about your campus. Have each person in the group choose a few documents and analyze them—comparing and contrasting—according to the principles and approaches in Chapters 1 and 2.
6. **Group Internet Activity:** Go to various websites related to government agencies and ethics, choose a site, and analyze its key ethical principles. Then compare the various websites with each other. Some of the sites are these:

Department of Agriculture
http://www.usda-ethics.net/

U.S. Department of Justice
Departmental Ethics Office
http://www.usdoj.gov/jmd/ethics/

The Council of Governmental Ethics Law
http://www.cogel.org/

United States Office of Government Ethics
http://www.usoge.gov/index.html

Government Ethics Training
http://www.ethics.gov

7. **Group Activity:** Find style guides for various agencies and organizations and have everyone in the group choose one, make a list of characteristics of that style guide, and share with the group what they found.

Works Cited

Addison, Wesley, Longman. *Author's Guide*. New York: Addison, Wesley, Longman, 1998.

American Psychological Association. Publication Manual of the American Psychological Association (APA) 5th ed. Washington, D.C.: APA, 2001.

Bascetta, Cynthia A. "Clarity of Letters to Claimants Needs to be Improved." *Report to the Ranking Democratic Member, Committee on Veterans' Affairs, House of Representatives.* United States General Accounting Office. 23 Apr. 2002: 3.

Bailey, Bob. "The Usability of Punched Ballots." Dec. 2000. 11 Dec. 2005 <http://webusability.com/article_usability_of_punched_ballots_12_2000.htm>.

Barbour, Philip L. *The Jamestown Voyages Under the First Charter 1606–1606.* Vol. 1. Second Series. No. CXXXVI. The Hakluyt Society. London: Cambridge U.P., 1969.

Bowdon, Melody and J. Blake Scott. *Service-Learning in Technical and Professional Communication.* The Allyn & Bacon Series in Technical Communication. New York: Addison Wesley Longman, 2003.

CENDI. "Frequently Asked Questions about Copyright: Issues Affecting the U.S. Government." CENDI Copyright Working Group. Edited and updated by Bonnie Klein and Gail Hodge. Oak Ridge, TN: CENDI Secretariat Information International Associates, Inc., Jan. 2002, updated Mar. 2007. 23 May 2007 <http://www.cendi.gov/publications/04-8copyright.html#222>.

Compston, Christine, and Rachel Filene Seidman, eds. *Our Documents: 100 Milestone Documents from the National Archives.* New York: Oxford UP, 2003.

Council of Scientific Editors Style Committee. CSE Manual for Authors, Editors, and Publishers. 7th ed. Reston, VA: Council of Scientific Editors, June 2006.

Dragga, Sam. "Is It Ethical? A Survey of Opinion on Principles and Practices of Document Design." *Technical Communication* 43.3: (Aug. 1996) 255–65.

—. "A Question of Ethics: Lessons from Technical Communications on the Job." *Technical Communication Quarterly* 6.2 (Spring 1997): 161–78.

Environmental Protection Agency "National Priorites List." 24 Feb. 2006. 21 May 2007 <http://www.epa.gov/superfund/sites/npl/index.htm>.

Flower, Linda. "Revising Writer-based Prose." *Journal of Basic Writing* 3.3 (1981): 62–74.

—. "Writer-Based Prose: A Cognitive Basis for Problems in Writing." *College English* 41 (Sept. 1979): 19–37.

Gibaldi, Joseph. *MLA Handbook for Writers of Research Papers.* 6th ed. New York: MLA, 2003.

—. *MLA Style Manual and Guide to Scholarly Publishing.* 2nd ed. New York: MLA, 1998.

Goldstein, Norm., ed. Associated Press Stylebook and Briefing on Media Law, Fully Revised and Updated. New York: Perseus Books, 2007.

Johnson-Sheehan, Richard. *Technical Communication Today.* New York: Pearson Education, 2005.

Jones, Sheila C. "A Cautionary Tale." *Intercom* Nov. 2005: 9.

Levin, Steve. "Pressure for Success Often Lures Researchers to Fudge the Truth." *Pittsburgh Post-Gazette*. 19 March 2006. 1 May 2007 <http://www.post-gazette.com/pg/06078/672956.stm>.

Locke, Joanne. "A History of Plain Language in the United States Government (2004)." 20 May 2007 <http://www.plainlanguage.gov>.

Markkula Center for Applied Ethics. Jan. 2006. Webpages developed by Manuel Velasquez, Claire Andre, Thomas Shanks, S. J., and Michael J. Myer. 21 May 2007 <http://www.scu.edu/ethics/practicing/decision/whatisethics.html>.

Microsoft Corporation Editorial Style Board. Microsoft Manual of Style for Technical Publications. 3rd ed. Redmond, WA: Microsoft Corporation, 2004.

Miller-Jacobs, Hal. "Palm Beach County Ballot Illustrates Usability Problem." *The HFI User Interface Design Update Newsletter*. Nov. 2000. 28 Nov. 2005 <http://www.humanfactors.com/downloads/election.asp/>.

National Information Standards Organization. Scientific and Technical Reports—Preparation, Presentation and Preservation. ANSI/NISO Z39.18-2005. Bethesda, MD: NISO, 2005.

Osselton, N.E. "Hakluyt's Language." *The Hakluyt Handbook*. Vol. 1. Second Series No. 144. Ed. David Beers. The Hakluyt Society. London: University Printing House, Cambridge, 1974.

Oxford English Dictionary Online (OED) 2nd ed. 1989 "divers." Dec. 2006. <http://dictionary.oed.com>.

Plain Language website. 31 Jan. 2006 <http://plainlanguage.gov/>.

Price, Alan R. "Cases of Plagiarism Handled by the United States Office of Research Integrity 1992–2005." *Plagiary: Cross Disciplinary Studies in Plagiarism, Fabrication, and Falsification*, 1(1): 1–11.

Reitz, Joan M. *Online Dictionary for Library and Information Science* (ODLIS). Def. of "Intellectual Property." Portsmouth, NH: Libraries Unlimited, 2004. 22 May 2007 <http://lu.com/odis>.

Rude, Carolyn D. *Technical Editing* 4th ed. The Allyn & Bacon series in Technical Communication. New York: Pearson Longman, 2006.

—. "Toward an Expanded Concept of Rhetorical Delivery: The Uses of Reports in Public Policy Debates." *Technical Communication Quarterly* 13.3: 271–88.

Shiyab, Siad. "Argument: An Alternative Model." *Lore: Rhetoric, Writing, Culture*. 2.2 (Nov. 2002). 21 May 2007 <http://www-rohan.sdsu.edu/dept/drwswebb/lore/2_2shiyab_arg.htm>.

Simpson, Doug. "Blanco's Katrina Correspondences Reveal Extent of Chaos." The Associated Press. AOL News. 4 Dec. 2005. 4 Dec. 2005 <http://aolsvc.news. aol.com>.

Tufte, Edward R. *The Cognitive Style of PowerPoint*. Cheshire, CT: Graphics Press, 2003. 9–12.

—. *Visual Explanations: Images, Quantities, Evidence, and Narrative*. Cheshire, CT, Graphics Press, 1997. 38–53.

University of Chicago Press. The Chicago Manual of Style. 15th ed. Chicago: U of Chicago P, 2003.

U.S. Air Force. The Tongue and Quill. (AFH 33-337). Maxwell AFB: Air Command and Staff College, 1 Aug. 2004. Available online at http://www.e-publishing.af.mil/pubfiles/af/33/afh33-337/afh33-337.pdf.

U.S. Copyright Office. 21 May 2007 <http://www.copyright.gov>.

—. *"Copyright Basics."* 22 May 2007 <http://www.copyright.gov/cirs/circ01.pdf/>.

U.S. Printing Office. *U.S. Government Printing Office Style Manual*. 29th ed. Washington, D.C., 2000. Available online at http://www.gpoaccess.gov/stylemanual/index.html.

U.S. Office of Government Ethics. 21 May 2007 <http://www.usoge.gov/index.html>.

PART 2

Writing to Make Policy

CHAPTER 3

Rules and Regulations

In October 2005, the City of Houston's Bureau of Air Quality Control received a complaint on behalf of blind and disabled citizens in an assisted-living facility— (City of Houston) about a crematorium at a funeral home, which was located nearby. The complainant alleged that there was ash and soot on cars in the parking lot and a horrible odor of burning bones, hair, and flesh in the air; the complainant also questioned why he had not been notified that a crematorium had been allowed to operate in the residential area (City of Houston). The City of Houston's Bureau of Air Quality Control investigated the complaint the next day, but when the investigator arrived, he did not smell the odor and could not confirm violations of any federal, state, or local rules (City of Houston). Within days, the complainant's allegations had spread throughout the city. The allegations were reported by the local news media and to the Houston City Council; one city council member stated, "I guess you don't think of a crematorium in your back yard" and suggested "the state needs to step in." (Click2Houston.com). According to the news report, the Texas Funeral Home Commission and the Texas Commission on Environmental Quality are also responsible for regulating these complaints. (Click2Houston.com).

As you read this sequence of events you might wonder:

Do government agencies consider affected communities when allowing businesses to operate close to homes or residential facilities?

How does the public learn about proposed rules that might affect their homes or incomes?

What roles do politicians play in developing and enforcing rules?

Are city, state, and federal agencies responsible for enforcing the same types of rules?

Most important for this textbook, you might wonder, who actually writes government rules?

In this chapter, we will answer many of your questions regarding rules and pay especially close attention to the purpose for rule writing, the audience for rules, ethical dilemmas faced by rule writers, and the contexts in which rules are written.

The Purpose of Rules

Rules, which are also commonly called **regulations,** are those local, state, and federal policies written and approved by governmental and administrative agencies to protect the various interests of the public and the communities we live in. For the purposes of this textbook, **policies** are the various types of government-mandated and agreed-upon requirements, including federal, state, county, and local rules and **laws.** In "Rulemaking Under Chapter 120, Florida Statutes," Glenda E. Hood, Florida's Secretary of State defines the term *rules* when she states, "In order to carry out the laws enacted by the Legislature, government agencies adopt legally binding rules. Rules are road maps for dealing with government, providing a path to the desired destination and conditions under which the trip must be made. Rules are intended to facilitate the governmental process, level the playing field, and protect the rights of all." We begin this chapter with the City of Houston Bureau of Air Quality Control example to help us examine some of the cultural, political, and rhetorical situations in which rules are written and enforced in cities and states across the United States.

Although the City of Houston employees in our example are responsible for enforcing air quality and environmental rules, they were not responsible for writing or defining the scope of rules that explain how funeral homes with crematoriums must operate to comply with air-quality standards in the State of Texas. Also, you should know that even though Congress and state legislators are responsible for making laws concerning our environment, few laws go into the details and specifics found in federal and state rules. The policies that City of Houston employees follow when enforcing environmental standards related to crematoriums are located in the Texas Administrative Code, which is where the State of Texas **codifies** state rules. Some examples of the very detailed and complex rules written and enforced to protect our interests include local health codes that require restaurateurs and food establishments to serve food and drinks under clean and healthy conditions, child care rules that outline the minimum standards for safe child care facilities under nurturing and healthy child care supervision, and federal and state rules written to limit the negative effects of businesses on the air you breathe, the water you drink, and the ground you walk on.

The City of Houston's Bureau of Air Quality Control narrative explains how environmental rules can protect citizens while simultaneously restricting the activities of those businesses required to follow rules. Government agencies are responsible for making sure that citizens are able to breathe clean air, but at the time these agencies must be careful that their interference does not restrict the public from their right to operate businesses in a free enterprise economy. In a sense, government rules are the compromise between regulated businesses and those constituents and communities that could be negatively impacted by the by-products generated in the production and distribution of goods and services. Rules represent an agreement among stakeholders outlining what business practices are acceptable in a given community. Government agencies achieve this implicit agreement between government agencies, regulated entities (businesses and individuals), and affected communities through an "open" process that allows citizens, business owners, advocacy groups, and other interested parties to comment on the rules that government agencies propose.

While each state has its own set of rules written to protect their constituents, federal rules are more authoritative and far reaching and are found in the *Code of Federal Regulations*. Before rules are codified there they are published in the *Federal Register* for review and comment by the public. Take a look at the proposed Federal Aviation Administration change as published in the *Federal Register* in Figure 3.1. We've included commentary to help you identify different parts of the proposed rule.

Rules or Laws?

Rules, like many other genres of technical communication, require the generation of ideas from internal and external sources. Although some people fail to differentiate rule writing from "legal writing" and mistakenly use the terms *rules and regulations* interchangeably with *laws,* rule writing is very different from the making of laws. While Congressional and state laws are developed by Congress and state legislatures, these legislative bodies give federal and state agencies the authority and latitude to write the very detailed rules needed to accomplish the specific goals of both the legislative bodies and the government agencies. In Table 3.1 take a look at an excerpt from section 50-13-1, a law that outlines the steps government agencies in Georgia must take to make rules and section 391-1-1-.04, a rule written at the Government Department of Natural Resources Environmental Protection Division:

In Table 3.1, you can see that the Georgia *law,* Section 50-13-3, establishes the scope of the *rule,* Section 391-1-1-.04, but does not attempt to provide the details provided in rule, which includes addresses, name of the agency, and a lot of other details that state legislators and their staff would not have the time or resources to provide for every regulatory agency in the State of Georgia.

An aspect of rule writing that differentiates it from other genres of technical communication such as report writing, proposal writing, and website design, is the fact that rule writing is a collaborative writing process that can be judged illegal if ideas from outside of the government organizations—external sources—are ignored. While reports and websites are genres of technical communication created for a countless number of reasons, by law, rules are written under very limited and heavily monitored conditions. The state law from the Texas Statutes

Federal Register / Vol. 70, No. 249 / Thursday, December 29, 2005 / Proposed Rules 77275

The text that precedes the proposed rule §401.5 is called the **rule preamble.** In this example, you can see several explanatory sections including, "International Trade Impact Assessment," "Unfunded Mandates Assessments," "Executive Order 13132, Federalism," "Environmental Analysis," and "Regulations that Significantly Affect Energy Supply, Distribution, or Use."

International Trade Impact Assessment

The Trade Agreement Act of 1979 prohibits Federal agencies from establishing any standards or engaging in related activities that create unnecessary obstacles to the foreign commerce of the United States. Legitimate domestic objectives, such as safety, are not considered unnecessary obstacles. Because this rulemaking would be largely consistent with current or prudent practice, it would not create obstacles. The statute also requires consideration of international standards and where appropriate, that they be the basis for U.S. standards. The FAA has assessed the potential effect of this proposed rule and determined that it would impose the same costs on domestic and international entities, and thus has a neutral trade impact.

Unfunded Mandates Assessments

The Unfunded Mandates Reform Act of 1995 (the Act) is intended, among other things, to curb the practice of imposing unfunded Federal mandates on State, local, and tribal governments. Title II of the Act requires each Federal agency to prepare a written statement assessing the effects of any Federal mandate in a proposed or final agency rule that may result in an expenditure of $100 million or more (adjusted annually for inflation) in any one year by State, local, and tribal governments, in the aggregate, or by the private sector; such a mandate is deemed to be a "significant regulatory action." The FAA currently uses an inflation-adjusted value of $120.7 million in lieu of $100 million. This proposed rule does not contain such a mandate. The requirements of Title II do not apply.

Executive Order 13132, Federalism

The FAA has analyzed this proposed rule under the principles and criteria of Executive Order 13132, Federalism. We determined that this action would not have a substantial direct effect on the States, on the relationship between the National Government and the States, or on the distribution of power and responsibilities among the various levels of government, and therefore would not have federalism implications.

Environmental Analysis

FAA Order 1050.1E identifies FAA actions that are categorically excluded from preparation of an environmental assessment or environmental impact statement under the National Environmental Policy Act in the absence of extraordinary circumstances. The FAA has determined this proposed rulemaking action qualifies for the categorical exclusion identified in paragraph (4i) appendix F and involves no extraordinary circumstances.

Regulations That Significantly Affect Energy Supply, Distribution, or Use

The FAA has analyzed this NPRM under Executive Order 13211, Actions Concerning Regulations that Significantly Affect Energy Supply, Distribution, or Use (May 18, 2001). We have determined that it is not a "significant energy action" under the executive order because it is not a "significant regulatory action" under Executive Order 12866, and it is not likely to have a significant adverse effect on the supply, distribution, or use of energy.

List of Subjects

14 CFR Part 401

Human space flight, Organization and functions (Government agencies), Space safety, Space transportation and exploration.

14 CFR Part 415

Human space flight, Rockets, Space safety, Space transportation and exploration.

14 CFR Part 431

Human space flight, Reporting and recordkeeping requirements, Rockets, Space safety, Space transportation and exploration.

14 CFR Part 435

Human space flight, Reporting and recordkeeping requirements, Rockets, Space safety, Space transportation and exploration.

14 CFR Part 440

Armed forces, Federal buildings and facilities, Government property, Indemnity payments, Insurance, Reporting and recordkeeping requirements, Space transportation and exploration.

14 CFR Part 450

Armed forces, Federal buildings and facilities, Government property, Human space flight, Indemnity payments, Insurance, Reporting and recordkeeping requirements, Space transportation and exploration.

14 CFR Part 460

Human space flight, Reporting and recordkeeping requirements, Rockets, Space safety, Space transportation and exploration.

IV. The Proposed Amendment

In consideration of the foregoing, the Federal Aviation Administration proposes to amend parts 401, 415, 431, 435, and 440; remove and reserve part 450 of Chapter III of title 14, Code of Federal Regulations; and add part 460 as follows—

PART 401—ORGANIZATION AND DEFINITIONS

1. The authority citation for part 401 continues to read as follows:

Authority: 49 U.S.C. 70101–70121.

2. Section 401.5 is amended by adding the following definitions in alphabetical order to read as follows:

§ 401.5 Definitions.

* * * * *

Crew means any employee or independent contractor of a licensee, transferee, or permittee, or of a contractor or subcontractor of a licensee, transferee, or permittee, who performs activities in the course of that employment directly relating to the launch, reentry, or other operation of or in a launch vehicle or reentry vehicle that carries human beings. A crew consists of flight crew and any remote operator.

* * * * *

Flight crew means crew that is on board a vehicle during a launch or reentry.

* * * * *

Operator means a holder of a license or permit under 49 U.S.C. Subtitle IX, chapter 701.

* * * * *

Pilot means a flight crew member who has the ability to control, in real time, a launch or reentry vehicle's flight path.

* * * * *

Remote operator means a crew member who

(1) Has the ability to control, in real time, a launch or reentry vehicle's flight path, and

(2) Is not on board the controlled vehicle.

* * * * *

Space flight participant means an individual, who is not crew, carried within a launch vehicle or reentry vehicle.

Suborbital rocket means a vehicle, rocket-propelled in whole or in part, intended for flight on a suborbital trajectory, and the thrust of which is greater than its lift for the majority of the rocket-powered portion of its ascent.

Suborbital trajectory means the intentional flight path of a launch vehicle, reentry vehicle, or any portion thereof, whose vacuum instantaneous impact point does not leave the surface of the Earth.

* * * * *

A rule's section symbol, §, is followed by a number that denotes the specific rule being changed or "amended." In this example, the amendment to §401.5 includes revised definitions relevant to human space flight.

"The Proposed Amendment" signals that the specifics of the proposed rule change follows.

FIGURE 3.1 Excerpt from "Proposed Rules, December 29, 2005." Source: *Federal Register*

Georgia Administrative Procedures Act	Georgia Department of Natural Resources Rule
50–13–3.	391–1–1–.04

Georgia Administrative Procedures Act

50–13–3.

(a) In addition to other rule-making requirements imposed by law, each agency shall:

(1) Adopt as a rule a description of its organization, stating the general course and method of its operations and the methods whereby the public may obtain information or make submissions or requests;

(2) Adopt rules of practice setting forth the nature and requirements of all formal and informal procedures available, including a description of all forms and instructions used by the agency;

(3) Make available for public inspection all rules and all other written statements of policy or interpretations formulated, adopted, or used by the agency in the discharge of its functions; and

(4) Make available for public inspection all final orders, decisions, and opinions except those expressly made confidential or privileged by statute.

(b) No agency rule, order, or decision shall be valid or effective against any person or party nor may it be invoked by the agency for any purpose until it has been published or made available for public inspection as required in this Code section. This provision is not applicable in favor of any person or party who has actual knowledge thereof.[1]

Georgia Department of Natural Resources Rule

391–1–1–.04

Method of Obtaining Information from, Making Submissions to or Requests of the Department. Amended.

(1) General Information concerning the Department's operations may be obtained from 205 Butler Street, S.E., Suite 1252, Floyd Towers East, Atlanta, Georgia 30334.

(2) More specific requests for information or submissions may be directed as follows:

(a) For licenses—fishing and hunting, 2189 Northlake Parkway, Building 10, Suite 108, Tucker, Georgia 30084.

(b) For boat registration—2189 Northlake Parkway, Building 10, Suite 108, Tucker, Georgia 30084.

(c) For coastal information—One Conservation Way, Suite 300, Brunswick, Georgia 31520–8687.

(d) For environmental information—205 Butler Street, S.E., Suite 1152 East, Atlanta, Georgia 30334.

(e) For state parks and historic sites information—205 Butler Street, S. E., Suite 1352 East, Atlanta, Georgia 30334.

(f) For historic preservation information—500 The Healey Building, 57 Forsyth Street, N.W., Atlanta, Georgia 30303.

(3) To request that the name and address of a person or organization be placed on a Division's mailing list maintained for advance notice of its rule-making proceedings pursuant to O.C.G.A. Section 50–13–4, a written request shall be mailed to the Director of that Division. The written request shall contain a complete and accurate mailing address of the person or organization to which advance notice is to be mailed. The written request may specify that the person or organization is to receive advanced notice of only the proposed rules or proposed amendments to rules of a specific program or branch of a Division, such as proposed rules or amendments to rules proposed by the Land Protection Branch of the Environmental Protection Division or the Hunting and Fishing Regulations proposed annually by the Wildlife Resources Division. Authority: O.C.G.A. § 50–13–3[2]

TABLE 3.1   Relationship Between Rules and Laws.

---

[1] Excerpt from "Georgia Code." Source: Official Code of Georgia Annotated
[2] Excerpt from "Georgia Department of Natural Resources" Source: Georgia Secretary of State

Government Code, Title 10, Subtitle A, Chapter 2001, Subchapter A, section 2001.021, is an example of a law that defines the parameters within which Texans must maneuver to write rules.

§ 2001.021. Petition for Adoption of Rules

(a) An interested person by petition to a state agency may request the adoption of a rule.

(b) A state agency by rule shall prescribe the form for a petition under this section and the procedure for its submission, consideration, and disposition.

(c) Not later than the 60th day after the date of submission of a petition under this section, a state agency shall:

(1) deny the petition in writing, stating its reasons for the denial; or

(2) initiate a rulemaking proceeding under this subchapter.

Within government agencies, administrators select writers from a group of diverse professionals including managers, subject-matter experts, attorneys, accountants, information technology professionals, and editors to write rules concerning subjects ranging from telecommunications to health care facilities.

Rule Writing in Cultural Contexts

Now that you have a basic idea of what rules are, it is important to understand that almost every good or service that you consume and every public space you operate in is regulated by some government agency. For example, each morning, even before you begin your school- or workday, you will likely encounter dozens of goods and services that are regulated by government agencies. Even this morning, you might have begun your day with a shower; read or listened to the morning news; fed your children eggs and milk; drank a cup of water, coffee or orange juice; filled up your gas tank at the corner gas station; dropped off your children at day care; and finally drove to your school or workplace. In that brief span of time, you drank and bathed in water in which quality is regulated by environment and health and safety agencies. You consumed food and beverages whose safety is regulated by the food and safety agencies, such as the Department of Agriculture. You read or listened to television, radio, or Internet news, whose fitness is regulated by the Federal Communications Commission. You purchased gasoline, whose consumption, production, and distribution is regulated by environmental and economic agencies, and drove on roads regulated by transportation agencies. You have placed your children in the care of day care providers, whose establishments are regulated by health and human services agencies. Finally, you have arrived at a school or workplace that is likely regulated by equal opportunity and workplace safety agencies.

Ideally, corporations and businesses would make every effort to protect their consumers from unhealthy food products, dangerous natural resources, and unqualified practitioners. Unfortunately, history and experience has taught us that some businesses fail to protect their consumers, due to lack of knowledge regarding what health and safety standards are most appropriate, while other business owners might operate from unethical perspectives that allow them to ignore their consumers' interests in order to maximize their own profits. Government agencies at the federal and state levels partner with businesses and individuals to draft rules that set parameters for businesses and individuals to produce and distribute goods, services, and by-products that will not harm the public.

In the opening narrative about the City of Houston's Bureau of Air Quality Control, you can see the number of different people who were affected and protected by environmental rules and their enforcement. Notice that this single incident affected the business owner and his customers, nonprofit organizations, other residents who live near the business, politicians responsible for protecting the interests of all of their constituents (residents, nonprofit organizations, and business owners), the media, and anyone in the City of Houston who was interested in the conflicts that arose as a result of the complaint. Conflicts or disagreements about rules or the enforcement of rules is common. Government personnel responsible for writing and enforcing rules are accustomed to handling these conflicts and have created clear guidelines for receiving and considering public opinions about the wording and enforcement of rules. We will discuss the collaborative nature of rule writing later in the chapter. In the meantime, it is important for you to know that you are part of the audience for rules. Whenever you hear about proposed rules or regulations enforced in your city or state, or even at the federal level, remember that you have a right to make written or oral comments about those rules to the government agency responsible for writing and enforcing them.

Audience for Rules

The primary audience for rules consists of those persons who actually read the rules because of these individuals' economic, social, or political interests in the scope and enforcement of the rules. Although we can all admit that we participate in daily activities that require government intervention and rules, this fact does not motivate most of us to actively read rules or even find out where to locate them. Clearly many residents of the United States of America have some idea of what rules and regulations are, but few take the time to read them, regardless of the impact of the rules on the health and safety of our families and children. Those persons who really take the time to read rules are most likely those who would suffer or benefit socially, politically, and economically from rule changes. The majority of people who take the time to locate rules and proposed changes to rules are business owners and licensed practitioners (physicians, attorneys, funeral home operators) and other professionals whose livelihoods would be severely impacted by changes in the way they distribute their goods and services.

Another reason that the general public or a nonexpert audience does not read rules as much as businesspersons and licensed practitioners regulated by rules is because, for the most part, rules are written for an expert audience who understand the specifics of the types of businesses addressed by any set of rules. Let's take a look at Figure 3.2, one of the actual regulations that the City of Houston Bureau of Air Quality Control investigator might have used to determine

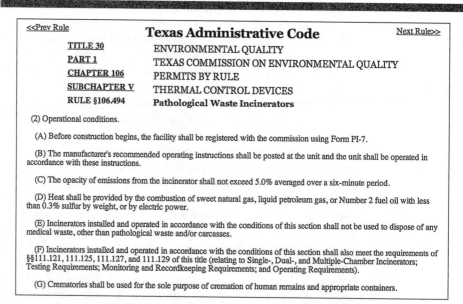

<<Prev Rule

Texas Administrative Code

Next Rule>>

TITLE 30	ENVIRONMENTAL QUALITY
PART 1	TEXAS COMMISSION ON ENVIRONMENTAL QUALITY
CHAPTER 106	PERMITS BY RULE
SUBCHAPTER V	THERMAL CONTROL DEVICES
RULE §106.494	**Pathological Waste Incinerators**

(2) Operational conditions.

(A) Before construction begins, the facility shall be registered with the commission using Form PI-7.

(B) The manufacturer's recommended operating instructions shall be posted at the unit and the unit shall be operated in accordance with these instructions.

(C) The opacity of emissions from the incinerator shall not exceed 5.0% averaged over a six-minute period.

(D) Heat shall be provided by the combustion of sweet natural gas, liquid petroleum gas, or Number 2 fuel oil with less than 0.3% sulfur by weight, or by electric power.

(E) Incinerators installed and operated in accordance with the conditions of this section shall not be used to dispose of any medical waste, other than pathological waste and/or carcasses.

(F) Incinerators installed and operated in accordance with the conditions of this section shall also meet the requirements of §§111.121, 111.125, 111.127, and 111.129 of this title (relating to Single-, Dual-, and Multiple-Chamber Incinerators; Testing Requirements; Monitoring and Recordkeeping Requirements; and Operating Requirements).

(G) Crematories shall be used for the sole purpose of cremation of human remains and appropriate containers.

FIGURE 3.2   Excerpt from § 106.494. Source: Texas Administrative Code

that the funeral home mentioned earlier in this chapter was not in violation of state rule—Texas Administrative Code, Title 30. Environmental Quality, Part I Texas Commission on Environmental Quality.

After reading this excerpt from the regulations, we can assume from the complexity of the rule that it was written for an expert audience who understands the operations, science, and technologies associated with thermal control devices. Quite frankly, most of us with access to the Internet or public libraries, where rules are most accessible, would not take the time to read a regulation on thermal control devices unless our homes, work, or families were directly affected by the regulation of these devices. The complexity of the language and specificity of the sentences like, "Heat shall be provided by the combustion of sweet natural gas, liquid petroleum gas, or Number 2 fuel oil with less than 0.3% sulfur by weight, or by electric power" does not encourage the casual perusal of rules by a general or uninterested audience. While some agencies are transitioning to a more plain style of rule writing in an effort to communicate to a broader audience, many government agencies have not allocated agency resources to hire technical writers to identify their audience and write with those audiences in mind.

Plainlanguage.gov is a government-sponsored website that encourages policy writers to use a plain and concise style of writing to reach a broad audience. When you use plain language, you choose words that most people know, avoid unnecessarily complex sentences, and create short sentences that can be read quickly. Figure 3.3 offers examples from the Plainlanguage.gov website, to compare rules written in the traditional "wordy" style of writing rules and rules written in the plain language style.

Plain Language.gov — Improving Communication from the Federal Government to the Public

Search — Powered by Google

Home | What is PL? | Why PL? | Using PL? | Examples | How To/Tools | Popular Topics | Resources

Examples > Before-and-After Comparisons > Reduce Wordiness

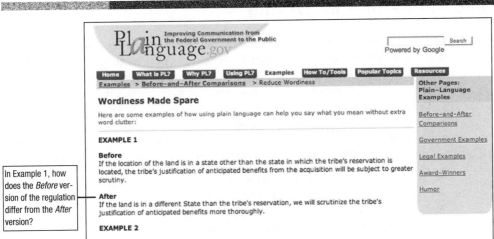

Wordiness Made Spare

Here are some examples of how using plain language can help you say what you mean without extra word clutter:

EXAMPLE 1

Before
If the location of the land is in a state other than the state in which the tribe's reservation is located, the tribe's justification of anticipated benefits from the acquisition will be subject to greater scrutiny.

After
If the land is in a different State than the tribe's reservation, we will scrutinize the tribe's justification of anticipated benefits more thoroughly.

> In Example 1, how does the *Before* version of the regulation differ from the *After* version?

EXAMPLE 2

Before
When the process of freeing a vehicle that has been stuck results in ruts or holes, the operator will fill the rut or hole created by such activity before removing the vehicle from the immediate area.

After
If you make a hole while freeing a stuck vehicle, you must fill the hole before you drive away.

> In Examples 2 and 3, do the *Before* and *After* versions communicate the same information?

EXAMPLE 3

Before
Under 25 CFR §1.4(b), the Secretary of the Interior may in specific cases or in specific geographic areas, adopt or make applicable to off-reservation Indian lands all or any part of such laws, ordinances, codes, resolutions, rules or other regulations of the State and political subdivisions in which the land is located as the Secretary shall determine to be in the best interest of the Indian owner or owners in achieving the highest and best use of such property.

After
Section 1.4(b) of 25 CFR allows us to make State or local laws or regulations apply to your off-reservation lands. We will do this only if we find that it will help you to achieve the highest and best use of your lands.

Making material into a list

Before
Sections 4.40 through 4.71 do not apply to Indian probate proceedings, heirship determinations under the White Earth Reservation Land Settlement Act of 1985, and other proceedings under subpart D of this part, except that §§ 4.40 through 4.71 do apply to cases referred to an administrative law judge pursuant to § 4.337(a)

After
Unless a case is referred to an administrative law judge under § 4.337(a), §§ 4.40 through 4.71 do not apply to:

1. Indian probate proceedings;
2. Heirship determinations under the White Earth Reservation Land Settlement Act of 1985; and
3. Other proceedings under subpart D of this part.

> Take a look at the *Before* and *After* versions under "Making material into list." Which versions are easier to read? Why?

Before
If a deponent fails to answer a question propounded, or a party upon whom a request is made under § 4.70, or a party on whom interrogatories are served fails to adequately respond or objects to the request, or any part thereof, or fails to permit inspection as requested, the discovering party may move the administrative law judge for an order compelling a response or inspection in accordance with the request.

After
You may move the administrative law judge for an order compelling a response or inspection if:

1. A deponent fails to answer a question;
2. A party upon whom you made a request under § 4.70, or a party on whom you served interrogatories either does not adequately respond or objects to the request; or
3. A party on whom you made a request under § 4.70, or a party on whom interrogatories are served does not permit inspection as requested.

Other Pages: Plain-Language Examples
- Before-and-After Comparisons
- Government Examples
- Legal Examples
- Award-Winners
- Humor

Home | About Us | Contact Us | Privacy and Other Policies | Feedback | Community | News | USA.gov

Site hosted by the Federal Aviation Administration and sponsored by the Web Content Management Working Group of the Interagency Committee on Government Information (ICGI).
An Official Site of the U.S. Government.

FIGURE 3.3 Examples of Plain Language Writing. Source: Plainlanguage.gov

Collaborative Nature of Rule Writing

In theory, government agencies and the public they serve work collaboratively to write rules. From political and economic theoretical perspectives, rules are public goods that are owned and authored by the public; however, some government documents such as memorandums and reports may be labeled *confidential*. Because proposed rules are open for public comment and have so many authors, these documents are arguably one of the most difficult genres of technical communication to write. The following list includes stakeholders and agency staff who are usually invited to engage in collaborative rule-writing workgroups:

- Agency directors or commissioners
- Policy specialists or subject matter experts
- Policy editors or regulation project managers
- Accountants, budget and fiscal analysts
- Agency commissions and boards of directors
- Legislative oversight bodies
- Agency attorneys
- Field staff
- Advocacy group representatives
- Business owners
- Consumers
- Researchers/academics
- Corporate and private attorneys

Although some government agencies do not receive as much public feedback or review by external sources as others, most agencies have some agreed-upon rule-writing processes that they use to make rule writing a less cumbersome process. Figure 3.4 is a visual representation of the rule-writing process at some agencies in the state of Texas.

Stakeholders in Rule Writing

In rule writing, stakeholders are those individuals or groups that are interested in helping to shape the language and intent of a rule. Some stakeholders may even advocate against the drafting of a rule or argue that a current rule should be deleted or **repealed.** The stakeholders' rationale for participating in the development of the rule is usually that they have some "stake" or vested interest in the outcome of the regulation. Stakeholders assume that the rule will have a negative or positive impact on their well-being. If there is no real affect on a particular person or group, they are not likely to spend the time and effort needed to advocate for or against the content or language used in a particular rule.

Let's reflect on the City of Houston Bureau of Environmental Quality Control example that we used to begin this chapter. Clearly, there are many stakeholders interested in where certain businesses are located, especially businesses that produce pollution, noise, and other by-products that might negatively affect those living near a business. In this particular example, the stakeholders would include

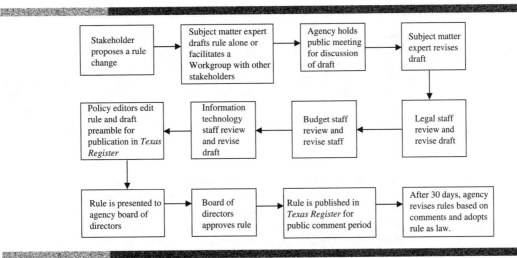

FIGURE 3.4 Adapted from the Texas Department of Human Services
Rule-Writing Process. Source: Texas Department of Human Services

the residents of the assisted-living facility; other neighbors who might be close enough to the funeral home to be bothered by its operations; the owners of the business; residents in the neighborhood who might appreciate the fact that there are businesses in the area that provide goods and services, employment, and tax revenues; politicians protecting the interests of business owners; politicians protecting the interests of residents, advocates for the physically disabled (some of the residents of the assisted-living facility were blind), environmentalists, and of course, the city, state, and federal agencies that write and enforce environmental policies.

Subject Matter Experts

In many state and federal agencies the first draft of a rule is written by someone with expertise in the policy area addressed in the rule. If the agency is a state agency with authorization to write environmental policies, it is very likely that the persons writing the initial drafts of rules will have educational and professional experience in environmental science or engineering. Subject matter experts are a type of stakeholder employed by federal and state agencies to write rules because of their knowledge of issues addressed in a rule. In both the disciplines of technical communication and public policy, the person with content-area expertise is often referred to as a subject matter expert. It is important for you to understand that the subjects addressed in rules are as diverse as those of any other genre of technical communication. From experience browsing the Internet, you know that the content of websites range from science and technology to social issues and the same can be said of the subjects addressed in rules. To see some of the varied subject areas covered by federal agencies with rulemaking authority, take a look at Table 3.2.

Executive Departments	Agency Within Each Executive Department	Subject Areas Addressed in Rule
Department of Agriculture (USDA)	Food Safety and Inspection Service (FSIS)	"The Food Safety and Inspection Service (FSIS) is the public health agency in the U.S. Department of Agriculture responsible for ensuring that the nation's commercial supply of meat, poultry, and egg products is safe, wholesome, and correctly labeled and packaged" (Food Safety and Inspection Service).
Department of Defense (DOD)	Missile Defense Agency	"The Missile Defense Agency's mission is to develop, test, and prepare for deployment a missile defense system" (Missile Defense Agency).
Department of Energy (DOE)	Federal Energy Regulatory Commission (FERC)	The Federal Energy Regulatory Commission regulates and oversees energy industries in the economic, environmental, and safety interests of the American public" (Federal Energy Regulatory Commission).
Department of Health and Human Services (HHS)	Food and Drug Administration (FDA)	"The FDA is responsible for protecting the public health by assuring the safety, efficacy, and security of human and veterinary drugs, biological products, medical devices, our nation's food supply, cosmetics, and products that emit radiation" (Food and Drug Administration).
Department of Homeland Security (DHS)	Federal Emergency Management Agency (FEMA)	"FEMA's continuing mission within the new department is to lead the effort to prepare the nation for all hazards and effectively manage federal response and recovery efforts following any national incident" (Federal Emergency Management Agency).
Department of the Treasury	Alcohol and Tobacco Tax and Trade Bureau (TTB)	"Our main responsibilities are protecting the public and collecting the revenue. We carry out these responsibilities by developing regulations, conducting product analysis, ensuring tax and trade compliance with the "Federal Alcohol Administration Act and the Internal Revenue Code" (Alcohol and Tobacco Tax and Trade Bureau).
Department of Transportation (DOT)	Federal Aviation Administration (FAA)	"We issue and enforce regulations and minimum standards covering manufacturing, operating, and maintaining aircraft. We certify airmen and airports that serve air carriers" (Federal Aviation Administration).
Independent Agencies	Environmental Protection Agency (EPA)	"The mission of the Environmental Protection Agency is to protect human health and the environment. Since 1970, EPA has been working for a cleaner, healthier environment for the American people" (Environmental Protection Agency).

TABLE 3.2 Subject Areas Covered by Agencies Within Executive Departments.

Table 3.2 contains some U.S. Executive Departments, representative agencies within each department, and the content addressed by subject matter experts who work for agencies within these **executive departments.** In addition to those federal agencies operating under executive departments, there are many independent agencies responsible for writing very important rules; these agencies include the Environmental Protection Agency (EPA), Federal Communications Commission (FCC), and Federal Trade Commission (FTC). Regardless of the type of federal agency, the content of federal rules, like state rules, are written by staff to inform or instruct specific audiences about policies and procedures that are often scientific and technical in nature. Because of the complexity of the content of rules and the fact that they inform and instruct their audiences, subject matter experts who write rules are technical communicators.

Legal, Fiscal, and Technology Experts

Attorneys, accountants, and information technology experts are not necessarily the subject matter experts for any particular set of rules, but government agencies depend on these professionals to analyze rules to assess the legal, fiscal, and technological impacts that rules will have on the public as well as the agencies responsible for writing and enforcing rules. Because of the very nature and purpose of rules, you have likely guessed that attorneys play a crucial role in the rule-writing process. While many agencies depend on attorneys to write their rules, others hire attorneys to review rules written by subject matter experts. The review of rules by attorneys is critical because legal experts can help agency officials determine if the rules they write are in fact enforceable in courts. If a rule is not enforceable, then it is not effective in protecting the public. Often, attorneys, in their role as rule reviewers, will make subtle changes to rules written by subject matter experts by adding or deleting a word or two, while other times attorneys need to make more substantive revisions that change the entire meaning and purpose of the rules. Therefore, it is necessary for attorneys to work very closely with subject matter experts so that the legal staff's revisions to rules do not compromise the subject matter expert's original intent. The same is true of the subject matter expert; these writers may have expert knowledge regarding the social, scientific, or technological complexities of the rules, but they must depend on attorneys to determine if the rule is enforceable.

Accountants, economists, and budget analysts are another group of professionals who lend their expertise in the rule writing. While in some agencies, like the Internal Revenue Service and Securities and Exchange Commission, financial experts may serve the role of subject matter experts, in other areas like health and safety rules, financial professionals are called upon to assess rules to see what economic impact a rule will have on the public. The role of fiscal experts and attorneys will certainly vary from agency to agency and state to state. In Figure 3.5, the State of Florida provides guidelines to employees responsible for writing rules and rule-related documents.

In Figure 3.5, in the sixth step of State of Florida's "Notice of Rulemaking" the "Statement of Estimated Regulatory Costs, if required" is the point where accountants, economists, budget analysts, or financial experts would participate in the rule making process by writing a document that explains the estimating costs of

Notice of Proposed Rulemaking
The Initial Rule Review File shall include the following documents:
1. Notices shall be submitted electronically through the F.A.W. article submission, found on the Florida Administrative Weekly Web site, http://election.dos.state.fl.us/fac/index.shtml or on diskette containing the notice and text of the rule. Call A.C.S. for assistance submitting online (850) 245-6270 or Suncom 205-6270.
See paragraph 1S-1.003(2)(a), F.A.C.
2. A cover memo identifying the proper agency for billing purposes.
3. Notice of proposed rulemaking (including the text of the rule).
See subsection 1S-1.003(4), F.A.C.
The following documents should be furnished to J.A.P.C.:
1. Copy of text of the rule;
2. Notice of Proposed Rulemaking;
3. Statement of Justification;
4. Summary of the rule;
5. Federal Standards Statement, if applicable;
6. Statement of Estimated Regulatory Costs, if required; and
7. Copies of any materials incorporated by reference, including forms.
See Section 120.54(3)(a)4., Florida Statutes

FIGURE 3.5   Notice of Rulemaking. Source: Florida Department of State

implementing rules on society or specific segments of society. Figure 3.6 provides an excerpt from the Florida statute, Section 120.541, which outlines the contents of the Statement of Regulatory Costs.

Other state agencies are required to submit similar documents, and although these documents may have different names (fiscal impact statement, economic impact statement, etc.), the purpose of the documentation is the same, to inform the public how a given proposed rule will impact small businesses and other stakeholders. In some agencies, information technology or computer experts are also called upon to assess the technological impact rule changes will have on government agencies, small businesses, and individuals. Evaluating how rule changes will impact information technology is especially important because some demographic groups have greater access to the Internet and computers than others.

The Public

The public, including business owners, advocacy groups, community activists, academic researchers, and other concerned constituents, can use federally and state-mandated **public comment periods** to make sure that **public comments** and their opinions are considered before proposed rules are adopted and implemented. This comment period gives us a chance to tell rule writers and other government agency officials our ideas about how new rules, changes to current rules, or repeals of rules would impact interested stakeholders. When government agencies publish public comments as well as agency responses to comments, the audience gets a glimpse of the contexts in which proposed and adopted rules are written, including conflicts and compromises made by various stakeholders. In Figure 3.7 you can see a summary of comments to a proposed EPA rule and the agency's response.

120.541 **Statement of estimated regulatory costs.**--

(1) [...]

(2) A statement of estimated regulatory costs shall include:

(a) A good faith estimate of the number of individuals and entities likely to be required to comply with the rule, together with a general description of the types of individuals likely to be affected by the rule.

(b) A good faith estimate of the cost to the agency, and to any other state and local government entities, of implementing and enforcing the proposed rule, and any anticipated effect on state or local revenues.

(c) A good faith estimate of the transactional costs likely to be incurred by individuals and entities, including local government entities, required to comply with the requirements of the rule. As used in this paragraph, "transactional costs" are direct costs that are readily ascertainable based upon standard business practices, and include filing fees, the cost of obtaining a license, the cost of equipment required to be installed or used or procedures required to be employed in complying with the rule, additional operating costs incurred, and the cost of monitoring and reporting.

(d) An analysis of the impact on small businesses as defined by s. 288.703, and an analysis of the impact on small counties and small cities as defined by s. 120.52.

(e) Any additional information that the agency determines may be useful.

(f) In the statement or revised statement, whichever applies, a description of any good faith written proposal submitted under paragraph (1)(a) and either a statement adopting the alternative or a statement of the reasons for rejecting the alternative in favor of the proposed rule.

FIGURE 3.6   Excerpt from Statement of Estimated Regulatory Costs. Source: Florida Department of State

COMMENT: Process-Based Models

Several commenters stated that the Emissions-Estimating Methodologies developed by EPA should be process-based models as suggested by the National Academy of Sciences (NAS). In addition, development of the Emissions-Estimating Methodologies should be an open process, with citizen and state involvement and peer review.

RESPONSE:

In the short term, the monitoring study is designed to produce scientifically sound emissions estimating methodology for making regulatory applicability decisions for AFOs. Our longer-term strategy involves development of process-based models that consider the entire animal production process, consistent with the recommendations from the NAS. The data collected in the monitoring study, along with other valid scientific studies that are available will be used to develop the process-based models.

EPA has not determined the process by which Emissions-Estimating Methodologies will be developed. EPA anticipates that the process will provide the opportunity for public input and review. However, the timing and extent of review have not been determined.

FIGURE 3.7   Example of Public Comment and Response. Source: EPA

Clearly, some agency staff person was responsible for summarizing comments from several different groups of individuals and responding to the public comment in a manner that is neither overly defensive of the proposed regulation nor adversarial. In Figure 3.7, you can see that the person responding to the proposed rule must be familiar with the subject matter of the rule and is likely a subject matter expert.

To increase participation in rule-writing activities, many government agencies have began to solicit input regarding rules online via *e-rulemaking* websites. (Shulman et al. 162–163). E-rulemaking websites allow citizens to express their opinions about rules through various websites, including Regulations.gov. Take a look at Figures 3.8 and 3.9, excerpts from the webpage of Regulations.gov, that allows stakeholders to browse the website for proposed federal rules and submit comments online.

Editors

Regardless of how the public decides to interact with government agencies—electronically or through traditional means (letters, public meetings, and email)—rule

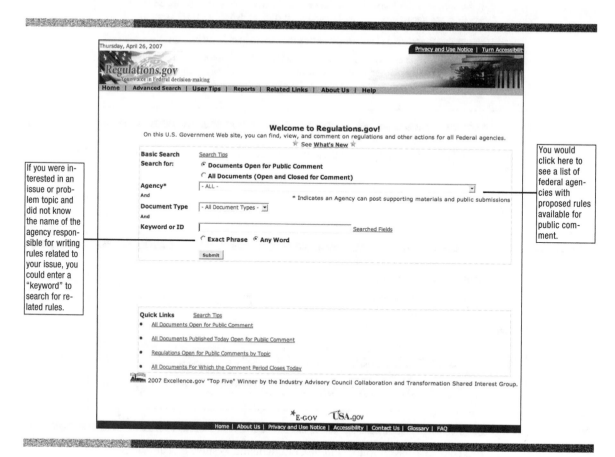

FIGURE 3.8   E-rulemaking website. Source: Regulations.gov

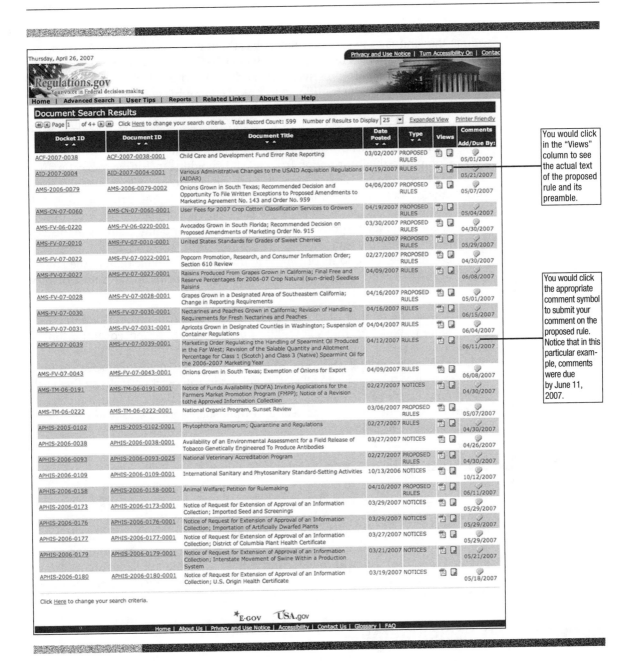

You would click in the "Views" column to see the actual text of the proposed rule and its preamble.

You would click the appropriate comment symbol to submit your comment on the proposed rule. Notice that in this particular example, comments were due by June 11, 2007.

FIGURE 3.9   E-rulemaking website. Source: Regulations.gov

editors must be able to handle the complexity of the policy addressed in rules as well as the language that the public, subject matter experts, attorneys, fiscal experts, and information technology specialists choose to use when drafting rules. In the editor's role as a liaison between the audience and the writers, the rule editor serves the same role as the traditional technical communicators in private industry. In some agencies, editors are responsible for the following tasks:

1. Editing the text of the rule for grammatical and punctuation errors and to comply with the appropriate state or federal style guide.
2. Compiling the information from all stakeholders, including subject matter experts, attorneys, fiscal experts, and the public into a *rule preamble*. Preambles include a summary explaining the purpose of a rule; legal, fiscal, and technological impacts of the rule; public comments received by the agency; agency responses to public comments; and any changes made as a result of public comments.
3. Editing the rule and its preamble to prepare it for publication in the *Federal Register* or state publication responsible for informing the public of proposed, adopted, and repealed rules.

Of course, the final draft of the rule preamble and rule is published in a federal or state publication that allows the public to view proposed and adopted rules as well as preambles, which explain the contexts in which the rules were created. To aid rule writers and rule editors in this task, many agencies provide handbooks and style guides to all staff involved in rule-writing tasks so that each government employee involved in rule writing can make sure that the content and structure of the rules are correct and publishable for the *Federal Register* or appropriate state registers.

Summary and Looking Forward

Rules are public policies written by government employees who work for government agencies at the federal and state levels. Rules are written to protect individuals, businesses, and other affected organizations. Because so many stakeholders are interested in the intent and language used in rules, government agencies are obligated to publish rules for review and comment by the public before rules can be adopted as public policy. In the next chapters, we'll closely examine other documents that evolve from rule writing.

Activities and Assignments

1. **Individual Internet Activity:** Browse the online versions of the *Federal Register* and *Code of Federal Regulations* to see if you can find the Federal Aviation Administration's revised definitions on human space flight mentioned in fig. 3.1 of this chapter or any information about 14 CFR § 401.5. Does this rule still exist? Were the proposed amendments to the rule adopted by the FAA? Has the rule been revised or repealed? Be prepared to discuss your findings with the rest of the class.

2. **Group Internet Activity:** Use Internet search engines (i.e., Google.com) and government agency websites to locate a rule from a government agency in the state you live in. After reading the rule and taking a look at the website for the agency that adopted the rule, identify the purpose, various audiences, and stakeholders for the rule. After you discuss the rule with your group members, be prepared to discuss your findings with the rest of the class.

3. **Individual Internet Activity:** Go to www.regulations.gov or browse the web to find another federal agency e-rulemaking website that allows you to submit a public comment to a proposed rule online. Then select a proposed rule that you have some stake in and would therefore be considered a stakeholder. Determine the audience for the rule and other potential stakeholders. Then, write a 150-200-word comment in response to the proposed rule. Do you agree with the rule? Is it clear? Your comment can be complimentary or critical, but it must be professional and well written. Your comment can also be in response to the content of the rule and/or the way the rule is written. (You are not required to submit the comment to the government agency, but be prepared to discuss your public comment with your classmates.)

4. **Individual Internet Activity:** Use www.plainlanguage.gov or some other government-sponsored plain language website to determine if the rule you read in Exercise 3 was written in plain language. In a one- to two-page essay, explain the following:

a. Who is the intended audience for the regulation?

b. Do you believe the regulation is written in plain or complex language? (Pull excerpts from the regulation to support your response to this question.)

c. Is the language used in the regulation appropriate for the intended audience?

Works Cited

Alcohol and Tobacco Tax and Trade Bureau. "About TTB." 5 Jan. 2007 <http://www.ttb.gov/about/index.shtml>.

City of Houston. "Service Request Summary Reports Related to Crematorium." 25 Oct. 2005 (2), 23 Nov. 2005, 11 Jan. 2006.

Click2Houston.com. "Crematorium Moves in Next to Apartment Complex." Nov. 2005. Local News. 9 Jan. 2007 <http://www.click2houston.com/news/5270062/detail.html>.

Environmental Protection Agency. "About EPA." 10 May 2007. 18 May 2007 <http://www.epa.gov/epahome/aboutepa.htm>.

Federal Aviation Administration. "What We Are." 10 March 2005. 18 May 2007 <http://www.faa.gov/about/mission/activities/>.

Federal Emergency Management Agency. "About FEMA." 27 Apr. 2007. 18 May 2007 <http://www.fema.gov/help/content_inventory.shtm>.

Federal Energy Regulatory Commission. "About FERC." 26 Sept. 2006. 5 Jan. 2007 <http://www.ferc.gov/about/about.asp>.

Florida Department of State. *Rulemaking Under Chapter 120 Statutes* "Statement of Estimated Regulatory costs." (Revised Feb. 2005): 63–64. 18 May 2007. <http://www.flrules.org/rmhb.pdf>.

—. "Notice of Rulemaking." (Revised Feb 2005): 4. 18 May 2007
    <http://www.flrules.org/rmhb.pdf>.

Food and Drug Administration. "FDA's Mission Statement." 18 May 2007
    <http://www.fda.gov/opacom/morechoices/mission.html>.

Food Safety and Inspection Service (FSIS)-United States Department of Agriculture.
    "About FSIS." 21 Mar. 2007. 18 May 2007 <http://www.fsis.usda.gov/
    About_FSIS/index.asp>.

Georgia Secretary of State. "Georgia Department of Natural Resources." 1 Dec. 2005
    <http://rules.sos.state.ga.us/docs/391/1/1/04.pdf>.

Hood, Glenda. *Rulemaking Under Chapter 120, Welcome Florida Statutes.* Feb. 2005. 18 May
    2007 <http://www.flrules.org/rmhb.pdf>.

Missile Defense Agency. "MDA Mission." 1 Dec. 2005 <http://www.mda.mil/mdalink/
    html/aboutus.html>.

Official Code of Georgia Annotated. Title 50. State Government Chapter 13. Administra-
    tive Procedure Article. 1. General Provisions. Section 50–13–1. *Georgia Code.* 2006.
    18 May 2007 <http://www.lexix-nexis.com/hottopics/gacode/default.asp>.

Plainlanguage.gov. "Before and After Comparisons." Mar. 2005. 5 Jan 2007
    <http://www.plainlanguage.gov/examples/before_after/index.cfm>.

"Proposed Rules." *Federal Register.* Dec. 2005. No.70.249. 29 Dec. 2005 <http://www.epa.gov/
    ttncaaa1/t3/fr_notices/organic_liquid_proposed122905.pdf>.

Regulations.gov. 5 Jan. 2007 <http://www.regulations.gov/fdmspublic/component/
    main>.

Shulman, Stuart W, David Schosberg, Steve Zavestoski, and David Courard-Hauri.
    "Electronic Rulemaking: A Public Participation Research Agenda for the Social
    Sciences." *Social Science Computer Review* 21.2 (2003): 162–78.

"Texas Administrative Code, Title 30. Environmental Quality, Part I, Chapter 106,
    Subchapter V, § 106.494." *Texas Administrative Code.* Sept. 4, 2000. 18 May 2007.
    <http://info.sos.state.tx.us/pls/pub/readtac$ext.ViewTAC>.

Texas Department of Human Services. "Adapted from the Texas Department of Human
    Services Rule-Writing Process." Workflow Process. 2001.

"Title 10, Subtitle A, Chapter 2001, Subchapter A, section 2001.021." *Texas Statutes
    Government Code.* 1 Sept. 1993. 18 May 2007 <http://www.tlo2.tlc.state.tx.us/
    statutes/gv.toc.htm>.

U.S. Environmental Protection Agency. "Response to Public Comment on the Animal
    Feeding Operation Air Agreement." 2 Mar. 2006. 18 May 2007
    <http://www.epa.gov/compliance/resources/agreements/caa/
    cafo-agr-response-com.html>.

Policy Handbooks, and Guides

On October 24, 2005, the headline for the PR Newswire read, "Medicare Agency Says Look for Important Handbooks in the mail; *Medicare & You Booklet* Provides Drug Plan Information." According to the author of this wire, "The handbooks are state specific and include a listing of the Medicare-approved prescription drug plans available in the beneficiary state" as well as information about "the new benefit and how to enroll." Two weeks before this announcement, *Modesto Bee* staff writer Ken Carlson's headline read, "*Medicare Handbook* is in Error, Charts Say No Monthly Fee For Drug Benefits; But Most Plans do Require Premiums." Carlson went on to write, "Despite what a government handbook says, only about 25% of the Medicare drug plans in Northern California have no monthly premiums for beneficiaries who qualify for financial help. *The Medicare & You Handbook* contains a significant error on the charts starting on page 97A, which give a comparison of the stand-alone drug plans that go into effect in 2006." Carlson's article explains that the federal government had shipped 35 million copies of this handbook in October 2005 alone and many handbooks had already arrived in the mailboxes of Medicare consumers, most of whom are elderly. So, how did the federal government allow handbooks to be shipped to Medicare consumers with an error that would likely confuse and mislead this audience? According to Carlson's article, "officials blamed the mistake on inadequate proofreading."

If you are unfamiliar with government handbooks, manuals, or guides, you may wonder:

> Who is responsible for writing and editing handbooks? Are local Medicare agencies or federal agencies responsible for making sure that the content is accurate and proofread?
>
> How would such an error be corrected? Is the review and editing process for government handbooks as extensive and collaborative as it is for those government rules we discussed in Chapter 3?

Is the audience for government handbooks and manuals always restricted to the public?

Under what circumstances does a government agency decide to publish a government handbook or manual?

In what formats are these documents produced?

In this chapter, we will provide responses to these questions as well as other questions you may have about government handbooks and manuals.

The Purpose of Government Handbooks

In the United States, federal, state, and local agencies use **government handbooks** to advise the public about how to abide by government rules and laws and how to take part in services provided by the government agencies. These same government agencies also have a history of publishing government handbooks and manuals for practical use by their own government employees to implement public policy. In the previous chapter, we discussed the differences between laws and rules and how government agencies write rules to provide the public with detailed explanations that are not thoroughly explained in laws promulgated either by state legislatures or at the federal level in Congress. Government handbooks go a step further by providing even more details about how to implement rules and laws as well as the actual instructions the public need to follow to benefit from public policy or to avoid violating laws and rules. For the purposes of this chapter, the terms *handbooks*, *manuals*, and *guides* are used interchangeably. Government agencies seldom differentiate between them regarding the functions of documents because in most cases, these terms are used synonymously; the audience for these documents can expect to find instructions, directives, and assistance.

One type of handbook that most of us are familiar with are human resource or personnel handbooks, which are used in corporate, not-for-profit, and government agencies to instruct us how to work productively and ethically in the organizations that employ us. Government personnel, including members of Congress, are given personnel handbooks to explain expectations for ethical and responsible behavior while working as public servants. For example, the Select Committee on Ethics published a 542-page manual, the 2003 edition of the *Senate Ethics Manual,* to provide senators specific standards of conduct while serving the public as elected officials (108th Congress' Senate Committee on Ethics). Government handbooks are useful in providing detailed instructions to a variety of audiences—from high-ranking elected officials, like senators, to citizens trying to figure out how to file taxes. Clearly, government handbooks have been around a lot longer than those published by the United States government; these documents have been used to instruct government officials and their constituents since Niccolo Machiavelli's *Prince,* where he provides detailed descriptions of how a monarchy was actually run in sixteenth-century Italy. The very practical and instructive purpose of Machiavelli's work is what allows us to describe it as an example of an early government handbook.

According to George Kennedy, classical rhetoricians wrote handbooks to instruct the Greek polis how to speak effectively in front of ancient Greek courts (33). Kennedy wrote, "First, we should admit that we know very little about the form and content of fifth-century handbooks," but he posits that handbooks included "illustrative examples, arranged by the parts of the oration in which they might be used..." (34). Although some scholars equate ancient Greek rhetoricians' "handbooks" with modern-day textbooks, these classical "handbooks" were written to teach citizens how to maneuver in interactions with government courts and officials; this differentiates these documents from the textbooks commonly found in contemporary classrooms. Today, the U.S. Attorney's Office Northern District of New York publishes *Victim and Witness Handbook* and the U.S. Attorney's Office Western District of Tennessee publishes *Victim & Witness Handbook*, both with information for victims of crime and witnesses of crime on the criminal justice system. They are examples of how contemporary governments still use handbooks to inform and instruct the public how to interact in courts and officials. In this chapter, you will see that contemporary government handbooks do share many characteristics with their ancient predecessors. The most obvious similarities are that government handbooks (1) include examples to communicate complex policies and procedures and (2) are directed to a very specific audience for very specific purposes. To begin our examination of these useful documents, take a look at the introduction of the U.S. Attorney's Office Northern District of New York's *Witness and Victim Handbook* in Figure 4.1.

This sentence identifies the primary audience for the handbook in the first sentence of the introduction.	**INTRODUCTION**	
	If you are a victim of or a witness to a crime, the Victim/Witness Assistance Program is designed to provide you with services while you are involved with the criminal justice system.	
	As a victim of crime, you may be experiencing feelings of confusion, frustration, fear, and anger. Our staff can help you deal with these feelings. We also will explain your rights as a victim or witness, and help you better understand how the criminal justice system works.	This paragraph describes some of the legal and political pressures that make this handbook necessary.
	One of the responsibilities of citizenship for those who have knowledge about the commission of a crime is to serve as witnesses at the criminal trial or one of the other hearings held in connection with the criminal prosecution. The federal criminal justice system cannot function without the participation of witnesses. The complete cooperation and truthful testimony of all witnesses are essential to the proper determination of guilt or innocence in a criminal case.	
This sentence states the purpose of the handbook.	Our office is concerned that victims and witnesses of crime are treated fairly throughout their contact with the criminal justice system. The United States Department of Justice and the United States Attorney's Office have taken several steps to make the participation by victims of crime and witnesses more effective and meaningful. One of these steps is the preparation of this handbook. We hope that it will provide you the answers to many of your questions and will give you sufficient general information to understand your rights and responsibilities. Another step has been to employ a Victim/Witness Coordinator who is available to answer any of your questions and to assist you where possible as you participate in the criminal justice process.	

FIGURE 4.1   Except from *Northern District of New York's Witness and Victim Handbook*.
Source: U.S. Attorney's Office Northern District of New York

Notice in Figure 4.1 that the *Northern District of New York's Witness and Victim Handbook* was written with a very specific audience in mind—victims of crime and witnesses to crime—and is written for a specific purpose: "We hope that it will provide you the answers to many of your questions and will give you sufficient general information to understand your rights and responsibilities." The writers of this handbook do more than discuss the purpose; they inform the audience of the intended audience, "a victim of or a witness to a crime," and some of the political and legal circumstances that make the handbook necessary. In the next section, we will discuss the varied contexts in which government agencies create handbooks and the audiences these handbooks address.

Policy Handbooks and Manuals in Cultural Contexts

In Herbert A. Simon's *The Proverbs of Administration,* he states, "Administrative efficiency is increased by grouping the [government] workers, for purposes of control, according to (a) purpose, (b) process, (c) clientele, (d) place" (127). In this description Simon describes the complexity of the structure of government agencies in that each department within each agency has different purposes, processes, and clientele, and each represents people in different places. Simon argues that government agencies should not simply depend on the economic theory of specialization as a means to achieving efficiency, but must "specialize in that particular manner along those particular lines which lead to administrative efficiency" (128). This very precise description of an efficient government agency and its unique structure provides us a framework to discuss the contexts in which government handbooks are created. Government handbooks, which are published by almost every major department within every federal, state, and local agency, define those specific purposes, processes, clientele, and places that government agencies address. Handbooks are the documentation that legitimize and certify the day-to-day procedures that government workers perform, policies they implement, and the everyday guidelines they expect the public to follow.

Examples of contemporary government handbooks include handbooks by the Department of Defense, Environmental Protection Agency, and New Jersey's bilingual handbook. The Department of Defense's handbook on security training, "requires service and Defense agencies for the first time to formally identify all employees with the responsibility for any aspect of IA [information assurance], assign them positions within a new organizational structure and ensure that each worker has the certifications required for that position" (Wait 2006). The Environmental Protection Agency's Office of Water's handbook is described as a document that "will help anyone undertaking a watershed planning effort, but it should be particularly helpful to persons working with impaired or threatened waters" (States News Service 2006). Bergen County,

New Jersey's bilingual handbook of government and nonprofit agencies is described as "a nod to the mushrooming population of Latino immigrants" in that the handbook provides "a list of phone numbers and other contact information for county and municipal departments, as well as an indication of the availability of Spanish-speaking staff" (Llorente 2006).

These handbooks address different purposes, processes, clientele, and places. Also, government handbooks are written by different government agencies that are authorized by different laws and rules. In the previous chapter, we discussed the differences between rules and laws. At this point, it is important to note that many government handbooks include references to or excerpts from laws and rules to explain the relationship between the procedures or requirements covered in the handbook and the laws and rules that give the agency the authority to implement handbook policies and procedures. Actually, if you examine any government handbook, you will likely find (1) an overview that includes references to laws and rules that give the government agency the power to implement specific policies and procedures outlined in the handbook; (2) guidelines for government agency personnel to conduct day-to-day procedures that implement laws and rules; and/or (3) instructions for the public to follow to benefit from or to avoid violation of government laws and rules.

The excerpts in Figure 4.2 are from the *Medicare & You 2006* booklet and demonstrate how government handbooks serve as a textual crossroad where public policy, the public, and government employees meet.

In Figure 4.3 notice the reference to "relevant laws, regulations, and rulings." The author of this handbook is informing the audience that there is additional "official" program information from which the content of this handbook is drawn. In contrast, some government agency handbooks are little more than verbatim copies of laws and rules renumbered into handbook format and include little explanatory text or visuals to help readers understand how these laws and rules are implemented. In most cases, placing laws and rules in traditional handbook binding is not effective in communicating to nonexpert audiences. While some laws and rules do provide instructions, these genres are legal documents that must be enforceable in a court of law; handbooks, on the other hand, should give government agencies the opportunity to go a step further and provide directives, explanatory information, and technical assistance that would not be appropriate for most rules and laws.

In Figure 4.2 the handbook writer addresses those persons in the public who might be affected by a new Medicaid plan and uses the question-and-answer format. In this format, the writer uses first person *I* and third person *you* to personalize the discussion and make the reader feel as if they are in conversation with the writer. The writer also provides specific information about what the audience must do to achieve specific objectives—including step-by-step instructions to respond to the anticipated question, "How Do I Switch My Plan"—telephone numbers, and relevant dates. In our next section, we will discuss how the content of government handbooks is shaped by the specific audience addressed.

Everyone needs to make a decision this year

Beginning January 1, 2006, Medicare will offer insurance coverage for prescription drugs through Medicare Prescription Drug Plans and other health plan options. Insurance companies and other private companies work with Medicare to offer these plans. **If you join by December 31, 2005, you won't miss a day of coverage.**

Because of changes in the Medicare Program, everyone with Medicare has to make a decision about prescription drug coverage this year. To learn more about these changes, see pages 39–54.

Even if you don't use a lot of prescription drugs now, you should still read the information about Medicare prescription drug coverage in this handbook and consider joining. As we age, most people need prescription drugs to stay healthy. For most people, joining now means you will pay a lower monthly premium in the future since you may have to pay a penalty if you choose to join later.

Keep this Handbook

This handbook describes important changes in Medicare. You can find basic information about the Medicare Program as well as specific information about each type of Medicare Advantage Plan or other Medicare Health Plan and prescription drug coverage choice.

This handbook is a good resource to have throughout the year.
The information is valid for 2006, but remember this year it's different than other years. Use it in place of any older version you have. Keep it where you can find it when you need it.

How can you find the information you need in this handbook?

There are two ways to find the information you need:

1. Look at the "Table of Contents." This lists topic areas by section, with page numbers.

2. Look at the "List of Topics" section after the table of contents. This is an alphabetical list of specific topics discussed in this handbook, with page numbers. This is the easiest way to find information.

Note: You may see words in blue in the text of this handbook. You can find definitions of these words on pages 89–92.

"Medicare & You 2006" explains the Medicare Program. It isn't a legal document. The official Medicare Program provisions are contained in the relevant laws, regulations, and rulings.

Reference to official program information

FIGURE 4.2 Excerpt from *Medicare & You* Handbook Reference Overview and Reference to Laws and Regulations. Source: *Medicare & You 2006*

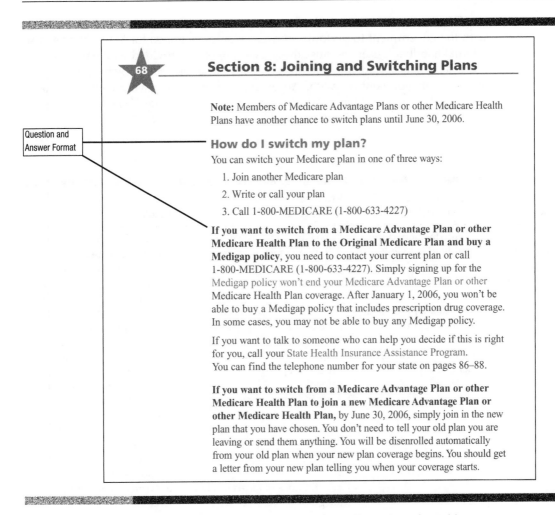

Question and Answer Format

Section 8: Joining and Switching Plans

68

Note: Members of Medicare Advantage Plans or other Medicare Health Plans have another chance to switch plans until June 30, 2006.

How do I switch my plan?

You can switch your Medicare plan in one of three ways:

1. Join another Medicare plan
2. Write or call your plan
3. Call 1-800-MEDICARE (1-800-633-4227)

If you want to switch from a Medicare Advantage Plan or other Medicare Health Plan to the Original Medicare Plan and buy a Medigap policy, you need to contact your current plan or call 1-800-MEDICARE (1-800-633-4227). Simply signing up for the Medigap policy won't end your Medicare Advantage Plan or other Medicare Health Plan coverage. After January 1, 2006, you won't be able to buy a Medigap policy that includes prescription drug coverage. In some cases, you may not be able to buy any Medigap policy.

If you want to talk to someone who can help you decide if this is right for you, call your State Health Insurance Assistance Program. You can find the telephone number for your state on pages 86–88.

If you want to switch from a Medicare Advantage Plan or other Medicare Health Plan to join a new Medicare Advantage Plan or other Medicare Health Plan, by June 30, 2006, simply join in the new plan that you have chosen. You don't need to tell your old plan you are leaving or send them anything. You will be disenrolled automatically from your old plan when your new plan coverage begins. You should get a letter from your new plan telling you when your coverage starts.

FIGURE 4.3 *Medicare & You* Handbook Instructions for Public. Source: *Medicare & You*

Audience for Policy Handbooks and Manuals

In this section, we discuss the specific audiences—both internal and external to government agencies—addressed by writers of government handbooks. **Internal handbook users** are those government employees required to read handbooks and follow the policies and procedures within handbooks to do their jobs. Government employees may use handbooks when inspecting private businesses to make sure businesses are in compliance with government regulations, to inform new government employees of their rights and responsibilities as civil servants, to explain custom-made software applications and technologies designed for use by government personnel, and to inform them of specific processes and work flow within their distinct units or departments within government agencies.

Government contractors, businesses, and nonprofit organizations that contract with the government to perform services or produce goods for the public are also internal handbook users because these users are often provided with handbooks to make sure that they are implementing public policies as defined by the government agency that they contract with. An example of internal government handbooks includes the Food and Drug Administration's *The Leveraging Handbook: An Agency Resource for Effective Collaboration*, which is described in Table 4.1.

Agency Handbooks	Purpose and Intended Audience	Processes and Procedures	Disclaimer
Food Safety and Inspection Service (FSIS)'s *Meat and Poultry Hazards and Control Guide*	"FSIS developed this Guide to help FSIS personnel to evaluate all aspects of an establishment's system for producing processed meat and poultry products" (Food Safety and Inspection Service September 2005, 3).	"The Guide consists of the following major sections: • alphabetical listing of process steps that may be used in the production of processed meat and poultry products and the page numbers where they can be found; • quick reference table of process steps by process category. . . • an individual listing of 27 processing steps with some currently identified common hazards and frequently used controls for each process step; and • definitions of terms used in the guide and a list of references for easy access to current information on regulations and other guidance material" (Food Safety and Inspection Service September 2005, 4).	"A set of suggested general and process-specific verification questions is included in this Guide. These questions will provide the FSIS personnel with an analytical thought process that may lead the FSIS personnel to ask additional questions in evaluating the process steps. FSIS personnel should use the general and process-specific questions in evaluating each process step. It is important for FSIS personnel to realize that these questions are not meant to be all inclusive but as a Guide to the types of questions that should be answered when verifying regulatory compliance" (Food Safety and Inspection Service September 2005, 3).
Missile Defense Agency's *Ballistic Missile Defense Organization Unsolicited Proposal Guide April 2000*	"It provides guidance to individuals assigned to the Ballistic Missile Defense Organization (BMDO) and potential offerors on procedures for submission and evaluation of unsolicited	"This Guide provides guidance to assist parties interested in preparing and submitting unsolicited proposals to the Ballistic Missile Defense Organization (BMDO). Within the Department of Defense, the BMDO	"This Guide is reissued under the authority of the Federal Acquisition Regulation (FAR) Subpart 15.6—Unsolicited Proposals" (BMDO 1).

TABLE 4.1   Examples of Federal Handbooks.

Agency Handbooks	Purpose and Intended Audience	Processes and Procedures	Disclaimer
	proposals. It also gives potential offerors instructions for identifying and marking proprietary information in their unsolicited proposals so that information is protected and restrictive legends conform to FAR requirements" (BMDO 1).	is responsible for managing, directing, and executing the Ballistic Missile Defense (BMD) Program" (BMDO 5).	
Federal Energy Regulatory Commission's *Handbook for Hydroelectric Project Licensing and 5 MW Exemptions from Licensing*	"This handbook is for all interested parties involved in the hydropower authorization process. It provides a step-by-step guide to applying for an original license, a new license or subsequent license (relicenses), and 5 MW exemption from licensing, and can be used to improve the quality and consistency of license or exemption applications" (FERC 1–1)	"The handbook presents an overview of the process for obtaining an original or new license in Chapter 2, followed by detailed information on the steps involved in the integrated, traditional, and alternative licensing processes in Chapters 3, 4, and 5, respectively. Detailed information on the steps for applying for exemptions from licensing is provided in chapter 6, and the Commission's rules of preference for competing applications are in chapter 7" (FERC 1–1)	"While this handbook provides helpful information about application procedures, it is not a substitute for the Commission's implementing regulations at 18 CFR Subchapter B. For specific guidance, prospective applicants and other participants in these proceedings should rely on the regulations, supplemented as necessary with legal advice" (FERC 1–1)
Food and Drug Administration's *Guidance for FDA Staff: The Leveraging Handbook: An Agency Resource for Effective Collaboration*	"This Handbook is a compendium of information and tools to support leveraging. It was developed for Agency staff and managers who may be involved in leveraging project development and implementation. It is intended to provide the reader with an introduction to and	"The chapters that follow describe how to establish a leveraged collaboration, what should be considered before, during and after implementing a project, and suggestions for managing legal and ethical issues. § Chapter 2–Quick Start for Leveraging—presents an informative question and answer section that should help those new to leveraging become	"FDA's guidance documents, including this guidance, do not establish legally enforceable responsibilities. Instead, guidances describe the FDA's current thinking on a topic and should be viewed only as recommendations, unless specific regulatory or statutory requirements are cited. The use of the word *should*

TABLE 4.1 *(continued)*

Agency Handbooks	Purpose and Intended Audience	Processes and Procedures	Disclaimer
	an overview of key leveraging topics and issues. This guidance finalizes the draft guidance of the same title dated November 2001" (FDA.1)	quickly acquainted with leveraging concepts and processes. The chapter also contains help for getting started. § Chapter 3–The Leveraging Process—provides an overview of basic steps in the process of leveraging, focusing on arrangements with outside organizations. The chapter addresses general issues related to the process of qualifying, negotiating with, and collaborating with others to achieve FDA goals. § Chapter 4–Leveraging Mechanisms—addresses concerns about controls and resource commitments, by providing an overview of existing contractual and financing mechanisms that can be used for leveraging. § Chapter 5–Legal and Ethical Points to Consider—addresses legal issues and ethical concerns regarding actual and perceived conflicts of interest. § Chapter 6–Internal Review and Sign-off—presents a process for the review of leveraging proposals and sign-off of leveraging projects. Appendices Documents and information referenced in the Handbook or that would be useful to implementing a leveraged collaboration" (FDA 7)	in FDA's guidances means that something is suggested or recommended, but not required" (FDA 1)
Federal Emergency Management Agency's *National Flood Insurance Program: Flood Insurance Claims Handbook*	This claims guide was created by the Federal Emergency Management Agency (FEMA), which oversees the National Flood	"This is a nine page handbook that covers the following topics: "What To Do Before A Flood, Check Your Policy, Prepare Lists And Documentation, Secure	"While every effort has been made to make sure the information in this handbook is correct, you should refer to your policy and its Declarations Page for

TABLE 4.1   *(continued)*

Agency Handbooks	Purpose and Intended Audience	Processes and Procedures	Disclaimer
	Insurance Program, to help you through the process of filing a claim and appealing the decision on your claim, if necessary (FEMA 1)	Important Papers, Talk To Your Insurance Agent, Plan An Emergency Contact, What To Do After A Flood, Steps to Take Immediately, Handling Your Claim, Filing Your Claim, Addressing Questions About Your Insurance Claim, and Four Steps To Appealing Your Claim" (FEMA 1-9)	specific information on coverage, limitations, restrictions and deductibles" (FEMA 1).
Alcohol and Tobacco Tax and Trade Bureau's *The (Beverage Alcohol Manual (BAM): A Practical Guide-Basic Mandatory Labeling Information for Distilled Spirits*	This manual goes straight into the labeling requirements without much discussion of the purpose of audience of the handbook. Based on the title of the handbook, we can assume that the handbook is directed to businesses who sell distilled spirits (ATTTB 1)	The manual is part 2 of a three-volume manual. The other manuals focus on wine and Malt Beverages. Volume II is organized in the following manner: Chapter 1: Mandatory Label Information Chapter 2: Type Size and Legibility Requirements Chapter 3: Type Size and Legibility Requirements for Health Warning Statement Chapter 4: Class and Type Designation Chapter 5: Name and Address Chapter 6: Standards of Fill Chapter 7: Coloring/Flavoring/Blending Materials Chapter 8: Statements of Age Chapter 9: Containers (ATTTB 1)	"GOVERNING LAWS AND REGULATIONS LAW IMPLEMENTING REGULATION REGULATION TITLE Federal Alcohol Administration Act (FAA Act) 27 USC 201 et seq. 27 CFR Part 5 Labeling and Advertising of Distilled Spirits Alcoholic Beverage Labeling Act of 1988 (ABLA) 27 USC 213 et seq. 27 CFR Part 16 Alcoholic Beverage Health Warning Statement 27 CFR Part 19 Distilled Spirits Plants 27 CFR Part 250 Liquors and Articles from Puerto Rico and the Virgin Islands 27 CFR Part 251 Importation of Distilled Spirits, Wine, and Beer Internal Revenue Code (IRC) 26 USC Chapter 51 27 CFR Part 252 Exportation of" (ATTTB 1)
Federal Aviation Administration's *Airplane Flying Handbook 2004*	"The *Airplane Flying Handbook* is designed as a technical manual to introduce basic	"This handbook conforms to pilot training and certification concepts established by the FAA. There are different	"It is essential for persons using this handbook to also become familiar with and apply the pertinent parts of

TABLE 4.1   *(continued)*

Agency Handbooks	Purpose and Intended Audience	Processes and Procedures	Disclaimer
	pilot skills and knowledge that are essential for piloting airplanes. It provides information on transition to other airplanes and the operation of various airplane systems. It is developed by the Flight Standards Service, Airman Testing Standards Branch, in cooperation with various aviation educators and industry. This handbook is developed to assist student pilots learning to fly airplanes. It is also beneficial to pilots who wish to improve their flying proficiency and aeronautical knowledge" (FAA iii)	ways of teaching, as well as performing flight procedures and maneuvers, and many variations in the explanations of aerodynamic theories and principles. This handbook adopts a selective method and concept of flying airplanes. The discussion and explanations reflect the most commonly used practices and principles. Occasionally the word "must" or similar language is used where the desired action is deemed critical. The use of such language is not intended to add to, interpret, or relieve a duty imposed by Title 14 of the Code of Federal Regulations (14 CFR)" (FAA iii)	14 CFR and the *Aeronautical Information Manual (AIM)*. . . Performance standards for demonstrating competence required for pilot certification are prescribed in the appropriate airplane practical test standard."(FAA iii).
Veterans Health Administration's *VHA Handbook 1200.06 Control of Hazardous Agents in VA Research Laboratories*	"This Veterans Health Administration (VHA) Handbook establishes policy and procedures related to select agents and toxins and the prevention and/or detection of terrorist events occurring in or originating from the Department of Veterans Affairs (VA) research laboratories" (VHA Cover)	"The procedures contained in this Handbook apply to all Research and Development (R&D) laboratories located within VA facilities, including leased space, and to space within a VA facility leased to a private entity. VA research laboratories located in approved off-site facilities such as affiliate universities are expected to comply with all VA and other Federal laws and regulations regarding security of both research laboratory facilities and select agents and toxins" (VHA Cover).	"This revised VHA Handbook incorporates new Federal regulations and addresses issues related to the security of VHA research laboratories. The changes related to these issues are extensive and are to be found throughout all sections of this Handbook" (VHA Cover).

TABLE 4.1   *(continued)*

Agency Handbooks	Purpose and Intended Audience	Processes and Procedures	Disclaimer
Environmental Protection Agency's *Handbook of Groundwater Protection and Cleanup Policies for RCRA Corrective Action (April 2004— Updated Version)*	"What does this Handbook do? This Handbook is designed to help you as a regulator, member of the regulated community, or member of the public find and understand EPA policies on protecting and cleaning up groundwater at Resource Conservation and Recovery Act (RCRA) corrective action facilities1. Who should use this Handbook? This Handbook is designed to help anyone who wants to develop a better understanding of EPA's groundwater cleanup policies for RCRA corrective action facilities. We wrote this Handbook for State and EPA regulators, owners and operators of facilities subject to RCRA corrective action, and members of the public. Throughout the rest of this Handbook we will refer to these three groups as "regulators," "facilities," and the "public," respectively. Sometimes, we will refer to all three	"How will this Handbook help me? If you are a regulator, the Handbook can help clarify key groundwater-related policies that you should consider, where appropriate, to guide investigations and cleanups at your assigned facilities (via permits, orders, or voluntary actions). EPA designed this Handbook to help you do your part in promoting a technically sound, reasonable, and consistent approach to protecting and cleaning up our Nation's groundwater. If you represent a facility, the Handbook can help you reduce your uncertainties about the actions a regulator may require of you. Reducing uncertainties can help you in your financial planning and project management. Clarity in EPA's expectations will allow you to phase your investigation and cleanup strategy in a manner consistent with the RCRA corrective Action Program priorities. These policies can help if you are currently undergoing RCRA corrective action under some form of regulatory oversight, or if you intend to begin cleanup in advance of oversight by an EPA or State regulator. If you are a member of the public, this Handbook can help you understand what EPA generally expects; regulators and facilities to do	"The statutory provisions and EPA regulations discussed in this Handbook contain legally binding requirements. This Handbook itself does not substitute for those provisions or regulations, nor is it regulation itself. Thus, this Handbook does not impose legally binding requirements on EPA, States, or the regulated community, and may not apply to a particular situation based upon the specific circumstances of the corrective action facility. EPA and State regulators retain their discretion to use approaches on a case-by-case basis that differ from this Handbook where appropriate. EPA and State regulators base their corrective action decisions on the statute and regulations as applied to the specific facts of the corrective action facility. Interested parties are free to raise questions and concerns about the substance of this Handbook and appropriateness of the application of recommendations in this Handbook to a particular situation. Whether or not the recommendations in this Handbook are appropriate in a given situation will depend on facility-specific circumstances" (EPA. ii-iii).

TABLE 4.1 *(continued)*

Agency Handbooks	Purpose and Intended Audience	Processes and Procedures	Disclaimer
	groups collectively as "stakeholders" (EPA. ii-iii).	during an investigation and cleanup of contaminated groundwater at a RCRA corrective action facility. EPA encourages you to use this Handbook as a tool in your interaction with regulators or facilities. In essence, EPA wrote this Handbook, in part, to help you influence decisions related to groundwater protection and cleanup at RCRA corrective action facilities" (EPA ii-iii).	

Also, government handbooks that are published for the public, including individuals and business, have specific audiences that we call **external handbook users**, since these audiences are not employed by or under contract with the government agency charged with the task of implementing public policy. Examples of external handbook users include the Medicare recipients we mentioned earlier in the chapter and pilots who read *The Airplane Flying Handbook* referenced in Table 4.1. Table 4.1, Examples of Federal Handbooks, lists a small sample of the current internal and external handbooks published by the federal agencies that were introduced in Chapter 3. The first column includes an excerpt from the handbook describing its purpose and intended audience; the second column is an excerpt from the handbook or its table of contents showing what processes or procedures are covered in the handbook; and the last column includes a disclaimer that alerts that audience that the handbook material does not override existing laws or regulations.

Style Guides and Organization of Policy Handbooks

Some government agencies have published and revised policy handbooks for decades and have established agency style guides to inform writers how to organize documents and write for their unique audiences (See Chapter 2). In this section, we will describe the main sections that most government agencies use to organize their handbooks, while remaining cognizant of the fact that history and experience with their unique audiences have led many agencies to include sections not mentioned in this textbook. We will limit our discussion to important handbook sections: handbook covers; overviews, forewords and prefaces; the body of the handbook; references; appendices; glossaries and definitions, and indexes.

Handbook Cover

Handbooks, whether in paper format or online, are usually bound with a front and back cover. The front cover includes the name of the government agency and the unit or department distributing the policy handbook. The front cover also includes the name of the handbook, month and year of distribution or revision, and the agency logo, symbol, or emblem (see Figures 4.4 and 4.5). In Figure 4.4, the cover from the Missile Defense Agency is representative of the basic layout that many government agencies use in the design of their handbook covers. Because many government handbooks are used daily by their users, government agencies often slip the paper covers into inexpensive plastic binders that can handle physical wear and frequent use.

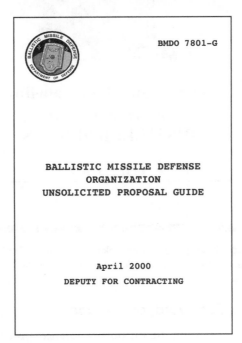

FIGURE 4.4　Example of Handbook Cover.　Source: *Ballistic Missile Defense Organization Unsolicited Proposal Guide April 2000*

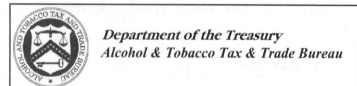

Department of the Treasury
Alcohol & Tobacco Tax & Trade Bureau

THE BEVERAGE
ALCOHOL MANUAL (BAM)

A Practical Guide

Basic Mandatory Labeling
Information For
DISTILLED SPIRITS

VOLUME 2

TTB P 5110.7 (04/2007)

FIGURE 4.5   Example of Handbook Cover. Source: *The Beverage Alcohol Manual (BAM): A Practical Guide—Basic Mandatory Labeling Information for Distilled Spirits*

Overview, Foreword, or Preface

Information regarding the purpose, audience, processes, and statutory authority of government handbooks and manuals are quickly accessible and located in prominent places in the handbooks, usually in the foreword, preface, or overview of the document. This is common practice in policy handbooks. So, once the reader opens the document, even before the table of contents, the reader will be welcomed to the handbook and provided a formal introduction to the document,

> **In this sentence, the handbook authors identify the intended audience (internal and external) for the handbook.**

FOREWORD

This Guide is reissued under the authority of the Federal Acquisition Regulation (FAR) Subpart 15.6—Unsolicited Proposals. It provides guidance to individuals assigned to the Ballistic Missile Defense Organization (BMDO) and potential offerors on procedures for submission and evaluation of unsolicited proposals. It also gives potential offerors instructions for identifying and marking proprietary information in their unsolicited proposals so that information is protected and restrictive legends conform to FAR requirements.

BMDO 7801-G, "Ballistic Missile Defense Organization Unsolicited Proposal Guide," July 1995, is hereby canceled.

This Guide applies to all offices, Directorates, and Deputates in the BMDO and to private (public) sector individuals and business concerns submitting unsolicited proposals to BMDO. It also applies to unsolicited proposals submitted by Defense Allies.

This Guide is effective immediately.

Send recommended changes to:

> Ballistic Missile Defense Organization
> Deputy for Contracting (BMDO/CT)
> 7100 Defense Pentagon
> Washington, DC 20301-7100

Nothing in this Guide is intended to conflict with coverage pertaining to unsolicited proposals in the Federal Acquisition Regulation.

This Guide will be available in the BMDO publication system. Interested public users may obtain copies by contacting the Deputy for Contracting at the above address.

FIGURE 4.6 Example of Handbook Foreword. Source: *Ballistic Missile Defense Organization Unsolicited Proposal Guide April 2000*

which is then followed by a table of contents. While some agencies title this section *overview*, *foreword*, or *preface*, other agencies begin with a letter or notice signed by agency personnel and directly addressing the audience. Figure 4.6 and Figure 4.7 are examples that demonstrate how different agencies introduce both internal and external audiences through forewords and prefaces.

Body

After the cover, overview (foreword, preface, or letter) and table of contents, the handbook writer is ready to walk the reader through the actual policy process. Of course, this is the most important part of the handbook. In reviewing numerous

PREFACE

The *Airplane Flying Handbook* is designed as a technical manual to introduce basic pilot skills and knowledge that are essential for piloting airplanes. It provides information on transition to other airplanes and the operation of various airplane systems. It is developed by the Flight Standards Service, Airman Testing Standards Branch, in cooperation with various aviation educators and industry.

This handbook is developed to assist student pilots learning to fly airplanes. It is also beneficial to pilots who wish to improve their flying proficiency and aeronautical knowledge, those pilots preparing for additional certificates or ratings, and flight instructors engaged in the instruction of both student and certificated pilots. It introduces the future pilot to the realm of flight and provides information and guidance in the performance of procedures and maneuvers required for pilot certification. Topics such as navigation and communication, meteorology, use of flight information publications, regulations, and aeronautical decision making are available in other Federal Aviation Administration (FAA) publications.

This handbook conforms to pilot training and certification concepts established by the FAA. There are different ways of teaching, as well as performing flight procedures and maneuvers, and many variations in the explanations of aerodynamic theories and principles. This handbook adopts a selective method and concept of flying airplanes. The discussion and explanations reflect the most commonly used practices and principles. Occasionally the word "must" or similar language is used where the desired action is deemed critical. The use of such language is not intended to add to, interpret, or relieve a duty imposed by Title 14 of the Code of Federal Regulations (14 CFR).

It is essential for persons using this handbook to also become familiar with and apply the pertinent parts of 14 CFR and the *Aeronautical Information Manual (AIM)*. The AIM is available online at **http://www.faa.gov/atpubs**. Performance standards for demonstrating competence required for pilot certification are prescribed in the appropriate airplane practical test standard.

The current Flight Standards Service airman training and testing material and subject matter knowledge codes for all airman certificates and ratings can be obtained from the Flight Standards Service Web site at **http://av-info.faa.gov**.

The FAA greatly acknowledges the valuable assistance provided by many individuals and organizations throughout the aviation community whose expertise contributed to the preparation of this handbook.

This handbook supersedes FAA-H-8083-3, *Airplane Flying Handbook*, dated 1999. This handbook also supersedes AC 61-9B, *Pilot Transition Courses for Complex Single-Engine and Light Twin-Engine Airplanes*, dated 1974; and related portions of AC 61-10A, *Private and Commercial Pilots Refresher Courses*, dated 1972. This revision expands all technical subject areas from the previous edition, FAA-H-8083-3. It also incorporates new areas of safety concerns and technical information not previously covered. The chapters covering transition to seaplanes and skiplanes have been removed. They will be incorporated into a new handbook (under development), FAA-H-8083-23, *Seaplane, Skiplane and Float/Ski Equipped Helicopter Operations Handbook*.

This handbook is available for download from the Flight Standards Service Web site at **http://av-info.faa.gov**. This web site also provides information about availablity of printed copies.

This handbook is published by the U.S. Department of Transportation, Federal Aviation Administration, Airman Testing Standards Branch, AFS-630, P.O. Box 25082, Oklahoma City, OK 73125. Comments regarding this handbook should be sent in e-mail form to **AFS630comments@faa.gov**.

AC 00-2, Advisory Circular Checklist, transmits the current status of FAA advisory circulars and other flight information publications. This checklist is available via the Internet at **http://www.faa.gov/aba/html_policies/ac00_2.html**.

> According to the preface, students and pilots are included in the audience for this handbook.

FIGURE 4.7   Example of Handbook Preface.   Source: Federal Aviation Administration's *Air Flying Handbook 2004*

local, state, and federal handbooks, we found that government handbook writers often organize this section using one or more of the following logical patterns:

1. *Regulatory Procedures*—Step-by-step instructions that describe the regulatory process in chronological order from licensing of businesses, to regulation of businesses, to citations for noncompliance rules, to revocations of licenses. This arrangement is effective for most handbooks that address regulated entities or government field staff who enforce rules.

2. *Directives and Policy Memorandums*—Some agencies frequently distribute directives or policy memos to agency staff and the public to clarify laws, rules, or other handbook material. These memorandums, which vary in length depending on the subject matter, are often filed in chronological order or by date. Handbooks comprised solely of policy memos are not the most user-friendly handbooks, especially when they lack tables of contents and indexes to the information they need.

3. *Distribution of Government Goods and Services Procedures*—Step-by-step instructions that describe how the public can interact with government agencies to obtain contracts, goods, and/or services from the government. Again, the handbook is organized in chronological order explaining what steps a business or individual must take to contract with the government or secure its goods or services. These instructions begin with discussions about who is eligible to participate, which is followed by a discussion of the bidding processes and/or application processes and explanations of how eligibility is determined; the instructions conclude with information about disbursement of contracts, goods, or services and/or fines inflicted on the public for providing false information.

4. *Question-and-Answer Format for Nonexpert Audiences*—A handbook organized in the question-and-answer format places the audience's frequently asked or anticipated questions in the order that they would arise in the process or procedure. This organizational pattern is effective for nonexpert audiences, like the general public, who are not familiar with legal or government jargon. The question-and-answer format is user-friendly and welcoming to readers who are unfamiliar with the subject matter.

5. *Alphabetical Order for Expert Audiences*—The alphabetical order format is where policy processes or procedures are given descriptive titles, which are then arranged in alphabetical order. This organizational pattern is most appropriate for experienced government field staff and regulated entities who are familiar with the subject matter and need to quickly leaf through the handbook to find the information they are looking for. Figure 4.8 is an excerpt from the *Federal Energy Regulatory Commission's Handbook for Hydroelectric Project Licensing and 5 MW Exemptions from Licensing* that uses the alphabetical and question and answer organizational patterns.

Within each of these organizational patterns, handbooks may be further segmented into even more specific processes. The handbook writers may decide to divide the policy handbook into subsections that address different constituencies

Notice that the handbook authors use relevant questions to guide the reader through the handbook.

APPLYING FOR A LICENSE

2.7   WHAT HAPPENS AFTER THE APPLICATION IS FILED?

2.7.1   APPLICATION REVIEW

Tendering Notice

Processing an application begins when the Commission issues a public notice of the tendering of the application for filing. The tendering notice will be published in the Federal Register, local newspapers, and directly with tribes and agencies. The content of the notice will vary slightly among the application processes. Regardless of the process, the notice will contain a preliminary schedule for processing the application.

18 CFR 5.19; 18 CFR 4.32(b)(7)

The tendering notice will also establish procedures and the deadline for submission of final amendments and a schedule for processing applications.[4]

18 CFR 5.19(a); 18 CFR 16.9(d)(2)

In the case of the traditional licensing process, the notice will notify agencies, tribes, and other persons that they have 60 days to identify additional scientific studies that they believe is necessary to form an adequate factual basis for completing an analysis of the application on its merits (see Chapter 4 for more details).

18 CFR 4.32(b)(7)

No similar provision is provided in the integrated or alternative licensing processes. Additional study requests are most often asked for during the second stage of consultation in the alternative licensing process, and thus are not requested again in the Commission's tendering notice.

Notice of Application Deficiencies

Within 30 days of filing the application, the Commission will notify the applicant by letter, or in the case of minor deficiencies, by telephone, describing any deficiencies in the application. The letter will establish a deadline for deficiency correction, generally 90 days after the date of the letter.

18 CFR 5.2(a)(2); 18 CFR 4.32(e)(1)

Last Date for Final Amendments

An applicant must make any final amendments to its application no later than the date specified in the Commission processing deadline notice or not later than 30 days after issuance of a ready for environmental analysis notice.

18 CFR 5.27(d); 18 CFR 16.9(c)

FIGURE 4.8   Example of Handbook Table of Contents. Source: *Handbook for Hydroelectric Project Licensing and 5 MW Exemptions from Licensing*

or segment it into categories that address even more specific policy areas within a given process or procedure.

References, Glossaries, Appendices, and Indexes

The final section of policy handbooks is very similar to that in other instructional materials, including this textbook: a policy handbook includes references where writers cite sources; a glossary to define unfamiliar words and concepts; one or more appendices that include helpful checklists, charts, telephone numbers, and other helpful resources; and an index to help the readers find information.

Government Agency Style Guides

As students, you have probably used one or more writing style guides when deciding what choices to make when writing and revising research papers and making in-text citations and works cited list. Commonly used style guides include Modern Language Association's *MLA Style Manual*, the *Publication Manual of the American Psychological Association's style guide (APA)*, and the *Chicago Manual of*

What Is a "Plain English" Document?

We'll start by dispelling a common misconception about plain English writing. It does not mean deleting complex information to make the document easier to understand. For investors to make informed decisions, disclosure documents must impart complex information. Using plain English assures the orderly and clear presentation of complex information so that investors have the best possible chance of understanding it.

Plain English means analyzing and deciding what information investors need to make informed decisions, before words, sentences, or paragraphs are considered. A plain English document uses words economically and at a level the audience can understand. Its sentence structure is tight. Its tone is welcoming and direct. Its design is visually appealing. A plain English document is easy to read and looks like it's meant to be read.

FIGURE 4.9 Excerpt from an Agency Style Guide. Source: U.S. Securities and Exchange Commission's *A Plain English Handbook: How to Create Clear SEC Disclosure Documents*

Style. While these manuals are still very useful in the professional workplaces, including government organizations, other government agencies create their own style guides for government staff and external audiences who communicate important information to the public. These government style guides include recommendations for using consistent and correct grammar and punctuation; clear and engaging instructions that make the audience feel at ease; scenarios and examples that help the audience to visualize a person complying with a policy or following a procedure; and the use of graphics, tables, and other visual and textual cues to guide the audience through the handbook. In Figure 4.9 we have an example of an agency style guide, the U.S. Securities and Exchange Commission's *A Plain*

English Handbook, which recommends plain style as described in an excerpt from the handbook.

Collaborative Nature of Handbook Writing

In Chapter 3 of this textbook, we discussed the collaborative nature of rule writing and the fact that stakeholders, internal and external to government agencies, were very much involved in developing rules. Handbook development is also collaborative, but it is a much more internal government process than rule writing. One reason is that there is no legal requirement, such as administrative procedures acts in rule writing, which require the government to include comments or perspectives of external stakeholders in handbook development. Another reason that handbook writing requires less interaction with the public is because many policy handbooks are internal government documents that address government employees; it is unlikely that the public, which does not frequently read documents written specifically for them, would be motivated to participate in the development of internal government documents. In those cases where there is negotiation between the government agency and external stakeholders about the content of policy handbooks, this negotiation is requested for purposes of clarification and usability testing by the subject matter experts before the documents are sent to government editors and web designers. Figure 4.10 and Figure 4.11 are visual representations of two handbook writing processes.

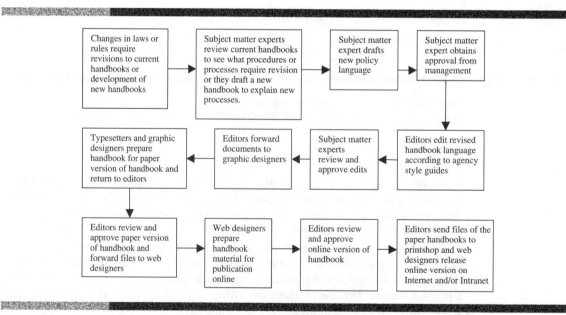

FIGURE 4.10 Handbook Development Process Using Graphic Designers. Source: Texas Department of Human Services

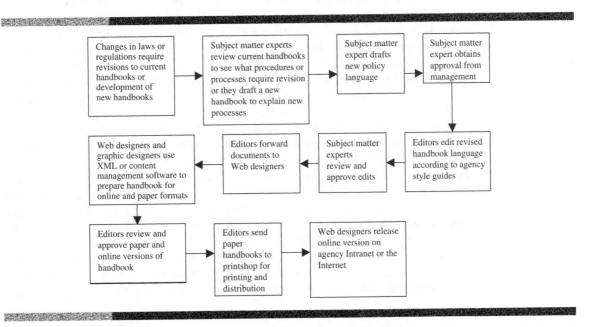

FIGURE 4.11   Handbook Development Process Using Content Management Software
Source: Texas Department of Human Services

Writing, Editing, and Publishing Policy Handbooks

Although there are fewer external stakeholders involved in writing public policy handbooks than there are in writing rules, this collaborative writing still requires negotiation between subject matter experts regarding the content of the handbooks, negotiation between editor and subject matter expert regarding the language used in the handbooks, and negotiation between all parties regarding the document design and distribution of the handbooks. As in all negotiation and collaborative writing processes, there are always interpersonal and intercultural conflicts that writers and managers must work diligently to overcome. These challenges can be remedied through the use of agency style guides that describe the "voice" of the agency, group meetings where writers and editors discuss and negotiate their varying ideas about what should remain in the handbook and what should be changed, and clear work flow and document approval processes that tell writers and editors where to go for final approval of handbooks. Policy writers and editors often have different styles of writing, different interpretations of the content of the policies, and different personalities that make negotiation difficult; it is important that these writers and editors remember that the goals of collaborative writing projects are the objectives of the government agency and much larger than meeting their individual aims. Policy handbook writing is a time-consuming, costly, and yet extremely important by-product of policy implementation and enforcement.

Government agencies are attempting to decrease the costs associated with printing and distributing handbooks by publishing more handbooks online and decreasing costs associated with printing, binding, and mailing handbooks to internal and external audiences. Still, agency officials are also aware of the fact that many handbook users prefer paper copies of handbooks because they are portable and more accessible for audiences, like the elderly and poor, who may not have access to the Internet. To serve both audiences, handbook users with access to the Internet as well as those without access, agencies use content management software or extensible markup language (XML) for **single-source publishing**. Single-source publishing increases efficiency in the production of handbooks by decreasing the duplication of work found in Figure 4.10, where typists for paper handbooks and web designers are both responsible for handbook content. In single-source publishing of handbooks, the handbook policies and procedures are stored in one file and available for use in online and paper handbooks. When both web designers and typists for paper documents are responsible for typing and formatting the same information for different audiences, there is an increased chance that their final products will be different. One of the two groups is likely to inadvertently leave out a word, edit a sentence, or make some change that will result in inconsistencies between the web content and paper content.

Summary and Looking Forward

Government handbooks have been used by governments throughout history to help the public and government employees to understand the complexities of government activities. Today, handbook writers use a variety of rhetorical strategies to communicate instructions and processes that help us to interact with government agencies. In the next chapter, we will discuss policy memorandums, a genre of technical communication that we briefly described in this chapter as being used to clarify laws, rules, or other handbook material.

Activities and Assignments

1. **Group Internet Activity:** Browse the Internet for examples of one internal agency handbook and one external agency handbook published by government agencies in your state or city. Once you find the examples, discuss the (a) purpose for each handbook, (b) procedures and processes explained in each handbook, (c) clientele addressed in each handbook, and (d) places or jurisdictions covered in each handbook. Be prepared to explain the differences and similarities between the two handbooks to the rest of the class.

2. **Group Activity:** In groups of three or four, create a six-to-seven-page policy guide that describes admission policies for prospective students who are considering applying to your university. (Feel free to consult your university's website as a resource for your handbook.) Identify a specific audience, and use one or more of the logical patterns for organizing the body of policy handbooks.

3. **Individual Internet Activity:** Use the Internet or your local library to find a policy handbook written by a government agency (see Appendix: U.S. Department of Justice List of Department and Agencies) that you have interacted with in the past year. Read the introduction to the handbook to see if it includes: (1) an overview that includes references to laws and rules that give the government agency the power to implement specific policies and procedures outlined in the handbook; (2) guidelines for government agency personnel to conduct day-to-day procedures that implement laws and rules; and/or (3) instructions for the public to follow the requirements needed to benefit from or to avoid violation of government laws and rules. What information do you find in the introduction? Is it useful? Report your findings to the rest of the class.

Works Cited

108th Congress' Senate Committee on Ethics. *Senate Ethics Manual.* 2003 Edition 15 Apr. 2006 <http://ethics.senate.gov/downloads/pdffiles/manual.pdf>.

Alcohol and Tobacco Tax and Trade Bureau. *The Beverage Alcohol Manual (BAM): A Practical Guide-Basic Mandatory Labeling Information for Distilled Spirits.* July 2001. 5 Jan. 2007 <http://www.ttb.gov/spirits/bam.shtml>.

Carlson, Ken."Medicare Handbook Is In Error: Charts Say No Monthly Fee for Drug Benefits; but Most Plans Do Have Premiums" *Modesto Bee*, 12 Oct. 2005. Lexis-Nexus Academic. 1 Apr. 2006.

Federal Aviation Administration. *Airplane Flying Handbook 2004.* 15 Apr. 2006 <http://www.faa.gov/library/manuals/aircraft/airplane_handbook/>.

Federal Emergency Management Agency. *National Flood Insurance Program: Flood Insurance Claims Handbook.* July 2005. 15 Apr. 2006 <http://www.fema.gov/pdf/nfip/f687_claimshdbk.pdf>.

Federal Energy Regulatory Commission. "Handbook for Hydroelectric project Licensing and 5MW Exemptions from Licensing" Apr. 2004. 18 May 2007. <http://www.ferc.gov/industries/hydropower/>.

Food Safety and Inspection Service (FSIS)—United States Department of Agriculture. *Meat and Poultry Hazards and Control Guide.* Sept. 2005. 5 Jan. 2007 <http://www.fsis.usda.gov/OPPDE/rdad/FSISDirectives/5100.2/Meat_and_Poultry_Hazards_Controls_Guide_10042005.pdf>.

Food and Drug Administration. "Guidance for FDA Staff The Leveraging Handbook: An Agency Resource for Effective Collaboration." (Feb. 2003-Corrected June 2003) 15 Apr. 2006 <http://www.fda.gov/oc/leveraging/handbook.html>.

Kennedy, George A. *A New History of Classical Rhetoric.* Princeton: Princeton UP, 1994.

Llorente, Elizabeth. "Bergen Handbook Bridges Language Gap for Latinos; Leaders Extol New Bilingual Format." *The Record.* 21 Mar. 2006. Lexis-Nexus Academic, 1 Apr. 2006.

Machiavelli, Niccolo. *The Prince.* London: Penguin Classics, 2003.

"Medicare Agency Says Look for Important Handbooks in the Mail: Medicare & You Booklet Provides Drug Information." *Pr NewswireUS.* Oct. 24 2005. Lexis-Nexus Academic. 5 Jan. 2007.

Missile Defense Agency. *Ballistic Missile Defense Organization Unsolicited Proposal Guide.* Apr. 2000. 5 Jan. 2007 <http://www.mda.mil/mdalink/pdf/proposal.pdf>.

Simon, Herbert A. "The Proverbs of Public Administration." *Classics of Public Administration* Eds. Jay M. Shafritz and Albert C. Hyde. Fort Worth: Harcourt Brace College Publishers, 1997. 127–41.

Texas Department of Human Services. "Handbook Development Process Using Graphic Designers." Workflow Process. 2001.

Texas Department of Human Services. "Handbook Development Process Using Content Management Software." Workflow Process. 2001.

U.S. Attorney's Office—Northern District of New York. *Victim and Witness Handbook.* 5 Jan. 2007 <http://www.usdoj.gov/usao/nyn/VW/VWHandBook.htm>.

U.S. Attorney's Office—Western District of Tennessee. *Victim and Witness Handbook.* 5 Jan. 2007 <http://www.usdoj.gov/usao/tnw/brochures/vwhandbook/vwhandbook.html>.

U.S. Department of Health and Human Services. *Medicare and You 2006.* 15 Apr. 2006 <http://www.medicare.gov/default.asp>.

U.S. Environmental Protection Agency. *Handbook of Groundwater Protection and Cleanup Policies for RCRA Corrective Action.* Apr. 2004. 15 Apr. 2006 <http://www.epa.gov/correctiveaction/resource/guidance/gw/gwhandbk/gwhndbk.htm#note>.

U.S. Securities and Exchange Commission-Office of Investor Education and Assistance. *A Plain English Handbook: How to Create Clear SEC Disclosure Documents.* 2 Apr. 2006 <http://www.sec.gov/pdf/handbook.pdf>.

Veterans Health Administration. *VHA Handbook 1200.06 Control of Hazardous Agents in VA Research Laboratories.* 21 Oct. 2005. 5 Jan. 2007 <http://www1.va.gov/vhapublications/ViewPublication.asp?pub_ID=1336>.

Wait, Patience. "DOD raises the bar on info assurance." *Post-Newsweek Media, Inc.* Feb. 2006. Lexis-Nexus Academic. 15 Apr. 2006 <http://www.gcn.com/>.

"Watershed Handbook Released." *States News Service.* Jan 6 2006. Lexis-Nexus Academic. 15 Apr. 2006 <http://www.lexisnexis.com/>.

5

Policy Memorandums

On January 25, 2001, Richard A. Clarke, former counter-terrorism advisor on the National Security Council, wrote a memorandum to then National Security Advisor Condoleezza Rice with a subject line that read "Presidential Policy/Initiative/Review—The Al-Qida Network." Months after September 11, 2001, this same memorandum was the center of much controversy regarding its intent and message—and, more importantly, its subsequent interpretation by Rice and other presidential staff. The first line of the memo read, "Steve asked today that we propose major Presidential policy reviews or initiatives. We _urgently_ need such a Principals level review on the al Qida network (Clarke)." Clarke went on to request that Rice have a "Principals' discussion of al Quida" to discuss its potential threat, strategies, budget issues, and other related foreign policy issues. Later, on March 24, 2004, Clarke testified before the National Commission on Terrorist Attacks Upon the United States, and he was asked if he received a response to this memo. "I did get a response," Clarke stated, "and the response was that in the Bush Administration, I should and my committee, counterterrorism security group, should report to the deputies committee, which is a sub-Cabinet level committee, and not to the principals and that, therefore, it was inappropriate for me to be asking for a principals' meeting" (CNN, Richard Clarke testifies).

The scheduling of a deputies' meeting instead of a principals' meeting, Clarke maintained, had a negative effect on the policy review process in that it "slowed it down enormously"—insinuating that a more timely or different response to this memo might have altered the tragic events of September 11, 2001 (CNN, Richard Clarke testifies). On April 8, 2004, Condoleezza Rice, the recipient of the memo, testified before the National Commission on Terrorist Attacks Upon the United States and stated, "In the memorandum that Dick Clarke sent me on January 25th, he mentions sleeper cells. There is no mention or recommendation of anything that needs to be done about them. And the FBI was pursuing them. And usually when things come to me it's because I'm supposed to do something about it, and there was no indicating that the FBI was not adequately pursing the sleeper cells" (CNN, Transcript of Rice's). While Clarke's testimony suggests that his memorandum's purpose was clear—to involve important decision makers in this review of policy—Rice argues that Clarke's memorandum was historical and informative. According to Rice, it failed to mention any action items relevant to her position.

After reading this narrative, you are likely to pose the questions:

> What caused the breakdown in communication between Clarke and Rice?
>
> Do government officials and personnel have certain expectations for the content that they receive in memorandums?
>
> Is there a particular rhetorical strategy or document design for policy memorandums that might alert government officials that some specific action is being requested from the writer?
>
> How does the public obtain access to memorandums pertaining to national security?

In this chapter, we will examine Clarke's memorandum to Rice as well as several other policy memos. Our objectives in evaluating these policy memos will be to better understand the purpose, contexts, and audience for policy memos and to explain how policy memos are different from memos we find in nongovernmental organizations.

Purpose of Policy Memos

In Chapter 3, we discussed public comments and the fact that the public can communicate with government agencies to inform government officials of their opinions about rules; this communication is usually expressed in public meetings, letters, and most recently through electronic rulemaking websites. In contrast, **policy memorandums** are government-initiated documents used to communicate about policy development, policy evaluation, and policy implementation at the local, state, and federal levels. Policy memorandums are written by government agency staff and officials within and across government agencies.

Today, when we hear that policy memorandums have been "leaked" to the press, our use of the term *leaked* supports the fact that although some government documents are public information, memorandums are initially written and addressed to a specific audience within a government agency or office and public review of these documents are not intended. In the United States federal government, memorandums have been used to communicate sensitive information between presidents and executive-level federal staff since Secretary of State William H. Seward sent President Abraham Lincoln a memorandum on April 1, 1861 titled, "Some Thoughts for the President's Consideration" (Sowle 234). Take a moment to read Seward's memorandum in Figure 5.1. After your initial reading of that memorandum to President Lincoln, you might believe that his purpose for writing the memo was to outline specific problems that he had with Lincoln's handling of domestic and foreign policy, to highlight the urgency of the situation, and to suggest specific policy-related action items that he would like for President Lincoln to consider. Take a look at Seward's memorandum and try to identity the problem, urgency of the situation, and action items. You will also find Lincoln's response to Seward, in Figure 5.2, which provides further evidence that this is a private, yet

MEMORANDUM FROM SECRETARY SEWARD, APRIL 1, 1861

Some thoughts for the President's Consideration,

First. We are at the end of a month's administration, and yet without a policy either domestic or foreign.

Second. This, however, is not culpable, and it has even been unavoidable. The presence of the Senate, with the need to meet applications for patronage, have prevented attention to other and more grave matters.

Third. But further delay to adopt and prosecute our policies for both domestic and foreign affairs would not only bring scandal on the administration, but danger upon the country.

Fourth. To do this we must dismiss the applicants for office. But how? I suggest that we make the local appointments forthwith, leaving foreign or general ones for ulterior and occasional action.

Fifth. The policy at home. I am aware that my views are singular, and perhaps not sufficiently explained. My system is built upon this idea as a ruling one, namely, that we must CHANGE THE QUESTION BEFORE THE PUBLIC FROM ONE UPON SLAVERY, OR ABOUT SLAVERY, for a question upon UNION OR DISUNION: In other words, from what would be regarded as a party question, to one of patriotism or union.

The occupation or evacuation of Fort Sumter, although not in fact a slavery or a party question, is so regarded. Witness the temper manifested by the Republicans in the free States, and even by the Union men in the South.

I would therefore terminate it as a safe means for changing the issue. I deem it fortunate that the last administration created the necessity.

For the rest, I would simultaneously defend and reinforce all the ports in the gulf, and have the navy recalled from foreign stations to be prepared for a blockade. Put the island of Key West under martial law.

This will raise distinctly the question of union or disunion. I would maintain every fort and possession in the South.

FOR FOREIGN NATIONS,

I would demand explanations from Spain and France, categorically, at once.

I would seek explanations from Great Britain and Russia, and send agents into Canada, Mexico, and Central America to rouse a vigorous continental spirit of independence on this continent against European intervention.

And, if satisfactory explanations are not received from Spain and France,

Would convene Congress and declare war against them.

But whatever policy we adopt, there must be an energetic prosecution of it.

For this purpose it must be somebody's business to pursue and direct it incessantly.

Either the President must do it himself, and be all the while active in it, or Devolve it on some member of his Cabinet. Once adopted, debates on it must end, and all agree and abide.

It is not in my especial province; But I neither seek to evade nor assume responsibility.

FIGURE 5.1 Memorandum from Secretary Seward. Source: http://www.gutenberg.org/files/2657/2657.txt

REPLY TO SECRETARY SEWARD'S MEMORANDUM

EXECUTIVE MANSION, APRIL 1, 1861

HON. W. H. SEWARD.

MY DEAR SIR:--Since parting with you I have been considering your paper dated this day, and entitled "Some Thoughts for the President's Consideration." The first proposition in it is, "First, We are at the end of a month's administration, and yet without a policy either domestic or foreign."

At the beginning of that month, in the inaugural, I said: "The power confided to me will be used to hold, occupy, and possess the property and places belonging to the Government, and to Collect the duties and imposts." This had your distinct approval at the time; and, taken in connection with the order I immediately gave General Scott, directing him to employ every means in his power to strengthen and hold the forts, comprises the exact domestic policy you now urge, with the single exception that it does not propose to abandon Fort Sumter.

Again, I do not perceive how the reinforcement of Fort Sumter would be done on a slavery or a party issue, while that of Fort Pickens would be on a more national and patriotic one.

The news received yesterday in regard to St. Domingo certainly brings a new item within the range of our foreign policy; but up to that time we have been preparing circulars and instructions to ministers and the like, all in perfect harmony, without even a suggestion that we had no foreign policy.

Upon your Closing propositions--that,

"Whatever policy we adopt, there must be an energetic prosecution of it.

"For this purpose it must be somebody's business to pursue and direct it incessantly.

"Either the President must do it himself, and be all the while active in it, or,

"Devolve it on some member of his Cabinet. Once adopted, debates on it must end, and all agree and abide"--

I remark that if this must be done, I must do it. When a general line of policy is adopted, I apprehend there is no danger of its being changed without good reason, or continuing to be a subject of unnecessary debate; still, upon points arising in its progress I wish, and suppose I am entitled to have, the advice of all the Cabinet.

FIGURE 5.2 Lincoln's Reply to Seward's Memorandum. Source: http://www.gutenberg.org/files/2657/2657.txt

official communication between a president and his secretary of state. (Note: The fact that the document is internal and clearly labeled as a memorandum alerts the reader that this is an official document and not a personal communication or letter.)

What is missing from these memorandums is the fact that, as Patrick Sowle states, "Seward, his old friend Thurlow Weed of the *Albany Evening Journal*, and

Henry J. Raymond, editor of the *New York Times*, planned to publish the memorandum together with Lincoln's reply [see Lincoln's reply in Figure 5.2], which they anticipated would endorse the Secretary's proposals" in an effort to promote public support for "peaceful reunification" of the states (Sowle 235). At the time, this particular memorandum was not "leaked" or published as was planned, but this important genre of technical communication has been used to negotiate domestic and foreign policy decisions and even public opinions for quite some time. Many historical memorandums are currently available for review by the public and analyzed by historians, journalists, and politicians. Historical documents have many uses, including providing us with examples of how former government officials and personnel made policy decisions that resulted in policy successes and failures.

The layout of the memorandum and language used in this historical document is somewhat different from what you might see in a contemporary policy memorandum, which would include information about who is writing to whom, the date, and a subject line at the top of the page. After that, the body of the memorandum would be separated into some logical structure under unique headers. In the example in Figure 5.3, we have taken the liberty to organize Sewall's memorandum using a more contemporary format that is supposed to be more user friendly and easier to navigate. Do you agree?

The formats or document designs for policy memorandums are as varied as government agencies and the departments within them; thus, this chapter will not focus as much on how memos are organized as on the purpose and content for policy memorandums. Also, most government agencies have memo templates and style guides that give government staff the preferred format and layout to use when writing internal memos and memorandums to other agencies. As you read the examples of policy memorandums in this chapter, take note of the subtle differences in format and style.

Take a look at the memorandum in Figure 5.4; it is a copy of the memorandum that we mentioned earlier in this chapter from Richard A. Clarke to Condoleezza Rice.

Now, consider the purpose of Clarke's memorandum, and how posing our questions to help analyze policy memos for intent and purpose on page 94 might help you to write policy memos with a clear intent and purpose:

You can also use these questions when analyzing policy memorandums to gain an understanding of the purpose of the document or what the audience is supposed to gain from reading it.

Clearly, all policy memorandums are not addressed to presidents of the United States or national security advisors. Most policy memos are written communications between mid-level management government employees and their staff and speak to policy issues that most of us would view as mundane and uninteresting. Also, we must acknowledge that many memos written within government agencies have little to do with public policy and are relevant to the same types of human resource or personnel issues communicated in private and nonprofit organizations. In this chapter, we will concentrate on those memorandums that are part of negotiating and implementing public policy. In the next section, we'll discuss the political, social, and historical contexts in policy memorandums, including those written by non-executive-level agency staff.

MEMORANDUM

TO: President Abraham Lincoln
FROM: Secretary Seward
DATE: April 1, 1861
SUBJECT: Some thoughts for the President's Consideration

Background (Problem)

We are at the end of a month's administration, and yet without a policy either domestic or foreign. This, however, is not culpable, and it has even been unavoidable. The presence of the Senate, with the need to meet applications for patronage, have prevented attention to other and more grave matters. But further delay to adopt and prosecute our policies for both domestic and foreign affairs would not only bring scandal on the administration, but danger upon the country. To do this we must dismiss the applicants for office. But how

Proposed Policy Change (General Discussion of How to Resolve the Problem)

I suggest that we make the local appointments forthwith, leaving foreign or general ones for ulterior and occasional action. The policy at home. I am aware that my views are singular, and perhaps not sufficiently explained. My system is built upon this idea as a ruling one, namely, that we must CHANGE THE QUESTION BEFORE THE PUBLIC FROM ONE UPON SLAVERY, OR ABOUT SLAVERY, for a question upon UNION OR DISUNION: In other words, from what would be regarded as a party question, to one of patriotism or union. The occupation or evacuation of Fort Sumter, although not in fact a slavery or a party question, is so regarded. Witness the temper manifested by the Republicans in the free States, and even by the Union men in the South.
I would therefore terminate it as a safe means for changing the issue. I deem it fortunate that the last administration created the necessity.

Action Items (Specific Steps to Resolve the Problem)

1. I would simultaneously defend and reinforce all the ports in the gulf, and have the navy recalled from foreign stations to be prepared for a blockade. Put the island of Key West under martial law. This will raise distinctly the question of union or disunion.

2. I would maintain every fort and possession in the South. FOR FOREIGN NATIONS,

3. I would demand explanations from Spain and France, categorically, at once.

4. I would seek explanations from Great Britain and Russia, and send agents into Canada, Mexico, and Central America to rouse a vigorous continental spirit of independence on this continent against European intervention.

5. And, if satisfactory explanations are not received from Spain and France,
Would convene Congress and declare war against them.

Conclusion

But whatever policy we adopt, there must be an energetic prosecution of it. For this purpose it must be somebody's business to pursue and direct it incessantly. Either the President must do it himself, and be all the while active in it, or Devolve it on some member of his Cabinet. Once adopted, debates on it must end, and all agree and abide. It is not in my especial province; But I neither seek to evade nor assume responsibility.

FIGURE 5.3   Adaptation of Seward's Memorandum in Contemporary Format

NATIONAL SECURITY COUNCIL
WASHINGTON, D.C. 20504

30009

January 25, 2001

INFORMATION

MEMORANDUM FOR CONDOLEEZZA RICE

C

FROM: RICHARD A. CLARKE

SUBJECT: Presidential Policy Initiative/Review -- The Al-
               Qida Network

Steve asked today that we propose major Presidential policy
reviews or initiatives. We _urgently_ need such a Principals
level review on the al Qida network.

Just some Terrorist Group?

As we noted in our briefings for you, al Qida is not some
narrow, little terrorist issue that needs to be included in
broader regional policy. Rather, several of our regional
policies need to address centrally the transnational challenge
to the US and our interests posed by the al Qida network.   By
proceeding with separate policy reviews on Central Asia, the
GCC, North Africa, etc. we would deal inadequately with the need
for a comprehensive multi-regional policy on al Qida.

al Qida is the active, organized, major force that is using a
distorted version of Islam as its vehicle to achieve two goals:

     --to drive the US out of the Muslim world, forcing the
withdrawal of our military and economic presence in countries
from Morocco to Indonesia;

     --to replace moderate, modern, Western regime in Muslim
countries with theocracies modeled along the lines of the
Taliban.

al Qida affects centrally our policies on Pakistan, Afghanistan,
Central Asia, North Africa and the GCC. Leaders in Jordan and
Saudi Arabia see al Qida as a direct threat to them.   The
strength of the network of organizations limits the scope of
support friendly Arab regimes can give to a range of US

Classified by: Richard A. Clarke
Reason: 1.5(d)(x6)
Declassify On: 1/25/25
Derived From: Multiple Sources

NSC DECLASSIFICATION REVIEW [E.O. 12958]
/X/ Exempt in part and redact as shown
by D.Sanborn Date 4/7/2004

FIGURE 5.4 Memorandum from Richard A. Clarke to Condoleezza Rice.
Source: George Washington University's National Security Archive. These materials are reproduced
from www.nsarchive.org with permission of the National Security Archive

2

policies, including Iraq policy and the Peace Process. We would make a major error if we underestimated the challenge al *Qida* poses, or over estimated the stability of the moderate, friendly regimes al *Qida* threatens.

Pending Time Sensitive Decisions

At the close of the Clinton Administration, two decisions about al *Qida* were deferred to the Bush Administration.

    -- First, should we provide the Afghan Northern Alliance enough assistance to maintain it as a viable opposition force to the Taliban/al Qida? If we do not, I believe that the Northern Alliance may be effectively taken out of action this Spring when fighting resumes after the winter thaw. The al Qida 55th Brigade, which has been a key fighting force for the Taliban, would then be freed to send its personnel elsewhere, where they would likely threaten US interests. For any assistance to get there in time to effect the Spring fighting, a decision is needed now.

    -- Second, should we increase assistance to Uzbekistan to allow them to deal with the al Qida/ IMU threat?

Operational detail, removed at the request of the CIA

Three other issues awaiting addressal now are:

    --First, what the new Administration says to the Taliban and Pakistan about the importance we attach to ending the al Qida sanctuary in Afghanistan. We are separately proposing early, strong messages to both.

    --Second, do we propose significant program growth in the FY02 budget for anti-al Qida operations by CIA and counter-terrorism training and assistance by State and CIA?

    --Third, when and how does the Administration choose to respond to the attack on the USS Cole. That decision is obviously complex. We can make some decisions, such as the those above, now without yet coming to grips with the harder decision about the Cole. On the Cole, we should take advantage of the policy that we "will respond at a time, place, and manner of our own choosing" and not be forced into knee jerk responses.

FIGURE 5.4 *(continued)*

Attached is the year-end 2000 strategy on al Qida developed by the last Administration to give to you. Also attached is the 1998 strategy. Neither was a "covert action only" approach. Both incorporated diplomatic, economic, military, public diplomacy and intelligence tools. Using the 2000 paper as background, we could prepare a decision paper/guide for a PC review.

I recommend that you have a Principals discussion of al Qida soon and addresss the following issues:

   1. Threat Magnitude: Do the Principals agree that the al Qida network poses a first order threat to US interests in a number or regions, or is this analysis a "chicken little" over reaching and can we proceed without major new initiatives and by handling this issue in a more routine manner?

   2. Strategy: If it is a first order issue, how should the existing strategy be modified or strengthened?

Two elements of the existing strategy that have not been made to work effectively are a) going after al Qida's money and b) public information to counter al Qida propaganda.

   3. FY02 Budget: Should we continue the funding increases into FY02 for State and CIA programs designed to implement the al Qida strategy?

   4. Immediate ██ Decisions: Should we initiate ██ funding to the Northern Alliance and to the Uzbek's?

Please let us know if you would like such a decision/discussion paper or any modifications to the background paper.

Concurrences by: Mary McCarthy, Dan Fried, Bruce Reidel, Don
                    Camp

Attachment
Tab A   December 2000 Paper: Strategy for Eliminating the Threat from the Jihadist Networks of al-Qida: Status and Prospects

Tab B   September 1998 Paper: Pol-Mil Plan for al-Qida

FIGURE 5.4   *(continued)*

Questions to Help Analyze Policy Memos for Intent and Purpose

1. Is the purpose stated clearly and in a prominent place in the policy memo?
2. Is the memo written to inform or persuade the audience about policy?
3. Is the memo written to help develop, evaluate, reconsider, or implement public policy?
4. Does the memo reference other information (historical, political, economic, and social) that might help you to better understand the purpose or intent of the memo?
5. Does the memo include adequate background information or a clear explanation of the policy or problems related to the policy?
6. Does the memo provide data or evidence to suggest that a policy needs to be developed, evaluated, reconsidered, or implemented?
7. Is there any mention of the urgency of the situation in the memorandum?
8. Does the memo request that specific actions be taken by the audience?
9. Does memo include alternatives to the requested actions?
10. Does the memo summarize the possible outcomes of the suggested policy actions?

Policy Memos in Cultural Contexts

Although Richard A. Clarke's memorandum to now Secretary of State Condoleezza Rice and Secretary of State William H. Seward's memorandum to President Abraham Lincoln span a difference of 140 years, both of these documents share many features. The most obvious similarity is that they were written by government staff with top-level appointments to an audience with even more authority and power. In considering the context in which government memorandums are written, we must consider the power and authority of those writing the memorandums as well as that of those receiving them. Unlike rules and handbook policy instructions, which have already been negotiated and are ready for implementation by the audience, the memorandum, when written by government official or staff with less power than the audience, is often in the form of a *proposal*; this same genre, when written by a government official or staff with more power than the audience, is often presented as a directive or instruction.

This issue of whether the memorandum is moving up the hierarchical ladder of bureaucracy or whether it is moving down this ladder is complicated further by the fact that many policy memorandums are written across agencies to government officials and staff with similar authorities and rank in civil and public service. We will continue with the ladder metaphor and present documents that are examples of memorandums both ascending the hierarchical ladder to superiors and descending the ladder to subordinates. As you examine these examples in Figure 5.5 through Figure 5.7, identify any differences in the memorandums including tone, formality, urgency, and format.

At this point, we'd like to discuss another type of policy memorandum that can help us to understand the contexts in which government memos are created. **Memorandums of understanding** are not policy proposals written by state agency staff to a federal agency or a directive from a manager to field staff but are

EXECUTIVE OFFICE OF THE PRESIDENT
OFFICE OF SCIENCE AND TECHNOLOGY POLICY
WASHINGTON, D.C. 20502

December 23, 2005

MEMORANDUM FOR THE SECRETARY OF STATE
THE SECRETARY OF DEFENSE
THE SECRETARY OF THE INTERIOR
THE SECRETARY OF AGRICULTURE
THE SECRETARY OF COMMERCE
THE SECRETARY OF HEALTH AND HUMAN
SERVICES
THE SECRETARY OF TRANSPORTATION
THE SECRETARY OF HOMELAND SECURITY
ADMINISTRATOR, ENVIRONMENTAL PROTECTION
AGENCY
ASSISTANT TO THE PRESIDENT FOR NATIONAL
SECURITY AFFAIRS
DIRECTOR OF NATIONAL INTELLIGENCE
ADMINISTRATOR, NATIONAL AERONAUTICS AND
SPACE ADMINISTRATION
DIRECTOR, NATIONAL SCIENCE FOUNDATION

FROM: JOHN H. MARBURGER, III
DIRECTOR

SUBJECT: Landsat Data Continuity Strategy Adjustment

This memorandum is to inform you of the outcome of recent discussions among affected agencies and Executive Office of the President (EOP) offices regarding the Landsat program. This memorandum updates and revises the guidance provided in my memorandum of August 13, 2004. That memorandum directed agencies to incorporate Landsat-type sensors on the National Polar-orbiting Operational Environmental Satellite System (NPOESS), and was based on preliminary analysis performed by an interagency study group. Please refer to that memorandum for additional background on the Landsat program leading up to this round of decision-making.

Detailed analysis leads to strategy adjustment

Consistent with the actions outlined in my August 13, 2004 memorandum, the National Aeronautics and Space Administration (NASA), working with the National Oceanic and Atmospheric Administration (NOAA) and other agencies, undertook a detailed analysis of the proposal to incorporate Landsat-type sensors on two selected NPOESS platforms. The results of that technical analysis indicated that the complexities of incorporating Landsat-type sensors on the NPOESS platforms significantly exceeded earlier assessments and made that option less

FIGURE 5.5 Example of Memo "Ascending the Ladder." Source: National Aeronautics and Space Association

2

suitable to the goals of both programs. After careful consideration in interagency discussions, all parties agreed that adjustments to the current near-term strategy and development of a new long-term strategy are required in order to ensure the continuity of Landsat-type data.

Ensuring near-term data continuity

The objective of ensuring continuous availability of scientifically sound Landsat-type data can be realized in the near term by revising the Landsat data continuity mission strategy and establishing a plan for data continuity over the longer term. In particular, the Departments of Commerce, Defense, the Interior and NASA will take the following near-term actions:

- Proceed with the NPOESS program without incorporating a Landsat-type instrument;

- NASA will acquire a single Landsat data continuity mission in the form of a free-flyer spacecraft to collect the required land surface data and deliver its data to the Department of the Interior (DOI) / United States Geological Survey (USGS);

- DOI, through the USGS, will be responsible for the operations of the Landsat data continuity mission and for the collection, archiving, processing, and distribution of the land surface data to U.S. Government and other users; and

- The detailed roles and responsibilities of DOI and NASA for this near-term Landsat data continuity mission will be ratified by the two agencies and will be commensurate with the final acquisition approach and selection. The agencies will seek to implement an approach for this mission in a manner that does not preclude a long-term solution for continuity of Landsat-type data.

Ensuring long-term continuity

It remains the goal of the U.S. Government to transition the Landsat program from a series of independently planned missions to a sustained operational program funded and managed by a U.S. Government operational agency or agencies, international consortium, and/or commercial partnership. Concurrent with the actions cited above, the National Science and Technology Council, in coordination with NASA, DOI/USGS, and other agencies and EOP offices as appropriate, will lead an effort to develop a long-term plan to achieve technical, financial, and managerial stability for operational land imaging in accord with the goals and objectives of the U.S. Integrated Earth Observation System.

FIGURE 5.5   *(continued)*

State of California
DEPARTMENT OF TRANSPORTATION

Business, Transportation and Housing Agency

M e m o r a n d u m

Flex your power!
Be energy efficient!

To: DEPUTY DISTRICT DIRECTORS
FOR ENVIRONMENTAL
DISTRICT OFFICE BRANCH CHIEFS
FOR ENVIRONMENTAL

Date: September 20, 2004

File: Biology

From: GARY B. WINTERS
Chief
Division of Environmental Analysis

Subject: Guidance for Combined Essential Fish Habitat and Endangered Species Act Consultation
Process

The attached table and flowchart provided by the Federal Highway Administration
(FHWA) California Division, gives additional guidance for implementation of the
combined Endangered Species Act (ESA) and Essential Fish Habitat (EFH) consultation
process. This memo is also intended to further clarify the responsibilities of the FHWA
and the California Department of Transportation (Department).

This information is provided as a follow up to the May 21, 2004 letter, in which the
FHWA authorized the Department to consult, as its *non-Federal representative*, with the
National Oceanic and Atmospheric Administration's National Marine Fisheries Service
(NOAA-Fisheries) under particular circumstances for EFH. On June 7, 2004, the
Division of Environmental Analysis sent a memo to the Districts identifying the
circumstances in which the Department would consult on behalf of the FHWA for EFH.
The letter identified those scenarios where combined EFH and ESA consultation was
necessary.

These documents can be referenced in the Department's Standard Environmental
Reference (SER) using the following web address: *http://www.dot.ca.gov/ser*

For more information please contact Gregg Erickson, Chief, Office of Biology and
Technical Assistance, at (916) 654-6296 or Deborah McKee, Senior Environmental
Planner, at (916) 653-8056.

Attachment

"Caltrans improves mobility across California"

FIGURE 5.6 Example of Memo "Descending the Ladder." Source: California
Department of Transportation

EFH CONSULTATION MATRIX:

Endangered Species Act (ESA)	Essential Fish Habitat (EFH)	
	No Adverse Effect	**Adverse Effect[1]**
No Effect	No consultation for ESA or EFH	Caltrans conducts consultation on EFH, (no consultation for ESA)
Not Likely to Adversely Affect	Caltrans conducts informal consultation for ESA (no consultation for EFH)	Caltrans conducts informal consultation for ESA and consults on EFH
Likely to Adversely Affect	FHWA conducts formal consultation on ESA (no consultation on EFH per Caltrans determination)	FHWA conducts formal consultation on ESA and EFH
Document Type	BA for ESA (include documentation of EFH determination in Section 4.2.x of NES following guidance for EFH analysis)	BA for ESA, including EFH assessment

Source-Federal Highway Administration, California Division

[1]EFH Adverse Effect Process Flowchart

FIGURE 5.6   *(continued)*

<u>[1]EFH Adverse Effect Process Flowchart</u>

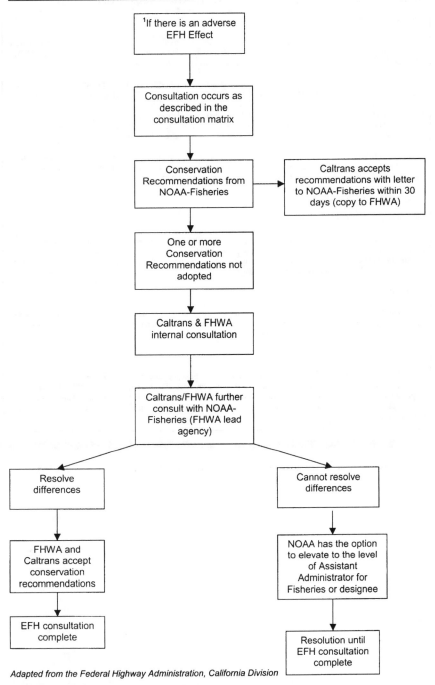

Adapted from the Federal Highway Administration, California Division

FIGURE 5.6 *(continued)*

MEMORANDUM OF UNDERSTANDING BETWEEN THE EMPLOYMENT STANDARDS
ADMINISTRATION AND THE EQUAL EMPLOYMENT OPPORTUNITY COMMISSION

I. Background and Purpose

The purpose of this Memorandum of Understanding (MOU) is to maximize the effectiveness of those laws enforced
by the Employment Standards Administration (ESA) and the Equal Employment Opportunity Commission (EEOC)
which prohibit unlawful compensation discrimination, and other unlawful compensation practices.

Historically, EEOC and ESA have maintained excellent working relationships in areas of mutual law enforcement
interest. EEOC enforces Title VII of the Civil Rights Act of 1964, and the Equal Pay Act of 1963, among other equal
employment opportunity laws. The ESA Office of Federal Contract Compliance
Programs (OFCCP) enforces Executive Order 11246, as amended, and other contract-based equal employment
opportunity laws. The ESA Wage and Hour Division (WHD) enforces the Fair Labor Standards Act, the Family and
Medical Leave Act (FMLA) and other laws establishing minimum wage and labor standards.

The agreement will enhance enforcement efforts to prohibit compensation discrimination and reduce duplication of
effort. It will also result in increased enforcement activity on the issue of compensation discrimination through the
training of ESA personnel, and through the sharing of information and data.

II. Agency Authorities and Responsibilities

Employment Standards Administration

Office of Federal Contract Compliance Programs: Executive Order 11246, as amended, and its implementing
regulations, prohibit covered federal contractors from discriminating in employment on the basis of race, color, sex,
religion, or national origin, and require them to take affirmative action to ensure that equal opportunity is provided in
all aspects of employment, including compensation.

Wage and Hour Division

The Fair Labor Standards Act of 1938 (FLSA) establishes minimum federal standards for wages and hours of work.
The Family and Medical Leave Act (FMLA) provides certain employees with up to 12 weeks of unpaid job-protected
leave a year for qualifying family leave reasons.

EEOC

The Equal Pay Act of 1963 prohibits employers from paying employees at a rate less than employees of the opposite
sex at the same establishment ``for equal work on jobs the performance of which requires equal skill, effort, and
responsibility, and which are performed under similar working conditions . . . 29 U.S.C. 206(d)(1). Title VII of the
Civil Rights Act of 1964 protects individuals from employment discrimination based on sex, race, color, religion, and
national origin.

FIGURE 5.7   Example of Memo Across Jurisdictions. Source: U.S. Department of Labor

III. Provisions

Training

Consistent with available resources, EEOC and ESA will develop and provide training to assist WHD enforcement staff in recognizing potential compensation discrimination. EEOC and ESA will determine the exact nature of the training, as well as costs and payment responsibilities, by consensus.

Transfer of Information

When, in the course of its enforcement activities, or through other sources, WHD learns of a potential issue of compensation discrimination, the WHD may, to the extent authorized by law, provide such information to OFCCP for a determination of the employer's contract status and for appropriate action. If OFCCP determines that the employer is not a federal contractor, but may be covered by the Equal Pay Act or Title VII, OFCCP may, to the extent authorized by law, provide the information to EEOC.

When in the course of its activities, OFCCP identifies potential issues of compensation discrimination, OFCCP may, to the extent authorized by law, share such information, as appropriate, with EEOC, as well as any other information that will enhance the effectiveness of the EEOC as an enforcement agency.

Likewise, when, in the course of its enforcement activities, EEOC identifies potential issues of compensation discrimination, EEOC may, to the extent authorized by law, share such information, as appropriate, with OFCP, as well as any other information that will enhance the effectiveness of the Employment Standards Administration's OFCCP and WHD as enforcement agencies or programs.

Exchanges of information will, generally, include any supporting documentation gathered during contact with employers, potential complainants, or other sources of information. The agency receiving information has the responsibility to ensure that any disclosures of the information are in conformance with all provisions of law that apply to the employees of the originating agency, including Section 706(b) and Section 709(e) of Title VII of the Civil Rights Act of 1964. The agency receiving the information is also bound to take all appropriate steps to assure that the information is protected from unauthorized disclosure or use.

ESA and EEOC will provide each other with semi-annual reports of actions taken on compensation discrimination referrals provided pursuant to this MOU. OFCCP and EEOC headquarters staff will meet periodically to coordinate enforcement on questions relating to compensation discrimination.

IV. Agreement

The provisions of this Memorandum of Understanding may be reviewed and jointly modified as appropriate when it is determined by ESA and EEOC that such review and modification is in the interest of their respective enforcement responsibilities.

FIGURE 5.7 *(continued)*

drafted to confirm an agreement or collaboration between different government agencies. The agreement shown in Figure 5.7 was published in April 1999 in the *Federal Register*, the same federal publication that publishes proposed and adopted rules for public comment.

Audience for Policy Memos

We've discussed the purpose of policy memorandums and the contexts in which these documents are used. Now, we will expand our discussion to describe various audiences for policy memorandums. The scope of audiences for policy memorandums is shaped by the Freedom of Information Act, which outlines the circumstances in which government information, including policy memorandums, are considered public information (accessible to the public), **classified** (made inaccessible to the public by the government), or **declassified** (removed from "classified" status and made accessible to the public). *Black's Law Dictionary* defines the Freedom of Information Act in the following terms; while this definition pertains to federal agencies, states have similar laws that set parameters for state agencies.

> The Freedom of Information Act (5 U.S.C.A. §552) provides for making information held by Federal agencies available to the public unless it comes within one of the specific categories of matters exempt from public discourse. Virtually all agencies of the executive branch of the Federal Government have issues regulations to implement the Freedom of Information Act. These regulations inform the public where certain types of information may be readily obtained, how other information may be obtained on request, and what internal agency appeals are available if a member of the public is refused requested information. This Act is designed to prevent abuse of discretionary power of federal agencies by requiring them to make public certain information about their workings and work product. (664).

When policy memorandums are accessible to the public, either as public information or declassified documents, the documents are susceptible to media analyses similar to that conducted on former FEMA Director Michael Brown's August 29, 2005 memo to Homeland Security Director Michael Chertoff, in which Brown characterized Hurricane Katrina disaster as "this near catastrophic event" (CNN, GOP leaders). CNN published an online article titled, "GOP leaders agree to joint Katrina hearings: Administration asks for $51.8 billion in Katrina aid" and the highlighted evidence would suggest that Michael Brown's memo did not communicate the urgency of the Hurricane Katrina disaster, but instead asked FEMA employees to "convey a positive image of disaster operations to government officials, community officials, and community organizations and the general public" (CNN, GOP leaders).

Many opinions, online and paper, were published that analyzed Brown's August 29, 2005 memo to Michael Chertoff, and these opinions were available to anyone in the public who was interested in the details of Hurricane Katrina and how it was handled by FEMA, a federal agency under the Department of Homeland Security. The same can be said of Richard A. Clarke's declassified memorandum to Condoleezza Rice, which we examined earlier in this chapter.

Once Clarke's memorandum was made public, Rice, the recipient of the memorandum, was questioned by Congress and asked to explain when and how she responded to Clarke's memorandum. So, policy memorandums that are made public or "leaked" to the media are often critiqued for tone, appropriate action items, urgency, and honesty—especially when the writer or their intended audience fail to communicate or receive a message that affects the health and safety of the public. Because the public and media shape public policy, policy memorandums that are public information or declassified have the potential to affect public policy decisions as much as policy memorandums that remain classified and only accessible to government personnel.

Components of Persuasive Policy Memorandums

Since policy memorandums are proposals or arguments for policy development, policy implementation, or reconsideration of a policy, government personnel who write policy memorandums should consider incorporating a basic structure for these arguments to aid in clarity and persuasion. In this section, we will use Stephen Toulmin's *The Uses of Argument* to describe the main parts of logical arguments, and show how we can use these parts to write thorough and well-thought-out policy memorandums. Toulmin defines his parts or "patterns of an argument" as follows: *claims* are "conclusions whose merits we are seeking to establish"; *data* are "the facts we appeal to as the foundation of the claim"; *warrants* are "rules, principles, inferences-licenses" that allow us to make claims based on certain types of data (90–91). Toulmin states, "standing behind our warrants . . . there will normally be other assurances, without which warrants themselves would possess neither authority nor currency—these other things we may refer to as the *backing* . . . for our warrants (96). Toulmin's *rebuttal* alerts the audience that as the memo writer, you are aware of alternatives and opposing views (93–94). See an example of a policy argument in Figure 5.3

In organizing a policy memorandum, a clear claim, data to support that claim, an explanation of the rationale that the writer uses to connect the claim to the supporting data, and anticipation of opposing views or proposed alternatives are useful in persuasion. Within the argument of a policy memorandum, Toulmin's parts of a logical argument could be translated as follows:

1. *Claim*—statement about the effectiveness or ineffectiveness of a current public policy.
2. *Data*—statistics or narratives that provide your audience evidence of that your claim is true.
3. *Warrant*—reference to public opinion, social, economic, or political beliefs that allow the audience to make a logical connection between your claim and the data you use to support your claim.
4. *Backing*—warrants should be "backed" or supported by whatever type of evidence is most appropriate for your given area of policy. For example, while an environmental policy writer might use statistical data from environmental impact studies to back public opinion, social, economic,

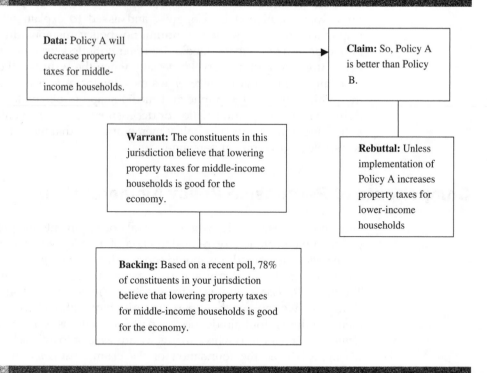

FIGURE 5.8 Using the Toulmin Model to Organize Your Policy Memorandum

or political beliefs, a policy writer in a child protective agency might use a narrative or news report about child deaths to explain public opinion, social, economic, or political beliefs.

5. *Rebuttal*—a statement that refutes your claim, warrant, or data. To make an effective argument, it makes sense to anticipate challenges to the logic of your claim, data, or warrant so that your audience knows that you are aware of other views about the subject.

Other important parts of a policy memorandum, not referenced in Toulmin's model, include clear action items that explain the specific actions that audiences should take as a result of reading the policy memorandum and the use of a tone and language that is appropriate for the situation.

Summary and Looking Forward

Policy memorandums communicate important information that audiences want to read quickly so that appropriate actions can be taken. To ensure that audiences read and understand your policy memorandums, you must know your audience and organize information in policy memorandums in a logical manner. In the next chapter, we will discuss policy reports, which are often more lengthy and complex documents than policy memorandums.

Activities and Assignments

1. **Individual Internet Activity:** Search the Internet to find your city or state's laws or regulations related to the Freedom of Information Act. Once you locate them, answer the following questions:

   a. What steps would you have to take to obtain copies of policy memorandums written by government personnel or officials within your state or city?
   b. Are there any restrictions placed on the type of memorandums that you are allowed to access? If so, what are those restrictions?
   c. Do you believe that your city or state has implemented a plan that makes it easy for citizens to obtain access to government policy memorandums? Explain your response.

2. **Group Activity:** In groups of three or four; use the Toulmin model to write a one-to-two-page policy memorandum that argues for at least one major change to your course syllabus. Your instructor is the primary audience for your policy memorandum.

3. **Group Activity:** Take a look at Richard Clarke's memorandum to Condoleezza Rice and William H. Seward's memorandum to President Lincoln.

   a. How has the language, tone, and organization of memorandums changed from Lincoln's time to the time Clarke wrote to Rice? What are some of the cultural factors (social, political, economic, and technological) that caused these changes?
   b. Use the "Questions to Help Analyze Policy Memos for Intent and Purpose" in this chapter to analyze the memorandum to see if it communicates a clear purpose to its intended audience.

Works Cited

Black, Henry Campbell. *Black's Law Dictionary 6th ed*. St. Paul: West Publishing Co. 1990.

Blanco, Kathleen Babineaux. "Letters." *Office of the Governor-State of Louisiana*. Dec. 2005. 15 Apr. 2006 <http://www.gov.state.la.us/>.

Clarke, Richard A. "Memorandum to Condoleezza Rice: Presidential Policy Initiative/ Review—The Al-Qida Network." *National Security Archive George Washington University*. January 2001. 15 Apr. 2006 <http://www2.gwu.edu/~nsarchiv/ NSAEBB/NSAEBB147/index.htm>.

"GOP leaders agree to joint Katrina hearings: Administration asks for $51.8 billion in Katrina aid." *CNN*. Sept. 2005. 15 Apr. 2006 <http://www.cnn.com/2005/POLITICS/ 09/07/katrina.congress/index.html>.

Lincoln, Abraham. "Lincoln's Reply to Seward's Memorandum". *The Project Gutenberg*. Apr. 1861. 15 Apr. 2006 <http://www.gutenberg.org/files/2657/2657.txt>.

"Richard Clarke Testifies Before 9/11 Commission." *CNN*. Transcript. Mar. 24, 2004. 30 May 2007 <http://transcripts.cnn.com/TRANSCRIPTS/0403/24/bn.00.html>.

Seward, William H. "Memorandum to President Lincoln: Some thoughts for the President's Consideration." *The Project Gutenberg*. Apr. 1861. 15 Apr. 2006 <http://www.gutenberg.org/files/2657/2657.txt>.

Sowle, Patrick. "A Reappraisal of Seward's Memorandum of April 1, 1861, to Lincoln." *The Journal of Southern History* 33.2 (May 1967): 234–39.

Toulmin, Stephen E. *The Uses of Argument.* New York: Cambridge UP, 1958.

"Transcript of Rice's 9/11 commission statement." *CNN*. Transcript. May 19, 2004. 30 May 2007 <http://cnn.com/2004/ALLPOLITICS/04/OB/rice/transcript/>.

U.S. Department of Labor. "Coordination of Functions; Memorandum of Understanding." Apr. 1999. 15 Apr. 2006 <http://www.dol.gov/esa/regs/fedreg/notices/99009066.htm>.

PART 3

Writing to Communicate Policy Issues to Agencies and the Public

Public Policy Reports

On July 22, 2004, *The 9/11 Commission Report: Final Report of the National Commission on Terrorist Attacks Upon the United States* was released to the public. The report was made available free of charge on the Internet and released for sale at bookstores. The authorized paperback copy of this report is 567 pages of meticulous detail, which in narrative form chronicles the events that led up to the tragedy of September 11, 2001, the United States of America's response to these events, and the Commission's recommendations based on an intense and thorough investigation that posed the simple yet complex questions: "How did this happen, and how can we avoid such tragedy again?" (National Commission xv).

In preparing the report, the commission held 12 public hearings and gathered testimonies from witnesses, survivors, victims' families, first responders, members of the military and intelligence communities, and Condoleezza Rice, who then served as Assistant to the President for National Security Affairs. After collection and analysis of these testimonies, for the National Commission on Terrorist Attacks Upon the United States—the authors of this report—wrote, "We present the narrative of this report and the recommendations that flow from it to the President of the United States, the United States Congress, and the American people for their consideration. Ten Commissioners— five Republicans and five Democrats chosen as elected leaders from our nation's capital at a time of great partisan division—have come together to present this report without dissent" (National Commission xv).

On November 15, 2005, Phillip D. Zelikow, Executive Director of the Commission, was interviewed on National Public Radio's *Tavis Smiley Show* about the very unusual fact that this lengthy government report was not only a *New York Times* bestseller but also nominated for the prestigious National Book Award (Tavis Smiley Show). In the interview, Zelikow acknowledged that the report was written under national security constraints that required the authors to "write in a way that we thought would not damage the national security, that we would not disclose anything damaging to national security," and revealed that he and his co-authors used guidelines and specific objectives to negotiate the language of the report. (Tavis Smiley Show) Zelikow explained, "we had the guideline of 'Be direct and concise.' Think really hard about just exactly what it is you want to say and then just say it . . . . And be prepared to back it up if it's a factual statement. So instead of characterizing that 'He did something well, he did something badly,' instead just say what it is the person did. And then if there's some specific critique, say the critiques. Don't just use general judgment words that obfuscate as much as they reveal" (Tavis Smiley Show). The authors' ability to walk a rhetorical tightrope between partisan politics, national security constraints, and fact finding make this report more than a well-written government document; it is possibly a model for government report writing. As with any government document with historical significance, only time and analysis of this report will tell us how worthy it is of acclaim, but for now, what lessons can we draw from it?

Did the "guideline" Zelikow mentions help five Democrats and five Republicans reach consensus on the contents and recommendations of a highly controversial subject and equally political document? What other rhetorical strategies do government writers use to negotiate the language and intent of government policy reports? While most government policy reports will never be nominated for National Book Awards nor become *New York Times* best sellers, there are obvious similarities between the 9/11 Commission report and other government policy reports that we will discuss in this chapter. Zelikow suggests that the authors of the Commission's 9/11 Report wrote under national security constraints; we will consider the constraints that government writers work under when writing other, less publicized government policy reports. In this chapter we will also review other historical and current contemporary government policy reports to identify the purposes, contexts, and audiences unique to this genre of technical communication.

Purpose of Government Policy Reports

We will begin our discussion of government **policy reports** by reflecting on the questions posed in the preface of the *The 9/11 Commission Report: Final Report of the National Commission on Terrorist Attacks Upon the United States*—"How did this happen, and how can we avoid such tragedy again?" (xv). By posing these questions, the authors created a framework to guide their investigation and to remind themselves of their mission or purpose. "How did this happen?" is an obvious reflection on very tragic events that warrant investigation and examination of past events, while "how can we avoid such tragedy again?" is a future-oriented question that is very much dependent on the answer to the first question—and on informed recommendations that can help decision makers thwart future terrorist attacks. Carolyn Rude explains that two major reasons for writing reports that inform public policy are to investigate a problem or make recommendations to solve a problem ("Report for Decision Making" 191–192). The questions posed in the early pages of the 9/11 Commission's report work towards both of these aims, both through investigation and recommendation.

Rude also explains that historically reports have focused on past events or symbolized a finalized project or study ("Environmental Policy Making" 78).

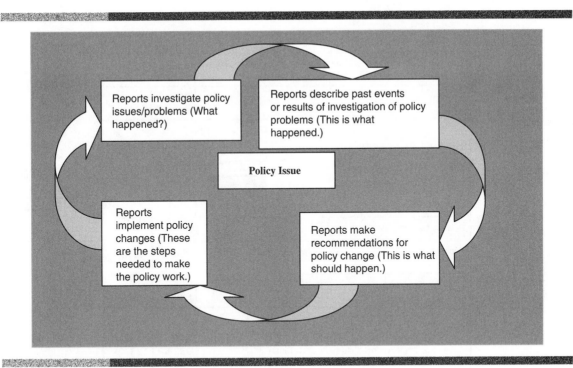

FIGURE 6.1   Uses for Government Policy Reports

Again we can turn to the 9/11 Commission's report, which uses the word *Final* in its title, to demonstrate that this genre of technical communication can represent the end of a project or reflection on past events. In the case of the 9/11 Commission Report, it was the end of this commission's study of the tragic event, but we must acknowledge that the 9/11 Commission Report and other government policy reports are more than a conclusion; they often attempt to prescribe future action with specific steps to implement change (Rude, "Toward an Expanded Concept of Rhetorical Delivery" 280). The model in Figure 6.1 is a visual representation of some of the most common uses for government policy reports, which were identified in Rude's research. The model should help you to view public policy report writing in government organizations as an ongoing process where reports serve "as a means to an end of change in policy and behavior" (Rude, "Toward an Expanded Concept of Rhetorical Delivery" 272).

Take a look at the excerpt in Figure 6.2 from the National Commission on the Terrorist Attacks Upon the United States' website (www.9-11commision.gov/) where it lists the table of contents for the 9/11 Commission Report. Notice areas that:

- investigate policy implementation and enforcement issues
- describe past events or results of investigation of policy problems
- make policy recommendations
- prescribe steps for policy implementation or enforcement.

Executive summaries give the audience an overview of the report.

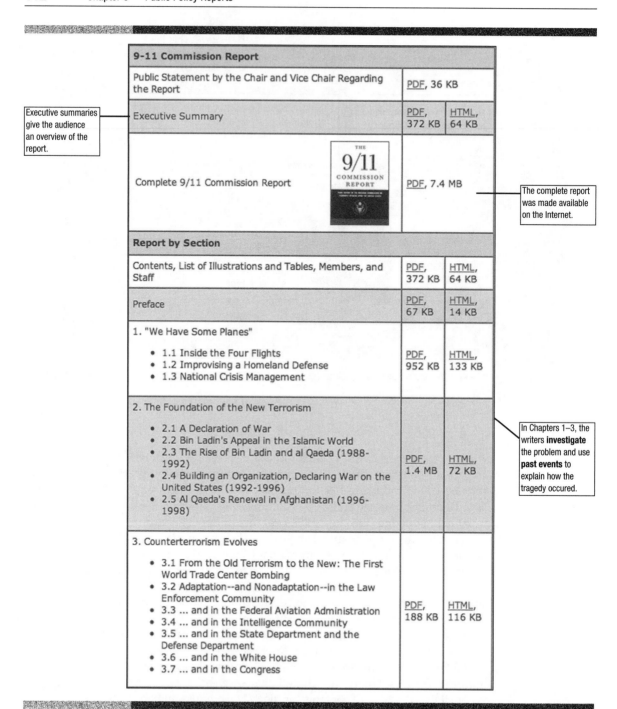

9-11 Commission Report		
Public Statement by the Chair and Vice Chair Regarding the Report	PDF, 36 KB	
Executive Summary	PDF, 372 KB	HTML, 64 KB
Complete 9/11 Commission Report	PDF, 7.4 MB	
Report by Section		
Contents, List of Illustrations and Tables, Members, and Staff	PDF, 372 KB	HTML, 64 KB
Preface	PDF, 67 KB	HTML, 14 KB

1. "We Have Some Planes"
  • 1.1 Inside the Four Flights
  • 1.2 Improvising a Homeland Defense
  • 1.3 National Crisis Management
	PDF, 952 KB	HTML, 133 KB

2. The Foundation of the New Terrorism
  • 2.1 A Declaration of War
  • 2.2 Bin Ladin's Appeal in the Islamic World
  • 2.3 The Rise of Bin Ladin and al Qaeda (1988-1992)
  • 2.4 Building an Organization, Declaring War on the United States (1992-1996)
  • 2.5 Al Qaeda's Renewal in Afghanistan (1996-1998)
	PDF, 1.4 MB	HTML, 72 KB

3. Counterterrorism Evolves
  • 3.1 From the Old Terrorism to the New: The First World Trade Center Bombing
  • 3.2 Adaptation--and Nonadaptation--in the Law Enforcement Community
  • 3.3 ... and in the Federal Aviation Administration
  • 3.4 ... and in the Intelligence Community
  • 3.5 ... and in the State Department and the Defense Department
  • 3.6 ... and in the White House
  • 3.7 ... and in the Congress
	PDF, 188 KB	HTML, 116 KB

The complete report was made available on the Internet.

In Chapters 1–3, the writers **investigate** the problem and use **past events** to explain how the tragedy occured.

FIGURE 6.2   Excerpt from the National Commission on the Terrorist Attacks Upon the United States' website. Source: http://www.9-11commission.gov/report/index.htm

4. Responses to Al Qaeda's Initial Assaults • 4.1 Before the Bombings in Kenya and Tanzania • 4.2 Crisis: August 1998 • 4.3 Diplomacy • 4.4 Covert Action • 4.5 Searching for Fresh Options	PDF, 185 KB	HTML, 113 KB
5. Al Qaeda Aims at the American Homeland • 5.1 Terrorist Entrepreneurs • 5.2 The "Planes Operation" • 5.3 The Hamburg Contingent • 5.4 A Money Trail?	PDF, 312 KB	HTML, 89 KB
6. From Threat To Threat • 6.1 The Millennium Crisis • 6.2 Post-Crisis Reflection: Agenda for 2000 • 6.3 The Attack on the USS *Cole* • 6.4 Change and Continuity • 6.5 The New Administration's Approach	PDF, 209 KB	HTML, 129 KB
7. The Attack Looms • 7.1 First Arrivals in California • 7.2 The 9/11 Pilots in the United States • 7.3 Assembling the Teams • 7.4 Final Strategies and Tactics	PDF, 949 KB	HTML, 119 KB
8. "The System Was Blinking Red" • 8.1 The Summer of Threat • 8.2 Late Leads--Mihdhar, Moussaoui, and KSM	PDF, 146 KB	HTML, 76 KB
9. Heroism and Horror • 9.1 Preparedness as of September 11 • 9.2 September 11, 2001 • 9.3 Emergency Response at the Pentagon • 9.4 Analysis	PDF, 2.3 MB	HTML, 130 KB

In Chapters 4–9, the writers continue with their **explanation of past events** to explain how and why the terrorist events were possible.

FIGURE 6.2 *(continued)*

10. Wartime • 10.1 Immediate Responses at Home • 10.2 Planning for War • 10.3 "Phase Two" and the Question of Iraq	PDF, 109 KB	HTML, 45 KB
11. Foresight--and Hindsight • 11.1 Imagination • 11.2 Policy • 11.3 Capabilities • 11.4 Management	PDF, 133 KB	HTML, 67 KB
12. What To Do? A Global Strategy • 12.1 Reflecting on a Generational Challenge • 12.2 Attack Terrorists and Their Organizations • 12.3 Prevent the Continued Growth of Islamist Terrorism • 12.4 Protect against and Prepare for Terrorist Attacks	PDF, 184 KB	HTML, 110 KB
13. How To Do It? A Different Way of Organizing the Government • 13.1 Unity of Effort across the Foreign-Domestic Divide • 13.2 Unity of Effort in the Intelligence Community • 13.3 Unity of Effort in Sharing Information • 13.4 Unity of Effort in the Congress • 13.5 Organizing America's Defenses in the United States	PDF, 158 KB	HTML, 79 KB
Appendices	PDF, 109 KB	HTML, 49 KB
Notes	PDF, 669 KB	HTML, 681 KB

In Chapter 12, the writers **make recommendations for policy change.**

In Chapter 13, the writers **prescribe steps for** change.

FIGURE 6.2   *(continued)*

Government Policy Reports Investigate a Problem

While the *9/11 Commission Report: Final Report of the National Commission on Terrorist Attacks Upon the United States* demonstrates that the aims of government policy reports are not mutually exclusive and that one report can have more than one aim, the excerpt in Figure 6.3 from a 1964 Surgeon General report, which is an

Foreword

Since the turn of the century, scientists have become increasingly interested in the effects of tobacco on health. Only within the past few decades, however, has a broad experimental and clinical approach to the subject been manifest; within this period the most extensive and definitive studies have been undertaken since 1950.

Few medical questions have stirred such public interest or created more scientific debate than the tobacco-health controversy. The interrelationships of smoking and health undoubtedly are complex. The subject does not lend itself to easy answers. Nevertheless, it has been increasingly apparent that answers must be found.

As the principal Federal agency concerned broadly with the health of the American people, the Public Health Service has been conscious of its deep responsibility for seeking these answers. As steps in that direction it has seemed necessary to determine, as precisely as possible, the direction of scientific evidence and to act in accordance with that evidence for the benefit of the people of the United States. In 1959, the Public Health Service assessed the then available evidence linking smoking with health and made its findings known to the professions and the public. The Service's review of the evidence and its statement at that time was largely focussed on the relationship of cigarette smoking to lung cancer. Since 1959 much additional data has accumulated on the whole subject.

Accordingly, I appointed a committee, drawn from all the pertinent scientific disciplines, to review and evaluate both this new and older data and, if possible, to reach some definitive conclusions on the relationship between smoking and health in general. The results of the Committee's study and evaluation are contained in this Report.

I pledge that the Public Health Service will undertake a prompt and thorough review of the Report to determine what action may be appropriate and necessary. I am confident that other Federal agencies and nonofficial agencies will do the same.

The Committee's assignment has been most difficult. The subject is complicated and the pressures of time on eminent men busy with many other duties has been great. I am aware of the difficulty in writing an involved technical report requiring evaluations and judgments from many different professional and technical points of view. The completion of the Committee's task has required the exercise of great professional skill and dedication of the highest order. I acknowledge a profound debt of gratitude to the Committee, the many consultants who have given their assistance, and the members of the staff. In doing so, I extend thanks not only for the Service but for the Nation as a whole.

SURGEON GENERAL

The words increasingly interested *signal an investigative purpose.*

The purpose of the report is to find answers to these questions.

The audience for the report consists of agency staff, other agencies, and the public.

The writer acknowledges the time constraints and other difficulties faced in writing this report.

FIGURE 6.3 Foreword to the 1964 report, *Smoking and Health: Report of the Advisory Committee to the Surgeon General of the Public Health Service Surgeon General Report: Reducing the Health Consequences of Smoking.* Source: http://www.cdc.gov/

investigation into the effects of smoking on health, is an example of a report that is not attempting to advocate a change in policy, describe past actions, or prescribe steps for policy implementation. The purpose of the 1964 report is to investigate a problem. Take a look at the foreword to the report to try to identify the issue under investigation.

Government Policy Reports Explain Past Events or Results of Investigations

In "Toward an Expanded Concept of Rhetorical Delivery: The Uses of Reports in Public Policy Debates," Rude states, "More influential than a single report was the cumulative effect of multiple reports and other initiatives over time" (272). You can certainly use multiple reports and their results to support facts in a report you are writing as illustrated in the 2006 report, *The Health Consequences of Involuntary Exposure to Tobacco Smoke: A Report of the Surgeon General*. Forty-two years after the 1964 report, *Smoking and Health: Report of the Advisory Committee to the Surgeon General of Public Health Service*, the Office of the Surgeon General presented the 2006 report, which includes charts listing the findings of previous reports by the Surgeon General and other organizations that support the Surgeon General Office's 2006 findings regarding the effects of secondhand smoke. The charts in Figure 6.4 and Figure 6.5, excerpted from the executive summary of the 2006 Surgeon General's Report, show us that results from other government and scientific reports, new and old, can be used to substantiate the findings or results of a more recent report.

Government Policy Reports Make Recommendations

While the 1964 Surgeon General report's foreword (see Figure 6.3) was clearly an attempt to investigate whether smoking was harmful to humans, the example in Figure 6.6 presents an argument against secondhand smoke and is more argumentative than the 1964 report because the 2006 report expresses a clear opinion on the issue. The 2006 Surgeon General's report does more than explain past events or results, as shown in the charts we have just discussed; it also serves as a tool to resolve the problem.

Government Policy Reports Prescribe Steps for Policy Implementation and Enforcement

So far, we've looked at excerpts from Surgeon General reports that promise to investigate a policy issue, explain the results of investigations, or persuade an audience that a policy issue exists. In the 1998 report, *Tobacco Use Among U.S. Racial/Ethic Minorities: A Surgeon General Report*, the writers use the report preface to promise more than an investigation of questions; they present to the audience, both the public and researchers, strategies to implement programs that will decrease smoking in U.S. ethnic/racial minorities in the United States. Read the excerpt in Figure 6.7 and make note of its various purposes.

Table 1.1 Conclusions from previous Surgeon General's reports on the health effects of secondhand smoke exposure

Disease and statement	Surgeon General's report
Coronary heart disease: "The presence of such levels" as found in cigarettes "indicates that the effect of exposure to carbon monoxide may on occasion, depending upon the length of exposure, be sufficient to be harmful to the health of an exposed person. This would be particularly significant for people who are already suffering from...coronary heart disease." (p. 7)	1972
Chronic respiratory symptoms (adults): "The presence of such levels" as found in cigarettes "indicates that the effect of exposure to carbon monoxide may on occasion, depending upon the length of exposure, be sufficient to be harmful to the health of an exposed person. This would be particularly significant for people who are already suffering from chronic bronchopulmonary disease...." (p. 7)	1972
Pulmonary function: "Other components of tobacco smoke, such as particulate matter and the oxides of nitrogen, have been shown in various concentrations to affect adversely animal pulmonary...function. The extent of the contributions of these substances to illness in humans exposed to the concentrations present in an atmosphere contaminated with tobacco smoke is not presently known." (pp. 7–8)	1972
Asthma: "The limited existing data yield conflicting results concerning the relationship between passive smoke exposure and pulmonary function changes in patients with asthma." (p. 13)	1984
Bronchitis and pneumonia: "The children of smoking parents have an increased prevalence of reported respiratory symptoms, and have an increased frequency of bronchitis and pneumonia early in life." (p. 13)	1984
Pulmonary function (children): "The children of smoking parents appear to have measurable but small differences in tests of pulmonary function when compared with children of nonsmoking parents. The significance of this finding to the future development of lung disease is unknown." (p. 13)	1984
Pulmonary function (adults): "...some studies suggest that high levels of involuntary [tobacco] smoke exposure might produce small changes in pulmonary function in normal subjects.... Two studies have reported differences in measures of lung function in older populations between subjects chronically exposed to involuntary smoking and those who were not. This difference was not found in a younger and possibly less exposed population." (p. 13)	1984
Acute respiratory infections: "The children of parents who smoke have an increased frequency of a variety of acute respiratory illnesses and infections, including chest illnesses before 2 years of age and physician-diagnosed bronchitis, tracheitis, and laryngitis, when compared with the children of nonsmokers." (p. 13)	1986
Bronchitis and pneumonia: "The children of parents who smoke have an increased frequency of hospitalization for bronchitis and pneumonia during the first year of life when compared with the children of nonsmokers." (p. 13)	1986

FIGURE 6.4 Excerpt from the 2006 report, *The Health Consequences of Involuntary Exposure to Tobacco Smoke: A Report of the Surgeon General*. Source: http://www.surgeongeneral.gov/library/secondhandsmoke/

Government Policy Reports in Cultural Contexts

Now that you've seen examples of policy reports that serve various purposes, we're ready to discuss the contexts in which these government policy reports are created. In Ken Baake's research on archeology reports he writes, "Technical writers can navigate the challenges of any writing task better if they can discern the contradictions sometimes present in the rhetorical situation. The first step involves knowing how closely a project is tied to the marketplace" (391). The same

Table 1.3	Selected major reports, other than those of the U.S. Surgeon General, addressing adverse effects from exposure to tobacco smoke	
Agency	Publication	Place and date of publication
National Research Council	*Environmental Tobacco Smoke: Measuring Exposures and Assessing Health Effects*	Washington, D.C. United States 1986
International Agency for Research on Cancer (IARC)	*Monographs on the Evaluation of the Carcinogenic Risk of Chemicals to Humans: Tobacco Smoking* (IARC Monograph 38)	Lyon, France 1986
U.S. Environmental Protection Agency (EPA)	*Respiratory Health Effects of Passive Smoking: Lung Cancer and Other Disorders*	Washington, D.C. United States 1992
National Health and Medical Research Council	*The Health Effects of Passive Smoking*	Canberra, Australia 1997
California EPA (Cal/EPA), Office of Environmental Health Hazard Assessment	*Health Effects of Exposure to Environmental Tobacco Smoke*	Sacramento, California United States 1997
Scientific Committee on Tobacco and Health	*Report of the Scientific Committee on Tobacco and Health*	London, United Kingdom 1998
World Health Organization	*International Consultation on Environmental Tobacco Smoke (ETS) and Child Health. Consultation Report*	Geneva, Switzerland 1999
IARC	*Tobacco Smoke and Involuntary Smoking* (IARC Monograph 83)	Lyon, France 2004
Cal/EPA, Office of Environmental Health Hazard Assessment	*Proposed Identification of Environmental Tobacco Smoke as a Toxic Air Contaminant*	Sacramento, California United States 2005

FIGURE 6.5 Excerpt from the 2006 report, *The Health Consequences of Involuntary Exposure to Tobacco Smoke: A Report of the Surgeon General.* Source: http://www.surgeongeneral. gov/library/secondhandsmoke/

can certainly be said of government policy reports because most government policy reports are created under some economic, sociopolitical, national security, scientific, and/or technological constraints. These constraints are very important in shaping the contexts in which government reports are written.

Economic Constraints

If you reflect on the foreword to the 2006 report, *The Health Consequences of Involuntary Exposure to Tobacco Smoke: A Report of the Surgeon General Report*, you might recall that the writer mentioned the economic benefits of the policy advocated. Although some reports may not mention economic constraints early on in the report, you can be assured that writers of most government policy reports consider the economic costs and benefits of the policies they investigate, recommend, or describe. Report writers must ask themselves: What are the costs of examining a describing, investigating this policy issue, and/or helping to implement policy?

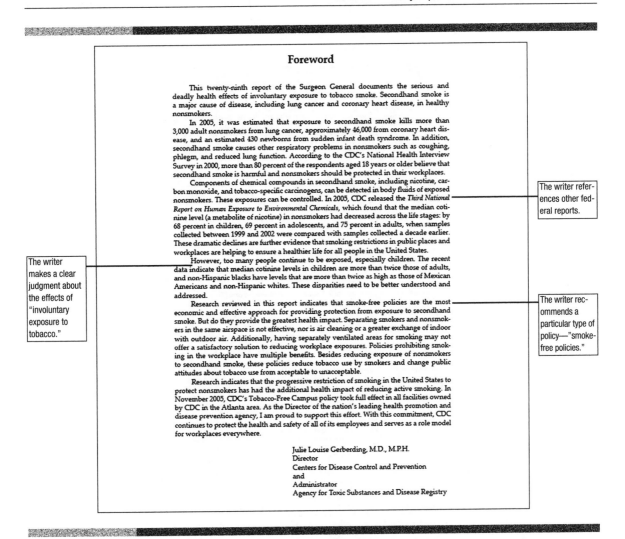

FIGURE 6.6   Excerpt from the 2006 report, *The Health Consequences of Involuntary Exposure to Tobacco Smoke: A Report of the Surgeon General*. Source: http://www. surgeongeneral.gov/library/secondhandsmoke/report/executivesummary.pdf

These economic analyses, even if not overtly acknowledged by the government writer, can determine the amount of time devoted to research and writing a report as well as the writers' word choice, tone, and style (Baake 395). Often, the greater the economic impact, the more time devoted to writing the report. Economic constraints can help to determine how much data is collected and analyzed in a given report, how many people, internal and external to the government agency, are involved in writing the document, and ultimately, how much time and resources are devoted to negotiating report recommendations.

Preface

from the Surgeon General,
U.S. Department of Health and Human Services

Effective strategies are needed to reduce tobacco use among members of U.S. racial/ethnic groups and thus diminish their burden of tobacco-related diseases and deaths. Cigarette smoking is the leading cause of preventable disease and death in the United States. There is enormous potential to reduce heart disease, cancer, stroke, and respiratory disease among members of racial and ethnic groups, who make up the most rapidly growing segment of the U.S. population.

This Surgeon General's report is the first to address the diverse tobacco control needs of the four major U.S. racial/ethnic minority groups—African Americans, American Indians and Alaska Natives, Asian Americans and Pacific Islanders, and Hispanics. This report is also the only single, comprehensive source of data on each group's patterns of tobacco use, physical effects related to tobacco smoking and chewing, and societal and psychosocial factors associated with tobacco use.

The findings detailed in this report indicate that if tobacco use is not reduced among members of these four racial/ethnic groups, they will experience increasing morbidity and mortality from tobacco use. The toll is currently highest for African American adults. Findings also suggest that some close, long-term relationships between tobacco companies and various racial/ethnic communities could hamper U.S. efforts to lower rates of tobacco use by the year 2000. Also notable is the support that members of racial/ethnic groups have shown for legislative efforts to control tobacco use, sales, advertising, and promotion.

As this report goes to press, discouraging news comes from a report published by the Centers for Disease Control and Prevention on the Youth Risk Behavior Survey about tobacco use among African American and Hispanic high school students. Past-month smoking increased among African American students by 80 percent and among Hispanic students by 34 percent from 1991 through 1997. The consistent decline once seen among young African Americans has sharply reversed in recent years. Past-month smoking prevalence increased from 13 percent to 23 percent among African Americans and from 25 percent to 34 percent among Hispanics.

Although cancer remains common in Americans of all racial and ethnic groups, the pattern of increasing lung cancer deaths in the 1970s and 1980s among African American, Hispanic, and some American Indian and Alaska Native subgroups has been halted or reversed for some groups from 1990 through 1995. Some encouraging news from *Cancer Incidence and Mortality, 1973–1995: A Report Card for the U.S.* was just published by the American Cancer Society, the National Cancer Institute, and the Centers for Disease Control and Prevention. The report described lung cancer trend data from 1990 through 1995 for African Americans, Asian Americans and Pacific Islanders, and Hispanics. Lung cancer death rates declined significantly for African American men and for Hispanic men and women from 1990 through 1995; death rates did not change significantly for African American women or for Asian American and Pacific Islander men or women. Although lung cancer trends may continue to decline among some racial/ethnic groups for several more years, recent increases in smoking prevalence among adolescent African Americans and Hispanics and among Asian American and Pacific Islander adolescent males, coupled with the lack of decline among American Indian and Alaska Native adults, do not bode well for long-term trends in lung cancer.

One purpose of this report is to guide researchers in their future efforts to garner more information needed to develop effective prevention and control programs. Several significant research questions need to be addressed. For example, why are African American youths smoking cigarettes in lower proportions than youths in other racial/ethnic groups? How does acculturation affect patterns of tobacco use among immigrants to the United States? What are the differential effects of gender on tobacco use among members of certain racial/ethnic groups? What racial- and ethnic-specific protective factors and risk factors will promote the development of culturally appropriate interventions to prevent and control tobacco use? And to what extent are culturally specific tobacco control programs necessary to curb tobacco use among racial/ethnic populations? While researchers are redirecting their focus, federal, state, and private tobacco control partners need to address program issues, such as how to develop and evaluate culturally appropriate prevention and cessation interventions.

This report includes examples of numerous racial- and ethnic-specific tobacco control programs used in communities across the country. These and other racial/ethnic group-specific programs must be disseminated to all areas of the country, where program planners can develop their own strategies, taking into consideration the cultural attitudes, norms, expectations, and values of the targeted cultural groups.

In each of these endeavors, we will succeed only if we are sensitive to our cultural differences and similarities. I challenge federal and state agencies as well as researchers and practitioners in the social, behavioral, public health, clinical, and biomedical sciences to join me in the pursuit of effective strategies to prevent and control tobacco use among racial/ethnic groups. By meeting this challenge, we will progress toward achieving the nation's year 2000 tobacco-related health objectives and will help to prevent the unnecessary disability, disease, and deaths that result from tobacco use.

This report is both investigative and prescriptive.

The report can be used to guide researchers in efforts to develop programs.

The report provides examples of programs as models for the public.

FIGURE 6.7 Preface to the 1998 report, *Tobacco Use Among U.S. Racial/Ethic Minorities: A Surgeon General Report.* Source: CDC http://www.cdc.gov/tobacco/sgr/sgr_1998/sgr-min-forpref.htm

Sociopolitical Constraints

Earlier in the chapter we discussed the fact that the 9/11 Commission Report was submitted "without dissent"—which of course does not mean that there were no disagreements, but "without dissent" does suggest that by the time the information was printed in the report, it had been debated and some consensus reached by members of the commission. The fact that the commission was made up of members from different political parties serving different constituencies makes negotiation and consensus-reaching difficult and sometimes impossible. The conflicts that arise from varying political ideologies, values, and motives in report writing can be described as a sociopolitical constraint.

In any collaborative writing project, the writers involved will likely have different levels of authority and areas of expertise, come from various cultural backgrounds, and embrace different ethical perspectives. In writing government policy reports, which address issues as diverse and controversial as health and safety, social programs, military and foreign affairs issues, the use and distribution of technology, and the national space program, report writing will certainly be bound by internal and external sociopolitical constraints. While internal social constraints will become obvious during discussion and debate by those writing the report—because of misunderstandings or disagreements, social and political pressures emerge from stakeholders *outside* of the writing process, including advocacy groups, protesters, legislators, political parties, and scientists. These stakeholders add to the conflicts that must be negotiated in the language and intent of policy reports. Writers who understand the purpose, context, and audience for a given report can certainly work to negotiate the interests of various stakeholders.

When negotiating the language of government policy reports, government writers should also be aware of their agency's relationship with their various intended audiences and consider this relationship in word choice, style, and tone. Rhetorical choices that evoke trust are especially important when communicating with audiences that do not trust government organizations because of past negative experiences with the writers' agency or other governmental bodies (Williams 163).

National Security Constraints

In the opening narrative of this chapter, we discussed the fact that Phillip D. Zelikow, Executive Director of the 9/11 Commission staff, acknowledged that the report was written under national security constraints that required the writers to "write in a way that we thought would not damage the national security, that we would not disclose anything damaging to national security" (Tavis Smiley Show). Many government organizations, at all levels, are responsible for writing reports that contain information that, if viewed by the wrong audience, could result in national security threats. When government agency staff and officials write reports, they must be cognizant of the fact that confidential information or information that might compromise national security must be left out of reports with public audiences. This rhetorical maneuver creates a problem for writers: they must present information ethically and honestly but without giving out information that decision makers have discussed as a potential threat to national security and labeled confidential.

Scientific and Technological Constraints

William C. Johnson describes technology assessments as "the effects on society that may occur when technology is introduced, extended, or modified with special emphasis on those consequences that are unintended, indirect, or delayed" (Johnson 329). Often, report writers must conduct technology assessments to evaluate science and technology and ethical dilemmas that scientific and technological innovations pose for agencies and the constituents they serve. Regardless of the purpose of the report (investigative, a tool for recommendations, descriptive, or prescriptive), writers of government policy reports must acknowledge that their constituents (individuals, members of the academic community, private businesses, etc.) have diverse opinions about the uses of science and technology and question which scientific and technological innovations should be considered in policy making decisions. The report writer must include more than the their agency's recommendations for the uses of science and technology, but consider opposing views.

Audience for Government Policy Reports

We began this chapter with a narrative about a very important report, the *The 9/11 Commission Report: Final Report of the National Commission on Terrorist Attacks Upon the United States*. Although we've mentioned that this report garnered a much broader audience than most government policy reports because of the magnitude and effects of the events of September 11, 2001, on the country and the world, the intended audience—"the American people"—is not much different from that of less publicized government policy reports. In this chapter, we've mentioned several reports from the Office of the Surgeon General, all of which were accessible to the American public and international audiences via the Internet. The *9/11 Commission Report* was unique because its target audience also included the president of the United States and Congress. From these examples, we can see that the audience for government policy reports include those persons or entities who need access to reports to make decisions or take action (i.e., government staff, including those who implement and enforce policy; private businesses; individuals; and law makers), those persons or entities to whom the government agency is accountable to (i.e., the American public, other state or federal agencies, law makers), and any persons or entities who might be interested in the outcome of policy actions associated with the report (i.e., scientists, academics, individuals, private businesses). While some reports include statistics and a lot of technical information easily understood by expert audiences or people with knowledge of the subjects under discussion, other reports include clear language and explanatory information appropriate for nonexpert audiences or the general public. Nonexpert audiences have a stake in the outcome of public policy reports and their interests and access to these documents should certainly be considered in report writing.

Although some government policy reports include hundreds of pages of technical information, there are certain parts of reports that make them accessible to a public that might not be interested in reading the entire report. In this chapter, we included excerpts from executive summaries, which serve as a summary of the report for audiences who may or may not want to read the full report but need a summary of it. We also included excerpts from forewords and prefaces to reports to show you how agencies can give an audience an idea of what is presented in an entire work before they begin reading the specific parts of a report. As in most book-length works, forewords and prefaces are located at the beginning of the report before its introduction, body, and other back matter (appendices, indexes, references, attachments). Some reports are book-length and take months to write and distribute to the public; other reports are published frequently on agency websites for expert audiences who visit the site often and are familiar with the agency's mission and purpose. Take a look at the Center for Disease Control report in Figure 6.8 and consider what audiences might be interested in reviewing and using this weekly report. What audiences might find this report difficult to comprehend?

Components of Government Reports

In this final section of the chapter, we will focus on the similarities in the format and content of these documents. The common components in government reports will help you to decide what information an audience usually needs and expects to see in government reports, regardless of the purpose of the report. In Crouch and Zetler's 1954 edition *A Guide to Technical Writing*, they present the following outline as a plan for organizing a formal report (117–18).

1. The cover sheet
2. The title page
3. The table of contents
4. The foreword or letter of transmittal
5. A short, often nontechnical, summary, or abstract
6. The body
   a. Purpose of the report (or introduction)
   b. Historical survey of the subject (if needed)
   c. Detailed analysis, giving all data necessary for a full understanding of the problem
7. Conclusions
8. Recommendations
9. Appendix
   a. Bibliography
   b. Charts, maps, graphs
   c. Supplementary mathematical data
   d. Other supplementary material.

If you look closely at the table of contents of the *9/11 Commission Report* you will notice that contemporary reports have not changed much since Crouch and Zelter's textbook. There are, of course, subtle differences between the outline

Weekly Report: Influenza Summary Update
Week ending May 20, 2006-Week 20

This is the final report of the 2005-06 season.

✉ Email this page
🖨 Printer-friendly version

Synopsis:

Influenza activity in the United States peaked in early March and continued to decrease during week 20 (May 14 – May 20, 2006)*. Fifty-one specimens (6.3%) tested by U.S. World Health Organization (WHO) and National Respiratory and Enteric Virus Surveillance System (NREVSS) collaborating laboratories were positive for influenza. The proportion of patient visits to sentinel providers for influenza-like illness (ILI) was below the national baseline. The proportion of deaths attributed to pneumonia and influenza was below the threshold level. Twenty-five states, the District of Columbia, New York City, and Puerto Rico reported sporadic influenza activity; and 25 states reported no activity.

> State health departments health departments, school districts, and hospitals would likely be interested in knowing which states had reported flu activity.

Laboratory Surveillance*:

> The "Laboratory surveillance" section is very technical and seems to be targeted to an expert audience.

During week 20, WHO and NREVSS laboratories reported 811 specimens tested for influenza viruses and 51 (6.3%) were positive. Of these, 1 was an influenza A (H3N2) virus, 1 was an influenza A (H1N1) virus, 8 were influenza A viruses that were not subtyped, and 41 were influenza B viruses.

Since October 2, 2005, WHO and NREVSS laboratories have tested a total of 135,973 specimens for influenza viruses and 17,068 (12.6%) were positive. Among the 17,068 influenza viruses, 13,857 (81.2%) were influenza A viruses and 3,211 (18.8%) were influenza B viruses. Five thousand six hundred forty-eight (40.8%) of the 13,857 influenza A viruses have been subtyped: 5,228 (92.6%) were influenza A (H3N2) viruses and 420 (7.4%) were influenza A (H1N1) viruses. During the past three weeks (weeks 18–20), the percentage of specimens testing positive for influenza has ranged from 16.4% in the West South Central region to 1.7% in the Mid-Atlantic region**. During this period, 66.4% of all isolates identified were influenza B viruses.

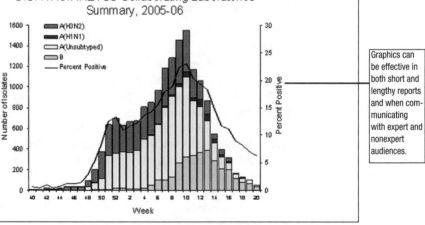

U.S. WHO/NREVSS Collaborating Laboratories Summary, 2005-06

> Graphics can be effective in both short and lengthy reports and when communicating with expert and nonexpert audiences.

FIGURE 6.8 *CDC Influenza Weekly Report* (Week ending May 20, 2006—Week 20).
Source: http://www.cdc.gov/flu/weekly/fluactivity.htm

Composition of the 2006-07 Influenza Vaccine:

WHO has recommended that the 2006-07 trivalent influenza vaccine for the Northern Hemisphere contain A/New Caledonia/20/99-like (H1N1), A/Wisconsin/67/2005-like (H3N2), and B/Malaysia/2506/2004-like viruses. The influenza A (H3N2) and the influenza B components have been changed from the 2005-06 season vaccine components. A/Wisconsin/67/2005 is an antigenic variant of the current vaccine strain A/California/07/2004. Influenza B viruses currently circulating can be divided into two antigenically distinct lineages represented by B/Yamagata/16/88 and B/Victoria/2/87 viruses. The updating of the influenza B component to B/Ohio/1/2005 (which is antigenically equivalent to B/Malaysia/2506/2004) represents a change to the B/Victoria lineage. This recommendation was based on antigenic analyses of recently isolated influenza viruses, epidemiologic data, and post-vaccination serologic studies in humans.

Antigenic Characterization:

CDC has antigenically characterized 828 influenza viruses [503 influenza A (H3N2), 88 influenza A (H1), and 237 influenza B viruses] collected by U.S. laboratories since October 1, 2005.

Of the 503 influenza A (H3N2) viruses, 381 (75.7%) were characterized as A/California/07/2004-like, which is the influenza A (H3N2) component recommended for the 2005-06 influenza vaccine, and 122 (24.3%) viruses showed reduced titers with antisera produced against A/California/07/2004. Of the 122 low-reacting viruses, 96 were tested with antisera produced against A/Wisconsin/67/2005 (the H3N2 component selected for the 2006-07 vaccine), and 70 are A/Wisconsin-like.

The hemagglutinin proteins of 85 (96.6%) of the 88 characterized influenza A (H1) viruses were antigenically similar to the hemagglutinin of the vaccine strain A/New Caledonia/20/99, and the other 3 (3.4%) showed reduced titers with antisera produced against A/New Caledonia/20/99.

Fifty-two (21.9%) of the 237 influenza B viruses that have been characterized belong to the B/Yamagata lineage: 8 were similar to B/Shanghai/361/2002, the recommended influenza B component for the 2005-06 influenza vaccine, 43 were characterized as B/Florida/07/2004-like, and 1 showed reduced titers with antisera produced against both B/Shanghai/361/2002 and B/Florida/07/2004. B/Florida/07/2004 is a minor antigenic variant of B/Shanghai/361/2002. One hundred eighty-five (78.1%) of the 237 influenza B viruses were identified as belonging to the B/Victoria lineage: 184 were similar to B/Ohio/1/2005, the influenza B component selected for the 2006-07 vaccine, and 1 showed reduced titers with antisera produced against B/Ohio/1/2005.

Pneumonia and Influenza (P&I) Mortality Surveillance*:

During week 20, 6.3% of all deaths reported by the vital statistics offices of 122 U.S. cities were due to pneumonia or influenza. This percentage is below the epidemic threshold of 7.4% for week 20.

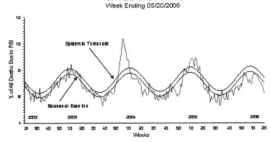

Pneumonia and Influenza Mortality
for 122 U.S. Cities
Week Ending 05/20/2006

Influenza-Associated Pediatric Mortality*:

During October 2, 2005 – May 20, 2006, CDC received reports of 35 influenza-associated pediatric deaths, 33 of which occurred during the current influenza season.

Influenza-Associated Pediatric Hospitalizations*:

Laboratory-confirmed influenza-associated pediatric hospitalizations are monitored in two population-based surveillance networks[†]: Emerging Infections Program (EIP) and New Vaccine Surveillance Network (NVSN). During October 1, 2005 – April 30, 2006, the preliminary influenza-associated hospitalization rate reported by EIP for children aged 0-17 years was 1.21 per 10,000. For children aged 0-4 years and 5-17 years, the rate was 2.76 per 10,000 and 0.38 per 10,000, respectively. During October 30, 2005 – April 29, 2006, the preliminary laboratory-confirmed influenza-associated hospitalization rate for children aged 0-4 years in NVSN was 5.4 per 10,000. EIP and NVSN hospitalization data collection have ended as of April 30, 2006. Rate estimates are preliminary and may continue to change as data are finalized.

FIGURE 6.8 *(continued)*

provided by Crouch and Zetler and the 9/11 Commission Report. Take a look at Table 6.1 to see a comparison of the type of information and organization of information presented in the *The 9/11 Commission Report: Final Report of the National Commission on Terrorist Attacks Upon the United States.*

Crouch and Zetler present their table to describe a common format used by many report writers, but they also highlight the fact that all reports will not look the same, they state that reports do not always follow set rules; they must be

Common Components in Government Reports	*The 9/11 Commission Report: Final Report of the National Commission on Terrorist Attacks Upon the United States*
Cover Page, Title Page, Table of Contents, Foreword	Contents, List of Illustrations, Tables, Members and Staff
Summary: Present your audience with a snapshot of the entire document.	Executive Summary
Purpose or Introduction: Give the audience background information regarding the policy problem.	In Chapter 1, "We Have Some Planes," the authors describe, in meticulous detail, the tragic events of September 11, 2001.
Historical Survey of the Subject: Describe important events (past, present, or future) that warrant consideration of a policy change. Depending on the scope of your report, you may want to provide audience with a detailed description of the tasks you completed to collect and analyze data in your reports.	In Chapters 2 through 10, the writers provide a detailed narrative of the various political, social, and national security issues that preceded the September 11, 2001 tragedy.
Detailed Analysis: Examine the various interpretations of the problem or event under scrutiny.	In Chapter 11, titled, "Foresight—And Hindsight" the authors begin their analysis of the tragic events by stating, "We believe the 9/11 attacks revealed four kinds of failures: in imagination, policy, capabilities, and management" (9/11 Commission Report 339).
Conclusions: Explain the implications of your analysis.	Also in Chapter 11, the authors provided a detailed explanation of how each identified failure— "imagination, policy, capabilities, and management" contributed to the tragic events of September 11, 2001 (9/11 Commission Report 339).
Recommendations: Present a decision, recommendations, or argument for change, which is strengthened by the other parts of the report.	Chapter 12 is titled, "What to Do? A Global Strategy," chapter presents recommendations with illustrations and examples of how their recommendations might be implemented.
	Chapter 13, "How to Do It? A Different Way of Organizing the Government," presents prescriptive recommendations for organizing the government to respond to the problem.

TABLE 6.1

tailored to the circumstances under which they are written and the requirements of their readers (114).

Summary and Looking Forward

In this chapter, we've introduced public policy reports—government policy reports that play an important part in policy development and can address a wide and diverse audience. Before writing policy reports, you should consider audiences as well as their goals for reading your report. Also, remember that some audiences are accustomed to common components in policy reports to help them to easily navigate these often lengthy documents. In the next chapter, we will discuss government grants and grant proposals, which help implement public policy and address a unique and specific audience.

Activities and Assignments

1. **Individual Internet Activity:** Search the Internet for a federal report that addresses a policy issue that concerns you. Read the foreword or preface of the report and try to determine the purpose of the report. Is it investigative? Does it recommend a particular policy? Does the report describe past events or results of past investigations? Does the report provide instructions for implementing a policy? Does the public policy report attempt to achieve more than one of these aims? After you determine the purpose for the report, browse through the report to see if you can determine the audience for the report and identify any constraints the writers faced while writing the report. Be prepared to share your findings and analysis with the rest of the class.

2. **Group Internet Activity:** Browse through today's local newspaper and identify a policy issue posing a problem at the local, state, or federal level. Then, search the Internet to see if you can find an investigative policy report that attempts to address a related policy problem. What questions did the public policy report writers use to resolve a similar policy issue? What methods or activities did the report writers use to gather data in the policy report? Then, reflect on the policy issue you identified in today's newspaper. Identify at least three questions that need to be investigated to resolve the policy problem in today's newspaper. What steps would you need to take to obtain answers to these questions? Be prepared to share your findings and analysis with the rest of the class.

3. **Individual Activity:** Locate the *9/11 Commission Report: Final Report of the National Commission on Terrorist Attacks Upon the United States* on the Internet or the school or local library. The writers of the report identify members of the public as part of their intended audience. Since you are a member of the public, analyze a chapter of the report by completing the following tasks:

In a two-to-three-page, double-spaced essay, (1) provide a brief summary of one chapter of the report and (2) make strong argument about the credibility or *ethos* of the writers. In this portion of your essay, you are asking yourself, "Do I trust the writers?" "What makes this chapter convincing?" Provide examples of effective or ineffective rhetorical choices (tone, word choice, use of stories, use of statistics) to support your argument about the authors' credibility. Feel free to reference information in the front matter (preface, foreword, table of contents) of the document to support your argument.

4. **Group Activity:** Locate three to four public policy reports. Be sure to select reports from different agencies, across jurisdictions (city, state, and local), and of various lengths and purposes. After reading the foreword, preface, table of contents, and introduction of the reports, make a note of any major differences in the cultural contexts of the reports. Specifically, make note of the technological and scientific, sociopolitical, economic, and national security constraints that the writers and stakeholders faced in writing and distributing these reports. Be prepared to provide your classmates with a oral description of the purpose of each report and explain any constraints that you believe the writers faced in addressing their audiences.

5. **Individual Activity:** Search newspaper archives and locate at least three articles and/or editorials that reference government policy reports. As you read these articles, make note of how journalists use the reports. Are the reports used as evidence to support the journalists' claims about a policy issue? Are the reports used to refute or support claims by nongovernmental bodies (advocacy groups, businesses, individuals, etc.)? Based on these articles, how do you believe journalists and the media use policy reports? Bring your newspaper clippings and a one-page essay explaining your examples of media use of policy reports to class. Be prepared to discuss your findings orally with your classmates.

6. **Group Activity:** In this chapter, we discussed the fact that Figure 6.8, CDC Influenza Weekly Report, is written for an "expert audience." This weekly report includes language and statistics that most nonexpert audiences would not understand. In a group, identify a nonexpert audience (elementary school teachers, school principals, day care workers, etc.) who might find some of the content of the report useful. Then, as a group, develop a one-page plan for rewriting the report to address your identified nonexpert audience. As you develop the plan to the report, consider the following questions:

a. What information is important to this audience?
b. What type of evidence (statistics, stories, examples) might this audience need to understand the report?
c. Is the tone and word choice in the original report appropriate for the new audience?
d. What information can be deleted or left out of the report?
e. What information needs to be added for this audience?
f. What constraints might make rewriting this report for a new audience difficult?

Works Cited

Baake, Ken. "Archaeology Reports: When Context Becomes an Active Agent in the Rhetorical Process," *Technical Communication Quarterly* 12.4 (Fall 2003): 389–402.

Centers for Disease Control and Prevention. *Smoking and Health: Report of the Advisory Committee to the Surgeon General of the Public Health Service.* 1964. Aug. 2006 <http://www.cdc.gov/tobacco/sgr/sgr_1964/1964%20SGR%20Intro.pdf>.

—. "CDC Influenza Weekly Report." May 2006-Week 20. 1 Aug. 2006 <http://www.cdc.gov/flu/weekly/fluactivity.htm>.

—. *Tobacco Use Among U.S. Racial/Ethic Minorities: A Surgeon General Report.* 1998. 1 Aug. 2006 <http://www.cdc.gov/tobacco/sgr/sgr_1998/sgr-min-forpref.htm>.

Crouch, W. George and Robert L. Zetler. *A Guide to Technical Writing.* 2nd ed. New York: The Ronald Press Company, 1954.

Johnson, William C. *Public Administration: Policy, Politics, and Practice.* Guilford: The Dushkin Publishing Group, Inc. 1992.

National Commission on Terrorist Acts Upon the United States. *The 9/11 Commission Report: Final Report of the National Commission on Terrorist Attacks Upon the United States.* 22 July 2004. 1 Aug. 2006 <http://www.9-11commission.gov/>.

"Philip Zelikow discusses his work on 'The 9/11 Commission Report' following its National Book Award nomination." *The Tavis Smiley Show.* National Public Radio. 15 Nov. 2004.

Rude, Carolyn. "Environmental Policy Making and the Report Genre." *Technical Communication Quarterly* 6.1 (Winter 1997): 77–90.

—. "The Report for Decision Making: Genre and Inquiry." *Journal of Business and Technical Communication* 9 (1995): 170–205.

—. "Toward an Expanded Concept of Rhetorical Delivery: The Uses of Reports in Public Policy Debates." *Technical Communication Quarterly* 13.3 (Summer 2004): 271–88.

United States Department of Health and Human Services. *The Health Consequences of Involuntary Exposure to Tobacco Smoke: A Report of the Surgeon General.* 27 June 2006. 1 Aug. 2006 <http://www.surgeongeneral.gov/library/secondhandsmoke/>.

Williams, Miriam F. "Tracing W.E.B. Dubois' 'Color Line' In Government Regulations." *The Journal of Technical Writing and Communication* 36.2 (2006): 141–65.

Government Grants and Proposals

In 1998, policy writers at a State of Texas agency met to consider translating recently revised rules into Spanish so that the business owners who read or spoke English as a second language would be able to easily follow rules. Texas has one of the largest Spanish-speaking populations in the United States and some of the Spanish-speaking business owners regulated by this agency were having difficulty deciphering the rules written in English. While some of the agency's policy writers argued that obtaining translations of the rules into Spanish should be a cost incurred by the business owners, other policy writers argued that the agency should at least find out how much it would cost the agency to translate the rules. After consultation with another State of Texas agency's translation department, the policy writers determined that it would be too costly to hire staff or contract with translations services to translate on an ongoing basis. At the time, translation services were too expensive for this small agency, especially since this particular agency was in the process of rewriting hundreds of rules.

To remedy the problem, one policy writer suggested that the agency consider writing a grant proposal to federal agencies interested in increasing the number of minority-owned businesses or improving intercultural communication. As this policy writer surfed the Internet for federal agencies willing to fund these types of projects, he discovered a grant award notice describing a recent grant that his own agency had awarded a nonprofit organization in his community. The policy writer wondered why his agency, which had funding needs of its own, was funding local organizations.

In this chapter, we will attempt to answer several important questions regarding federal, state, and local agencies and their roles as funding organizations. Specifically, this chapter will respond to the questions:

Under what circumstances do government agencies write proposals to receive grants from other government agencies?

Which government agencies are considered funding agencies?

How does a proposal writer find information about grants available from government agencies?

What rhetorical strategies can proposal writers use to increase their chances of funding without compromising ethical standards or codes of conduct?

Do government funding agencies provide guidelines for proposal writers to follow?

Under what conditions might government personnel write proposals, and who are the audiences for these proposals?

In this chapter we'll address these questions as well as the purpose, contexts, and audiences for grant proposals.

Purpose of Government Grants and Grant Proposals

In the opening narrative of this chapter, we describe **government grants** in terms of their potential benefit to other government agencies, but government grants actually have a variety of beneficiaries, including other government entities, private businesses, researchers and students in most academic disciplines, nonprofit organizations, and organizations and individuals willing to provide goods and services to the public on behalf of government agencies. The United States operates under a "federal system," or *federalism*, which "denotes a system in which the powers of the government are divided among one authority that governs the whole nation and several that govern its political subdivisions (Johnson 114). Over the decades, our federal system has become increasingly influenced by constituents and interest groups who encourage government entities, especially the federal government, to use grants to fund "programs in education, health, transportation, urban development, and the environment" (Johnson 121).

Grant-seeking behavior is influenced by ever-changing economic, social, and political factors. An example of the type of influence of interest groups and constituents in health matters is evident in the operations of the United States Public Health Service, which disbursed $30 billion in 2004, according to the Office of Research Integrity. Because federal, state, and local government agencies do not have the personnel, time, or expertise to provide their constituents with all of the goods and services these agencies are authorized or committed to perform, they disperse grants. The purpose of some federal, state, and local grants is to fund other government entities through grants and to fund individuals and organizations in the public.

Grants-In-Aid

William C. Johnson suggests "the major feature of fiscal federalism is the **grant-in-aid,** a transfer of money from one government to another, generally national to state, national to local, and state to local. Nearly always it is conditional: it must be spent for the purpose and by the procedures specified in law or the rules of the granting agency" (122). Because the federal government does not have the

FIGURE 7.1   Senator Collins' Grant Information: Constituent Services webpage.

Source: http://collins.senate.gov/public/continue.cfm?FuseAction=ConstituentServices.
GrantInformation

authority under a federal system to provide every government good or service demanded at the state and local levels, other jurisdictions are gifted grants to provide goods and services to their constituents. In Figure 7.1, Senator Susan Collins of Maine encourages municipalities in Maine to apply for federal grants and includes references to potential funding sources.

Figure 7.2 is an excerpt from the Environmental Protection Agency (EPA), the federal agency responsible for regulating environmental rules and regulations; it presents a list of the types of institutions that were recipients of EPA grants over the last ten years (U.S. Environmental Protection Agency). Take a look at the EPA grants listed in Figure 7.2 that are **grants-in-aid** and notice the large amounts of grant money awarded to city, county, and state governments.

In Chapter 3, we introduced you to the *Federal Register*, which is the federal publication that announces proposed and adopted federal regulations. The *Federal Register* is also responsible for publishing **requests for proposals (RFPs)** and **requests for applications (RFAs)**—public announcements of new grant opportunities, contracting opportunities, and grant awards. As we mentioned in Chapter 3, state governments also have publications that are the state equivalent of the *Federal Register* and publish proposed rules and regulations and announce new grants and grant awards. The request for application from the *New York State Register* shown in Figure 7.3 is an example of how states announce funding opportunities from local governments.

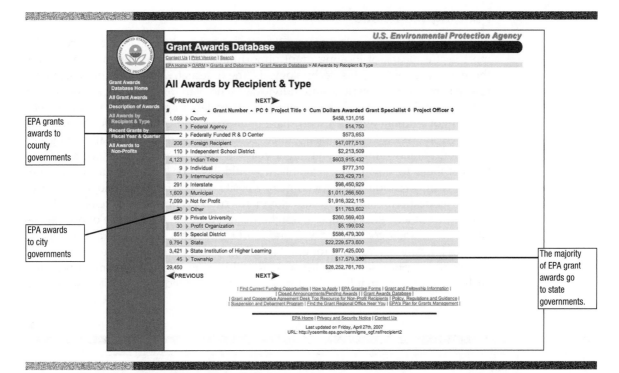

FIGURE 7.2 EPA *Grant Awards Database* webpage for awards during a ten-year period.
Source: http://yosemite.epa.gov/oarm/igms_egf.nsf/recipient2?OpenView

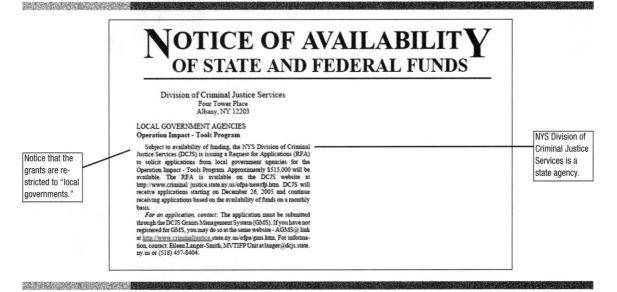

FIGURE 7.3 Excerpt from the January 11, 2006 *New York State Register*.
Source: http://www.dos.state.ny.us/info/register/2006/jan11/pdfs/availability.pdf

Funding the Public

The pubic also seeks grant opportunities through a variety of sources. One of the most useful means of locating grant opportunities and grant announcements, for those with access to this technology, is the Internet. Nonprofit organizations, researchers, business owners, and individuals who plan to implement a project with positive implications for their communities or society in general can visit the websites of government agencies who share their goals and objectives. For example, if you were interested in pursuing a grant to fund a weekend adult education program in a small rural community, you might visit the Department of Education's website to see if there are any grants available. It would likely be a waste your time to look for government funding at a government website with no interests or logical connection to education, community development, rural community development, job training, or other issues related to adult education. To see an example of how agencies publicize their goals, objectives, and funding interests, take a look at the Department of Education's resource for grant funding opportunities in Figure 7.4.

Another option for the grant-seeking public is to find a government website, such as Grants.gov, that list all grant opportunities for federal agencies. According

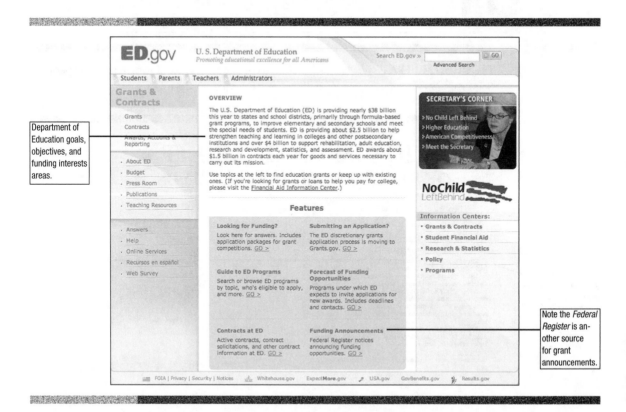

FIGURE 7.4   Department of Education Funding Opportunities Webpage.

Source: http://www.ed.gov/fund/landing.jhtml?src=ln

The U.S Department of Health and Human Services is responsible for managing the site.

FIGURE 7.5   Grants.gov homepage. Source: http://www.grants.gov/

to Grants.gov, "Grants.gov was born as a governmental resource named the E-Grants Initiative, part of the President's 2002 Fiscal Year Management Agenda to improve government services to the public . . ."

Grant Proposals

Now that we've addressed the two main purposes of government grants—to provide funds to other government agencies and to fund programs initiated by the public—we need to discuss the genre of technical communication used to apply for grants, **grant proposals**. Grant proposals are the genre of technical communication used to convince funding sources (both government agencies and private donors) that a project can be implemented and meets the objectives of the funding organizations. Grant proposals addressed to government agencies are unique in that they must persuade the government agency personnel that the proposed projects, whether academic, entrepreneurial, or community-based initiatives, provide society with some public good.

To aid proposal writers in their efforts and define the scope of the proposal, government agencies provide specific instructions and criteria for writers to use in their writing process; these instructions are called **proposal guidelines.** In most cases, the proposal guidelines are part of the RFP or RFA document, but in some cases, proposal guidelines are in a separate booklet or hyperlink that is referenced in the RFA. Although there are common elements in grant proposals (introduction, needs statements, objectives, methods or activities, budget, schedule, references, etc.), a successful proposal writer will be sure to address *specific* instructions and questions requested in proposal guidelines and not deviate from those instructions. Thus, the purpose of grant proposals is to provide persuasive, clear, and comprehensive responses to proposal guidelines. Writing persuasive proposals can be challenging, but if your proposal is comprehensive and clear, the benefits of a grant proposal can be twofold: it can be a means of persuading a government funding agency of the need for a project and it can serve as a blueprint for the implementation of the proposed project. Although proposal guidelines vary depending on the purpose of a specific grant proposal and the funding agency's proposal guidelines, as a proposal writer, you can expect to address some common questions when reading proposal guidelines. These common questions are often arranged in the following order and allow you to introduce your organization to the funding agency and describe how the organization's proposed project will be implemented.

Section 1 *Background or History:*

What is your organization's history?

What background information can you use to present your organization as credible and able to successfully complete your proposed project?

Section 2 *Problem or Needs Statement:*

What problem or need will be addressed with grant funding?

Can you convince the funding agency, through the use of narratives, examples, and statistics, that there is a real problem that needs to be addressed?

Section 3 *Goals and Objectives:*

Does the funding agency's mission statement, strategic plan, or grant funding intiative address the problem or need your organization is trying to solve? If so, what are your organizational goals or project goals and objectives?

Can you convince the funding agency that your proposed project is aligned with their mission statement or the issue addressed in the request for proposal?

Section 4 *Activities, Methods, or Tasks:*

What tasks will you need to complete to meet your objectives?

What steps will you need to take to make your objectives a reality?

Section 5 *Means of Evaluating the Success of the Proposed Project:*

As you complete each task or step of the project, what methods will you use to determine if you've done a good job?

How will you evaluate your tasks to make sure that you're not wasting the funding agency's money?

Section 6 *Schedule:*
How long will the project take?
What are the activities that you need to perform to implement your project and by what dates do you plan to complete these activities?

Section 7 *Budget:*
How do you plan to spend the funds?
How much does each budget item cost?

Section 8 *Qualifications:*
Who will serve as the principal investigator or person in charge of the project?
What other personnel will need to be hired?
What are their qualifications?

If the proposal guidelines include additional sections or suggest a different organization of these sections, be sure to provide the information and arrangement suggested in the proposal guidelines. In a sense, following proposal guidelines is your first chance to show the funding agency that you can follow instructions. If you fail to follow instructions, it is not likely that funding agencies will view you or your organization as credible. Another way to lose the respect or confidence of your audience is to fail to proofread your proposal, to use jargon or language that your audience will not understand, and to fail to cite outside sources. Your proposal is the proposal reviewer's first and sometimes only opportunity to test your ability to use their grant money correctly, so your proposal must address all of the questions or sections outlined in the proposal guidelines, be written in a style that is understandable to a general audience, and present you and your organization in a favorable and honest manner. In the next section, we will explain the contexts in which proposals are written, including examples of proposal guidelines, which set the parameters for a proposal.

Proposal Writing in Cultural Contexts

Proposal writing is a genre of technical communication that many writers find challenging, not because proposals are more difficult to write than other technical documents, but unfortunately many writers perceive a level of inaccesibility associated with this genre of technical communication. However, the reality is that proposal writing may be one of the most publicly recognized and accessible genres of technical communication. It is a genre attempted by school teachers interested in starting after-school programs, clergy wanting to fund community-based programs with the help of their congregations, community activists interested in providing shelter for the homeless, and a variety of other professionals and nonprofessionals who want to provide some good or service to the public. To aid in the accessibility of this genre of technical communication, there are numerous workshops, books, courses, and Internet sites on the subject, unlike the other genres of technical communication covered in this textbook. Take a look at Figure 7.6, which is the website resource that the National Institute of Neurological Disorders and

Grants

- **Request for Applications (RFA)**
  Requests for Applications (RFAs) are typically one-time solicitations for grant applications addressing a defined research topic. Each RFA specifies the scope and objectives of the research to be proposed; application requirements and procedures; and the review criteria to be applied in the evaluation of applications submitted in response to the RFA. Although there are exceptions, these types of solicitations offer only one Application Receipt Date.

  > "Application requirements and procedures" are essentially proposal guidelines.

- **Program Announcements (PA)**
  A Program Announcement (PA) is used by the institute to announce its interest in building or enhancing its research program in a particular area. The PA typically is an ongoing solicitation, accepting applications for multiple receipt dates, for up to three years. The PA specifies the scope and objectives of the research of interest, application requirements and procedures, and review criteria to be applied. There are two variations of the standard PA, a Program Announcement with Set-Aside Funds (PAS) and a Program Announcement Reviewed by an Institution (PAR)

  > What is the difference between a RFA and PA?

  - **PAS Mechanism**
    A PAS is a program announcement with a specific dollar amount set aside by the Institute to fund select applications that receive a score beyond the **payline**. Set-aside funds will be distributed across the duration of the PAS.

  - **PAR Mechanism**
    A PAR is a program announcement whose applications will be reviewed by the Institute, rather than the NIH Center for Scientific Review.

- **Notices**
  Notices are announcements published in the NIH Guide which provide policy or other information relevant to funding. The availability of supplemental funding for current grantees is sometimes announced through a notice.

Contracts

- **Notices**
  Many types of "notices" are used in the contract process. Notices are used to: initiate advance acquisition planning and facilitate market research; disseminate information on the availability of new contract opportunities; notify the public of modifications/additions under existing contracts for additional supplies/services; announce subcontracting opportunities and contract awards.

  Federal Business Opportunities (FedBizOpps) website. This website is the government-wide point of entry (GPE) and is the primary location for the government to publish contract opportunities.

> Website for finding contracting opportunities

Our competitive proposed contract opportunities are also listed in the **NIH Guide for Grants and Contracts (NIH Guide)**. The NIH Guide is distributed free of charge to organizations which request inclusion on the **mailing list**.

> Free resources for proposal writers

The following are contract notices primarily used by the NINDS:

- **Pre-Solicitation Notices:**

  - **Request for Information (RFI)** - used for market research purposes and for the exchange of information with industry prior to receipt of proposals. RFI's are used as one means of obtaining and collecting information about capabilities within the market to satisfy our contract needs. The results of market research help identify sources potentially capable of satisfying the requirement; determine if the contract need is available as a commercial item; the extent the final product/service could be augmented by or with commercial or nondevelopmental items; and helps the Government to understand the practice and standards of the firms, businesses, organizations engaged in the industry that would respond to the requirement.

  - **Sources Sought (R&D Advance Notice)** - used as an advance notice of an Institute's interest in potential Research & Development (R&D) programs whenever market research efforts do not produce a sufficient number of potential sources to obtain adequate competition. Sources sought notices enable potential sources to learn of R&D programs and provide organizations an opportunity to submit information that will permit evaluation of their capabilities. Sources who respond are usually added to the appropriate solicitation mailing list.

FIGURE 7.6 Excerpt from NINDS Funding Opportunities. Source: http://www.ninds.nih.gov/funding/differences_pr.htm

As a matter of practice, we publish both of the notices mentioned above at FedBizOpps and in the NIH Guide

- **Request for Proposals (RFP) Availability:**
  This notice announces the pending posting and release of a RFP. RFP availability notices are published at FedBizOpps site and in the NIH Guide.

- **Contract Award**
  This notice is used to disseminate award information on all contract actions exceeding $25,000 and those awards likely to result in the award of lower tier subcontracts. The name of the organization and dollar amount of the contract award are published. Award notices are only published at the FedBizOpps site.

- **Request for Proposals (RFP)**
  A RFP is the Government's official solicitation document that communicates to prospective offerors, what it is the Government needs to buy/acquire, and formally invites the submission of proposals. The purpose of the RFP is to convey all information that prospective offerors need to prepare a proposal. In addition to a description of what it is the Government needs to buy, the RFP also contains various representations and certifications that are required of prospective offerors, proposed terms and conditions that would be applicable to any resultant contract, instructions on how to prepare proposals, and information as to how the Government will evaluate proposals and determine who is selected for award.

| What is a RFP? |

Additional Contract-related Terms and Definitions

What is meant by Acquisition?
Acquistion is the process, through the award of contracts, by which the Government acquires or obtains goods, supplies, products, or services for its direct benefit or use, or who in-turn provides these results or end products for use by non-Government parties, including the general public.

| What is a contract? |

What is a Contract?
A contract is an award instrument establishing a mutually binding legal relationship between the Government (buyer) and a Contractor (seller), obligating the seller to furnish/deliver goods, supplies, or services whose functional and performance qualities are defined in the contract, and the buyer to pay for them.

What is a Research and Development Contract?
R&D contracts are awarded for specific scientific inquiry directed towards particular areas of research and development needed by the Government. R&D contracts typically involve: 1) a systematic search, specific scientific inquiry, or intensive study directed towards gaining new or fuller scientific knowledge or understanding; 2) use of knowledge and understanding gained from research, directed towards creating useful materials, devices, methods, models, or systems to meet scientific/research requirements, including procedures to accomplish novel enhancements to existing equipment and systems; 3) feasibility of disseminating or applying R&D findings to community or other group situations, e.g., establish effectiveness of health diagnosis, treatment, or prevention approaches to improve public health; or 4) the design of equipment prototypes and demonstration of processes, procedures, techniques and activities that directly support the conduct of research and development.

FIGURE 7.6 *(continued)*

Stroke (NINDS) provides as technical support for prospective proposal writers and applicants. Government employees are responsible for writing the information included in websites that assist prospective proposal writers, which includes definitions explaining the differences between grants and contracts and between RFAs and RFPs, and which answers a variety of questions that novice proposal writers might need to better understand the grant development process.

So, with so many resources available to potential applicants, why does proposal writing make so many writers uncomfortable? We believe writers often find proposal writing challenging for the following reasons: (1) It requires adherence to strict, complex, and sometimes vague guidelines; (2) it is competitive in nature; (3) it requires personal and professional accountability; and (4) the length and complexity of the proposal development process can be intimidating. Clearly, these constraints are not exclusive to proposal writing, but the presence of all of these factors in one genre is challenging.

Adherence to Strict and Complex Guidelines

As we've mentioned earlier in the chapter, proposal guidelines tell you how the funding agency would like you to frame or organize your arguments. Because some proposal writers find these instructions difficult to follow, most proposal guidelines include the name and telephone number of a contact person, often called a program officer, who is responsible for answering questions about the proposal guidelines and providing any other technical assistance that the proposal writer may need. Before accessing the proposal guidelines, you must find a request for proposal that describes funding appropriate for your needs. Requests for proposals are usually written by government employees who are subject matter experts in the policy area addressed in the announcement and edited by agency personnel. Figure 7.7 is an

---

Services to Unaccompanied Alien Children

| Synopsis | Full Announcement | How to Apply |

The synopsis for this grant opportunity is detailed below, following this paragraph. This synopsis contains all of the updates to this document that have been posted as of **06/01/2006**. If updates have been made to the opportunity synopsis, update information is provided below the synopsis.

If you would like to receive notifications of changes to the grant opportunity click send me change notification emails. The only thing you need to provide for this service is your email address. No other information is requested.

Any inconsistency between the original printed document and the disk or electronic document shall be resolved by giving precedence to the printed document.

Document Type:	Grants Notice
Funding Opportunity Number:	HHS-2006-ACF-ORR-ZU-0007
Opportunity Category:	Discretionary
Posted Date:	Jun 01, 2006
Creation Date:	Jun 01, 2006
Original Closing Date for Applications:	Jul 10, 2006 See link to full announcement for details. IMPORTANT NOTE: Applications submitted electronically via Grants.gov must be submitted no later than 4:30 p.m., eastern time, on the due date referenced above.
Current Closing Date for Applications:	Jul 10, 2006 See link to full announcement for details. IMPORTANT NOTE: Applications submitted electronically via Grants.gov must be submitted no later than 4:30 p.m., eastern time, on the due date referenced above.
Archive Date:	Aug 09, 2006
Funding Instrument Type:	Cooperative Agreement
Category of Funding Activity:	Income Security and Social Services
Category Explanation:	
Expected Number of Awards:	4
Estimated Total Program Funding:	$7,577,000
Award Ceiling:	$5,387,000
Award Floor:	$315,360
CFDA Number:	93.676 -- Unaccompanied Alien Children Program
Cost Sharing or Matching Requirement:	No

> The agency is expecting to award four grants.

FIGURE 7.7   Services to Unaccompanied Alien Children Grant Announcement.
Source: Grants.Gov

Eligible Applicants

Unrestricted (i.e., open to any type of entity above), subject to any clarification in text field entitled "Additional Information on Eligibility"

Additional Information on Eligibility:

Prospective applicants would look here to see if they're eligible to apply.

Eligibility is open to all types of domestic applicants other than individuals. Faith-based and community organizations are eligible to apply. Non-profit organizations (including faith-based and community organizations) and for-profit organizations are eligible to apply. Organizations must be appropriately licensed (at the time of submission of the application) as facilities for the provision of shelter care and other related services to dependent children. For-profit organizations must clearly demonstrate that they are only charging the program actual costs incurred and will not realize a profit at the expense of the Federal Government. The U.S. Government is opposed to prostitution and related activities, which are inherently harmful and dehumanizing, and contribute to the phenomenon of trafficking in persons. U.S. non-governmental organizations, and their sub-grantees, cannot use U.S. Government funds to lobby for, promote or advocate the legalization or regulation of prostitution as a legitimate form of work. It is the responsibility of the primary grantee to ensure these criteria are met by its sub-grantees. Accordingly, the grant application must ensure that no monies, if awarded, will be used for these unallowable purposes.

Agency Name

Administration for Children and Families

This is the government agency soliciting proposals for a grant. This agency will also select reviewers to evaluate proposals and disburse grant money to the winning applicant.

Description

One of the functions of the Office of Refugee Resettlement (ORR) Division of Unaccompanied Children's Services (DUCS) is to provide temporary shelter care and other related services to children in ORR custody. Shelter care services will be provided for the period beginning when DUCS accepts the child for placement and custody and ending when the child is released from custody, a final disposition of the child's immigration case results in removal of the child from the United States, or the child turns 18 years of age. Shelter care and other child welfare related services in a State-licensed residential shelter care program will be provided in the least restrictive setting appropriate to the Unaccompanied Alien Children's (UAC) age and special needs. While the majority of UAC remain in care for an average of 45 days, some will stay for shorter or longer periods of time. This announcement provides the opportunity to fund providers of basic shelter and/or group homes.

Link to Full Announcement

Proposal guidelines are usually listed in the "Full Announcement."

http://www.acf.hhs.gov/grants/open/HHS-2006-ACF-ORR-ZU-0007.html

If you have difficulty accessing the full announcement electronically, please contact:

Tsegaye Wolde
twolde@acf.hhs.gov
Tsegaye Wolde

FIGURE 7.7 *(continued)*

excerpt from the Department of Health and Human Services Administration for Children and Families' request for applications to fund a program to aid children who enter the U.S. unaccompanied by adults.

Next, take a look at an excerpt from the 44-page full announcement (Figure 7.8).

Competitive Nature of Proposal Writing

In a market economy, competition is necessary and expected, but although many Americans thrive in competition in a variety of settings (job interviews,

IV. APPLICATION AND SUBMISSION INFORMATION

1. Address to Request Application Package:

Sylvia M. Johnson, Grants Officer
U.S. Department of Health and Human Services
ACF - Office of Grants Management
Division of Discretionary Grants
370 L'Enfant Promenade, S.W.
Aerospace Building, 6th Floor-East
Washington, DC 20447
Phone: 202-401-4524
Email: sjohnson@acf.hhs.gov
URL: http//www.Grants.gov

2. Content and Form of Application Submission:

> It is not clear which of the following persons are willing to answer questions or provide technical assistance to prospective applicants.

Letters of intent are encouraged but not required. Letters of intent to apply are expected to be received by 4:30 pm EST, 15 calendar days after publication of the announcement. Letters should state the funding opportunity number, the Applicant's name and contact information, the location of the proposed site and the type of facility for which the Applicant is applying. One letter for each facility type that is being applied for should be submitted.

Letters of intent should be sent to the attention of Tsegaye Wolde at Office of Refugee Resettlement, Administration for Children and Families, 370 L'Enfant Promenade, S.W., 6th Floor-East, Washington, D.C., 20447. Letters may also be sent by facsimile to: 202-401-1022 or by Email to: twolde@acf.hhs.gov.

Application Format

- Please do not include organizational brochures or other promotional materials, slides, films, clips, etc. A limited number of photographs of the proposed site are encouraged.

- The font size may be no smaller than 12-point, and the margins must be at least one inch on all sides.

- Number all application pages sequentially throughout the package, beginning with the abstract of the proposed project as page number one.

- For those submitting in hard copy, submit application materials on white 8.5 x 11 inch paper only. Do not use colored, oversized or folded materials.

- Please present application materials either in loose-leaf notebooks or in folders with pages two-hole punched at the top center and fastened separately with a slide paper fastener.

> In addition to the narrative, proposal writers must complete several forms to apply for this grant.

- Completed Standard Form 424 -- signed by an official of the organization applying for the grant who has authority to legally obligate the organization.

- Standard Form 424A -- Budget Information-Non Construction Programs.

- Narrative Budget Justification -- for each object class category required under Section B, Standard Form 424A.

- Project Narrative -- A narrative that addresses issues described in the "Project Description" and the "Evaluation Criteria" sections of this announcement. Please see Section V, Application Review Information for further information on these requirements.

> There are other sections of this 44-page grant announcement, like Section V, that must be read and understood to complete a competitive proposal.

- Table of Contents.

> If the proposal writer fails to pay attention to these requirements, it is not likely that their organization will be awarded a grant.

- Each application narrative should not exceed 30 pages double-spaced.

- Attachments and appendices should not exceed 30 pages and should be used only to provide supporting documentation such as administration charts, position descriptions, resumes, and letters of intent or partnership agreements.

- A table of contents and an executive summary should be included but will not count in the page limitations.

- Each page should be numbered sequentially, including the attachments and appendices.

FIGURE 7.8   Services to Unaccompanied Alien Children Grant Announcement.
Source: Grants.Gov

- This limitation of 30 pages should be considered as a maximum, and not necessarily a goal.

- Application forms are not to be counted in the page limit. Any pages that go beyond the 30-page limit will not be considered in the review process.

- Please do not include books or videotapes as they are not easily reproduced and are therefore inaccessible to the reviewers. The review panel will not consider submitted material which exceeds the 30-page limit.

Forms and Certifications

The project description should include all the information requirements described in the specific evaluation criteria outlined in this program announcement under *Section V*. Application Review Information. In addition to the project description, the applicant needs to complete all of the Standard Forms required as part of the application process for awards under this announcement.

Applicants seeking financial assistance under this announcement must file the appropriate Standard Forms as described in this section. All applicants must submit SF-424, Application for Federal Assistance. For non-construction programs, applicants must also submit SF-424A, Budget Information and SF-424B, Assurances. For construction programs, applicants must also submit SF-424C, Budget Information and SF-424D, Assurances. The forms may be reproduced for use in submitting applications. Applicants must sign and return the standard forms with their application.

Applicants must furnish prior to award an executed copy of the SF-LLL, Certification Regarding Lobbying, when applying for an award in excess of $100,000. Applicants who have used non-Federal funds for lobbying activities in connection with receiving assistance under this announcement shall complete a disclosure form, if applicable, with their application. Applicants must sign and return the certification with their application.

Applicants must also understand that they will be held accountable for the smoking prohibition included within Public Law (P.L.) 103-227, Title XII Environmental Tobacco Smoke (also known as the PRO-KIDS Act of 1994). A copy of the *Federal Register* notice that implements the smoking prohibition is included with this form. By signing and submitting the application, applicants are providing the necessary certification and are not required to return it.

Applicants must make the appropriate certification of their compliance with all Federal statutes relating to nondiscrimination. By signing and submitting the application, applicants are providing the necessary certification and are not required to return it. Complete the standard forms and the associated certifications and assurances based on the instructions on the forms. The forms and certifications may be found at: http://www.acf.hhs.gov/programs/ofs/forms.htm.

Private, non-profit organizations are encouraged to submit with their applications the survey located under *Grant Related Documents and Forms: Survey for Private, Non-Profit Grant Applicants, titled, Survey on Ensuring Equal Opportunity for Applicants,* at: http://www.acf.hhs.gov/programs/ofs/forms.htm.

Those organizations required to provide proof of non-profit status, please refer to *Section III.3.*

Please see *Section V.1* for instructions on preparing the full project description.

Please reference *Section IV.3* for details about acknowledgement of received applications.

Electronic Submission

You may submit your application to us in either electronic or paper format. To submit an application electronically, please use the http://www.Grants.gov site.

If you use Grants.gov, you will be able to download a copy of the application package, complete it off-line, and then upload and submit the application via the Grants.gov site. ACF will not accept grant applications via facsimile or email.

IMPORTANT NOTE: Before you submit an electronic application, you must complete the organization registration process as well as obtain and register "electronic signature credentials" for the Authorized Organization Representative (AOR). Since this process may take more than five business days, it is important to start this process early, well in advance of the application deadline. **Be sure to complete all Grants.gov registration processes listed on the Organization Registration Checklist, which can be found at** http://www.acf.hhs.gov/grants/registration_checklist.html.

Applicants are accountable to federal laws.

FIGURE 7.8   *(continued)*

Please note the following if you plan to submit your application electronically via Grants.gov:

- Electronic submission is voluntary, but strongly encouraged.

- You may access the electronic application for this program at http://www.Grants.gov. There you can search for the downloadable application package by utilizing the Grants.gov FIND function.

- **We strongly recommend that you do not wait until the application deadline date to begin the application process through Grants.gov.** We encourage applicants that submit electronically to submit well before the closing date and time so that if difficulties are encountered an applicant can still submit a hard copy via express mail.

- To use Grants.gov, you, as the applicant, must have a D-U-N-S number and register in the Central Contractor Registry (CCR). You should allow a minimum of five days to complete the CCR registration. **REMINDER: CCR registration expires each year and thus must be updated annually. You cannot upload an application to Grants.gov without having a current CCR registration AND electronic signature credentials for the AOR.**

- The electronic application is submitted by the AOR. To submit electronically, the AOR must obtain and register electronic signature credentials approved by the organization's E-Business Point of Contact who maintains the organization's CCR registration.

- You may submit all documents electronically, including all information typically included on the SF-424 and all necessary assurances and certifications.

- Your application must comply with any page limitation requirements described in this program announcement.

- After you electronically submit your application, you will receive an automatic acknowledgement from Grants.gov that contains a Grants.gov tracking number. ACF will retrieve your application from Grants.gov.

- ACF may request that you provide original signatures on forms at a later date.

- You will not receive additional point value because you submit a grant application in electronic format, nor will we penalize you if you submit an application in hard copy.

- If you encounter difficulties in using Grants.gov, please contact the Grants.gov Help Desk at: 1-800-518-4726, or by email at support@grants.gov to report the problem and obtain assistance.

- Checklists and registration brochures are maintained at http://www.grants.gov/GetStarted to assist you in the registration process.

- When submitting electronically via Grants.gov, applicants must comply with all due dates **AND** times referenced in *Section IV.3.*

Hard Copy Submission

Applicants that are submitting their application in paper format should submit one original and two copies of the complete application. The original and each of the two copies must include all required forms, certifications, assurances, and appendices, be signed by an authorized representative, have original signatures, and be unbound.

Non-Federal Reviewers

Since ACF will be using non-Federal reviewers in the review process, applicants have the option of omitting from the application copies (not the original) specific salary rates or amounts for individuals specified in the application budget as well as Social Security Numbers, if otherwise required for individuals. The copies may include summary salary information.

If applicants are submitting their application electronically, ACF will omit the same specific salary rate information from copies made for use during the review and selection process.

3. Submission Dates and Times:

Due Date For Letter of Intent: 06/12/2006

Due Date for Applications: 07/10/2006

Explanation of Due Dates

The due date for receipt of applications is referenced above. Applications received after 4:30 p.m., eastern time, on the due date will be classified as late and will not be considered in the current competition.

Margin notes:

Pay attention to bold text that includes recommendations and reminders. The words "strongly recommend," should signal actions that a competitive proposal writer will not ignore.

This grant application can be submitted electronically or via hardcopy.

Proposal writers must submit both a letter of intent and a proposal to apply for this grant.

FIGURE 7.8 *(continued)*

Applicants are responsible for ensuring that applications are mailed or hand-delivered or submitted electronically well in advance of the application due date and time.

Mail

Applications that are submitted by mail must be received no later than 4:30 p.m., eastern time, on the due date referenced above at the address listed in *Section IV.6.*

Hand Delivery

Applications hand carried by applicants, applicant couriers, other representatives of the applicant, or by overnight/express mail couriers must be received on or before the due date referenced above, between the hours of 8:00 a.m. and 4:30 p.m., eastern time, at the address referenced in *Section IV.6.*, between Monday and Friday (excluding Federal holidays).

Electronic Submission

Applications submitted electronically via Grants.gov must be submitted no later than 4:30 p.m., eastern time, on the due date referenced above.

ACF cannot accommodate transmission of applications by facsimile or email.

Late Applications

Applications that do not meet the requirements above are considered late applications. ACF shall notify each late applicant that its application will not be considered in the current competition.

ANY APPLICATION RECEIVED AFTER 4:30 P.M., EASTERN TIME, ON THE DUE DATE WILL NOT BE CONSIDERED FOR COMPETITION.

Extension of Deadlines

ACF may extend application deadlines when circumstances such as acts of God (floods, hurricanes, etc.) occur; when there are widespread disruptions of mail service; or in other rare cases. A determination to extend or waive deadline requirements rests with the Chief Grants Management Officer.

Receipt acknowledgement for application packages will not be provided to applicants who submit their package via mail, courier services, or by hand delivery. Applicants will receive an electronic acknowledgement for applications that are submitted via http://www.Grants.gov.

Checklist

You may use the checklist below as a guide when preparing your application package.

What to Submit	Required Content	Required Form or Format	When to Submit
Letter of Intent	See Section IV.2	Found in Section IV.2	30 days after publication.
SF-424	See Section IV.2	See http://www.acf.hhs.gov/programs/ofs/forms.htm	By application due date.
SF-424A	See Section IV.2	See http://www.acf.hhs.gov/programs/ofs/forms.htm	By application due date.
SF-424B	See Section IV.2	See http://www.acf.hhs.gov/programs/ofs/forms.htm	By application due date.
Assurances	See Section IV.2		By date of award.
Project Abstract	See Sections IV.2 and V	Found in Sections IV.2 and V	By application due date.
Table of Contents	See Section IV.2	Found in Section IV.2	By application due date.
Budget Narrative/Justification	See Sections IV.2 and V	Found in Sections IV.2 and V	By application due date.

> At the beginning of the writing process, proposal writers can use the checklist to decide what sections they'll need to include in the proposal. Of course, this list is also helpful at the end of the writing process to make sure that all pertinent information is included.

FIGURE 7.8   *(continued)*

Project Description	See Sections IV.2 and V	Found in Sections IV.2 and V	By application due date.
Support Letters	See Sections IV.2 and V	Found in Sections IV.2 and V	By application due date.
Third-Party Agreements	See Sections IV.2 and V	Found in Sections IV.2 and V	By application due date.
Proof of Non-Profit Status	See Section III.3	Found in Section III.3	By date of award.
SF-LLL Certification Regarding Lobbying	See Section IV.2	See http://www.acf.hhs.gov/programs/ofs/forms.htm	By date of award.
Certification Regarding Environmental Tobacco Smoke	See Section IV.2	See http://www.acf.hhs.gov/programs/ofs/forms.htm	By date of award.

Additional Forms

Private, non-profit organizations are encouraged to submit with their applications the survey located under *Grant Related Documents and Forms: Survey for Private, Non-Profit Grant Applicants, titled, Survey on Ensuring Equal Opportunity for Applicants,* at: http://www.acf.hhs.gov/programs/ofs/forms.htm.

What to Submit	Required Content	Required Form or Format	When to Submit
Survey for Private, Non-Profit Grant Applicants	See form.	See http://www.acf.hhs.gov/programs/ofs/forms.htm	By application due date.

FIGURE 7.8   *(continued)*

athletics, academics, sales, entertainment, etc.), others would prefer that their efforts have more definite and accessible goals. As a proposal writer, you must face the reality that even if you write a persuasive proposal according to the very specific proposal guidelines provided by a government agency, it may not be a winning proposal. For some proposal writers, this is a harsh reality that they would rather avoid; others realize that their chances of having a winning proposal will increase with experience and learning from proposal reviewer's feedback. We will discuss proposal review panels and their duties later in the chapter.

Length and Complexity of the Proposal Development Process

Although grant seeking and proposal writing can be rewarding and beneficial to both the government and society, it can also be a lengthy process that involves

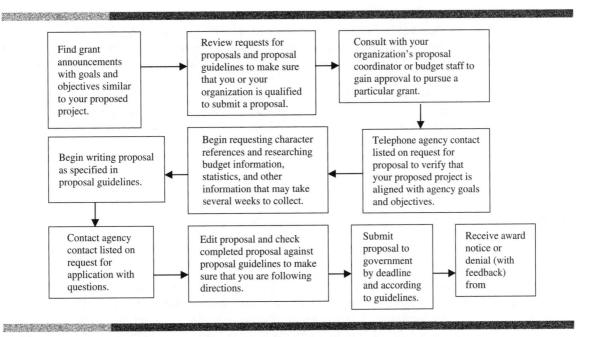

FIGURE 7.9   Grant Proposal Development Process.

several steps. Each step in Figure 7.9 can take days, weeks, or months to complete depending on the scope of the proposed project and the complexity of the targeted funding agency's proposal guidelines, willingness to provide technical assistance to the prospective applicant, and the time allotted for the proposal review and award process.

Personal Accountability and Ethical Dilemmas

Another interesting and unique aspect of proposal writing is the fact that the proposal writer is not always the grant applicant (person authorized to administer the proposed program with the prospective grant). Often, prospective applicants will hire a skilled or trained proposal writer to complete grant applications. The distinction between these two roles, writer and applicant, is important because there are personal and ethical issues that the applicant is responsible for and, thus, although the applicant might not write the proposal, both writer and applicant must be involved in the proposal writing process. For example, in the proposal guidelines in Figure 7.8, there is a reference to federal laws related to smoking prohibition and discrimination that the applicant must be willing to abide by (U.S. Department of Health and Human Services). Both the proposal writer and applicant should be aware of these stipulations in writing the proposal and, if awarded the grant, in the implementation of the funded project. The applicant should also acknowledge their inherent vulnerability in trusting another person to write without plagiarism, without fabricating research, and without violating the applicant's standards of ethical behavior.

If the grant applicant decides to write the proposal without the help of another writer, there are of course issues of ethics and honesty that the applicant should adhere to, regardless of temptations to exaggerate or even fabricate data or information to enhance the chances of funding.

Audience for Government Proposals

At this point, we've mentioned quite a few government agencies that fund proposal writers and applicants through federal agencies and state funding sources. We've provided examples of funding opportunities presented by the Office of Public Health and Science, National Institutes of Health, Environmental Protection Agency, Department of Education, Department of Health and Human Services Administration, even the State of New York's Division of Criminal Justice Services to demonstrate the breadth of government funding available to applicants. In addition to the numerous state and city agencies with funding capabilities, federal agencies provide funding opportunities. Take a look at the list of federal agencies listed on Grants.gov in Figure 7.10.

When these agencies announce funding opportunities through requests for applications and proposal guidelines, they are prepared to receive numerous proposals and are responsible for reviewing each proposal that meets their guidelines and applicant qualifications, selecting the best proposals for grant awards, and providing feedback to those proposal writers who do not win the award. To review grant proposals, government funding agencies select a group of professionals and/or community representatives with some expertise in the program or policy area addressed in the grant announcement. Proposal review panels or teams then use established criteria to evaluate proposals to determine which proposals are worthy of award. Take a look at the excerpt in Figure 7.11 from the 2006 National Science Foundation Proposal Review schedule.

Once the reviewers make their selections and government agencies award grants to applicants, the challenging work of actually implementing the proposed projects finally begins. If the winning proposal was comprehensive and clear, the document can serve as a reference to help the grant winner in scheduling and completing relevant tasks, purchasing necessary materials, managing grant funds, hiring of staff, and of course, staying focused on the objectives of the project. If you do not win the grant, you can certainly benefit from reading proposal reviewer's feedback and comments that explain the strengths and weaknesses of your proposal. Understanding your audience and their preferences is critical in learning to write persuasive proposals.

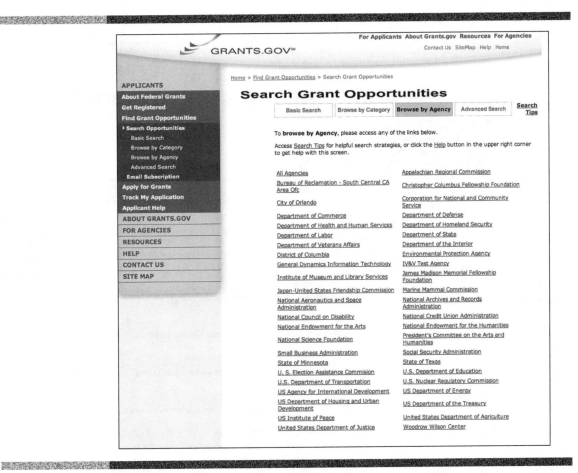

FIGURE 7.10 Grants.gov "Search Grant Opportunities: Browse by agency."
Source: http://www.grants.gov/search/agency.gov

Summary and Looking Forward

In this chapter, we have attempted to introduce you to a very complex, yet important genre of technical communication that is beneficial to government agencies as well as the public. To walk you through the grant announcement and proposal development processes, we often referenced government websites that make this information available to the public. In the next chapter, we will discuss government websites, which is another genre of technical communication that serves the needs of both government agencies and the public.

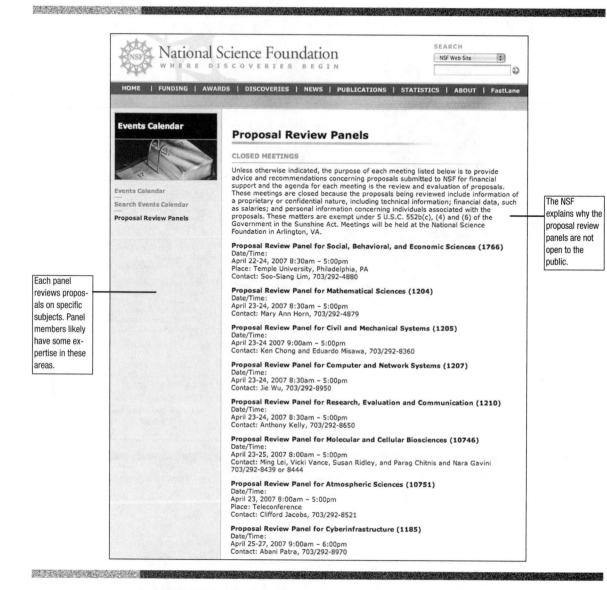

Each panel reviews proposals on specific subjects. Panel members likely have some expertise in these areas.

The NSF explains why the proposal review panels are not open to the public.

FIGURE 7.11   NSF.gov "Proposal Review Panels."   Source: http://www.nsf.gov/events/advisory.jsp

Activities and Assignments

1. **Individual Internet Activity:** Search www.grants.gov or another free government grant portal to find a RFA with proposal guidelines. Try to find an RFA that addresses a policy area of interest to you. Use the following questions to determine the level of difficulty a prospective applicant might experience when applying for this grant. Be prepared to discuss your findings with your classmates.

   a. Who is the audience for the RFA?
   b. Does the RFA contain language appropriate for an expert or nonexpert audience?
   c. What is the purpose of the grant?
   d. Who is eligible to apply for the grant? What qualifications or credentials are required?
   e. Are the proposal guidelines available online? If so, are the proposal guidelines easy to understand?
   f. Does the agency offer technical assistance through an agency contact person?

2. **Individual Exercise:** Search the *Federal Register* to find at least one RFA related to a policy issue of interest to you. Use the proposal guidelines to create a checklist or outline that would help you to write a competitive grant proposal. To create this proposal writing tool, complete the following tasks:

   a. Search the proposal guidelines for mention of particular sections that the proposal reviewers will expect to see. Examples of these sections include abstract, introduction, problem statement, budgets, proposed activities, evaluation section, and qualifications. These sections will serve as section headers in your proposal.
   b. After you've identified the sections, arrange the sections in your proposal outline in the same order that they appear in the proposal guidelines.
   c. Under each section, brainstorm or list the data or evidence that you believe proposal reviewers will find persuasive. For example, under the "introduction" section, jot down a list of important facts about your organization or project that would give the proposal audience the background information that they need.
   d. Make a list of forms or attachments that you are required to include in the proposal.
   e. If available, consult proposal writing resources listed on the funding agency's website for help with unfamiliar terminology in the proposal guidelines or on forms.

3. **Group Exercise:** Find four RFAs, including proposal guidelines, from four different government agencies. As a group, analyze these four documents and identify the following:

   a. How are the sets of proposal guidelines similar? What common information do the government agencies expect to see in the proposals? Do the request for applications and accompanying proposal guidelines have similarities in language, content, or tone?

b. How are the sets of proposal guidelines different? Identify information, forms, or sections of proposals requested in RFAs for some agencies that are not mentioned in other agency RFAs.

c. Pretend that you are a fictional government agency that provides a specific good or service to your community. Use the information that you collected from your analysis in *a* and *b* (both similarities and differences) to develop a fictional RFA (including proposal guidelines) soliciting competitive proposals. Your audience and potential applicants should include individuals, businesses, and nonprofit groups from your community.

Works Cited

Collins, Susan. "Grant Information: Constituent Services." 1 Aug. 2006 <http://collins.senate.gov/public/continue.cfm?FuseAction=ConstituentServices.GrantInformation>.

Johnson, William C. *Public Administration: Policy, Politics, and Practice*. Guilford, Connecticut: The Dushkin Publishing Group, Inc. 1992.

National Institute of Neurological Disorders and Stroke. "NINDS Funding Opportunities: Know the Differences." 5 Jan. 2007 <http://www.ninds.nih.gov/funding/differences.htm>.

"Notice of Availability of State and Federal Funds." *New York State Register* 11 Jan. 2006. Division of Criminal Justice Service. 1 Aug. 2006 <http://www.dos.state.ny.us/info/register/2006/jan11/pdfs/availability.pdf>.

Office of Research Integrity. "About ORI." U.S. Department of Health and Human Services. 1 Aug. 2006 <http://ori.dhhs.gov/about/index.shtml>.

"Proposal Review Panels." *National Science Foundation*. 1 Aug. 2006 <http://www.nsf.gov/events/advisory.jsp>.

U.S. Department of Education. "Department of Education Funding Opportunities." 1 Aug. 2006 <http://www.ed.gov/fund/landing.jhtml?src=ln>.

U.S. Environmental Protection Agency. "EPA Awards Database." 1 Aug. 2006 <http://yosemite.epa.gov/oarm/igms_egf.nsf/recipient2?OpenView>.

U.S. Department of Health and Human Services. "About Grants.gov." 1 Aug. 2006 <http://www.grants.gov/aboutgrants/about_grants_gov.jsp>.

—. "Grants.gov homepage." 1 Aug 2006. <http://www.grants.gov>.

—. "Search Grant Opportunities: Browse by Agency." 1 Aug. 2006 <http://www.grants.gov/search/agency.do>.

—. "Services to Unaccompanied Alien Children." 1 Aug. 2006 <http://www.acf.hhs.gov/grants/open/HHS-2006-ACF-ORR-ZU-0007.html>.

8

Government Websites

In 2004, the Pew Internet & American Life Project research study reported that, excluding the act of turning in a tax return, more than half of all Americans contact the government in a given year (Horrigan iii). With the U.S. population breaking the 300 million mark in 2006 that means some 150 million people contact the government in a given year.

In July 2003, the time of the study, 77% of Internet users, or 97 million Americans, went online to search for information from government agencies or to communicate with them. This was a 50% increase from the same time in 2002 (Horrigan v). Thirty-five percent of Internet users and nonusers contacted state government, 32% contacted federal government, 19% contacted local government, and 7% contacted a combination of levels of government (Horrigan 4).

These are a few of the findings from the Pew research report, "How Americans Get in Touch with Government," spearheaded by John B. Horrigan, Senior Research Specialist, of 2,925 Americans, aged 18 and older, about how Americans contact their government—by telephone, website, in person, email, or letter. Although more people are turning to the Internet and government websites for information, to solve problems, and complete transactions, there are large segments of the population who cannot or do not. In 2003, nearly one-third of Americans did not have Internet access. Even Internet users indicated they preferred to use the telephone in contacting the government, especially with sensitive personal issues like taxes, urgent, or complex matters (i).

About 80% of the disabled in the survey preferred to contact the government by phone, in person, or letter, not online (14–15). Regardless of Internet use, the education and race of the users contributed to how many had successful encounters with government. Sixty-eight percent of the college graduates felt they had a successful encounter with the government, but only 48% of those with a less than a high school education said

	2000	2001	2002	2003	2004	2005	2006
Phone Contact Info.	91%	94%	96%	--	--	--	--
Address Info	88	93	95	--	--	--	--
Links to other Sites	80	69	71	--	--	--	--
Publications	74	93	93	98	98	98	98
Databases	42	54	57	80	87	67	82
Audio Clips	5	6	6	8	17	12	10
Video Clips	4	9	8	10	21	18	28

TABLE 8.1   Percentage of Websites Offering Publications and Databases.

Source: "State and Federal E-Government in the United States, 2006:4." http://www.insidepolitics.org/egovt06us.pdf

they had a successful encounter. In addition, while 66% of whites had a successful result with their last contact with government, only 51% of non-Hispanic blacks and 55% of Hispanics had a successful result (9).

In another research study of e-government, "State and Federal E-Government in the United States, 2006," Darrell M. West, the John Hazen Professor of Public Policy and Political Science of the Taubman Center for Public Policy at Brown University, compared features that are available online through state and federal government websites, using a detailed analysis of 1,503 state websites and 48 federal government legislative and executive sites, and 13 federal court sites—a total of 1,564 sites—and compared the 2006 results with those from the years 2000–2005.

The report says, "In looking at the availability of basic information at American government websites, we found that access to publications and databases is excellent. Ninety-eight percent of the sites provide access to publications (the same as [2005], while 82% have databases, compared to 67% in 2005)" (West 4). In 2000, only 74% had access to publications, while only 42% had access to databases.

West tallied a number of categories of characteristics of sites, and the top five federal government sites in order were USA.gov, Department of Agriculture, Department of Housing and Urban Development, Department of Commerce, and Department of the Treasury, and the top five state sites in order were Texas, New Jersey, Oregon, Michigan, and Utah. Table 8.1 compares the features in the state and federal government websites from 2000 to 2006.

A summary of other key findings are these:

■ Fifty-four percent of federal sites (up from 44% [in 2005] and 43% of state sites (up from 40% [in 2005]) met the **World Wide Web Consortium (W3C)** disability guidelines.

■ Thirty percent of the sites offer some type of foreign language translation, up from 18% the year before.

■ Sixty-four percent of government websites are written at the twelfth-grade reading level, which is a much higher level than most Americans read.

■ One percent of the sites are accessible through personal digital assistants, pagers, or mobile phones, which is the same as 2005 (West 3).

We begin this chapter with these two studies of electronic or "e"-government because they indicate some important aspects about government websites:

1. The enormous growth in numbers of people looking for government information online
2. The effect of the Internet on people's increased interactivity with the government
3. The growth in the types of online transaction activities and documents available to online users
4. The importance of personal contact, on the telephone or in person, to solve sensitive, urgent, or complex matters
5. The large number of people who are left out of the online information because of disability and/or socioeconomic barriers

The findings from these studies represent some of the potential and problems for government websites. There are literally hundreds of books, articles, and websites offering information and advice on writing and designing websites. A single chapter about government websites cannot cover in detail any one aspect of website development; however, because our text focuses on writing for the government, we show how the principles of knowing an audience, having a clear purpose, and understanding the cultural context of a website come into play in writing and designing effective government websites. This chapter is an introduction to writing and designing government websites for the lone webmaster for a small town community website, or for someone starting as part of a team for a large federal government agency website.

Because the writing and designing of websites are so closely related, the chapter also presents introductory information about website designing. Throughout this chapter we may refer to writers, designers, developers, and website masters, in interchangeable ways. A website for a small town, for instance, can be planned, written, designed, and maintained by one person, who may be called a "webmaster," while another person may be one of many on a large team of a large website. Those large sites could include positions with titles such as web project manager, content manager, graphic designer, editor, infrastructure manager, programmer, documentation specialist, technical support technician, and usability specialist. Regardless of where they work, knowledgeable website writers, designers, and developers understand that these websites are more than information portals; they are a means for Americans to be closer to and more involved with their government.

Audience, Purpose, and Cultural Contexts

Whatever the title or position of the person working on a website, his or her knowledge of the audience and its needs are vital to creating an effective site. We will discuss audience awareness and purpose in upcoming sections of this chapter, but the cultural context of the website is very important also. The research studies at the beginning of the chapter speak to the cultural environment that government website developers work in today, and just as with paper documents, a website's content and design are influenced by the culture of the time in which it is created and presented, and, in turn, website change and development can affect culture. For example, among the factors affecting website content and design are changes in technology available to users. It has only been in the last decade that **Portable Document Format Files (PDFs)** have been easily made available and **broadband** fast access has been able to reach more Americans. At the same time, the fact that there is so much more information online means Americans expect their government websites to increasingly provide current, readily available information and interactive features. In a similar fashion, laws change over time and what was acceptable practice say 20 years ago is no longer.

Website developers for governmental entities need to keep abreast of new rules and regulations pertaining to online communication. Not only are accessibility requirements for the disabled for government websites in place now; as the percentage of the population grows older and disabilities increase, there will be the need to make disability accommodation common practice for all new software, multimedia, and other yet-to-be-developed technological devices.

Genre and Purpose

Genres of Websites

As we discussed in previous chapters, the genre of a document and the purpose for which it is written are inextricably linked. This is the same for websites. Website developers typically spend a lot of time looking at other sites to see what has worked and become standard categories of information, such as homepages with "About Us" or "**FAQs**," and they then incorporate those features into sites because users have become familiar with them. Over time these features evolve into *genres*—the conventions of websites that users expect. But genres can also change over time, especially with emerging technologies, and savvy website developers, who observe how information can be provided in more useful, clear, and effective ways, will change the features and begin to transform the genre of websites. What's more, it is important to know that websites can fall into more than one genre. In *Principles of Web Design*, David K. Farkas and Jean B. Farkas list these genres for websites:

Education such as online tutorials and instruction

Entertainment for celebrity news, sports, and games

News, public information, and specialized information

E-commerce for selling, marketing, and promotion

Web portals, specialized websites that are starting points for web users

Persuasive sites to promote political, social, religious, and cultural matters

Community building and sustaining for users with specialized interests

Personal and artistic expressive sites (5–8).

Purpose

The purpose of government websites is chiefly to provide public information, but they can educate users, build and sustain community, and even at times provide space for artistic expression. For example, health agency websites could provide information on a specific cancer such as breast cancer, have an illustration for women on the procedure for doing a breast cancer self-exam, and also provide a place for cancer survivors to post poetry and other personal expressions about their experiences.

Our textbook has emphasized that writing is inherently rhetorical and persuasive: effective writing draws in its readers because it meets their needs. However, the kind of persuasion listed above as a genre is an overt politically motivated approach with the expressed purpose of validating or changing someone's beliefs. As you can imagine, government web content writers and designers need to be very careful not to impose their own political, social, and religious views on a government website. Because government sites are paid for by tax dollars, they cannot be forums for web content writers and designers' personal, political, social, or religious views. There are numerous other legal and ethical matters to take into consideration when writing, designing, and developing a government site, which will be more fully discussed later in the chapter. Regardless of the genre, though, each site needs to work hand in hand with the mission of the agency or organization; the content and design of a website represents the agency or organization to its constituency.

As the numbers of Americans looking for government information online soared, the federal government's Interagency Committee on Government Information (ICGI) in 2004, established the Web Content Management Working Group, now called the Web Managers Advisory Committee, a group of about 40 senior web managers representing every cabinet-level agency, some independent agencies, and the judicial and legislative branches. The purpose of the group is to recommend policies and procedures for all federal public websites and to ensure that sites comply with the 2002 E-Government Act, which outlines how to improve methods by which government information is "organized, preserved, and made accessible to the public" including information on the Internet (http://www.archives.gov). The group's goals include enhancing the content of government websites so they are "on par with the best websites in the world" (http://www.usa.gov/webcontent/). They manage a website, called Webcontent.gov, which provides information, advice, and resources for federal government web managers. The Advisory Board includes representatives from agencies as diverse as the Centers for Disease Control and Prevention, Department of Defense, Department of Housing and Urban Development, Department of Homeland Security, Department of Labor, Federal Aviation Administration, the Library of Congress, National Aeronautics and Space Administration, Office of the Comptroller, and the U.S. Forest Service (http://www.usa.gov/webcontent/). Although this website is directed to federal governments websites, it offers resources and information useful to website development at any level of government.

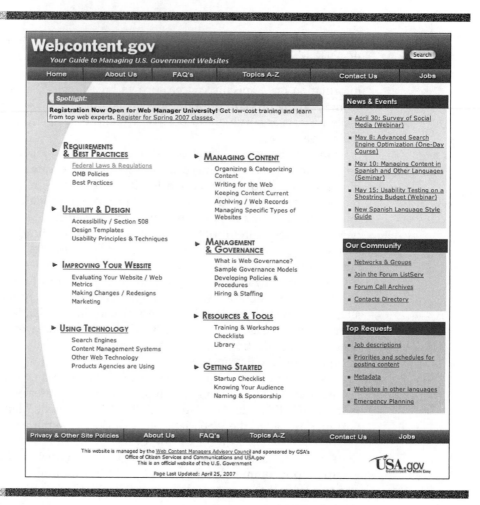

FIGURE 8.1   Source: Webcontent.gov. http://www.usa.gov/webcontent/

Writing Website Content

How Users Read Websites

For the web content writer's perspective, one of the most important things to know is that people do not go to websites intending to read everything closely and carefully. Instead, eye-tracking research—in which research participants wear headgear with cameras that track their eye movements as they move across websites—has shown the opposite; the vast majority of people scan sites for the information that meets their needs (Nielsen, "How Users Read"). If users are looking for longer documents, they usually save them or print them for more comfortable reading (Lynch and Horton). However, individuals with lower reading levels may be an important exception to this predictable scanning behavior in reading websites. Researchers found that individuals with lower reading levels did not scan but read word for word, "plowing" carefully through the text (Nielsen "Lower-Literacy Readers").

Because of how users read and view websites, content is written in a way different from the conventional linear sequential writing style that you may be used to doing. A key strategy for writing web content is to do **"chunking"** of information—placing information and text together in like groups so that they can be placed appropriately on a webpage or within a website. "Concise chunks of information are better suited to the computer screen, which provides a limited view of long documents. Long web pages tend to disorient readers; they require users to scroll long distances and to remember what is off-screen (Lynch and Horton). Chunking writing style and other writing strategies will be discussed in detail later in the chapter.

Readability Analysis of Websites

West's study at the opening of the chapter showed that 64% of the websites were written at a twelfth grade level, which is higher than the average citizen reads. West cites that about half of Americans read at the eighth grade level. "Only 14% [of the sites] fell at the eighth grade level or below, which is the reading level of half the American public, compared to 10% [in 2005]" (6). West analyzed reading levels using the Flesch-Kincaid test, which rates word syllables and sentence length on a 100-point scale with 100 being the easiest to understand. Then the test evaluates the grade level of a passage, and a score of 8.0, means an eighth grade reading level. For some writers the idea of "dumbing down" prose may sound distasteful, but effective writers understand the importance of writing to meet the needs of the reader.

Plain Language Movement

Because of the importance of the readability of text for websites, web content writers and designers need to write in "plain language." As we discussed earlier in the book, the Plain Language Movement consists of individuals concerned about how well government writing is read and understood. The Plain Language Movement has been around for many decades, but in 1998, President Bill Clinton wrote an Executive Memo requiring agencies to write in plain language. The Plain Language (also called Plain English) website describes it as "communication your audience can understand the first time they read or hear it. Language that is plain to one set of readers may not be plain to others. Written material is in plain language if your audience can find what they need, understand what they find, and use what they find to meet their needs. . . . No one technique defines plain language. Rather, plain language is defined by results—it is easy to read, understand, and use" (http://plainlanguage.gov/whatisPL/index.cfm).

Writing in plain language not only helps the reader, it also helps government employees because it decreases the number of phone calls, letters, and documents that need to be attended to because readers do not understand a message.

Army Regulations:

G2/Counterintelligence and Security Division, Department of the Army, Handbook Information Security Program Handbook

This rewritten version of an Army Information Security manual makes good use of sub-sections and white space and eliminates irrelevant information.

Before

Methods of Transmission or Transportation: 7-301. Secret Information.

Administrative procedures shall be established by each DoD Component for controlling Secret information and material originated or received by an activity; distributed or routed to a sub-element of such activity; and disposed of by the activity by transfer of custody or destruction. The control system for Secret information must be determined by a practical balance of security and operating efficiency and must meet the following minimum requirements:

 a. It must provide a means to ensure that Secret material sent outside a major subordinate element (the activity) of the DoD Component concerned has been delivered to the intended recipient...
 b. It must provide a record of receipt and dispatch of Secret material by each major subordinate element. The dispatch record requirement may be satisfied when the distribution of Secret material is evident and addressees or distribution lists for classified documentation...
 c. Records of receipt and dispatch for Secret material shall be retained for a minimum of 2 years...

After

Transmission, Methods: 4-102. Secret.

 A. You may send secret information by US Registered Postal Service mail within and between the United States and its Territories.
 B. You may use Federal Express and U.S. Post Service Express Mail for transmitting secret mail within the United States and between the United States and its Territories under the following STRICT condition security:
  1. Mail should meet the weight and size limits of the carrier used.
  2. You should follow the inner wrappings and receipt requirements in this handbook.
  3. You should ensure delivery by Friday so that the carrier is not in possession of the package over the weekend.

FIGURE 8.2   Before and After Army Regulations. Source: Plainlanguage.gov. http://www.plainlanguage.gov/examples/before_after/govregarmy.cfm

Furthermore, there has been litigation about overly complex language in government. In Walters v. Reno, in 1998, the U.S. 9th Circuit Court of Appeals found that the Immigration and Naturalization Service forms were so confusing and misleading that they violated a person's due process rights. Figure 8.2 is a comparison of an excerpt from a U.S. Department of Army *Information Security Program Handbook* before and after writers revised it in plain language.

Plain Language advocates say that it is even more important that government website content be written in plain language because users typically scan website content rather than reading it closely, and the typical reader of government websites are looking for information to help them complete tasks—this makes users want to find the information quickly in order to act quickly (http://www.plainlanguage.gov/whyPL/web_writing/index.cfm).

Languages Other Than English

West's study also found that "[t]hirty % of the sites offered some type of foreign language translation, up from 18% [in 2005]" (3). Increasingly government websites are providing translations of information for people who are non-English speakers or speak English as a second language. One of the requirements for federal websites is to provide information to those with limited English proficiency. The number of people who are not proficient in English is growing dramatically every year. The 2000 U.S. Census reports more than 20 million people in the United States consider themselves as not speaking English "well" or "very well" or they do not speak English at all. The federal government's Webcontent.gov recommends that web developers determine how much information needs to be provided in other languages based on an assessment of their website users. Government website developers should provide information for individuals who are not proficient in English because it is required for government sites, because those individuals are entitled to government services, and because it encourages their participation in government.

Writing Techniques for the Web

As we have seen, research on how users read websites, the importance of plain language, and the reading levels of most Americans make writing for the web different from the longer expository, linear, sequential writing style you may be familiar with reading and doing. Web writing has some qualities similar to the inverted journalism pyramid style of writing and the conventions of language usage for publications for a widespread readership.

The homepage from the National Institutes of Health clinical trials website, Figure 8.3, has technical materials for medical professionals but the language, navigation, and description is appropriate for the general public (http://www.usa.gov/webcontent/). The Clinicaltrials.gov website contains information on 31,700 clinical studies by the National Institutes of Health, other federal agencies, and private industries in 50 states and 130 countries. There are eleven million page views with 29,000 visits daily (http://clinicaltrials.gov).

Effective web writing

- Places the main idea first and the remaining ideas in priority
- Has a conversational tone, uses "you" when appropriate
- Uses straightforward, concrete words, not complex wording or jargon
- Anticipates readers' questions and provides answers
- Has short (even one-sentence) paragraphs
- Has headings to grab the reader's attention and segment information

- Uses headings as signals to the reader where to go next
- Has more headings but less information under each heading
- Has the majority of sentences in active voice (not passive voice)
- Uses specific examples to explain information
- Is visually pleasing

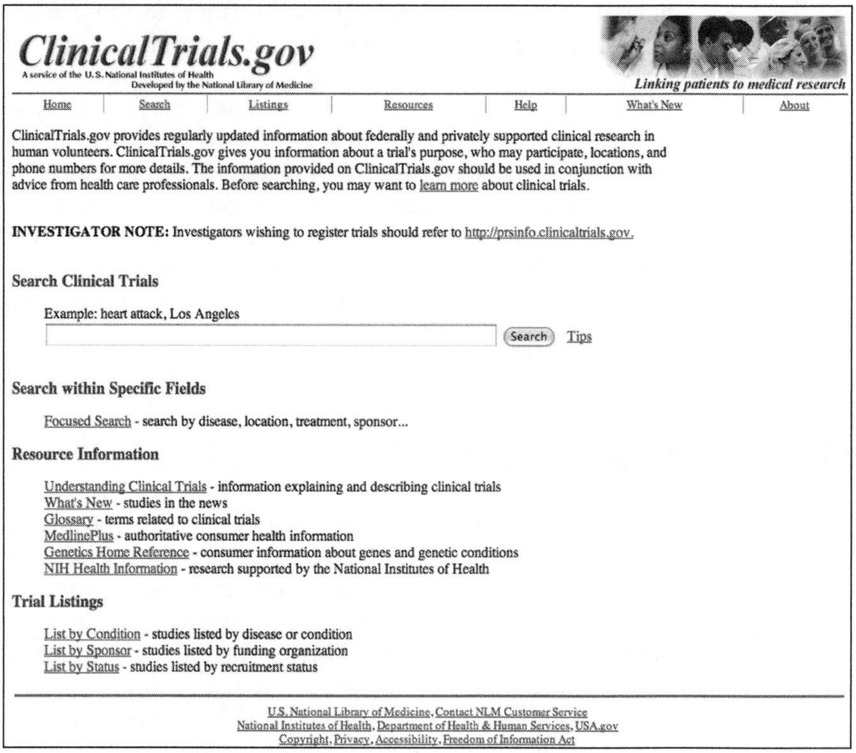

FIGURE 8.3   Source: ClinicalTrials.gov website. http://clinicaltrials.gov

The Clinicaltrials.gov homepage categorizes thousands of topics of information within a few clear headings and subheadings. Notice the introductory section consists of only five sentences and uses *you*. The language is clear and simple. The navigation bar at the top lists categories of information that users would be interested in finding. The search feature is distinctive, and the tip: "Example: heart attack, Los Angeles" lets the user know that she or he can type in a familiar medical term to find information. There is plenty of white space to make the page seem approachable rather than overly busy with an overwhelming amount of choices.

Chunking Style of Writing

As mentioned earlier, writing for websites is not the conventional expository style that you may be used to writing. "Chunking" information means grouping text into sentences, paragraphs, sections, or topics, and/or visuals that relate to each other, similar to writing strong paragraphs. Later in the chapter when we discuss **Information Architecture,** these chunks (or **nodes** as they can be called) pertain to one webpage in a conceptual website diagram drawing, but for the sake of writing and designing webpages, chunking means pieces of related information which

- appear within one webpage and/or
- are spread out through different webpages, and/or
- are used for deciding where links will be placed in the site.

One approach to chunking information and visuals and deciding where they go on a website is the journalism technique of answering *who, what, when, where, why,* and *how.*

1. *Who* is the primary audience for this material? Is it just about everyone who comes to the website or only a small segment?
   If it is for the typical website user perhaps it belongs on the homepage. If it is for someone who would only come to the site occasionally then it could go several levels down in the website hierarchy.
2. *What* do the users need to know? Does it answer important questions or solve major problems for the site's constituency, or is the information tangential to the users' needs?
   If it is vital information, then it needs to go on or near the homepage. If it is not vital then it goes down in the website hierarchy or maybe not at all on the site.
3. *When* do users need to know this information? Is it urgent, does it have a deadline, or does it belong in the website archives, where users can find it by searching the archives?
   If it is urgent, then it goes on the homepage. If it is historical, then it goes in the site's archives.
4. *Where* are users likely to go to find this information, on your website or on another?
   If there is useful information on other websites, linking to those maybe an answer to assist readers.
5. *Why* is this information useful?
   This kind of question helps you sort out information that may not even be on the website or redundant to what is already there.
6. *How* is this information useful? Does it solve a problem? Does it instruct? Does it update older information?
   These are also factors in deciding how to present information. If it solves a problem that many users have, maybe it belongs on the Frequently Asked Questions (FAQ) page. If it is instructional, then it may be presented as a step-by-step process. If it updates important older information, maybe there needs to be an alert placed on the homepage, or if it is not so important a note on the page where the information was before—or simply changing the update information at the bottom of a webpage may suffice.

Card Sorting as Organizing

Another challenge in developing web content is organizing content—deciding what belongs as a particular chunk or part of a chunk and how users might prioritize and/or categorize different chunks of information themselves. One method for organizing content is by index card sorting or "sticky notes" (Farkas and Farkas 54), in which users of the site or potential users review topics from a website on index cards, and then group the various topics on the cards into categories that makes sense to them. There are two kinds of card-sorting activities—an open sort, in which participants decide on the categories, and a closed sort, in which they put the cards into predetermined categories. Sometimes a closed sort can come after an open sort, which is used to create the categories. This kind of activity helps content developers understand what is important to users. It can be a central point for creating and up-dating a homepage and second-and lower-level pages (http://usability.gov/) as well as a means of creating a prototype or model of your website. Website prototypes can be as informal as a series of drawings or a few representative pages so users can click through them to try them, or as formal as a fully functioning website.

Chunking and Sorting Activity Example

Let's begin with a simple chunking and sorting activity to clarify the process. Suppose Beth McDonald is a student in a course like yours on a large campus in the Midwest. She and her classmates are pretending to create their own government agency and its website to advise future students about this course. They take stock of everything that might be helpful for future students to know: prerequisites for the course, assignment requirements, books and materials, faculty informa-tion, date, time, location of class meeting, class and campus resources, computer hardware and software needs, other media equipment, and even types of desks in the room. They write each topic onto sticky notes as the "chunks" of content for a website.

Then they begin to sort through the items to determine the most important ones among them. They decide that prerequisites, assignments, and faculty infor-mation would be at the top of the list. But what about something like location? It would certainly be important but not as important as these other items. Therefore, it would go in the second level of priority, and in this way, they go, about sorting and prioritizing.

After the first sort, they discuss location and realize that, although location is not at the top of the priority list, it is important—not only for the obvious reason that students need to know where they are going to go to class, but they also need to know how to reach it to get to class on time. On such a large campus classes can be miles apart, and they need to know how long it takes to walk or if they need to ride the campus buses. So Beth and her classmates decide to expand this location topic to include not just the address but also a photo of the building where the class meets, Stanford Hall.

They take it further by deciding to include an interactive map of the campus that has the times listed that it takes to get from one building to the next. So the chunking and sorting on the sticky notes and discussion looks like the flowchart shown in Figure 8.4.

Content Writing, Visual Thinking, and Headings

Because web content is both written and visual, writers should be thinking of ways to communicate messages visually as well as in text to create "scannable text"

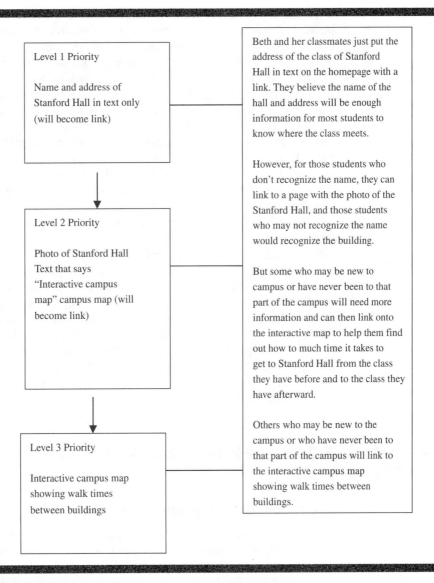

FIGURE 8.4   Chunking and Sorting Activity Example

(Nielsen "How Users Read"). Consider what graphics and pictures will help communicate your message. Some of the usual visual aids to web writing are meaningful **headings** and subheadings, bulleted lists, and highlighted keywords for links or variation in colors (Nielsen "How Users Read"). An upcoming section of this chapter shows some other common types of graphics that have been used in print publications and are now found frequently on the web. The visual display section is to spur your thinking on other visuals that could help communicate a message.

Headings and subheadings have become especially important in websites because of how people seek information. Effective websites have meaningful and useful headings and subheadings for content comprehension. Headings catch readers' attention and help direct them quickly to the information they need. Consistency among the headings is also important for comprehension. Headings should be short enough to provide the needed information but not too short to compromise clarity. Researcher Ginny Redish says, "[H]eadings need to make connections to the user. Questions are better as headings than are nouns or noun phrases. People come to documents with questions so raising the question creates the link that helps users say 'yes, this is where I want to be; this is what I need to read'. . . single nouns or noun phrases that have no people and no verbs in them do not do well as headings. However, this does not mean that questions are always the best type of heading" ("Headings").

When people are trying to do tasks, action verbs with phrases are the best headings for the steps of instructions. Redish says, "Other headings that work well are verb phrases such as 'Filling out the Application'; sentences such as 'You must Get a Permit to Operate a Center,' and phrases that have pronouns and verbs, such as 'What You Must Do First.'" She also recommends that headings be parallel in structure at the level of the heading. For example, all headings at the top level could be questions, and then subheadings could begin with verbs. Although it is best to avoid nouns or noun phrases for headings, if they are specific titles and proper names, or terms that are self-evident to the reader, then they may work too. For example, in the Clinicaltrials.gov website homepage earlier in the chapter the headings are clear about what kinds of information to expect when a user clicks on the link.

Methods of Getting to Know Your Audiences and Their Needs

Feedback, Usability, and Personas

Throughout the website development process, website developers need to be in contact with their audiences to receive feedback. Depending on what information web developers are looking for, how much time they have, and what their budget offers, feedback can be informal or formal or a combination. Web developers can collect information and data on their audiences to better understand their needs with these approaches:

- Surveys asking a variety of questions from demographic data to basic information as to why they come to a site
- Focus groups, which are small groups that can provide useful insights into the site's effectiveness
- Market research collected and analyzed by experts
- Web server logs providing data about who is coming to the site and from where
- Email, phone calls, letters, and other types of contact with the public

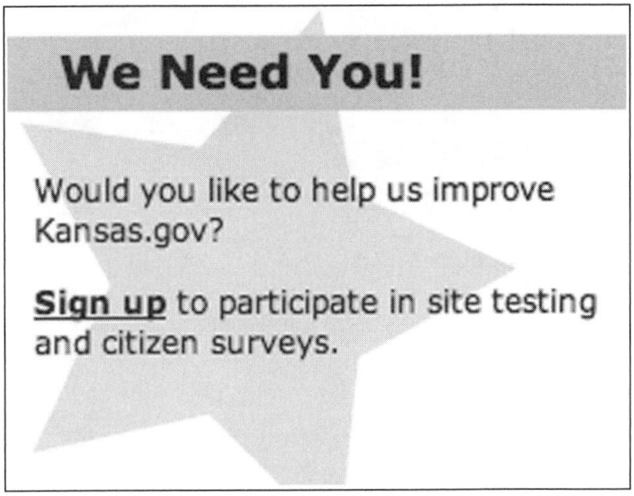

FIGURE 8.5   Source: Kansas government website. http://www.state.ks.us

- Other web content managers' experience, which you can solicit during individual email conversations, organizational meetings, or on listservs

The following two examples are also informal ways to get to know an audience and its needs. Usability.gov website says this about contextual interviews:

> Contextual interviews are natural and realistic. They are also usually quite informal. In a contextual interview, you watch and listen as the user does his or her own work. You don't usually impose tasks or scenarios on the user. The observer listens to the user but may also ask clarifying questions and probe to gain greater understanding of what the user is doing and thinking. The results are usually qualitative rather than quantitative. (http://usability.gov/methods/contextual.html)

Figure 8.5 is from the State of Kansas homepage to get feedback on how well a website is working. They were asking users to participate in site testing and surveys. This is an informal but quick and easy feedback method.

Usability Testing

Usability testing is research on how users or potential users of a website, software program, hardware device, or other type of technology are able to quickly and easily find the information they need, work the device, or apply the software to their needs. The research approach draws from the idea of "user-centered design," meaning that the website matches the needs of the audience or user. In a kind of "grass roots" strategy, this approach is about meeting users' needs to determine whether the website, software, hardware, and so forth "works"—instead of writers and designers working in isolation and distanced from users. Usability testing tends to be

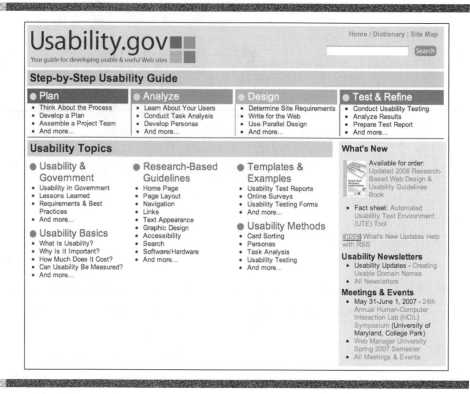

FIGURE 8.6   Source: Webcontent.gov. http://www.usa.gov/webcontext/

formal research strategies and methodologies, such as with users in computer laboratory testing situations while testers watch through one-way mirrors and/or computer screens, but for small and beginning efforts website developers can get useful feedback in even informal situations, such as users completing surveys.

Usability testing can uncover a wide array of trouble spots to help improve a website, from large-scale changes like overhauling the navigation procedure to fine-tuning the prose. It can also pinpoint what is useful and effective on a website. Web developers should involve users of the site from the planning to the maintenance to the evaluation to the redesign stage. For more information, there is a federal government website devoted to usability matters. (See Figure 8.6.)

Personas

One of the results of feedback and usability testing is that web developers can create a composite of the typical website user; this is called a "**persona**." The persona can include a fictional name and demographic characteristics such as age, education, ethnicity, family status, professional background, and expertise. Some site developers even use a photo from clip-art or licensed stock files to create a visual image of the person for web team members. Having a persona to talk about and focus on keeps the writers and designers attentive to their user. Many government sites service users from different backgrounds, so there can be a number of different personas. For example, the persona for the user of a website section with highly technical documents would be dissimilar to that of a children's section of a website. Furthermore, web teams have to follow trends in changes in who might be users of sites. An example would be that during natural disasters the types of people seeking information from a site about emergencies could be different from those users of the site on a typical day.

Applying Personas   The U.S. Department of Agriculture *Web Presence Initiative Audience Analysis* is a report on how the agency created and uses customer personas. The report says that personas serve as representations of its customer groups to create a shared understanding of the USDA's targeted audiences. Personas "help ensure the most important customer groups are adequately served, simplify design decisions by focusing on customers' needs, … provide a disciplined approach to [website] design" (N.1). The methodology for creating the personas, says the report, was from input from key stakeholders—with most of the data from the USDA Marketing and Grower Relations Assessment, USDA eGovernment Readiness Assessment, ERS User Personas, US Census Bureau data, FNS.USDA.gov., and the NASS Census of Agriculture 1977. Figures 8.7–8.9 show three of 11 personas from the report.

PRODUCERS:
PHILIP MACON USER PERSONA

Philip is a 53-year-old farmer in Walla Walla, Washington. He has a high school education, but was always more interested in farming than academics. He doesn't like getting tied up with paperwork; he would rather be working outdoors. He goes to his local Farm Service Agency (FSA) office somewhat regularly to fill out paperwork and get information on specific programs. He likes talking face-to-face with people, so he doesn't mind making the trip to the office occasionally. When he has a quick question he would prefer to use a faster avenue.

Though he has limited computer experience, Philip owns a desktop computer. At his tech-savvy neighbor's urging, he recently got a dial-up Internet connection and an email account which he shares with his wife. When Philip has a simple question, he wants to go online and find the information quickly. He also wants to be able to fill out necessary forms without having to interrupt his work schedule too much. He requires easy-to-understand navigation and quickly loading pages.

Philip also likes to keep up-to-date on farming news and programs but does not always have time to sit down and read lengthy articles or new government legislation. He would like to access current news from his local FSA Web site about the Farm Bill and other programs or changes that may affect his region. He would be interested in receiving email notices about relevant news.

Customer Characteristic	Conclusion
Relies on intermediaries to support interaction with USDA	Would benefit from additional support tools from USDA.gov
Feels paperwork pulls him from farm duties	Wants swift access to information and applications
Recently gained Internet access	Requires a simple interface and intuitive navigation
Does not currently leverage the Web for research	Could benefit from additional education on USDA's online offering and capabilities

FIGURE 8.7   Source: USDA Web Presence C.3. http://www.usa.gov/webcontent/documents/USDA_Audience_Analysis.pdf

LOW-INCOME FAMILIES AND INDIVIDUALS: SELENA MARTIN PERSONA

Selena is a single mother of two who lives in rural Maryland. She cannot afford to purchase a computer. She uses the computers at her town's public library, even though she usually has to wait for a computer to become available. She gained a fair amount of knowledge about computer applications and the Internet through a training class, but still considers herself a novice. She is particularly hesitant to use sites that require a login since she uses a shared computer. She is also hesitant to enter personal information in a public computer. She would feel embarrassed if someone caught a glimpse of her income or other sensitive data.

She has a Web-based email account but is only able to check it every few weeks. Because of this, she is frustrated when she has to request information by email rather than simply locate it online.

Selena needs to find the latest information on food stamps and rural housing programs. She knows limited English. Her first language is Spanish and she has a lot of trouble finding resources she can confidently decipher. She is further inhibited by a time limit on computer use at the library. She does not have a lot of time to search around, but must get the information she needs quickly. Filling out forms online is an especially difficult process because she often does not have all the information she needs. She must then retrieve it from home and start all over again, beginning with the wait in line.

Customer Characteristic	Conclusion
Does not check email regularly	▪ Needs an instant response to queries
Does not feel completely confident reading in English	▪ Would prefer resources in her primary language
Still feels like a computer novice	▪ Values ease-of-use and might leave any site that feels too frustrating
Only has access to a public computer	▪ Is uneasy entering personal data, like annual income, in a public space
Does not use a home computer	▪ Does not always have data readily available

FIGURE 8.8   Source: USDA Web Presence E.3. http://www.usa.gov/webcontent/documents/ USDA_Audience_Analysis.pdf

Information Architecture

In website development vernacular, Information Architecture, at times abbreviated I.A., is the arrangement and organization of text, information, and data on a webpage or in a website. Websites typically have four types of pages:

- A **homepage,** which introduces users to the agency or organization
- Navigation pages such as site maps, indexes, Help, and search engines
- Basic content pages for information users are looking for
- Pages that begin sections of websites.

Also, understanding how users navigate government websites helps developers create more effective and efficient ones. According to Webcontent.gov, users navigate through government websites by topic, task or service, audience group, geographic location, or a combination of these factors (Webcontent.gov "Organize Content"). Although there are clearly differences between paper documents and

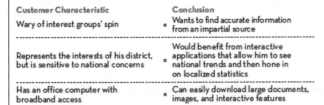

POLICY MAKERS AND INFLUENCERS: ADAM WEBER PERSONA

Thirty-four-year-old Adam is a legislative assistant to the congresswoman representing Ohio's 9th district. Another congressman in the House has asked for her help in drafting a wetlands protection bill that could affect the thousands of agricultural producers and rural residents in the 9th district. Always politically cautious, the representative asks Adam to give the issue thorough due diligence before she decides whether to associate herself with this legislation.

Adam wants to find statistics on wetland acreage and usage that would help him assess whether this initiative would serve the interests of citizens not only in his district, but nationwide. While environmental and agricultural lobby groups provide information on the issue, he is apprehensive about the accuracy of their data. He needs un-slanted, unbiased information to steer his decision.

Adam first researches existing legislation on the Library of Congress' THOMAS system, he then navigates to USDA.gov. He locates raw data on the issue provided by National Agricultural Statistic Service (NASS). He then locates in-depth reports from Economic Research Service (ERS) on the links between agriculture and the environment. An ERS map shows him the geographic areas with high proportions of wetlands, so he can quickly recognize the parts of the country that would be most affected by the proposed law. A variety of resources on wetlands provided by Natural Resource Conservation Service (NRCS) help complete his view of the public debate. By the end of the day, USDA's site has provided him the balanced view he needs to determine the representative's stance on the issue.

Customer Characteristic		Conclusion
Wary of interest groups' spin	▪	Wants to find accurate information from an impartial source
Represents the interests of his district, but is sensitive to national concerns	▪	Would benefit from interactive applications that allow him to see national trends and then hone in on localized statistics
Has an office computer with broadband access	▪	Can easily download large documents, images, and interactive features

FIGURE 8.9 Source: USDA Web Presence I.3. http://www.usa.gov/webcontent/documents/USDA_Audience_Analysis.pdf

websites, Table 8.2 demonstrates that there some similarities that are helpful in comparing the two. (Also see Johnson-Sheehan 384).

As discussed earlier, effective websites have information divided into related groups or "chunks," prioritized according to the needs of the audience. These chunks can form the basis for the way text is presented, how pages are differentiated, and how a site is navigated through its links. Pieces of information or chunks are separate files in which related ones are connected by hypertext **links**. The menu of topics on sites show the connections between these separate files of information. Information Architecture moves from abstract ideas to a visual diagram of the proposed webpages or an amendment to current webpages on a website. These visual representations are called **node-link diagrams.** The chunks of content are called nodes, which are "more or less equivalent to a Web page, and like a Web page, a node is not restricted to any particular content type," and, "[l]inks are pathways connecting nodes" (Farkas and Farkas 11). Most often website users work their way from the top node—the homepage—downward through the hierarchy. Although there may not be arrows

Website	Paper-based Document
Homepage	Introduction, or TOC
Node page	Chapter or Section
Page	Page
Site Index	Index
Menu	Table of Contents or Index
Search engine	Index
Site Map	Table of Contents
Navigation Bar or tabs	Table of Contents
Linking	Turning a page
Gifs, jpegs, tiffs	Graphics, pictures, drawings

TABLE 8.2   Comparing paper and website features. Source: Adapted from Johnson-Sheehan 384

pointing in both directions on the diagrams, the assumption is that users can also go backward to the page they were on before—just as you do when you push the back button to return to the previous page on a website. For the sake of applying these abstract concepts, we have used the word *node* as Johnson-Sheehan does for a particular type of webpage: pages that open sections of websites. Figure 8.10 is a diagram of a simple website hierarchy.

Just as websites can fit into several genres, many websites have some variety of these diagrams. Large websites are not only places for users to find information, they often are complex databases where many types of files are stored and where the website software "adapts" to the needs of the user as he or she goes through the site by storing user's preferential information in the database. Many websites fit into a hierarchical structure, which then goes into a different structure further down in the levels of webpages. Lynch and Horton, authors of the *Web Style Guide*, present three main types of information architectural structures: linear, hierarchy, and web. Lynch and Horton's *Web Style Guide* shows the three types of information structures. As these authors say, even though most users will likely click through a site in a free-form

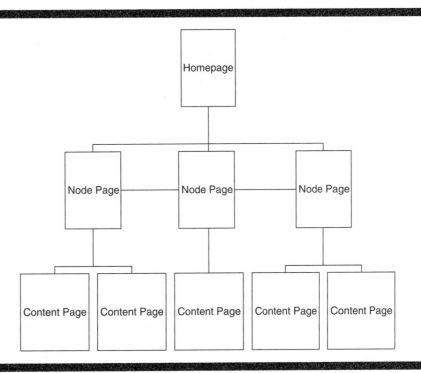

FIGURE 8.10 Simple Website Hierarchy

manner, it does not mean the site should not have a clear, consistent, and organized structure. The chart in Figure 8.11 "summarizes three basic organization patterns against the 'linearity' of narrative and the complexity of content" (Lynch and Horton).

Site Indexes and Maps

Creating a website diagram also helps in developing the site map and/or site index. A *site index* functions much like an index in a book in that it is alphabetically arranged based on keywords related to the website; *site maps* are graphic or text displays of the website's hierarchy, much like a Table of Contents, and often found on the homepage to help the user locate information. Figure 8.12 is the site map for Usability.gov.

An excerpt from the site index for USA.gov, the web portal for the federal government's websites is shown in Figure 8.13. Similar to a "mock up" or layout for print documents, a **wireframe** is the visual representation of all the elements of one web page from a site. Figure 8.14 is the wireframe from Usability.gov. when it was in the development stage.

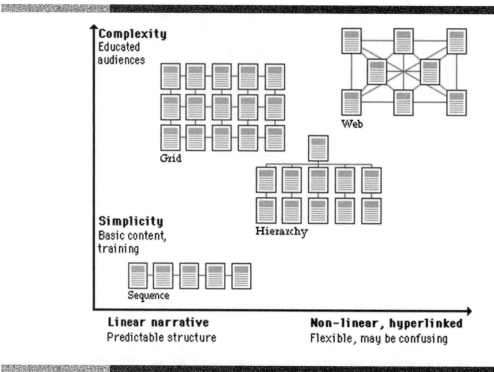

FIGURE 8.11   Three Basic Organization Patterns. Source: *Web Style Guide*,
www.webstyleguide.com, Copyright 2002 Patrick J. Lynch and Sarah Horton

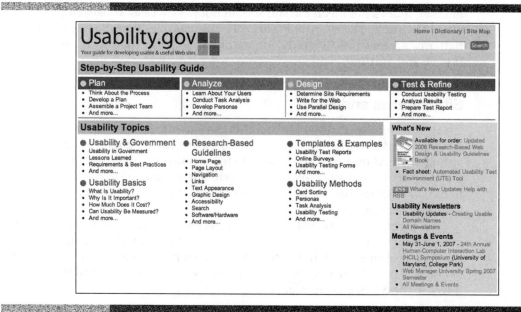

FIGURE 8.12   Source: Usability.gov. http://usability.gov

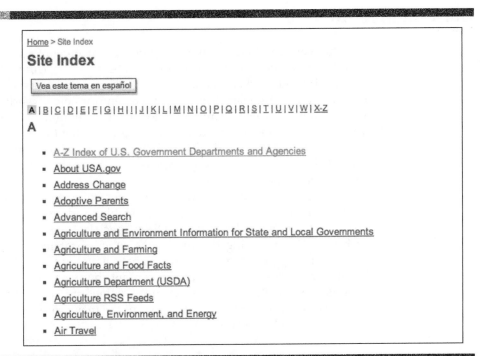

FIGURE 8.13   Source: USA.gov. http://www.usa.gov/Site_Index.shtml

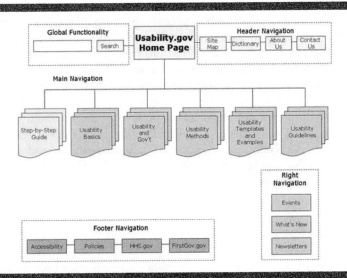

FIGURE 8.14   Source: Usability.gov. http://usability.gov

Content Inventory

Whether you are a lone website developer or a member of a large team, a key part of the Information Architecture of a website is the **Content Inventory**. The Content Inventory can be as simple as a list for a small website or as complex as a database for a large site. The Content Inventory helps website developers find gaps in content as well as areas with too much or redundant information. Web developers must anticipate readers' questions and what they need to know because the "content must be available" and "[t]he means of searching must be obvious and reliable" (Rude 370). If users cannot find the content they need, then the content, no matter how comprehensive, is not useful.

The Content Inventory helps in other important website development strategic matters such as budget, timetable, and technical decisions. These strategic matters can be part of a **Site Specifications** planning document for websites. This planning document has concise statements of goals, audience characteristics, web strategies to meet goals, how the site will be maintained, the number of pages, the scope of the content, budgets, timetable, and technical aspects of a website. "The best site specifications are very short and to the point, and are often just outlines or bullet lists of the major design or technical features planned" (Lynch and Horton).

Content Management System (CMS)

Many agencies and organizations are implementing Content Management Systems (CMS). CMS are applications that allow a website manager or writer to create, modify, or update content without having to know **HTML, Java,** or other programming language or **code**. Typically the system can also automatically update, format, revise, and index the content for database information and search engine function. In addition, agencies and organizations can create their own templates, **wizards,** and other tools. From the content writer's perspective, one of the key attributes of the CMS is that multiple writers can work on a website without inadvertently overwriting someone else's work. There is also version control of content so writers will know who made the latest changes and when they were made. According to Webcontent.gov, the Department of Defense Finance and Accounting Service, Department of Energy, Department of Homeland Security, Department of Justice, National Oceanic and Atmospheric Administration, and the U.S. Air Force are some of the federal agencies and departments that have used CMS ("Content Management Systems"). The state of Oregon is also using a CMS. (See Figure 8.15.)

Technology Inventory

Whether you are planning a small website on your own or are part of a team designing a large one, understanding the potential and limitations of your own software and hardware and that of your audiences is important. Considering that

What is content management?
Content management is the process of creating, updating, distributing and publishing information on a Web site. It does this by creating a central storage area for files, templates, images, and other material used to build a Web site.

The E-government content management system helps you create and update Web pages without knowing HTML and Java. You can focus on what you want your Web page to say, not how it looks. Just by using the templates provided, your Web pages will be consistent with the Brand Oregon standards used across the state.

You use a content management system to make sure that all Web page content has been reviewed and approved before it is published.

Why is content management important?
Your agency's online information must be periodically updated. You may add services, prices for your product may change or your agency sponsors a public event. You want to get this information to your customers as quickly and easily as possible. A content management process makes this easier.

In addition, our content management system helps you control what content is on your Web site.   All content must go through the workflow.

1. Contribution – Content is written and placed in the Web page.
2. Approval – Content is reviewed and approved or rejected.
3. Publishing – Content is sent to the live site.

At each step in the work flow - contribution, approval, and publishing – someone must sign off. These sign-offs help you ensure accountability for your content.

Finally, our content management system provides you with total control of your content. You don't have to wait for technical assistance to add or update your content. You decide what to update and when you want it updated.

FIGURE 8.15   Source: Oregon.gov. http://www.oregon.gov/DAS/EISPD/EGOV/ faq_content_mgmt.shtml

many government websites have a wide range of audiences with a wide range of technical skill and access, you'll need to make sure that your website works on different operating systems, browsers, **cross-computer platforms**, connection speeds, screen resolutions, and printing capabilities. Other technological considerations are the bandwidth available to users, advanced code and program language features such as Java, database access for users, and technological support for both users and yourself. You'll also want to consider whether the website's server is in-house or outsourced to another provider and related concerns such as support and maintenance of it as well as what a search engine is appropriate. All of these factors can affect the content, design, budget, and timetable of the website's development. If, for example, webpages are designed so users cannot easily print them, then the webpages have not met the audience's needs.

Code

Today website developers do not need to know how to program a webpage using code because they can create sites with web-authoring software. Some of the most common commercial software programs are Adobe GoLive, Macromedia

Dreamweaver, and MS FrontPage, which use a **WYSIWYG,** or "What You See Is What You Get" interface to design pages. But knowing at least something about code takes the mystery out of it and helps you consider what might be a problem when written or design features do not show up on the computer screen as you had expected. We offer this very basic introduction to coding to give you a place to begin to "read" code so you can pinpoint coding problems. As you work with code, you can learn to read it easier. Moreover, if you are working on a team or hiring an outside contractor to develop a website, you should know what tools and programming language (or code) the website developer is using and whether you are going to be able to easily maintain the site once the contract is over. The most common code are the tags in HTML (hypertext markup language), but other languages such as SGML (Standard Generalized Markup Language), XML (Extensible Markup Language), and an emerging XHTML (Extensible Hypertext Markup Language) is also used on the web.

Reading HTML

HTML "tags" are labels within the < and > brackets and provide the instructions for putting information on the web. Tags come in pairs with ones that begin and end an instruction or set of instructions. The opening bracket is followed by an "element," a browser command telling it what element to show, and then "attributes," describing the properties of the element, then an equal sign, enclosed in quotes, with a closing bracket. For example, in this code: <font face="Arial, sans-serif">, *font face* tells the browser to show a typeface; while, the attributes of that font is Arial, sans-serif type style. Meta tags are tags with keywords and information inserted into the "head" area of webpages that are not seen by the viewer but can be "seen" by certain search engines. Therefore, whatever information is in those tags is important so the search engine will "hit" the page, and it will appear on the user's screen.

The bare structure of HTML coding is as follows:

<HTML>	Begins a HTML page.
<HEAD>	Contains information about the page such as the TITLE and META tags, which are used for search engines to find the page, STYLE tags that set up the page layout, and JavaScript coding for special effects.
<TITLE>	The TITLE of the page that shows up in the browser title bar.
</TITLE>	Closes the HTML <TITLE> tag.
</HEAD>	Closes the HTML <HEAD> tag.
<BODY>	This is where to begin writing your document and placing your other HTML codes.
</BODY>	Closes the HTML body of the document.
</HTML>	Closes the <HTML> tag at the beginning of the document.

Other commonly used basic HTML codes are shown in Table 8.3.

HTML Code	Action	Example
 	line break, begins a new line without a double space between	Contents of page Contents of page
<EMBED>	embedded object, usually used with video or music files	<EMBED src="file.mid" width="75" height="25" align="center">
<H1>	heading 1, large heading	<H1>Heading 1 example</H1>
<H2>	heading 2, small heading or subheading	<H2>Heading 2 example</H2>
<href>	link inside or outside site	<href>url</href>
<IMG>	image alt = alternative text to describe image for accessibility	<IMG SRC="tree.gif" WIDTH="21" HEIGHT="21" BORDER="0" ALT="a sentence about site"
<L1>	Bulleted list with circle bullets	<MENU> <LI type="circle">List 1 </MENU>
<Menu>	Menu for lists with disc, circle, and square bullets	<MENU> <LI type="disc">List item 1 <LI type="circle">List item 2 <LI type="square">List item 3 </MENU>

TABLE 8.3 Basic HTML Codes.

<Menu>	Menu for lists with disc, circle, and square bullets	<MENU> <LI type="disc">List item 1 <LI type="circle">List item 2 <LI type="square">List item 3 </MENU>
<Meta>	meta	<Meta name= "Description" content= "Description of site> <Meta name= "keywords describing site">
<P>	Paragraph begins a new paragraph with a line between	<p> looks like this.
<Table> and </Table>	Table	<Table>displays a table</Table>
<TD ...> and </TD>	Set a single table cell	<TD>table cell data</TD>
<Tr> and </Tr>	Table Row	<Tr> displays a table row</table row>
<!>	Comment that is not read by the browser	<! This is a comment line>

TABLE 8.3   *(continued)*

Two examples from Lynch and Horton's *Web Style Guide* compare the readability of a display of codes to demonstrate that most people would find Example 1 easier to read. (See Figure 8.16.)

Code often appears in commercial software website design programs laid out like Example 2, but you can begin to read code by having it laid out as in Example 1 because the code is broken up into shorter segments. By using the **code or source** view feature on your browser, you can practice reading code. HTML tables are frequently used for webpage layout; these tables are similar to ones you are familiar with in a word processing program, such as the one earlier listing codes, but HTML tables are used with webpages to divide up the space on the page for text and design purposes. (Sometimes you will see websites with SHTML extensions rather than HTML. Information which can be modified by a server may

Example 1

```
<! — START OF SCHEDULE TABLE ======= — >

<table summary="Human Investigations Committee II schedule, FY 2001."
border="0" width="100%" cellspacing="0" cellpadding="1">
<tr valign="top">
<! — =============================== — >
<td width="50%">
<p class="tabletext">
Deadline for Submissions</p>
</td>
<td width="2%">
 
</td>
<td width="48%">
<p class="tabletext">
Meeting Dates 2001</p>
</td></tr>
<! — =============================== — >
```

Example 2

```
<table summary="Human Investigations Committee II schedule, FY 2001."
border="0" width="100%" cellspacing="0" cellpadding="1"><tr valign="top"><td
width="50%"><p class="tabletext">Deadline for Submissions</p></td><td
width="2%"> </td><td width="48%"><p class="tabletext">Meeting Dates
221</p></td></tr>
```

FIGURE 8.16 Source: *Web Style Guide*, www.webstyleguide.com, Copyright 2002 Patrick J. Lynch and Sarah Horton

have a SHTML extension). If you work as a lone web developer for a small governmental unit, you will want to learn what web-authoring software package is best for your employer, and a good method for making the decision is to look at other similar sites and talk with their webmasters for advice. If you work for a larger agency or organization, it will likely have its own programmers; yet, you should become familiar enough with programming language or code to be able to predict and detect problems in web content and design.

Design Inventory

When creating a Content Inventory, it may be useful to separate out the design requirements from the other elements of the site. When we talk about websites today, we often refer to "web design," rather than "web writing" because the writing of content and the designing of the sites often go hand-in-hand. In large website development, there can be both content writers and editors as well as "designers." Whatever the job position, a person with an understanding of how the written language and visual language work together ensures an effective website that communicates clearly to the user. An inventory of design needs and features can go into greater detail about the design criteria. Here are some design topics:

- How the agency or organization's name is to appear
- Font styles and sizes for headings and subheadings
- Font styles and sizes for body text
- How white space will be used
- What kinds of tabs might be used
- How lists will be formatted
- The kinds and sizes of images
- The details for including forms

The Design Inventory can also include the features of the different page designs for the site such as details about home page design, navigation pages that are designed specifically to direct users to other pages, frequently asked questions pages, and error reporting, as well as others. Webcontent.gov recommends the following common content for federal government websites:

- Contact Information ("Contact us" page)
- Organizational Information ("About us" page)
- Site Map or A-Z Index
- Frequently Asked Questions (FAQs)
- Online Services
- Forms and Publications
- Jobs and Employment Information
- Information about Regulations
- Information about Grants and Contracts
- Site Policies and Notices. (Webcontent.gov)

The Homepage Undoubtedly, a homepage is the most important webpage. "Research shows that more than half of all web users evaluate websites based on homepages alone. If you have an ineffective homepage, many visitors will immediately be turned off and may never come back to your site. . . . Web users are impatient. They don't want to be distracted by text or graphics that don't help them find what they want or that increase download time" (Webcontent.gov) "Homepages."

Because a homepage is the first page users visit, it should create a positive impression to reflect well on the agency or organization it represents; the text should be straightforward, and to the point; the features should provide quick guideposts to other pages; all federal, state, or local requirements should be met; and when changes have been made to the site, alerts should be on the page for the user.

A beginning point in designing a homepage is looking at other homepages that are similar to the one on which you are working. See Figure 8.17 for a homepage with details and annotations from the USDA Food Safety and Inspection Secure (FSIS) Style Guide that helps explain parts of the page.

Visual Displays

Many types of visual displays explain, inform, and enhance data and content. Graphics should supplement writing not supplant it. Just as in paper documents, graphics need to be placed as close as possible to the text to which they relate. To help web content writers and designers think about ways to incorporate visuals, the following are some familiar ones.

Charts Charts show components of an organization, object, or steps in a process. An *organizational chart* shows the hierarchical or linear structure of an organization. A flowchart shows the steps in a process. An organizational chart of the Internal Revenue Service (IRS) is shown in Figure 8.18. The flow chart in Figure 8.19 is from the North Carolina Department of Transportation showing the steps in the planning and development of a transportation project.

Drawings Drawings are helpful in representing the structure of an object. There are four basic types: (1) translucent ("see through"); (2) cutaways, where the front of the object has been removed and the internal structure is shown (see Figure 8.20); (3) a cross-section of an object, one in which the object appears cut in half crosswise; and (4) exploded drawings, ones in which parts of an object are separated to show how they are connected to each other (see Figure 8.19).

Graphs Types of graphs include area, bar, line, and pictorial. Some graphs show how quantities change usually over time. Graphs are series of points on a coordinate system in which the Y or vertical axis indicates a quantity and the X axis, which is horizontal, indicates category, item, or time. Figure 8.22 is an

4.1 Homepage Template

This template is used primarily to create the FSIS Homepage. Its unique characteristics include the agency tagline graphic and a particular construct for featuring content in the center content area. This template is also used when creating Footer pages.

The FSIS home page contains the following areas of information: *Introduction Text, In the News, I Want To, Promotion Area,* and *Spotlight: Fact Sheets.*

1. **Introduction Text**
2. **I Want To**

3. **In the news**

4. **Promotion Area**

5. **Spotlights**

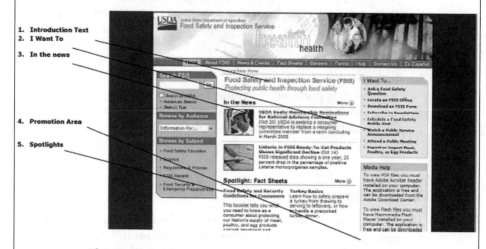

Template Components

1. **Introduction Text**
   The *Introduction Text* is slightly larger than other body text on the Web site. It can be used as an introduction to your agency or a mission statement. The Introduction can be two to four lines in length.

   Attributes: Font: Verdana Regular / Size: 16px / Color: # 4D8544 / Text-Decoration: none / Hover: none / Image: fsis_mission.gif / Width: 368/ Height: 70px / Cutsheet Name: text_intro.psd

2. **I Want To**
   This is a section in the Right Navigation Column that lists common and important tasks relevant to FSIS, such as *Ask a Food Safety Question, Locate an FSIS Office, Download an FSIS Form, Subscribe to Newsletters, Schedule a Food Safety Mobile Visit,* etc. Topics should be limited to a maximum of ten.

   Overall Size: Width: 188px / Variable height / Content: "I Want To" image and bulleted list of various tasks.

   Navigation Headings: Text: "I Want To" / Font: Helvetica Medium / Size 14px / Color: #313131 / Rollover: none / Rollover Color: none / Image: l_c_iwanttio.gif / Width: 188px / Height 23px / Cutsheet Name: nav_columns.psd

FIGURE 8.17 Source: USDA "Style Guide for the FSIS Website": 33–34.
http://www.usa.gov/webcontent/documents/FSIS_Styleguide.pdf

Homepage Template continued

3. In the News

This section highlights the top two current news releases and should be updated frequently. News release headlines are bold text and are HTML links. Use of imagery or summary is optional. When a summary is shown, it will always end with the news release date.

A. Headline bars

Overall Size: Width: 368px / Height: 23px

Headings: Text: "In the News" / Font: Helvetica Medium / Size: 15px / Color: #000000 / Rollover: none / Rollover Color: none / Image: content_head_inthenews.gif / Width: 368px / Height: 23px /
Cutsheet Name: subheads.psd

B. Headlines

Attributes: Font: Verdana Bold / Size: 11px / Color: #000099 / Text-Decoration: none / Hover: underline

C. Body text

Attributes: Font: Verdana Regular / Size: 11px / Color: #000000 / Text-Decoration: none / Hover: none

D. Images

Attributes: not required / Portrait Orientation: Width 70px, Height 80px /
Landscape Orientation: Width 80px, Height 70px

4. Promotion Area

This is a section in the Right Navigation Column that features a promotional item. When the redesigned site is launched, this area will be used to feature USDA and FSIS programs. The messages promoted in this area are temporary and will be updated on a regular basis.

Overall Size: Width: 188px / Height: 153px

Attributes: Text: "Questions about food safety? Ask Karen" / Font: Helvetica Medium / Size: 15px / Color: #FFFFFF / Rollover: none / Rollover Color: none / Image: l_c_promotion_questions.gif /
Width: 188px / Height: 153px / Cutsheet Name: promotion.psd

5. Spotlight: Fact Sheets

Spotlights contain important programs that will appear on the homepage for a longer period of time than
News & Events. Each program headline is a bold HTML link. Use of imagery or summary is optional.

A. Headline bars

Overall Size: Width: 368px / Height: 23px

Headings: Text: "Spotlight: Fact Sheets" / Font: Helvetica Medium / Size: 15px / Color: #000000 / Rollover: none / Rollover Color: none / Image: content_head_spotlight_facts.gif / Width: 368px /
Height: 23px / Cutsheet Name: subheads.psd

B. Headlines

Attributes: Font: Verdana Bold / Size: 11px / Color: #000099 / Text-Decoration: none / Hover:

FIGURE 8.17 *(continued)*

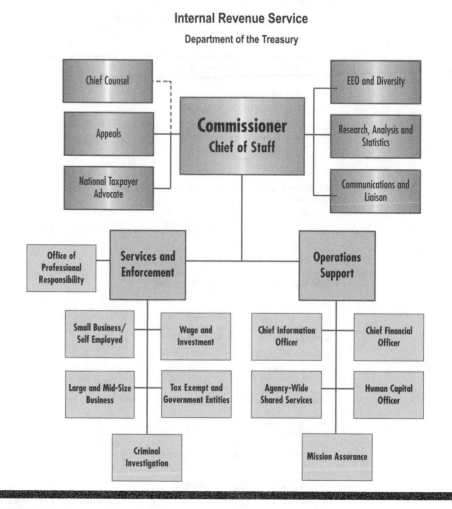

FIGURE 8.18 Organizational Chart. Source: IRS.gov. http://www.irs.gov/

example of a line graph showing a change in nonfarm jobs in Minnesota from April 2003 to October 2006. Next to it is an explanation of the change.

Maps Maps show spatial relationships of places. The map of Central Park in New York City (see Figure 8.23) was generated through an interactive feature on the city website.

Tables Tables in documents are used to categorize, summarize, and allow for comparison of parts of specific data—text or figures—within a small space. (Tables are also used in websites for design formats.) Columns are vertical and rows are horizontal. The table shown in Figure 8.24 is from the state of Pennsylvania website.

Transportation Program Life Cycle

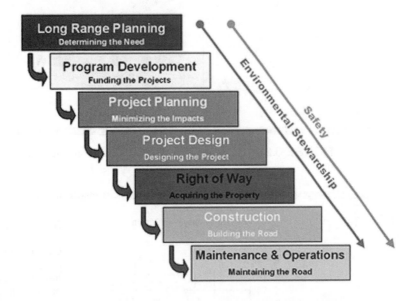

FIGURE 8.19   Flowchart. Source: North Carolina Department of Transportation.
http://www.ncdot.org/projects/roadbuilt/road.html

An Exploded Drawing by NASA

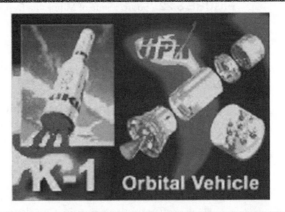

FIGURE 8.20   Artist's concept of Rocketplane-Kistler's K-1 Orbital Vehicle.
Source: NASA

A Cutaway Drawing by NASA

FIGURE 8.21 Cutaway diagram of the space shuttle. Source: NASA

Line Graph

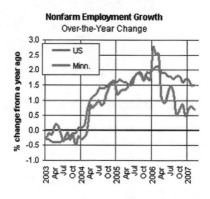

Nonfarm Jobs

Over the year Minnesota added 41,500 jobs in **May**. This translates into a growth rate of 1.5 percent, up from last month's over-the-year growth rate of 1.3 percent. The nation grew 1.4 percent over the year in May. Minnesota's strong performance once again brings the state's over-the-year growth rate above that of the nation's.

FIGURE 8.22 Source: State of Minnesota Department of Employment and Economic Development. http://www.deed.state.mn.us/lmi/Home.htm

Multimedia

Government websites increasingly include multimedia. Most multimedia requires a plug-in or third-party software package to view or listen to the media. Some common formats of multimedia are these:

- mp3 (audio), wav (audio)
- rm (Real media, Real player)
- wmv (windows movie, windows media player)
- mov (Quicktime movie, Quicktime player)

If you embed or link outside media, you should always include a recommendation of what media player should be used to open the file. Several state sites have

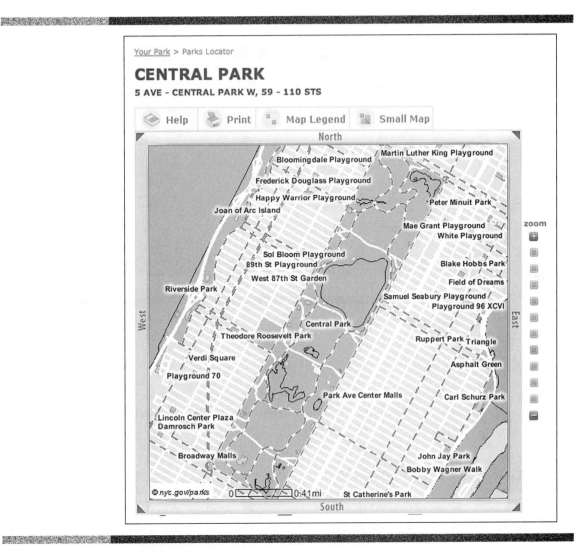

FIGURE 8.23 Map. Source: New York City Government website. http://gis.nyc.gov/parks/lc/NYCParkMapIt.do

Budget Materials:

2006-07 Governor's Executive Budget [PDF]	**Pennsylvania Cares Slide Presentation** (9MB) [PDF]
2006-07 Budget in Brief [PDF]	**Pennsylvania Competes Slide Presentation** (1 Edward G. Rendell, Governor
2006-07 Executive Budget Slide Presentation (Color) [PDF]	**2006-07 Budget Fact Sheets, Talking Points and FAQs**
2006-07 Executive Budget Slide Presentation (black & white) [PDF]	

FIGURE 8.24 Table. Source: State of Pennsylvania website. http://www.governor.state.pa.us/governor/cwp/view.asp?a=1101&q=445371

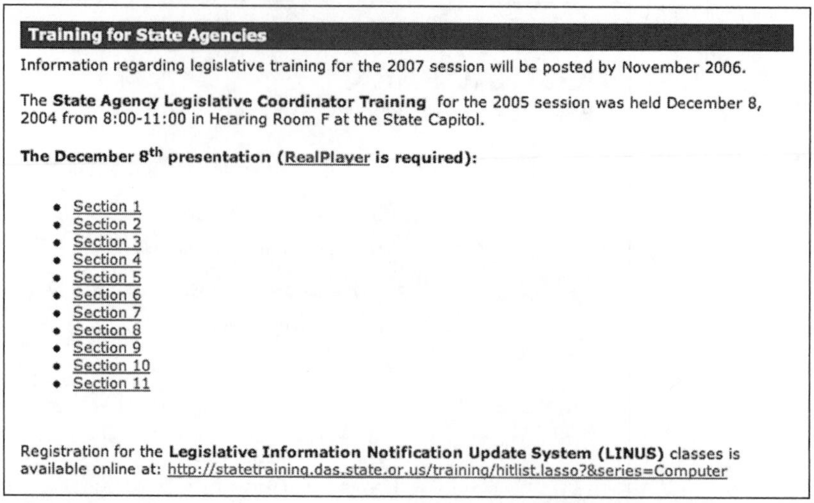

Training for State Agencies

Information regarding legislative training for the 2007 session will be posted by November 2006.

The **State Agency Legislative Coordinator Training** for the 2005 session was held December 8, 2004 from 8:00-11:00 in Hearing Room F at the State Capitol.

The December 8th presentation (RealPlayer is required):

- Section 1
- Section 2
- Section 3
- Section 4
- Section 5
- Section 6
- Section 7
- Section 8
- Section 9
- Section 10
- Section 11

Registration for the **Legislative Information Notification Update System (LINUS)** classes is available online at: http://statetraining.das.state.or.us/training/hitlist.lasso?&series=Computer

FIGURE 8.25 Oregon State website. Source: http://www.oregon.gov/DAS/legcoord.shtml

online chat features where users can talk in real time with state employees. Among other multimedia features, the Oregon website has video of legislative training sessions as shown in Figure 8.25.

Style Guides and Templates

As we discussed in earlier chapters, every professional publication and government website needs to adhere to a professional style guide or to have style guidelines created for it. Moreover, because of the interrelationship between text and visuals and between writing and design in websites, style guides for websites incorporate detailed information about graphics as well. Style rules for websites serve the same purpose as ones for the print industry. Consistency in written content and design characteristics help website users read and comprehend text and visuals easily, efficiently, and effectively.

Style Guides for Government Websites

Because large agencies have employees all over the country with thousands of clients, their large websites can have their own style guides. These guides can be hundreds of pages of style choices and include templates to help website developers throughout the country meet the needs of the audience and ensure consistency throughout the agency's websites. The U.S. Department of Health and Human Services has a 292-page, comprehensive guide for web developers, *Research-Based*

FIGURE 8.26   Source: *Research-Based Web Design and Usability Guidelines*. U.S. Department of Health and Human Services: xi–xiii. http://www.usability.gov/pdfs/guidelines.html

Web Design and Usability Guide. Among the topics in the table of contents for this guide are ones shown in Figure 8.26. They show the guide covers written and design advice and requirements.

Figure 8.27 is the Table of Contents from the *Food Safety and Inspection Service Style Guide* of the U.S. Department of Agriculture, showing what this guide covers.

Useful style guides for agencies and organizations also contain essential information on ethical and legal issues that government writers and web developers need to know. These style books serve as valuable resources for government employees to turn to for advice about a myriad of topics.

Style Sheets

If you are building a site on your own for a small governmental unit or organization or even if you are on a large website team, you can use an established style

Table of Contents

FIGURE 8.27   Source: USDA Style Guide for the FSIS Website: 2. http://www.usa.gov/webcontent/placements/FSIS_Styleguide.pdf

guide. You may want to create your own list of rules for the content and design features specifically for your website, which is sometimes called a *project style sheet* (Farkas and Farkas 67). In this way, when new employees work on the site, the style rules help them make the writing and design features of the site consistent. A simple style sheet might include rules such as whether *website* will be one word or two, if the word *street* would be spelled out in addresses or abbreviated, or under what circumstances numbers would be spelled out. A website style sheet would also have the design conventions like the background color on the site, the type of fonts used on it, and the size of the fonts for headings and subheadings, and other items like those listed in the Design Inventory section. Style sheets and any style guides about websites need to be "organic documents" in that they change and evolve over time. This is especially important for content and design criteria in the rapidly changing technological world.

Cascading Style Sheets (CSS)

Word processing and desk top publishing programs have used **cascading style sheet** features for many years. For example, in Microsoft Word, on the Formatting toolbar on the left-hand side at top of the screen is the type of typeface, size, and style for whatever you are working on at the time. By pressing the down arrow next to the box, you can see the various style formats. You can apply the same style in the list to other text by selecting the text you wish to modify, and then selecting the style you want from the menu. Or if you want to create your own styles, you can do so by going to the Styles and Formatting task pane at the top of a document and modifying the styles that appear on the right hand side of the screen. For example, suppose you wanted the subtitles for a secondary heading, *Heading Level 2*, to be in 14-point Times New Roman bold. Every time you want a secondary heading to appear in the document with those type attributes, it would have the same typeface, size, and style as every other one. If you wanted to change any of the attributes, you'd change them in the Styles and Formatting feature, and in every instance where the text has been "tagged," it would automatically change, embedding the instructions as code into the document. Having headings, subheadings, body text, and so forth with consistent appearance throughout a document enhances comprehension.

Cascading Style Sheets for websites do much the same thing as the Styles and Formatting feature on Word, but they can also work for much larger and more complex projects. Cascading Style Sheets are also a collection of specifications either embedded in a webpage or stored in a separate file that determine the appearance of particular HTML elements. Cascading style sheets are becoming increasingly important for websites because they can maintain consistency among thousands of webpages. Because of their consistency CSS are part of Content Management Systems (CMS). There can be some difficulty with disability accessibility requirements for websites and CSS, but these problems are being worked out.

Templates

Because of the vast mixture of websites, many government agencies and organizations have developed *templates* incorporating design specifications, based on usability testing and feedback from users. Templates, like those for paper documents, are predetermined formats for websites. Templates correspond to the genre of the website—the conventions of the agency or organization. Templates assist web developers because there is a pattern already established from which to work. The main drawback to using templates is that sometimes they are not easy to change, and some cannot be changed at all. This could mean they allow for consistency for agency websites design but not for differences among sites.

Legal and Ethical Inventory

Accessibility

Meeting government mandated rules and regulations are an important part of all government websites not only because they are part of the government, but also because they should serve as examples for other websites. Take the issue of accessibility. The Federal Rehabilitation Act requires all federal agencies to make sure their websites are accessible to individuals who have difficulty hearing, seeing, or making precise movements. The U.S. Department of Health and Human Services says, among other things, websites need to provide text equivalents for nontext elements, enable users to skip repetitive navigation links, ensure that plug-ins and applets meet the requirements for accessibility, provide client-size image maps, and synchronize all multimedia elements (U.S. Department of Health and Human Services 46). For government websites, mandated rules and regulations should also be in style guides. More information about accessibility section 508 can be found at http://www.section508.gov or for the Americans with Disabilities Act (ADA) http://www.ada.gov.

Other Requirements and "Best Practices"

Federal government websites have many rules and regulations to follow. State and local governments are obligated to meet the requirements within their own states as well. According to Webcontent.gov the following are some highlights of other requirements for federal government websites:

- The appropriate domains for the URLs:,gov, .fed,us, or .mil
- Clear notification of an agency involvement with a site
- A linking policy within and outside the site
- A policy of not allowing private advertising
- A practice of establishing and maintaining communications with the public
- A "Privacy Act Statement" telling visitors the legal authority for collecting personal data and how it will be used

- Compliance with required electronic security protocols
- Compliance with Freedom of Information (FOIA) existing laws and directives
- Access for individuals with limited English proficiency
- Compliance with digital records and copyright laws ("Webcontent.gov" "Best Practices").

Templates for government sites should already incorporate the various rules, regulations, and other requirements into their format but website developers should always double-check. A copy of a **Best Practices** form from the U.S. Interagency Committee on Government Information (ICGI) for websites is provided in Figure 8.28 because it is a checklist of federal government website writing and government mandated rules and regulations. Since this form is directed to the federal government, it may not be as applicable to state or local government

Checklist of ICGI Web Content Policy and Guideline Recommendations

Recommendation	Do You Do This?	
	Yes	No
1a. Use public domains (.gov, .mil, .fed.us)		
1b. Show U.S. sponsorship		
1c. Follow linking requirements:		
o Linking policy posted on website		
o Notification that visitors are leaving,		
o Disclaimers for non-federal sites		
o Established link review schedule stated in linking policy		
1d. Must show that it is current		
2a. Organized for citizens and intended audiences (topics, audience groups, location)		
2b. Written/organized from audience point of view		
2c. No employee info		
2d. Common content/terminology		
o Contact Us		
o About HUD		
o Site map or index		
o Common questions		
o Online services		
o Forms/publications		
o Jobs		
o Regulations (link to regs.gov)		
o Grants/contracts		
o Required policies and links		
2e. Evaluate customer satisfaction and usability		
3a. Provide common access		
3b. Plain language		
3c. Provide access in appropriate file formats		
3d. Provide appropriate access to data		
3e. Consistent navigation		
3f. Search engine on every page		
3g. Use standard metadata		
3h. Inform audiences of website changes		
3i. Ensure continuity during emergencies		
4a. Avoid duplication of other websites		
4b. Collaborate on cross-agency portals		
4c. Link to appropriate portals		
4d. Provide link back to homepage		
4e. Link to FirstGov		
5a. Develop and post priorities/schedule for posting new content		
6a. Comply with privacy requirements		
6b. Have security protocols		
6c. Ensure access for people with disabilities		
6d. Comply with FOIA requirements		
6e. Comply with Information Quality Guidelines		
6f. Provide access for people with limited English proficiency		
6g. Comply with Paperwork Reduction Act (OMB approval on forms/surveys)		
6h. Comply with Government Paperwork Elimination Act (electronic forms, etc.)		
6i. Comply with records management requirements		
6j. Comply with digital rights, copyright, trademark, and patent laws		
6k. Comply with Government Performance and Results Act (post annual performance plans)		
6l. Comply with No Fear Act (post employee discrimination complaint info)		
6m. Comply with Small Business Paperwork Relief Act (post small bus contact)		
6n. Comply with restrictions on lobbying		
6o. Comply with upcoming requirements for categorization of info		

FIGURE 8.28   Source: U.S. Interagency Committee on Government Information from Webcontent.gov. http://www.usa.gov/webcontent/rego_bestpractices/checklist/short.pdf

or organization websites. Nevertheless, knowing what is considered "Best Practices" at the federal level is useful to everyone who works for any level of government.

Other Important Legal and Ethical Matters

The Internet has provided access to more information than conceivable by earlier generations; yet, as we have discussed in this textbook, copyright and other matters pertaining to intellectual property have become more complex because of the growing digital world. Government information is unique in that almost all of what is written, printed, and distributed falls within the public domain, meaning that it cannot be copyrighted. Think of it like information that "belongs" to the public because taxpayers paid for it. However, everyone who works on government websites needs to know that not every document on the web is public and not everything on the web, including what is in government websites, can be reproduced and distributed without permission of a copyright holder. The burden of determining whether something is copyrighted rests with the user.

"Don't Keep the Public Guessing: Best Practices in Notice of Copyright and Terms & Conditions of Use for Government Website Content," by the CENDI, an interagency cooperative organization composed of scientific and technical information (STI) managers in government agencies, points out that "[m]any government agencies give no notice about the copyright status or terms and conditions of use for information and content on agency websites" (vi).

The CENDI report says, "A work is not in the public domain simply because it does not have a copyright notice. Additionally, the fact that a privately created work is, with permission, included in a U.S. Government work does not place the private work into the public domain. For example, works produced by contractors and grantees for the government are often protected by copyright" (v).

Key recommendations by CENDI for government websites are that government agencies:

- "inform the public that information on agency websites may be copyrighted and subject to various terms and conditions of use" (vi).
- clearly state any "[l]imitations on the rights of the public to use, reproduce, and redistribute any copyrighted information presented on the government website"(vi). . .
- "clearly, consistently and prominently provide access to a Copyright Policy statement from their homepage via a link to a stand-alone web page" (vi) . . .
- "establish policies and procedures whereby their employees, contractors and grantees that create individual works, such as documents, images, etc., must upon creation, mark such works with the copyright status". . . (vi).

This advice is relevant for graphics, music, video, as well as text. Web designers, for instance, should be aware that paraphrasing or redrawing a figure even in a minor way "is still considered a derivative of the original or an adaptation, and permission must be obtained" (Addison 30). It would seem unnecessary to say but government website writers need to be careful not to post untruths, misinformation, data inaccuracies, and other types of content displays that could mislead readers or negatively reflect on an agency's or organization's mission.

Aside from the agency or organization's style guide, website writers, developers, and designers can also turn to their professional organizations for ethical codes and guidelines. The government copyright office website at http://www.copyright.gov has more detailed information.

Government Websites in the Future

As the research at the beginning of this chapter indicates, the number of Americans who visit government websites will continue to grow as will their expectations for what is available on the sites. Not only will they be looking for information, they will also expect to make online transactions, express opinions, and interact with governmental employees in "real" time. Websites will be both their window and gateway to their government.

Knowledgeable website writers, designers, and developers understand that these websites are more than information portals; they are a means for Americans to be closer and more involved with their government. Website personnel need to keep their thumbs on the pulse of Americans' expectations, desires, and changes in demographics and technological ideas. With this approach to websites' development, individual or team government website members will continually look for new ways to address their audience's needs and the needs of that large segment of the population who may not have the ability, language, or access to technology. Any new strategies will certainly include more multimedia as well as more personal, telephone, or mail connections to those who cannot access websites. Regardless, though, of any changes in websites' structures, planning, writing, designing, or development, the rhetorical principles and approaches of knowing your audience, having a clear purpose, and understanding the cultural context will always be the deciding factors in whether any communication message—no matter what the medium—to any audience is heard and understood.

Activities and Assignments

1. **Group or Individual Internet Activity Assignment:** Go online and look for government websites at the federal, state, and local levels. Consider the principles of understanding an audience, having a clear purpose, and comprehending the cultural context of each site. Address as many of these questions as possible:

Audience

Who do you think the primary audience is for the site? Who might be the stakeholders for the site or an issue on the site? What might be some of the demographic characteristics of the audience members? How inviting is the site for its audience or audiences? Does it seem to cater to certain people and not others? How so? Does the site contain language specific to a particular group or audience (such as acronyms)? If it does, provide some examples. Specifically what features make you think it is inviting or not? What *ethos* does the site portray of the agency or organization?

Purpose

What purpose or purposes are there for the site or some of its webpages? How useful it is it in finding information? What features make it useful? Which do not? Does the site contain features for a type of website genre? What are those features, and do you think users would recognize them and be able to use them naturally without hesitating to think about them? In the terminology of website development, how "intuitive" are they for the user?

Cultural Context

What kinds of economic, historical, political, social, ethical, and/or technological aspects do you believe contribute to the usefulness of the site (or it not being useful)? For instance, is the site accessible for the disabled? Does it have features for non-native English speakers? What kinds of technological features does it offer? Do those help communicate its messages or get in their way? How so? If you can tell, how might the site have changed over time? What do you attribute to that change? What features on the site stimulate input from the public or stakeholders? If it is a federal government site, does the site include the various recommendations listed on the ICGI checklist in Figure 8.28?

2. **Individual Internet Activity:** After you and your classmates discuss the various sites, write a paper addressing the questions for a site and/or compare and contrast several the sites. Subdivide the sections of the paper up into audience, purpose, and cultural contexts. If you want and your teacher agrees, you could choose other sites than those discussed with your classmates. Be sure to include a section on your paper of any suggestions you have about changing the sites.
3. **Group Internet Activity:** Go online to look for government websites in your state. Compare them and list the differences.
4. **Individual and/ or Small Group Activity:** In the "Chunking and Sorting Activity Example" of the chapter, Beth McDonald and her classmates took on the activity of deciding what should be on a hypothetical government website for future students who would be taking the course. Break into small groups, and pretend your classmates and you are creating a government agency website to advise future students about the class. Create a basic Content Inventory for the site. Include in the inventory everything you think is

pertinent. Then write the topics of this inventory onto note cards or sticky notes as if they are the "chunks" of content for a website.

Individually sort the topics according to priority as if you were deciding what would be on the homepage or linked to lower levels of the website hierarchy. As you sort the materials ask yourself the *who, what, when, where, why,* and *how* questions in the section on chunking information. After everyone has completed the list and sorting, share yours with your classmates. Web content managers call the practice of individuals sorting on their own and then sharing with each other, "parallel designing." After sorting, use the best ideas from each person to improve yours. Repeat the process several times until the group is satisfied with the final product. Then either individually or as a group effort draw a rough sketch of a wireframe or, if the software is available, create a prototype of a homepage or several pages. After the assignment is complete, share what your group learned with the entire class.

If you want to take the assignment further, find some prospective students and interview them or ask them to participate in a sorting activity. Then compare what your group or class did with the prospective student input and revise the wireframe or the prototype.

5. **Individual or Group Activity:** The beginning of this chapter presents a great deal of statistical information about how Americans go about contacting their government. Try doing your own research study among your classmates or on campus. On a random basis students if they have contacted the local, state, or federal government in the past year, aside from sending in their income tax forms. See how many contacted local, state, or federal government agencies by telephone, email, website, letter, in person, or a combination. Then compare what you find with these studies. Write up a research paper for your class. Share your findings with your classmates.

6. **Individual Assignment:** Most word processing programs have a readability features. On Microsoft Word, for example, when it completes checking the spelling or grammar of a section of text it can display the reading level, word count, and Flesch Kincaid Grade level of the text, etc. Using the readability feature on a word processing program, take a variety of your own writing samples, and check them against the readability scale. What is the level for each sample? If there is a difference in the readability levels, how would you explain the difference? Find a government website at any level, copy the text into a word processing document, and check it against the readability scale. Share with your classmates what you find out.

7. **Individual Assignment:** Interview someone in your local government who is in charge of the website. Find out what he or she expects from web content writing and designing. Write up a description of what you find out. Share what you learned with your classmates.

8. **Individual Assignment:** You can begin to practice reading code by viewing the source coding for a website. In Internet Explorer, for instance, open a website, go to View on the Explorer menu at the top, and click on Source. The code for the website will then appear. Don't be taken aback if there is a lot of code that you cannot read. You are not expected to read code, just to get a sense of what it looks like. Go to several government websites on all levels of

government. Open the source code on each government site, and jot down the types of coding on the site, and other things you can readily see and tell about the codes. See if you can tell what web design software program was used, such as Dreamweaver or FrontPage. Then compare site coding for each site. Share what you learn with your classmates.

9. **Individual or Group Assignment:** Visit the campus Office of Disability Services or an organization that supports the disabled and find out what kinds of accessibility features they think are needed on websites for disabled students. Check the campus website and other local government websites to see if they are accessible. Report your findings to your class and to the campus website master, if needed.

10. **Individual or Group Assignment:** Go to government websites to find language that is complex and confusing to the average website viewer. Rewrite those passages into "plain language."

11. **Individual or Group Assignment:** Go to government websites for the same agency or similar agencies on different levels of government and compare the structure and features of the sites. Identify the text and visual design features of the sites. What might these features indicate about the primary audience? How are they similar or different? Which do you think is more effective and why?

12. **Individual Assignment:** Some people have suggested that ethnographic research about users can help create representations of actual people who use a website and prevent stereotypes of users. What is ethnographic research, and how might it aid in a realistic depiction of users? Research this topic, write up what you find, and share it with your classmates.

13. **Individual Assignment:** Write a research paper on one of the following topics: Plain Language Movement, Accessibility, or the World Wide Consortium (W3C).

Works Cited

Addison, Wesley, Longman. *Author's Guide*. New York: Addison, Wesley, Longman, 1998.

Americans with Disabilities Act (ADA) 4 June 2007 <http://www.ada.gov>.

CENDI: "Don't keep the Public Guessing: Best Practices in Notice of Copyright and Terms and Conditions of Use for Government Website Content." CENDI Copyright and Intellectual Property Working Group. 19 Oct. 2004. 29 June 2007 <http://www.cendi.gov/publications /04-04website_policy.pdf>.

Census 2000 Brief. U.S. Census Bureau. U.S. Department of Commerce. "Language Use and English Speaking Ability: Census 2000." 15 Oct. 2003 12 Aug. 2007 <http://www.census.gov/prod/2003pubs/c2kbr-29.pdf>.

Clinicaltrials website. 2 June 2007 <http://clinicaltrials.gov>.

"E-Government Act of 2002." The U.S National Archives and Record Administration 16 Oct. 2006 <http://www.archives.gov>.

Farkas, David K. and Jean B. Farkas. *Principles of Web Design*. New York: Pearson Education, 2002.

Horrigan, John. B. "How Americans Get in Touch with Government: Internet Users Benefit from the Efficiency of E-government, but Multiple Channels are Still Needed for Citizens to Reach Agencies and Solve Problems." Pew Internet & American Life Project 202-296-0019 24 May 2004. 29 June 2007 http://www.pewinternet.org/pdfs/PIP_E-GOV_Report_0504.pdf.

Internal Revenue Service (IRS) U.S. Department of Treasury. 15 Nov. 2006 <http://www.irs.gov/>.

Johnson-Sheehan, Richard. *Technical Communication Today.* New York: Pearson Longman, Inc., 2005.

Kansas state Website. 15 Nov 2006 <http://www.state.ks.us/>.

Lynch, Patrick and Sarah Horton. *Web Style Guide.* 2nd ed. Copyright 2004 Lynch and Horton <http://webstyleguide.com>.

Minnesota Department of Employment and Economic Development website. 15 Nov. 2006 <http://www.deed.state.mn.us/lmi/Home.htm>.

National Aeronautics and Space Administration (NASA) 15 Nov. 2006 <http://www.nasa.gov/mission_pages/exploration/news/COTS_selection.html>.

New York City Government website. 15 Nov 2006 <http://www.nyc.gov/portal/site/nycgov/>.

Nielsen, Jakob. "How Users Read on the Web." 1 Oct. 1997. Useit.com Alertbox. Copyright © 1997 by Jakob Nielsen. ISSN 1548-5552. 2 June 2007. <http://www.useit.com/alertbox/9710a.html>.

—. "Lower-Literacy Readers." Useit.com Alertbox. 14 Mar. 2005. Copyright © 2005 by Jakob Nielsen. ISSN 1548-5552 2 June 2007 <http://www.useit.com/alertbox/20050314.html>.

North Carolina Department of Transportation. 15 Nov. 2006 <http://www.ncdot.org/projects/roadbuilt/road.html>.

Oregon State Website. "Training for State Agencies." 10 Oct. 2006 <http://www.oregon.gov/DAS/legcoord.shtml>.

—. "What is Content Management?" 10 Oct. 2006 <http://www.oregon.gov/DAS/IRMD/EGOV/Faq_Content_mgmt.shtml>.

Pennsylvania state website. 3 June 2007. <http://www.usa.gov/webcontent/managing_content/organising/audience_viewpoint.shtml>. 15 Nov. 2006 <http://www.state.pa.us/>.

Plain Language website. 31 Jan. 2006 <http://plainlanguage.gov/>.

Rude, Carolyn D. *Technical Editing.* 4th ed. New York: Pearson Education, 2006.

Redish, Ginny. "Headings." PlainLanguage.gov 18 Nov. 2006 <http://www.plainlanguage.gov/howto/guidelines/headings.cfm>.

Section 508 "The Road to Accessibility" 4 June 2007 <http://www.section508.gov/index.cfm>.

Usability.gov website. 2 June 2007 <http://usability.gov>

USA.gov website. The Government's Official Web Portal "Site Index." 3 June 2007 http://www.usa.gov/site_index.shtml.

U.S. Copyright Office of the U.S. Library of Congress website. 5 June 2007. <http://www.copyright.gov/>.

U.S. Department of Agriculture (USDA). "Style Guide for the FSIS Web Site." 4 June 2007 <http://www.usa.gov/webcontent/documents/FSIS_styleguide.pdf>.

—. USDA *Web Presence Initiative Audience Analysis* 3 June 2007 <http://www.usa.gov/webcontent/documents/USDA_Audience_Analysis.pdf>.

U.S. Department of Health and Human Services. *Research-Based Web Design and Usability Guidelines*, 2003. 26 Oct. 2006 <http://www.usability.gov/pdfs/guidelines.html>.

Walters v. Reno. No. 9636304 U.S. 9th Circuit Court of Appeals. 18 May 1998.

Webcontent.gove. 3 Aug. 2007. 8 Aug. 2007
   <http://www.usa.gov/webcontent/index.shtml>.

—. "Best Practices." 14 Dec. 2005. 4 June 2007
   <http://www.usa.gov/webcontent/reqs_bestpractices/best_practices.shtml>.

—. "Checklist of ICGI Web Content Policy and Guidelines Recommendations." Aug. 2005.
   4 June 2007 <http://www.usa.gov/webcontent/reqs_bestpractices/
   checklist/short.pdf>.

—. "Content Management Systems Used by Government Agencies." 18 Jan. 2007. 8 Aug.
   2007 <http://www.usa.gov/webcontent/technology/products/cms.shtml>.

—. "Homepages." 12 Jan. 2007. 8 Aug. 2007 <http://www.usa.gov/webcontent/
   managing_content/organizing/homepages

—. "Organize Content Based on Audience Needs." 14 Dec. 2005. 4 June 2007
   <http://www.usa.gov/webcontent/managing_content/organizing/audience_
   viewpoint.shtml>.

—. "Requirements and Best Practices" 19 June 2007. 8 Aug. 2007
   <http://www.usa.gov/webcontent/reqs_bestpractices/best_practices.shtml>.

West, Darrell M. "State and Federal E-Government in the United States, 2006." Taubman
   Center for Public Policy, Brown University, August 2006. 5 June 2007
   <http://www.insidepolitics.org/egovt06us.pdf>.

Case Studies

CASE STUDY 1: Hurricane Katrina

Hurricane Katrina is arguably the worst natural disaster in American history. "Katrina was an extraordinary powerful and deadly hurricane that carried a wide swath of catastrophic damage and inflected a large loss of life" (Knabb, Rhome, and Brown). The official death toll in August 2006 stood at 1,810, of which some 1,464 were dead in Louisiana, and there were 135 people still missing (Louisiana Department of Health), making Katrina rank as one of the deadliest hurricanes in the nation's history (*World Almanac*). The property devastation estimate from Katrina topped $75 billion, the costliest in the nation's history, nearly double that of the next costliest hurricane—Andrew, which hit south Florida in August 1992 (Knabb, Rhome, and Brown).

Katrina formed August 23, 2005, in the central Bahamas; it had become a Category 1 storm when it hit south Florida, moved into a Category 5 storm in the Gulf of Mexico, made landfall as a Category 3 storm in Louisiana with 127-mph winds (Pain), and finally dissipated August 31, 2005, over the eastern Great Lakes on its way into Canada. During its course, it wreaked havoc, destruction, and death through the Bahamas, south Florida, Cuba, Louisiana, Mississippi, Alabama, the Florida Panhandle, and throughout eastern North America.

The greatest amount of damage and what the media captured most was the human suffering that resulted when levees breached and pumping stations stopped in the flood protection system for the "Crescent City," New Orleans, which is primarily situated below sea level at a bend in the Mississippi River, with Lake Pontchartrain on the north and Lake Borgne on the east. Originally colonized by the French, New Orleans has a unique history and culture in the United States. It is the home of jazz, uniquely American music, and some of the best food in the world. It is one of the country's major ports and has ranked as a key commercial and industrial center in the Southeast. It has been the headquarters for oil and chemical distribution and shipping, food processing, and shipbuilding and repairing. It has had many universities, and every year the city celebrates the legendary Mardi Gras.

The storm surges formed by Hurricane Katrina caused overtopping of floodwalls and the 18-foot-high levees, while erosion of the soil beneath the levees from the flooding led to more failures and breaches. Surge levels were measured as high as 18 to 25 feet (Seed, Nicholson, Dalrymple, et al. 1-5). Approximately 75 percent of the city was flooded (Seed, Nicholson, Dalrymple, et al. iv). Subsequently, Katrina moved inland and its high winds cut a diagonal path across Mississippi causing damage to almost the entire state and parts of Alabama.

More than 1.2 million people were under orders to evacuate before the hurricane's landfall near Buras-Triumph, Louisiana, at 6:10 A.M. CDT on Monday, August 29, 2005. By 11 A.M. that day the levees around New Orleans began to collapse. What unfolded was the worst-case scenario described in publications such as the 2002 Special Report series in the *The Times-Picayune* called "Washing Away," and in an emergency hurricane drill that included local, state, and federal emergency personnel only a year before for a hypothetical hurricane named Pam (Federal Emergency Management Agency).

Not only did the water from the breaches rise to rooftops, it became a toxic nightmare stew of untreated sewage, decomposing human bodies, dead animals, and chemicals and oils. People who had not evacuated were left stuck on their house tops, trapped in their attics, or stranded in the Louisiana Superdome or the Ernest N. Morial Convention Center, where the daily living conditions for thousands became horrific as supplies of food and water ran out, electricity and air conditioning failed, sanitary conditions deteriorated, and violence—or rumors of violence—ensued. Hospitals lost power and hospital staff took heroic measures to care for as many patients as they could. Many of the stranded were poor, African American, children, elderly, and the disabled. Some had not evacuated because they had no transportation and not enough money to leave. Some had gone through numerous hurricanes without major problems and decided to try to ride this one out too, and some stranded tourists did not have any way to evacuate once the transportation system in the city became overwhelmed and buckled.

Eventually, the Louisiana Department of Wildlife and Fisheries, the U.S. Coast Guard, other branches of the military, various organizations, and hundreds of volunteers began rescue efforts. The American Red Cross, the Salvation Army, and many volunteers began relief efforts. Within a couple of months of Katrina's landfall, evacuees were residing in all 50 states; some vowed to return to New Orleans and rebuild, and some vowed never to return. Ultimately, 1.5 million people were dislocated—the largest displacement of Americans because of a single incident since the 1927 flooding of the southern Mississippi River, which ultimately may have displaced as many as 700,000 (Von Drehle and Salmon). People had no homes, nowhere to work because businesses were lost, and nowhere to get funds because banks and government offices were closed. They had lost family, friends, community, and tradition (Mehren). Many people simply were left only with what they had on their backs.

Aside from the vast human suffering, the long-term economic impact to the region has been overwhelming. Tourism in the "Big Easy," one of its lifebloods, has been irreparably damaged; oil production and distribution have been affected; transportation and regional infrastructure such as railroads require extensive repair.

Not only did Katrina spawn widespread disaster, it created serious controversies, particularly over the delay in getting help to the people of New Orleans, the surrounding parishes, and all of the Gulf Coast affected by the storm. Michael D. Brown, the former director of the Federal Management Agency (FEMA) came under national scrutiny and resigned his post. Race and class became an issue. The 2000 U.S. census shows that the city of New Orleans was 67% black or African American and 28% white. In addition, the census indicated that 23.7% of families were below the poverty level (U.S. Census). Surveys after Katrina indicated the majority of African Americans believed race was the factor in the slow response by officials to the disaster, and whites believed that race was not a factor (Saad).

In addition to the question of racial bias in the delay about responding to the crisis, among the many other issues raised were these:

- The responsibility of the military in national rescue efforts
- The lack of coordination between local, state, and federal officials
- The failure of communication systems—cell phone towers that fell, lack of satellite phones, the lack of Internet service, etc.
- The role—both positive and negative—of the New Orleans police in the event

- How the new Department of Homeland Security, which oversees FEMA and has received billions in funding after 9-11, performed so inadequately
- The susceptibility of the elderly and the disabled in large-scale evacuations
- The vulnerability of the levees and how funding for shoring them up might have been used in the past for other projects
- How and why evacuation plans were not followed
- What to do about the tremendous amount of damaged or destroyed homes
- How to solve the hardship of families having to abandon pets because they were not allowed to evacuate with them

When Louisiana Gov. Kathleen Blanco's office handed over documents in December 2005 to Congressional committees investigating the government's failure in preparing for and responding to Hurricane Katrina, among the 100,000 pages of documents were emails, police reports, weather reports, logs of calls to be rescued, public statements, and many other documents (Simpson).

Activities and Assignments

1. **Individual or Group Activity:** Case Study 1 focuses on some of the early key documents and images associated with the Katrina disaster as they relate to the principles and approaches described in Chapter 1 and Chapter 2 of *Writing for the Government*. For each of them here, consider these questions:

   - Who is the audience (or stakeholders)?
   - What might be the demographics of the audience? Their level of knowledge and expertise? Their personal and professional needs for the document's information?
   - Who wrote the document and/or what agency released it? Who might have contributed to its writing, editing, design, and release? How does who is involved with the writing, editing, design, and distribution affect its presentation, communication, and credibility?
   - What is the tone and style of the language of the document? Are they appropriate for the audience?
   - What is the cultural context—the historical, political, social, economic, technological, and ethical possibilities and constraints—surrounding the writing and distribution of the document?
   - What are the characteristics of the genre for the document?
   - What kinds of ethical issues might have had to be dealt with in writing this document?
   - What technological factors contributed to the distribution of the document?

   After you compose answers to these questions, summarize your responses, and analyze whether you think the document or image's message was effective or not. Not every question may be relevant, but if you think a document or image is effective, provide evidence from the document to support your points. If you think it is not effective, describe what you think would make it communicate better. You may need to do some research about the document and the hurricane before making your decision. Included with the title for each of the documents are other questions to consider and address and/or to focus on as well as the questions above. After you have written your responses, share them with your classmates.

Document 1: "Hurricane Pam Exercise Concludes"

This document is a Federal Emergency Management Agency (FEMA) public relations piece released following an emergency preparedness exercise about a major hurricane hitting the New Orleans area. As you consider the previous questions, also consider these questions:

- When was this document released?
- Who was involved in this drill?
- How realistic were the parameters of the exercise?
- How is the document formatted to incorporate a lot of information?

(Please note that Col. Michael L. Brown, Deputy Director for Emergency Preparedness, Louisiana Office of Homeland Security and Emergency Preparedness, is someone different from Michael D. Brown, the former Director of Federal Emergency Management (FEMA).)

Find examples of other emergency drill documents, and compare them in terms of audience, purpose, cultural context, language, and format. Then write a report about what you find, and share it with your classmates.

Documents 2 and 3: "Governor Blanco Declares State of Emergency"

This document is a Proclamation. A Proclamation is a genre.

- What is the format of this genre for the document? What are its characteristics?
- Is it a useful genre? Why or why not?

Compare this document to "Governor Blanco asks President to Declare an Emergency for the State of Louisiana due to Hurricane Katrina." This document is the text of the official request for help from Governor Blanco to President Bush. Both of these documents were made available on the governor's website.

- Why do you think these were posted on there?
- What do you make of the opening sentences of them?
- What about the specifics in them?

Research proclamations from officials on various levels of government—local, state, and federal. Compare them for format, audience, purpose, and cultural context. Share what you find with your classmates.

Create your own Proclamation for something or some event, possibly related to your class or campus. Compare yours with your classmates' proclamations.

Document 4: "Memorandum to Michael Chertoff"

This memo from former FEMA Director, Michael D. Brown, to Michael Chertoff, the head of FEMA, created a great deal of controversy when it was released to the public.

- Can you tell why?
- What is the date of it, and what was happening at the time that could have sparked such controversy?
- What about the style and tone of it?

Compare it with the principles presented in Chapter 5 on writing memorandums. Write a research paper about what you find, and share it with your classmates.

Document 5: "Nagin tells Feds to Get off Their Asses"

This radio transcript is a different kind of document because it is an interview with Mayor Ray Nagin of New Orleans, which was taped in a New Orleans radio station, on Thursday night, September 1, 2005, four days after the hurricane hit New Orleans. Because of the natural disaster and electrical crisis in the city, many radio stations pooled together to broadcast emergency information.

- What do you think about Nagin's language?
- Considering the circumstances that New Orleans was in at the time, is Nagin's style and tone effective?
- Why or why not?

Write a short report with your opinion about the situation, citing reasons for your opinion based on research and/or personal experience. Cite specific information and quote from the transcript in your report.

Document 6: "President Outlines Hurricane Katrina Relief Efforts"

This document is an excerpt from the original on the White House webpage. Go online to view the full document. It is from the Office of the Press Secretary.

- What strikes you about the presentation of information and the language in it?
- How does it compare with President Bush's weekly radio addresses, for instance?
- What about the photo that accompanies the statement?

Discuss your ideas with a group of your classmates and share them with the entire class.

Document 7: Photos and emails

These are a series of photos of the Hurricane Katrina disaster in New Orleans and some email messages among FEMA employees to each other and to Michael Brown, then director of FEMA, during Hurricane Katrina and its aftermath. The emails here, which are a few of the many that have been released, have created controversy in and of themselves. The photos and the emails are from a Senate committee investigation.

- What do you make of the emails from Monty Bahamonde, who was one of the FEMA employees in New Orleans and who spent days and nights in the Louisiana Superdome?
- What do you think about the language and tone of the exchanges?
- What about some of the responses or lack thereof by Brown to concerns expressed by employees?

Discuss your ideas with your classmates.

Document 8: Preliminary Report

This document is the cover, "Executive Summary," is from a "Preliminary Report on the Performance of the New Orleans Levee System in Hurricane Katrina on August 29, 2005."

- Why is this document different from the previous ones?
- How many authors does it have? Does that matter? Why or why not?
- What about the language is different?
- What is the purpose of this document?

Find this report online and compare it with the information in Chapter 6 on Policy Report Writing. Write up what you find, and share it with your classmates.

2. **Individual or Group Activity:** Many parts of the United States have the potential for or experience natural disasters: tornados, wildfires, hot and cold weather–related deaths, floods, and earthquakes. Individual students or in groups can contact various

emergency and first responders in your communities to find out what they do to assist citizens in disastrous situations. Write a research paper and make a presentation to your classmates about your findings.

3. **Individual or Group Activity:** Investigate documents and research the other controversial issues mentioned earlier in the bulleted list on page 210–213, analyze them in a similar manner, write what you find, and share it with your classmates.

Works Cited

Knabb, Richard D., Jamie R. Rhome and Daniel P. Brown. "Tropical Cyclone Report, Hurricane Katrina, 23–30 Aug. 2005." National Hurricane Center. TCR-AL122005_Katrina.pdf. 6 Jan. 2006 <http://www.nhc.noaa.gov/2005atlan.shtml?>.

Federal Emergency Management Agency (FEMA). "Hurricane Pam Concludes." News Release. 23 July 2004. Release Number: R6-04-093. 28 Sept. 2005 <http://www.fema.gov/news/newsrelease_print.fema?id=13051>.

Louisiana Department of Health and Hospitals. "Hurricane Katina Deceased Reports. Reports of Missing and Deceased Aug. 2 2006." 8 Jan. 2007 <http://www.dhh.louisiana.gov/offices/page.asp?ID=192&Detail=5248>.

Mehren, Elizabeth. "Study: Katrina Evacuees Having Trouble Coping." From the *Los Angeles Times Seattle Times Online* 6 Jan. 2006. 6 Jan. 2006 <http://www.seattletimes.com>.

National Ocean and Atmospheric Agency (NOAA). National Hurricane Center. "Tropical Weather Summary." 5 Jan. 2006 <http://nhc.noaa.gov/archive/2005/tws/MIATWSAT_augshtml?>.

Pain, John. "Researchers Say Katrina was Weaker than Believed." Associated Press. 21 Dec. 2005. AOL news. 21 Dec. 2005 <http://aolsvc.news.aol.com/>.

Seed, Raymond B., Peter G. Nicholson, Robert A. Dalrymple, et al. *Preliminary Report on the Performance of the New Orleans Levee Systems in Hurricane Katrina on August 29, 2005* 1.2 17 Nov. 2005. Report No. UCB/CITRIS-05/01. 11 Jan. 2007 <http://hsgac.senate.gov/_files/Katrina/Preliminary_Report.pdf>.

Saad, Lydia. "Blacks Blast Bush for Katrina Response." The Gallup Poll. 14 Sept. 2005. 6 Jan. 2006 <http://galluppoll.com/content/default.aspx?ci=18526>.

Simpson, Doug. "Blanco's Katrina Correspondence Reveals Extent of Chaos." Associated Press. 4 Dec. 2005. AOL news. 4 Dec. 2005 <http://aolsvc.news.aol.com/Dec.2005>.

World Almanac and Book of Facts, The. "Some Notable Hurricanes, Typhoons, Blizzards, Other Storms." Section: Disasters. Oclc FirstSearch database. 25 June 2007 <http://firstsearch.oclc.org>.

U.S. Census Bureau, Census 2000. "Table DP-1. Profile of General Demographic Characteristics: 2000." Geographic area: New Orleans city, Louisiana. 6 June 2006 <http://www.census.gov/>.

U.S. Senate. Hurricane Katrina: A Nation Still Unprepared: Special Report of the Committee on Homeland Security and Governmental Affairs. United States Senate together with Additional Views. 109th Cong. 2nd sess. Rept. 109–322. Washington: GPO, 2006. <http://hsgac.senate.gov/_files/Katrina/FullReport.pdf>.

Von Drehle, David and Jacqueline Salmon. "Displacement of Historic Proportions." 02 Sept. 2005. 2 Sept. 2005 <http://www.washingtonpost.com/wp-dyn/content/article/2005/09/01/AR2005090102406_pf.html>.

"Washing Away." *The Times-Picayune.* 23-27 June 2002. 6 Jan. 2006 <http://www.nola.com/hurricane/?/washingaway/>.

Hurricane Pam Exercise Concludes

Release Date: July 23, 2004
Release Number: R6-04-093

BATON ROUGE, La. -- Hurricane Pam brought sustained winds of 120 mph, up to 20 inches of rain in parts of southeast Louisiana and storm surge that topped levees in the New Orleans area. More than one million residents evacuated and Hurricane Pam destroyed 500,000-600,000 buildings. Emergency officials from 50 parish, state, federal and volunteer organizations faced this scenario during a five-day exercise held this week at the State Emergency Operations Center in Baton Rouge.

The exercise used realistic weather and damage information developed by the National Weather Service, the U.S. Army Corps of Engineers, the LSU Hurricane Center and other state and federal agencies to help officials develop joint response plans for a catastrophic hurricane in Louisiana.

"We made great progress this week in our preparedness efforts," said Ron Castleman, FEMA Regional Director. "Disaster response teams developed action plans in critical areas such as search and rescue, medical care, sheltering, temporary housing, school restoration and debris management. These plans are essential for quick response to a hurricane but will also help in other emergencies."

"Hurricane planning in Louisiana will continue," said Colonel Michael L. Brown, Deputy Director for Emergency Preparedness, Louisiana Office of Homeland Security and Emergency Preparedness. "Over the next 60 days, we will polish the action plans developed during the Hurricane Pam exercise. We have also determined where to focus our efforts in the future."

A partial summary of action plans follows:

Debris

- The debris team estimates that a storm like Hurricane Pam would result in 30 million cubic yards of debris and 237,000 cubic yards of household hazardous waste
- The team identified existing landfills that have available storage space and locations of hazardous waste disposal sites. The debris plan also outlines priorities for debris removal.

Sheltering

- The interagency shelter group identified the need for about 1,000 shelters for a catastrophic disaster. The shelter team identified 784 shelters and has developed plans for locating the remaining shelters.
- In a storm like Hurricane Pam, shelters will likely remain open for 100 days. The group identified the resources necessary to support 1000 shelters for 100 days. They planned for staff augmentation and how to include shelterees in shelter management.

- State resources are adequate to operate shelters for the first 3-5 days. The group planned how federal and other resources will replenish supplies at shelters.

Search and Rescue

- The search and rescue group developed a transportation plan for getting stranded residents out of harm's way.
- Planners identified lead and support agencies for search and rescue and established a command structure that will include four areas with up to 800 searchers.

Medical

- The medical care group reviewed and enhanced existing plans. The group determined how to implement existing immunization plans rapidly for tetanus, influenza and other diseases likely to be present after a major hurricane.
- The group determined how to re-supply hospitals around the state that would face heavy patient loads.
- The medical action plan includes patient movement details and identifies probable locations, such as state university campuses, where individuals would receive care and then be transported to hospitals, special needs shelters or regular shelters as necessary.

Schools

- The school group determined that 13,000-15,000 teachers and administrators would be needed to support affected schools. The group acknowledged the role of local school boards and developed strategies for use by local school officials.
- Staffing strategies include the use of displaced teachers, retired teachers, emergency certified teachers and others eligible for emergency certification. Displaced paraprofessionals would also be recruited to fill essential school positions.
- The group discussed facility options for increasing student population at undamaged schools and prioritizing repairs to buildings with less damage to assist in normalizing operations
- The school plan also calls for placement or development of temporary schools near temporary housing communities built for hurricane victims.

The Hurricane Pam scenario focused on 13 parishes in southeast Louisiana-Ascension, Assumption, Jefferson, Lafourche, Orleans, Plaquemines, St. Bernard, St. Charles, St. James, St. John, St. Tammany Tangipahoa, Terrebonne. Representatives from outside the primary parishes participated since hurricane evacuation and sheltering involve communities throughout the state and into Arkansas, Mississippi and Texas.

On March 1, 2003, FEMA became part of the U.S. Department of Homeland Security. FEMA's continuing mission within the new department is to lead the effort to prepare the nation for all hazards and effectively manage federal response and recovery efforts following any national incident. FEMA also initiates proactive mitigation activities, trains first responders, and manages the National Flood Insurance Program and the U.S. Fire Administration.

Last Updated: Friday, 23-Jul-2004 15:05:38

State of Louisiana

EXECUTIVE DEPARTMENT

PROCLAMATION NO. 33 KBB 2007

LIMITED EXTENSION OF STATE OF EMERGENCY - HURRICANE KATRINA

WHEREAS, Proclamation No. 48 KBB 2005, issued on August 26, 2005, declared a state of emergency for the state of Louisiana due to Hurricane Katrina's potential to cause severe storms, high winds, and torrential rain that could cause flooding and damage to private property and public facilities, and threaten the safety and security of the citizens of Louisiana;

WHEREAS, On August 29, 2005, Hurricane Katrina struck Louisiana resulting in severe flooding, damage, and the interruption in the delivery of utility services to the southeastern part of the state of Louisiana, which has threatened the safety, health, and security of the citizens of the state of Louisiana, along with private property and public facilities;

WHEREAS, the extreme damage caused by Hurricane Katrina continues to cause disaster and emergency conditions, as indicated above, in the most affected areas, as evidenced, for example, by the deployment of the Louisiana National Guard for peacekeeping measures, the extraordinary housing across the state of inmates evacuated from parishes affected by the disaster, the continued assessment and remediation of the environmental impact of the disaster, and the use of property to expedite levee repair and reconstruction;

WHEREAS, it is necessary to renew Proclamation No. 48 KBB 2005, as extended by subsequent proclamations, to further extend the state of emergency due to the continuation of emergency/disaster conditions;

NOW THEREFORE I, KATHLEEN BABINEAUX BLANCO, Governor of the state of Louisiana, by virtue of the authority vested by the Constitution and laws of the state of Louisiana, do hereby order and direct as follows:

SECTION 1: Pursuant to Title 29 of the Louisiana Revised Statutes of 1950 and the Louisiana Homeland Security and Emergency Assistance and Disaster Act, R.S. 29:721, *et seq*., a state of emergency/disaster is declared to continue to exist in the state of Louisiana due to Hurricane Katrina and its aftermath, which resulted in severe storm damage and extreme flooding to private property and public facilities, and continues to threaten the safety, health, and security of the citizens of the state of Louisiana;

SECTION 2: The state of emergency/disaster is extended for an additional thirty (30) days through Friday, May 18, 2007, unless terminated sooner.

IN WITNESS WHEREOF, I have hereunto set my hand officially and caused to be affixed the Great Seal of the state of Louisiana, at the Capitol, in the city of Baton Rouge, on this 16th day of April, 2007.

/S/ Kathleen Babineaux Blanco
GOVERNOR OF LOUISIANA

ATTEST BY
THE GOVERNOR

/S/ Jay Dardenne
SECRETARY OF STATE

PRINT   << BACK

Aug 27, 2005

Governor Blanco asks President to Declare an Emergency for the State of Louisiana due to Hurricane Katrina

BATON ROUGE-Today Governor Kathleen Babineaux Blanco forwarded a letter to President Bush requesting that he declare an emergency for the State of Louisiana due to Hurricane Katrina. The full text of the letter follows:

August 27, 2005

The President The White House Washington, D. C.

Through: Regional Director FEMA Region VI 800 North Loop 288 Denton, Texas 76209

Dear Mr. President:

Under the provisions of Section 501 (a) of the Robert T. Stafford Disaster Relief and Emergency Assistance Act, 42 U.S.C. ïï 512 1-5206 (Stafford Act), and implemented by 44 CFR ï 206.35, I request that you declare an emergency for the State of Louisiana due to Hurricane Katrina for the time period beginning August 26, 2005, and continuing. The affected areas are all the southeastern parishes including the New Orleans Metropolitan area and the mid state Interstate I-49 corridor and northern parishes along the I-20 corridor that are accepting the thousands of citizens evacuating from the areas expecting to be flooded as a result of Hurricane Katrina. In response to the situation I have taken appropriate action under State law and directed the execution of the State Emergency Plan on August 26, 2005 in accordance with Section 501 (a) of the Stafford Act. A State of Emergency has been issued for the State in order to support the evacuations of the coastal areas in accordance with our State Evacuation Plan and the remainder of the state to support the State Special Needs and Sheltering Plan.

Pursuant to 44 CFR ï 206.35, I have determined that this incident is of such severity and magnitude that effective response is beyond the capabilities of the State and affected local governments, and that supplementary Federal assistance is necessary to save lives, protect property, public health, and safety, or to lessen or avert the threat of a disaster. I am specifically requesting emergency protective measures, direct Federal Assistance, Individual and Household Program (IHP) assistance, Special Needs Program assistance, and debris removal. Preliminary estimates of the types and amount of emergency assistance needed under the Stafford Act, and emergency assistance from certain Federal agencies under other statutory authorities are tabulated in Enclosure A.

The following information is furnished on the nature and amount of State and local resources that have been or will be used to alleviate the conditions of this emergency: ï Department of Social Services (DSS): Opening (3) Special Need Shelters (SNS) and establishing (3) on Standby. ï Department of Health and Hospitals (DHH): Opening (3) Shelters and establishing (3) on Standby. ï Office of Homeland Security and Emergency Preparedness (OHSEP): Providing generators and support staff for SNS and Public Shelters. ï Louisiana State Police (LSP): Providing support for the phased evacuation of the coastal areas. ï Louisiana Department of Wildlife and Fisheries (WLF): Supporting the evacuation of the affected population and preparing for Search and Rescue Missions.

Mr. President Page Two August 27, 2005

ï Louisiana Department of Transportation and Development (DOTD): Coordinating traffic flow and management of the evacuations routes with local officials and the State of Mississippi.

The following information is furnished on efforts and resources of other Federal agencies, which have been or will be used in responding to this incident: ï FEMA ERT-A Team en-route.

I certify that for this emergency, the State and local governments will assume all applicable non-Federal share of costs required by the Stafford Act.

I request Direct Federal assistance for work and services to save lives and protect property.

(a) List any reasons State and local government cannot perform or contract for performance, (if applicable).

(b) Specify the type of assistance requested.

In accordance with 44 CFR ï 206.208, the State of Louisiana agrees that it will, with respect to Direct Federal assistance:

1. Provide without cost to the United States all lands, easement, and rights-of-ways necessary to accomplish the approved work.

2. Hold and save the United States free from damages due to the requested work, and shall indemnify the Federal Government against any claims arising from such work;

3. Provide reimbursement to FEMA for the non-Federal share of the cost of such work in accordance with the provisions of the FEMA-State Agreement; and

4. Assist the performing Federal agency in all support and local jurisdictional matters.

In addition, I anticipate the need for debris removal, which poses an immediate threat to lives, public health, and safety.

Pursuant to Sections 502 and 407 of the Stafford Act, 42 U.S.C. ïï 5192 & 5173, the State agrees to indemnify and hold harmless the United States of America for any claims arising from the removal of debris or wreckage for this disaster. The State agrees that debris removal from public and private property will not occur until the landowner signs an unconditional authorization for the removal of debris.

I have designated Mr. Art Jones as the State Coordinating Officer for this request. He will work with the Federal Emergency Management Agency in damage assessments and may provide further information or justification on my behalf.

Sincerely,

Kathleen Babineaux Blanco Governor Enclosure

ENCLOSURE A TO EMERGENCY REQUEST

Estimated requirements for other Federal agency programs: ï Department of Social Services (DSS): Opening (3) Special Need Shelters (SNS) and establishing (3) on Standby. Costs estimated at $500,000 per week for each in operation. ï Department of Health and Hospitals (DHH): Opening (3) Shelters and establishing (3) on Standby. Costs estimated at $500,000 per week for each in operation. ï Office of Homeland Security and Emergency Preparedness (OHSEP): Providing generators and support staff for SNS and Public Shelters. Costs estimated to range from $250,000-$500,000 to support (6) Shelter generator operations. ï Louisiana State Police (LSP): Costs to support evacuations - $300,000 for a non-direct landfall. ï Louisiana Department of Wildlife and Fisheries (WLF): Costs to support evacuations - $200,000 for a non-direct landfall. ï Louisiana Department of Transportation and Development (DOTD): Costs to support evacuations - $2,000,000 for a non-direct landfall.

Totals: $ 9,000,000 Estimated Requirements for assistance under the Stafford Act: Coordination: $0 Technical and advisory assistance: $0 Debris removal: $0 Emergency protective measures: $ 9,000,000 Individuals and Households Program (IHP): $0 Distribution of emergency supplies: $0 Other (specify): $0 Totals: $ 9,000,000 Grand Total: $ 9,000,000

The Louisiana Disaster Recovery Foundation (LDRF), Louisiana's fund for Louisiana's people, has been established by Governor Kathleen Babineaux Blanco in order to support long-term family restoration and recovery and help provide assistance to our citizens in need through a network of Louisiana charities and non-profit agencies.

1-877-HELPLA1 (877-435-7521) www.louisianahelp.org

Office of the Under Secretary
U.S. Department of Homeland Security
500 C Street, SW
Washington, DC 20472

FEMA

August 29, 2005

MEMORANDUM TO: Michael Chertoff
                  Secretary of Homeland Security

FROM: Michael D. Brown
                  Under Secretary

SUBJECT: DHS Response to Katrina

We are requesting your assistance to make available DHS employees willing to deploy as soon as possible for a two-week minimum field assignment to serve in a variety of positions. We anticipate needing at least 1000 additional DHS employees within 48 hours and 2000 within 7 days. Attached is a list of requirements that employees will have to meet before deploying.

It is beneficial to use DHS employees as it allows us to be more efficient responding to the needs of this disaster and it reinforces the Department's All-Hazard's Capabilities. Also, DHS employees already have background investigations, travel cards and badges, all items that normally delay filling our surge workforce. FEMA Response and Recovery operations are a top priority of the Department and as we know, one of yours.

We will also want to identify staff with specialized skills such as bilingual capabilities, Commercial Driver's License (CDL), and logistics capabilities.

Thank you for your consideration in helping us meet our responsibilities in this near catastrophic event.

Attachment

cc: Michael P. Jackson
     Deputy Secretary

     Janet Hale
     Under Secretary for Management

www.fema.gov

Attachment

Requirements:

You must have your supervisor's approval.
Contact your Human Resource Office to follow-up with FEMA Human Resource Office
You must be physically able to work in a disaster area without refrigeration for
medications and have the ability to work in the outdoors all day.
Must be willing to work long hours under arduous conditions.

Role of Assigned Personnel:

Establish and maintain positive working relationships with disaster affected communities
and the citizens of those communities.
Collect and disseminate information and make referrals for appropriate assistance.
Identification of potential issues within the community and reporting to appropriate
personnel.
Convey a positive image of disaster operations to government officials, community
organizations and the general public.
Perform outreach with community leaders on available Federal disaster assistance.

Training will be provided:

A roster of available personnel will be developed and made available as components
identify personnel for deployment.
Selected personnel from the roster will be given training in Emmitsburg, Maryland,
Atlanta, Georgia and Orlando, Florida, before you are deployed to the field.
You will be expected to use government credit cards (in good standing) for
transportation, lodging, meals and other incidentals.
Contact your agency financial officer for information on obtaining government credit
card (if you do not hold one).

Point of Contact to accept and process your assignment:

Human Resource Operations Branch, 202-646-4040
You will be walked through the system for further processing and deployment.

Deployment Information:

Selected personnel will either go to Atlanta, Georgia for Community Relations Training
or Orlando, Florida for all other Training and assignments. After which they will be
deployed to a disaster Joint Field Office (FCO) when conditions are safe. Some
organizational clothing and equipment will be supplied.

Type of personal supplies you should bring:

Sunscreen
Sun hat
Sun Glasses
Walking shoes
Mosquito repellant
Medication (both over the counter and prescriptions)
Valid driver's license
Government ID
Cash (ATMs may not be working)
Government equipment (cell phones, computers, blackberries, etc)
Appropriate clothing (walking shorts acceptable)
Rain gear

Nagin transcript

The following is a transcript of part of an interview done over WWL-AM Radio by Garland
Robinette with New Orleansí Mayor Ray Nagin on the evening of Thursday, Sept. 1, 2005, four days
after Hurricane Katrina ravaged the city and the Gulf Coast. During that time, WWL was one of the
only radio stations in the area remaining on the air, and its emergency coverage, which was
simulcast on numerous other local radio stations, was called, "The United Radio Broadcasters of
New Orleans." The United Radio Broadcasters are a partnership between Entercom and Clear
Channel Communications.

[announcer cues up second half of interview with Nagin]

NAGIN: ...and to give me executive powers to authorize me to dictate and to manage military resources down here and I'll
fix this for ya. You call him right now and you call the governor, and you tell him to delegate the power that they have to
the mayor of New Orleans and we'll get this damn thing fixed. (pause) It's politics man, and they're playing games and
they're spinning. They're out there spinning for the cameras.

WWL: But, but..

NAGIN: And..

 WWL: But, can't they, can't they just if nothing else look at 25% of their energy coming from the state is not flowing
through the pipelines? We're on the verge of anarchy? Can't they understand that there, if nothing else they're going to
be hurt politically?

NAGIN: I don't know what they're doing. I mean the air conditioning must be good, because I haven't had any in five
days. Uh, and maybe, so maybe there's some, some smoke coming out from the air conditioning units that's clogging
some folks, uh, you know, their vision.

WWL: Have you talked with the president?

NAGIN: I've talked directly with the president.

WWL: What is he saying?

NAGIN: I've talked with the head of homeland security. I've talked to everybody under the sun. I've been out there man,
I've flew these helicopters, been in the crowds talking to people crying don't know where their, where their relatives are.
I've done it all, man, and I'll tell you, man, Garland, I keep hearing that it's comin. This is coming, that is coming, and
my answer to that, today, is: B.S. Where is the beef?

WWL: What?

NAGIN: Because there is no beef in this city. There is no beef anywhere in Southeast Louisiana and these goddamn ships
that are coming, I don't see them.

WWL: What did you say to the president of the United States and what did he say to you?

NAGIN: I basically told him we had an incredible, uh, crisis here and that his flying over in Air Force One does not do it
justice. And that I have been all around this city, and I am very frustrated because we are not able to marshal resources
and we're outmanned in just about every respect. You know the reason why the looters got out of control? Because we
had most of our resources saving people, thousands of people, for, that were stuck in attics, man, old ladies... when you
pull off the doggone ventilator vent and you look down there and they're standing in there in water up to their fricking neck.

And they don't have a clue what's going on down here. They flew down here one time, two days after the doggone event
was over with TV cameras, AP reporters, all kind of goddamn -- excuse my French everybody in America, but I am
pissed.

WWL: Did you say, did you say to the president of the United States, "I need the military in here"?

NAGIN: I said, "I need everything." Now, I will tell you this -- and I give the president, uh, some credit on this -- he sent
one John Wayne dude down here that can get some stuff done, and his name is Gen. Honore. And he came off the
doggone chopper, and he start cussing and people start moving. And he's gettin some stuff done. They ought to give that
guy -- if they don't want to give it to me--give him full authority to get the job done, and we can save some people.

WWL: What do you need, right now, to get control of this situation?

NAGIN: I need reinforcements, I need troops, man. I need 500 buses, man. We ain't talking about -- you know, one of the
briefings we had, they were talking about getting, uh, you know, public school bus drivers to come down here and bus

Source: Excerpt from Nagin Interview by Garland Robinette. Source: Broadcast over WWL-AM
Radio. 1 Sept. 2005. Transcript by Jennifer R. Johnson. January 2006.

Nagin transcript

people out here. I'm like, "You got to be kidding me. This is a national disaster. Get every doggone Greyhound bus line in the country and get their asses moving to New Orleans." That's -- they're thinking small, man. And this is a major, major, major deal. [pause] And I can't emphasize it enough, man. This is crazy. I've got 15 to 20 thousand people over at the convention center. It's bursting at the seams. The poor people in Plaquemines Parish, theyíre, theyíre air-vaccing people over here in New Orleans. We don't have anything, and we're sharing with our brothers in Plaquemines Parish. It's awful down here, man.

WWL: Do you believe that the president is seeing this, holding a news conference on it but can't do anything until Kathleen Blanco requested him to do it? And do you know whether or not she has made that request?

NAGIN: I have no idea what they're doing. But I will tell you this: You know, God is looking down on all this, and if they are not doing everything in their power to save people, they are going to pay the price; because every day that we delay, people are dying. And they're dying by the hundreds; I'm willing to bet you. They're, we're getting reports and calls that is breaking my heart, from people saying, "I've been in my attic. I can't take it anymore. The water is up to my neck. I don't think I can hold out." And that's happening as we speak. And, you know what really upsets me, Garland? We told everybody the importance of the 17th Street Canal issue. We said, "Please, please take care of this. We don't care what you do. Figure it out."

WWL: Who'd you say that to?

NAGIN: Everybody: the governor, you know, Homeland Security, FEMA. You name it, we said it. And, you know, they allowed that pumping station next to it, Pumping Station 6 to, to go under water. Our sewage and water board people, Marcel St. Martin stayed there and endangered their lives. And what happened when that pumping station went down, the water started flowing again in the city, and it starting getting to levels that probably killed more people. In addition to that, we had water, uh, flowing through the pipes in the city. That's a power station over there. So there's no water flowing anywhere on the east bank of Orleans Parish. So our critical water supply was destroyed because of lack of action.

WWL: Why couldn't they drop the 3,000-pound sandbags or the containers that they were talking about earlier? Was it an engineering feat that just couldn't be done?

NAGIN: It, it, they said it was some pulleys that they had to manufacture. But, you know, in a state of emergency, man, you you are creative, you figure out ways to get stuff done. Then they told me that they went overnight, and they built seventeen, seventeen concrete structures and they had the pulleys on them and they were going to drop them. I flew over that thing yesterday, and it's in the same shape that it was after the storm hit. There is nothing happening. And they're feeding the public a line of bull and they're spinnin, and people are dying down here.

WWL: If some of the public called and they're right, that there's a law that the president, that the federal government can't do anything without local or state requests, would you request martial law?

NAGIN: I've already called for martial law in the city of New Orleans. We did that a few days ago.

WWL: Did the governor do that, too?

NAGIN: I don't know. I don't think so. But we called for martial law when we realized that the looting was getting out of control. And we redirected all of our police officers back to patrolling the streets. They were dirt dead-tired from saving people, but they worked all night because we thought this thing was going to blow wide open last night. And so we redirected all of our resources, and we hold it under check. I'm not sure if we can do that another night with the current resources. And I am telling you right now: They're showing all these reports of people looting and doing all that weird stuff, and they are doing that, but people are desperate. And they're trying to find food and water, the majority of them. Now you got some knuckleheads out there, and they are taking advantage of this lawless -- this situation where, you know, we can't really control it, and they're doing some awful, awful things. But that's a small majority of the people. Most people are looking to try and survive. And you've got, and one of the things people have -- nobody's talked about this. Drugs flowed in and out of New Orleans and the surrounding metropolitan area so freely it was scary to me, and that's why we were having escalation in murders. People don't want to talk about this, but I'm going to talk about it. You have drug addicts that are now walking around this city looking for a fix. And that's the reason why they were breaking in hospitals and drugstores. They're looking for something to take the edge off of their jones', if you will. And right now, they don't have anything to take the edge off. And they've found, theyíve probably found guns. So what you're seeing is drug-starving crazy addicts: drug addicts that are wrecking havoc. And we don't have the manpower to adequately deal with it. We can only target certain sections of the city and form a perimeter around them and hope to God that we're not overrun.

WWL: Well, you and I must be in the minority. Because apparently there's a section of our citizenry out there that thinks because of a law that says the federal government can't come in unless requested by the proper people, that everything that's going on to this point has been done as good as it can possibly be.

NAGIN: Really?

WWL: I know you don't feel that way.

Nagin transcript

NAGIN: Well, did the tsunami victims request? Did it go through a formal process to request? Uh, you know, did the Iraqi people request that we go in there?

WWL: They..

NAGIN: Did they ask us to go in there? What is more important? This is ...and I'll tell you, man, I'm probably going get in a whole bunch of trouble. I'm probably going to get in so much trouble it ain't even funny. You probably won't even want to deal with me after this interview is over.

WWL: You and I will be in the funny place together.

NAGIN: But we authorized $8 billion to go to Iraq: lickety quick. After 9/11, we gave the president unprecedented powers lickety quick to take care of New York and other places. Now, you mean to tell me that a place where most of your oil is coming through, a place that is so unique when you mention New Orleans anywhere around the world, everybody's eyes light up -- you mean to tell me that a place where you probably have thousands of people that have died and thousands more that are dying every day, that we can't figure out a way to authorize the resources that we need? Come on, man. You know, I'm not one of those drug addicts. I am thinking very clearly. And I don't know whose problem it is. I don't know whether it's the governor's problem. I don't know whether it's the president problem, but somebody needs to get their ass on a plane and sit down, the two of them, and figure this out right now. [pause]

WWL: What can we do here?

NAGIN: Keep talking about it.

WWL: We'll do that. What else can we do?

NAGIN: Organize people to write letters and make calls to their congressmen,

WWL: E-mails

NAGIN: To the president, to the governor. Flood their doggone offices with requests to do something. This is ridiculous.

WWL: You know

NAGIN: I don't want to see anybody do anymore goddamn press conferences. Put a moratorium on press conferences.

WWL: Who do I

NAGIN: Don't do another press conference until the resources are in this city. And then come down to this city and stand with us when there are military trucks and troops that we can't even count. Don't tell me 40,000 people are coming here. They not here. [pause] It's too doggone late. Now get off your asses and let's do something, and let's fix the biggest goddamn crisis in the history of this country.

WWL: I'll say it right now, you're the only politician that's called and called for arms like this. And if -- whatever it takes, the governor, president -- whatever law precedent it takes, whatever it takes, I bet that the people listening to you are on your side.

NAGIN: Well, I hope so, Garland. I am just -- I'm at the point now where it don't matter. People are dying. They don't have homes. They don't have jobs. The city of New Orleans will never be the same [2 second pause] in this time.

[15 second pause] sounds of breathing, hitching catching breath.

WWL: [in wavering voice, sounds of sobbing in background] We're both pretty speechless here.

NAGIN: [sob] Yeah, I don't know what to say. I got to go.

WWL: [wavering] OK. Keep in touch. Keep in touch.

(Transcript by Jennifer R. Johnson. January 2006)

For Immediate Release
Office of the Press Secretary
September 15, 2005

President Discusses Hurricane Relief in Address to the Nation
Jackson Square
New Orleans, Louisiana

8:02 P.M. CDT

THE PRESIDENT: Good evening. I'm speaking to you from the city of New Orleans -- nearly empty, still partly under water, and waiting for life and hope to return. Eastward from Lake Pontchartrain, across the Mississippi coast, to Alabama into Florida, millions of lives were changed in a day by a cruel and wasteful storm.

In the aftermath, we have seen fellow citizens left stunned and uprooted, searching for loved ones, and grieving for the dead, and looking for meaning in a tragedy that seems so blind and random. We've also witnessed the kind of desperation no citizen of this great and generous nation should ever have to know -- fellow Americans calling out for food and water, vulnerable people left at the mercy of criminals who had no mercy, and the bodies of the dead lying uncovered and untended in the street.

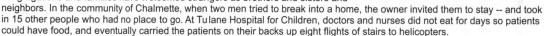

These days of sorrow and outrage have also been marked by acts of courage and kindness that make all Americans proud. Coast Guard and other personnel rescued tens of thousands of people from flooded neighborhoods. Religious congregations and families have welcomed strangers as brothers and sisters and neighbors. In the community of Chalmette, when two men tried to break into a home, the owner invited them to stay -- and took in 15 other people who had no place to go. At Tulane Hospital for Children, doctors and nurses did not eat for days so patients could have food, and eventually carried the patients on their backs up eight flights of stairs to helicopters.

. . .

The work of rescue is largely finished; the work of recovery is moving forward. In nearly all of Mississippi, electric power has been restored. Trade is starting to return to the Port of New Orleans, and agricultural shipments are moving down the Mississippi River. All major gasoline pipelines are now in operation, preventing the supply disruptions that many feared. The breaks in the levees have been closed, the pumps are running, and the water here in New Orleans is receding by the hour. Environmental officials are on the ground, taking water samples, identifying and dealing with hazardous debris, and working to get drinking water and waste water treatment systems operating again. And some very sad duties are being carried out by professionals who gather the dead, treat them with respect, and prepare them for their rest.

The Department of Homeland Security is registering evacuees who are now in shelters and churches, or private homes, whether in the Gulf region or far away. I have signed an order providing immediate assistance to people from the disaster area. As of today, more than 500,000 evacuee families have gotten emergency help to pay for food, clothing, and other essentials. Evacuees who have not yet registered should contact FEMA or the Red Cross. We need to know who you are, because many of you will be eligible for broader assistance in the future. Many families were separated during the evacuation, and we are working to help you reunite. Please call this number: 1-877-568-3317 -- that's 1-877-568-3317 -- and we will work to bring your family back together, and pay for your travel to reach them.

In addition, we're taking steps to ensure that evacuees do not have to travel great distances or navigate bureaucracies to get the benefits that are there for them. The Department of Health and Human Services has sent more than 1,500 health professionals, along with over 50 tons of medical supplies -- including vaccines and antibiotics and medicines for people with chronic conditions such as diabetes. The Social Security Administration is delivering checks. The Department of Labor is helping displaced persons apply for temporary jobs and unemployment benefits. And the Postal Service is registering new addresses so that people can get their mail.

To carry out the first stages of the relief effort and begin rebuilding at once, I have asked for, and the Congress has provided, more than $60 billion. This is an unprecedented response to an unprecedented crisis, which demonstrates the compassion and resolve of our nation.

Our second commitment is to help the citizens of the Gulf Coast to overcome this disaster, put their lives back together, and rebuild their communities

. . .

Our third commitment is this: When communities are rebuilt, they must be even better and stronger than before the storm. Within the Gulf region are some of the most beautiful and historic places in America. As all of us saw on television, there's also some deep, persistent poverty in this region, as well. That poverty has roots in a history of racial discrimination, which cut off generations from the opportunity of America. We have a duty to confront this poverty with bold action. So let us restore all that we have cherished from yesterday, and let us rise above the legacy of inequality. When the streets are rebuilt, there should be many new businesses, including minority-owned businesses, along those streets. When the houses are rebuilt, more families should own, not rent, those houses. When the regional economy revives, local people should be prepared for the jobs being created.

Americans want the Gulf Coast not just to survive, but to thrive; not just to cope, but to overcome. We want evacuees to come home, for the best of reasons -- because they have a real chance at a better life in a place they love.

. . .

In the long run, the New Orleans area has a particular challenge, because much of the city lies below sea level. The people who call it home need to have reassurance that their lives will be safer in the years to come. Protecting a city that sits lower than the water around it is not easy, but it can, and has been done. City and parish officials in New Orleans, and state officials in Louisiana will have a large part in the engineering decisions to come. And the Army Corps of Engineers will work at their side to make the flood protection system stronger than it has ever been.

. . .

The cash needed to support the armies of compassion is great, and Americans have given generously. For example, the private fundraising effort led by former Presidents Bush and Clinton has already received pledges of more than $100 million. Some of that money is going to the Governors to be used for immediate needs within their states. A portion will also be sent to local houses of worship to help reimburse them for the expense of helping others. This evening the need is still urgent, and I ask the American people to continue donating to the Salvation Army, the Red Cross, other good charities, and religious congregations in the region.

. . .

Four years after the frightening experience of September the 11th, Americans have every right to expect a more effective response in a time of emergency. When the federal government fails to meet such an obligation, I, as President, am responsible for the problem, and for the solution. So I've ordered every Cabinet Secretary to participate in a comprehensive review of the government response to the hurricane. This government will learn the lessons of Hurricane Katrina. We're going to review every action and make necessary changes, so that we are better prepared for any challenge of nature, or act of evil men, that could threaten our people.

. . .

In this place, there's a custom for the funerals of jazz musicians. The funeral procession parades slowly through the streets, followed by a band playing a mournful dirge as it moves to the cemetery. Once the casket has been laid in place, the band breaks into a joyful "second line" -- symbolizing the triumph of the spirit over death. Tonight the Gulf Coast is still coming through the dirge -- yet we will live to see the second line.

Thank you, and may God bless America.

END 8:28 P.M. CDT

New Orleans residents and tourists line up at the Superdome, established as refuge of last resort. Source: FEMA photo From: Hurricane Katrina: A Nation Still Unprepared http://hsgac. senate.gov/_files/Katrina/FullReport.pdf

Abandoned cars sit in the flooded downtown area, near S. Robertson street.
Source: U.S. Senate Hurricane Katrina Exhibits http://hsgac.senate.gov/_files/
102005HrgExhibits.pdf

Man rescued after Hurricane Katrina flooding by a Louisiana Wildlife and Fisheries team. Source: FEMA photo From: Hurricane Katrina: A Nation Still Unprepared http://hsgac. senate.gov/_files/Katrina/FullReport.pdf

Evacuees fill Superdome. Source: FEMA photo From: Hurricane Katrina: A Nation Still Unprepared http://hsgac.senate.gov/_files/Katrina/FullReport.pdf

---

Bahamonde, Marty

From:	Bahamonde, Marty
Sent:	Sunday, August 26, 2005 4:40 PM
To:	'Michael-Heath1@dhs.gov'
Subject:	Re:

There are currently 2000 inside the dome with about 300 special needs.National guard Is setting up cots. Oklahoma-1DMAT is around midnight to supply medical needs. Medical staff at the dome say they expect to run out of oxygen in about two hours and are looking for alternatives. There are still lines outside the dome waiting to get in.

CG has confirmed they will pick me up at the superdome at first Tuesday morning weather permitting expected at get light

Contact: 202–041–1750
          617-212-5149

Sent from my Blackberry Wireless Handheld

Source: U.S. Senate Hurricane Katrina Exhibits http://hsgac.senate.gov/_files/102005HrgExhibits.pdf

Bahamonde, Marty

From:	Bahamonde, Marty;
Sent:	Sunday, August 28,2005 9:20 PM
To:	'Clndy.taytor@dhs.gov'
Subject:	Fw: Potential hot issue

I thought you would like this

Sent from my BlackBerry Wireless Handheld

-----Original Message----
From: Rule, Natalie <Natalie.Rule@Dema.gov>
To: Passey, David <David. Passeyf)fema.qov>
CC: Bahamonde, Marty <Marty. 8ahamonde() fema.gov>
Sent: Sun Aug 28 21:58: 18 2005
Subject: RE: Potential hot issue

It feels a little like I am living in the middle of a horror movie...hope you are doing
okay. Please let us know how we can support. I am going to my house, but will be up on
computer again as soon as I get there.

From: Passey, David
Sent: Sunday, August 28. 2005 9: 58 PM
TO: Rule, Natalie
Cc: Bahamonde, Marty
Subject: RE: Potential hot issue

Our intel is that neither the OK-l DMAT nor the public health officers staged in Memphis
will make it to the Superdome tonight. Oxygen supply issue has not been solved yet either.

From: Rule, Natalie
Sent: Sunday, August 28. 2005 B: 55 PM
To: Passey, David
Cc: Bahamonde, Marty
Subject: RE: Potential hot issue

Thanks Dave...and I believe marty is aware of this and that is why the Oklahoma DMAT team
was supposed to immediately deploy there. . though not sure if they are going to make it .. but
talked to front office and was told that "'was the"solution.

From:	Lowder, Michael
Sent:	Monday, August 29,20059:53 AM
To:	Brown, Michael D; Lokey, WlUIam; Jones, Gary; Robinson, Tony; Heath, Michael; Rhode, Patrick; EST-ESF03-A; EST-ESFO3-8; EST-ESFO3C
Subject:	FW: Information
Importance:	High

FYI

ML

From:	Green, Matthew
Sent:	Monday, August 29, 2005 9:50 AM
To:	BuIkema, Edward
Cc:	Lowder, Michael
Subject:	RE: Information

From WWL lV

" A LEVEE BREACH OCCURRED ALONG THE INDUSTRIAL CANAL AT TENNESSEE STREET. 3 TO 8 FEET OF WATER IS EXPECI'ED DUE TO THE BREACH....LOCATIONS IN THE WARNING INCLUDE BUT ARE NOT LIMITED TO ARABI AND 9TH WARD OF NEW ORLEANS.

Matthew Green
FEMA Hurricane Liaison Team Coordinator
National Hurricane Center
11691 SW 17th Street
Miami. Florida, 33165-2149 USA

From:	Buikema, Edward
Sent:	Monday, August 29, 2005 9:40 AM
To:	Green, Matthew
Cc:	Lowder, Michael
Subject:	Information

Matthew.

Please copy me on the spot report emails you send to Mike Lowder. That information is very helpful.

Thanks. Ed

Source: U.S. Senate Hurricane Katrina Exhibits http://hsgac.senate.gov/_files/102005HrgExhibits.pdf

Original Message
From:Brown, Michael D <Michael.D.Brown@dns.gov>
To:'Michael.Lowder@dns.gov <Michael.Lowder@dns.gov> 'Michael.D.Brown@dns.gov>
Sent:Monday. August 29. 200512:09 PM
Subject: Re: Information

I'm being told here water over not a breach

-----Original Message----
From: Lowder, Michael <Michael.Lowder@dns.gov>
To: 'Michael.D.Brown@dns.gov' <Michael.D.Brown@dns.gov>
Sent: Mon Aug 29 11:57:35 2005
Subject: Fw: Information

Not sure if you have this..

-----Original Message----
From: Heath, Michael <Michael.Heath@fema.gov>
To: Lowder, Michael <Michael.Lowder@fema.gov>
Sent: Mon Aug 29 11:51:18 2005
Subject: Re: Information

FYI. . .

From Marty. He has been trying to reach Lokey.

New Orleans FD is reporting a 20 foot wide breech on the lake ponchatrain side levy. The area is lakeshore
Blvd and 17th street.

Sent from my BlackBerry Wireless Handheld

Source: U.S. Senate Hurricane Katrina Exhibits http://hsgac.senate.gov/_files/102005HrgExhibits.pdf

---

Taylor, Cindy

From:	Taylor, Cindy
Sent:	Monday, August 29, 2005 2:19 PM
To:	'Worthy. Sharon'
Subject:	FW: Updates from Marty and Beeman

Fmm:	Taylor, Cindy
Sent:	Monday, August 29, 2005 1:38 PM
To:	Rule, Natalie; Widomski, Michael; Andrews, Nicole D.Public Affairs
Cc:	Passey, David; Hudak.Mary
Subject:	Updates from Marty and Beeman

From Marly (New Orleans):

- 17th Avenue Canal levee (running along border of Orleans and Jefferson Parishes broke through with waterflow" bad" into New Orleans side
- City will have feeding I sheltering issues with population at superdome (est.12K)
- Northside of city under est.11' water in residential area
- Estimate of 30,000 tourists in city holed up in hotel rooms
- Chanty Hospital all windows out; flooded, no power: have not been able to reach other 27 hospitals for capabilities
- Early estimate that power will be over a month to restore main hubs out of commission
- Hoping to get out in next hour, with helicopter tour to follow

From Beeman (Gulfport):

- Last broadcasting radio station was knocked off the air an hour ago
- Significant flooding occuring not far from where he's located with reports of people climbing into attics to escape waist deep and higher waters
- Been sitting desk forfour hours watching as the winds have torn apart the back of the building with pieces of the roof slamming into the posts that hold up the porch on his buildings.
- Trees dropping all around and six fence from a small park to left have been sailing by like frizzbies
- Power and water are both off

Source: U.S. Senate Hurricane Katrina Exhibits http://hsgac.senate.gov/_files/102005HrgExhibits.pdf

Eahamonde, Marty

From: **Bahamonde, Marly**
Sent: **Tuesday, August 30, 2005 7:02 AM**
To: **'Nicol.Andrews@dhs.gov':'Marty.Bahamonde@dhs.gov'**
Subject   **Re:Site search**

What is happening with the US travel this morning. When is he coming to New Orleans. The area the around superdome is filling up with water, now waist deep.The US can land and do a presser but then have to leave, there will be no ground tour, only flyover
----

Source: U.S. Senate Hurricane Katrina Exhibits http://hsgac.senate.gov/_files/102005HrgExhibits.pdf

From: **Brown, Michael D**
Sent: **Wednesday, August 31, 2005 12:24 PM**
To: **'Marty.Bahamonde@dhs.gov'**
Subject: **Re: New orleans**

Thanks for update. Anything specific I need to do or tweak?

----------Original Message----------
From: Bahamonde, Marty <Marty.Bahamonde@dhs.gov>
To: 'michael.d.brown@dhs.gov' <Michael.D.Brown@dhs.gov>
Sent: Wed Aug 31 12:20:20 2005
Subject: New orleans

Sir, I know that you know the situation is past critical. Here some things you might not know.
Hotels are kicking people out, thousands gathering in the streets with no food or water.
Hundreds still being rescued from homes.

The dying patients at the DMAT tent being medivac. Estimates are many will die within hours. Evacuation in process. Plans developing for dome evacuation but hotel situation adding to problem. We are out of food and running out of water at the dome, plans in works to address the critical need.

FEMA staff is OK and holding own. DMAT staff working in deplorable conditions. The sooner we can get the medical patients out, the sooner wecan get them out.

Phone connectivity impossible

More later

Sent from my BlackBerry Wireless Handheld

Source: U.S. Senate Hurricane Katrina Exhibits http://hsgac.senate.gov/_files/102005HrgExhibits.pdf

Taylor, Cindy

From:	**Taylor, Cindy**
Sent:	**Wednesday, August 31, 2005 2:27 PM**
To:	**Bahamonde, Marly; Widomski, Michael**
Subject:	**FW: Scarborough**

Let me preface by saying I know he needs down time, but how much time do each of you need for dinner, including travel time to the restaurants of your choice?

------- Original Message -------
From: Worthy, Sharon [mail to: Sharon.Worthy@dhs.gov]
Sent: Wednesday. August 31,2005 2:00 PM
To: 'Valerie.Smith@dhs.govl
Cc: 'natalie.rule.gov'; Andrews, Nicol D-Public Affairs; 'cindy.taylor@dhs.govl
Subject: Scarborough

Please schedule Joe Scarborough this evening for period. with his producer and told him to call you. Mr.Brown wants to do this one.

Also, it is very important that time is allowed for Mr. Brown to eat dinner. Given that Baton Rouge is back to normal, restaurants are getting busy. He needs much more that 20 or 30 minutes. We now have traffic to encounter to get to and from a location of his choice, followed by wait service from the restaurant staff, eating, etc.Thank you.

Sharon Worthy
Press Secretary

Source: U.S. Senate Hurricane Katrina Exhibits http://hsgac.senate.gov/_files/102005HrgExhibits.pdf

Taylor,Cindy

From:	Bahamonde, Marty
Sent:	Wednesday, August 31, 2005 2:44 PM
To:	Taylor, Cindy: Widomski, Michael
Subject:	Re: Scarborough

OH MY GOD !!!!!!!! NO won't go any further, too easy of a target. Just tell her that I just ate an MRE and in the hallway of the Superdome along with 30,000 other close friends so I understand her concern about busy restaurants. Maybe tonight I will have to move the pebbles on the parking garage floor so they don't stab me the back while try to sleep, but instead I will hope her wait at Ruthisshort. But I know she is stressed so I make a big deal it and you shouldn't either.

Sent from my BlackBerry Wireless Handheld

Source: U.S. Senate Hurricane Katrina Exhibits http://hsgac.senate.gov/_files/102005HrgExhibits.pdf

Taylor,Cindy

From:	Bahamonde, Marly
Sent:	Saturday, September 03, 2005 1:06 AM
To:	Taylor, Cindy
Subject:	Re: Airlift

The state told us we would run out of places, the army told us they had run out of places. The leadership from top down in our agency is unprepared and out of much. When told that superdome had been evacuated and would be locked, Scott Wells said we shouldn't lock it because people might still need it in an emergency. Myself and the general who had been there spoke up and told Scott that impossible to send any one back in there....is that not out of touch.But I am horrified at some of the cluelessness and self concern that persists, I try to focus on those that have put their lives on hold to help people that they have never met and never will. And while I sometimes think that can't work in this arena, I can't get out of my head the visions of children and babies I saw sitting there, helpless, looking at me and hoping I could make a difference and so I will and you must to. IC is not what we do that is as important as who we are and that's what Chose little kids faces were-counting on.

Sent from my BlackBerry Wireless Handheld

Source: U.S. Senate Hurricane Katrina Exhibits http://hsgac.senate.gov/_files/102005HrgExhibits.pdf

From: Brown, Michael D
Sent: Tuesday, September 06, 2005 11 :22 AM
To: Altshuler, Brooks; Lowder, Michael
Subject: FW: Medical Help

Can we use these people?

From: carolyn
Sent: Friday, September 02, 2005 5:57 PM
To: Michael D Brown; Michael D Brown
Subject: Medical Help

Mike,

Mickey and other medical equipment people have a 42ft trailer full of beds,
wheelchairs, oxygen concentrators,etc. They are wanting to take them where they can
be used but need direction.Mickey specializes in ventilator patients so can be very
helpful with acute care patients. If you could have someone contact him and let him
know if he can be of service, he would appreciate it. Know you are busy but they really
want to help. His number is

Carol

Source: U.S. Senate Hurricane Katrina Exhibits http://hsgac.senate.gov/_files/102005HrgExhibits.pdf

Preliminary Report on the Performance of the New Orleans Levee Systems in Hurricane Katrina on August 29, 2005

by

R.B. Seed, P.G. Nicholson, R.A. Dalrymple, J. Battjes, R.G. Bea, G. Boutwell, J.D. Bray,
B. D. Collins, L.F. Harder, J.R. Headland, M. Inamine, R.E. Kayen, R. Kuhr, J. M. Pestana, R. Sanders,
F. Silva-Tulla, R. Storesund, S. Tanaka, J. Wartman, T. F. Wolff, L. Wooten and T. Zimmie

Preliminary findings from field investigations and associated studies performed by teams from the University of California at Berkeley and the American Society of Civil Engineers, as well as a number of cooperating engineers and scientists, shortly after the hurricane.

Report No. UCB/CITRIS – 05/01
November 2, 2005

New Orleans Levee Systems
Hurricane Katrina
August 29, 2005

EXECUTIVE SUMMARY

This report presents the results of field investigations performed by several teams of researchers in the wake of the passage of Hurricane Katrina, to study the performance of the regional flood protection systems and the resulting flooding and damage that occurred in the New Orleans area. The principal focus of these efforts was to capture perishable data and observations related to the performance of flood control systems before they were lost to ongoing emergency response and repair operations.

The initial field investigations occurred over a span of approximately two and a half weeks, from September 28 through October 15, 2005. The starting date for these field investigations was determined by balancing the need to gather vital perishable data before it was damaged or obscured by emergency repair operations versus the need to avoid interference with such emergency operations, and issues associated with safe access, logistics, etc. It was fortunate that the main field investigation teams arrived when they did, as there were numerous occasions when team units arrived and investigated sites only days, or even hours, prior to the covering of vital information by ongoing emergency repair activities.

The storm surges produced by Hurricane Katrina resulted in numerous breaches and consequent flooding of approximately 75% of the metropolitan areas of New Orleans. Most of the levee and floodwall failures were caused by overtopping, as the storm surge rose over the tops of the levees and/or their floodwalls and produced erosion that subsequently led to failures and breaches.

Overtopping was most severe on the east side of the flood protection system, as the waters of Lake Borgne were driven west towards New Orleans, and also farther to the south, along the lower reaches of the Mississippi River. Significant overtopping and erosion produced numerous breaches in these areas. The magnitude of overtopping was less severe along the Inner Harbor Navigation Canal (IHNC) and along the western portion of the Mississippi River Gulf Outlet (MRGO) channel, but this overtopping again produced erosion and caused additional levee failures.

Field observations suggest that little or no overtopping occurred along most of the levees fronting Lake Pontchartrain, but evidence of minor overtopping and/or wave splashover was observed at a number of locations. There was a breach in the levee system at the northwest corner of the New Orleans East protected area, near the Lakeside Airport.

Farther to the west, in the Orleans East Bank Canal District, three levee failures occurred along the banks of the 17th Street and London Avenue Canals, and these failures occurred at water levels below the tops of the floodwalls lining these canals. These three levee failures were likely caused by failures in the foundation soils underlying the levees,

New Orleans Levee Systems
Hurricane Katrina
August 29, 2005

and a fourth "distressed" levee/floodwall segment on the London Avenue Canal shows signs of having neared the occurrence of a similar failure prior to the water levels having receded.

This report presents an overview of initial observations and findings regarding the performance of the New Orleans flood protection system, including observations regarding preliminary assessments of likely causes of failures and/or significant damage to levees and floodwalls at many sites. Although most of the failures/breaches that occurred were primarily due to overtopping and subsequent erosion, several major and costly breaches appear to have been the result of stability failures of the foundation soils and/or the earthen levee embankments themselves. In addition, it appears that many of the levees and floodwalls that failed due to overtopping might have performed better if relatively inexpensive details had been added and/or altered during their original design and construction.

Major repair and rehabilitation efforts are now underway to prepare the New Orleans flood protection system for future high water events. The next hurricane season will begin in June of 2006. Based on our observations, a number of initial comments are warranted concerning the rebuilding and rehabilitation of the levee system, and this preliminary report makes a number of observations and recommendations regarding ongoing flood system repair efforts. Preparing the levees for the next hurricane season should also include a review of how the system performed during Hurricane Katrina, so that key lessons can be learned and then used to improve the performance of the system.

The devastating damages and loss of life, wrought by the flooding produced by Hurricane Katrina will now lead to ongoing studies of the performance of the flood protection system in this catastrophic event, as well as efforts to improve the levels of reliability and safety of these types of defenses for the future. Several teams have been formed to perform the types of initial on-site studies reported herein, and these teams have announced intentions to continue their studies through the coming year. It must be hoped that the results of these studies will lead to a clear appreciation of what happened in Katrina, and that the lessons learned from this event will lead to improved protection in the future, not just in the New Orleans area, but throughout the nation and around the world.

CASE STUDY 2: Southwest Florida Water Management District

Every day Americans across the country turn on faucets without worrying whether clean and sanitary water will come out. We take for granted one of the most important resources to sustain life. Most people living in large urban areas get water from "surface" water sources such as reservoirs, lakes, and rivers, while others depend on water pumped from underground by private and public wells. Because water is such a necessity, the protection and adequate and equitable distribution of it is always a priority for local, state, regional, and federal authorities. On the federal level the responsibility for water quality primarily lies with the Environmental Protection Agency (EPA), which has offices on the state level, and, according to the EPA, "[T]he United States enjoys one of the cleanest drinking water supplies in the world." The EPA's role is to do the following:

- Regulate the quality of the nation's drinking water
- Issue and enforce safe drinking water standards
- Protect the watersheds—natural drainage basins into lakes and rivers—of drinking water supplies
- Regulate the release of pollutants into the environment
- Encourage water conservation
- Assist in developing plans for water emergencies (Environmental Protection Agency).

To fulfill its role, the EPA depends on partnerships with local, regional, state authorities, and community groups. Water resources and emergencies do not stop at city, county, or even state lines, and because of that, the protection and regulation of water is also done on a local and regional as well as state and national level. One regional water authority is the Southwest Florida Water Management District (SWFWMD), commonly called "swift mud"; it is one of five water management districts in Florida.

In 1972, after the worst drought in the state's recorded history, the Florida legislature established the five districts. This approach to water resources management is unique because it is written into the State Constitution that the districts have taxing powers, and they are not based on political boundaries but rather on hydrologic determinations of watersheds (Purdum 10, 13). Moreover, unlike other states where laws about water resources are primarily based on private ownership or private land ownership, in Florida, water is a resource of the state and not privately owned by anyone (Purdum 12), and because of that, "[a]ccording to some scholars, 'Florida's water management system has been the envy of many other states for over 25 years'" (qtd. in Regan 124).

Southwest Florida Management District

In 2006, with some 750 employees, SWFWMD had an annual budget of about $333.8 million total ("Fiscal Year 2006"). The district encompasses all or portions of 16 counties in west-central Florida—some 10,000 square miles, about 17% of the state's total land area with about one-quarter of the state's population (see Figure CS2.1). SWFWMD (not to be confused with the South Florida Water Management District, SFWMD, that covers the area of Miami, the Keys, and Everglades) stretches from Levy County in the north to Charlotte County in the south and inland from the Gulf counties to Highlands and Polk counties (SWFWMD).

Governed by an 11-member board (see Figure CS2.2) of unpaid citizen volunteers, appointed by the governor and confirmed by the state senate, SWFWMD's primary funding source is ad valorem taxes, although funding also comes from state and federal appropriations, permit fees, interest earnings, and other sources. The taxing capabilities of the District, established by the legislature, is one mil, or one dollar per thousand dollars of assessed value, which is also shared with eight of nine local basin boards—an organizational arrangement distinctive to SWFWMD.

Members of the Basin Boards, also appointed by the governor and confirmed by the senate, identify water-related issues in their localities and fund programs to address these issues. The ex officio member of each of the basin boards also serves as one of the 11 members of the District's governing board (SWFWMD, Issue Papers, "Basin Boards"). The relationship between the agency and basin boards is essential because of the important work done by the 98 local government groups in the district, including ones that operate critical water facilities.

Although water allocation and protection issues are different for different regions of the country and states, water resources can be the subject of great controversy and debate because clean, safe, and adequate water supplies impact almost every individual and industry. No state has had more of its share of potential and real problems with water resources than Florida. The drafters of the Florida's Model Water Code that laid the basis for the legal structure for the management districts wanted a legal system that balanced the water needs of humans and protection of the ecosystems (Regan 124). However, the increasing scarcity of water "intensified conflicts and made achieving this delicate balance even more difficult" (Regan 124).

Water Resources

On one hand, Florida has been blessed with some plentiful water resources. During the summer months, tropical storms almost every afternoon bring needed relief from the stifling heat, and, with an average rainfall of 53 inches per year, Florida is only second to Louisiana in rainfall amounts, making it one of the rainiest regions in North America (Purdum 1). To put the hydrological cycle simplistically, once rain falls to the earth, it either flows as diffused surface water or it percolates into the soil as groundwater. Water that stays in the uppermost part of the soil fills surface water bodies such as lakes and wetlands, while water that seeps down further goes into aquifers—deep underground rock formations through which water travels and/or where it is stored. Water is then pumped out from underground wells. Water that stays on the surface or reaches the surface again eventually returns to the atmosphere through evaporation or transpiration, and the cycle is repeated (see Figure CS2.3). Although some drinking water in Florida comes from surface streams and rivers, most of it comes from ground water in aquifers.

Florida's aquifers hold nearly quadrillion gallons of water, equivalent to one-fifth of all the water in all the Great Lakes (Purdum 49). The state also has some 700 natural springs (where water flows directly from underground aquifers to the surface), 13 major rivers, and 7,800 lakes (Purdum 49, 71), including Lake Okeechobee, in the southern region of the state, which is the fourth largest lake within the United States. Most importantly, though, for central and west-central Florida, between Tampa and Orlando, are the 560,000 acres of a unique, natural ecosystem with wetlands and mesic flatlands, known as the "Green Swamp." It is here that the Hillsborough, Withlacooche, Ocklawaha, and Peace rivers emerge, providing much of the central part of the state's water supply ("Green Swamp Interactive").

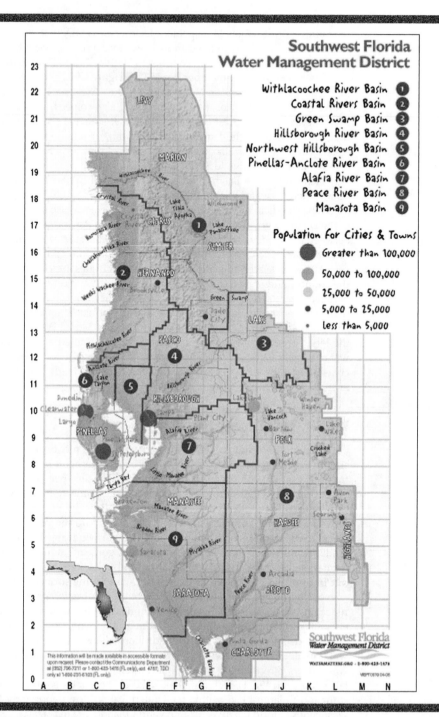

FIGURE CS2.1   Map of Southwest Florida Water Management District. Adapted from the Basin Map for Youth Poster. Source SWFWMD. http://www.swfwmd.state.fl.us./publications/type/poster

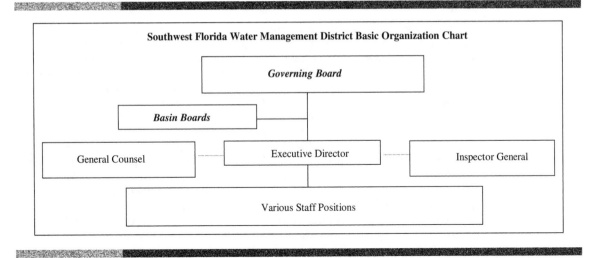

FIGURE CS2.2   Source: Adapted from SWFMD Organization Chart, July 2006

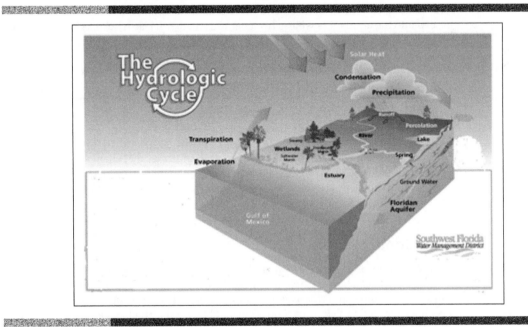

FIGURE CS2.3   Source: Adapted from SWFWMD graphic, July 2006

Unprecedented Growth

Florida is also a state with almost unprecedented growth. From 1900, with some 500,000 population—one of the smallest populations in the eastern part of the country—Florida grew to 16 million in 2000, making it the fourth largest state in the nation (Smith 2). Florida's population growth rate began to soar after World War II when many of the thousands of veterans who had trained there came back from duty to settle there (Purdum 27) and in the 1960s with the advent of residential air conditioning (Smith 9). In 1950, the population was 2,771,305; in 1960, it was 4,951,560, and in 2004, it was 17,516,732 (Smith Table 1). If the growth rate continues, as researchers expect, by the year 2010, with an estimated population of about 19 million, Florida will outdistance New York as the third most populated state behind California and Texas (Smith 16, Table 14). The population increase has largely been because of migration into Florida from people in Northern and Midwestern states. In the 1970s, 1980s, and 1990s, the people moving into the state accounted for approximately 85–90% of its population increase (Smith 6). SWFWMD's *Strategic Plan*, addressing the region's water priorities, estimates that by 2025 that region's population will be 5.8 million, a 45% increase from 2000. During the last 40 years, the state has also changed from a primarily agricultural, tourist destination, and retirement location, to a popular place for families to live and work. "Contrary to popular belief, most persons moving to Florida are young rather than elderly" (Smith 8) seeking employment and transferring to new jobs.

Its ecologically sensitive system of underground aquifers that feed drinking water supplies and its critical wetlands and estuaries (such as the Everglades in the southernmost part of the Florida peninsula) have been strained by the increasing demand for water, and a tireless tug-of-war has ensued among housing and real estate developers, agricultural interests, tourism, and other industries over water resources. At the same time, the state's drinking water sources and facilities are constantly needing protection, from storm water runoff pollutants such as those from agricultural, industrial, and road construction that can seep into the aquifers as well as from natural weather hazards such as hurricanes and periodic long-term drought. In parts of Florida, water demands are starting to exceed the natural supply (Purdum 14). Groundwater is being pumped out of the aquifers at an alarming rate, which creates problems ranging from sinkholes, where the ground suddenly collapses, to inadequate large-scale drinking water supplies. Paradoxically, at the same time, the largest city in the SWFWMD district, Tampa, with a name which some speculate comes from a Native-American term meaning "fire stick," is considered the lightening capital of the United States (Purdum 43–44); it is also in a region of the state now designated as a "Water Use Caution Area" because of a scarcity of available water (Purdum 75). Recent research in water use however indicates that changes in agricultural irrigation, industry, thermodynamic cooling, conservation efforts, water reclamation, and generally more efficient use of water resources is decreasing the amount of water usage (Purdum 79–80).

Water Controversies

Water regulation and protection raise large and long-standing technical and ethical questions—such as whether phosphate mining, which began in Florida in the late 1800s, should now be allowed in the watershed of a drinking water supply—as well as questions about regulation that impact on a personal and individual level—such as whether a resident should be allowed to water a newly planted yard during drought conditions. Thus, the allocation and protection of water resources is complex and often rife with political and economic consequences. Southwest central Florida and SWFWMD have had their share of water controversies. SWFWMD was originally created in 1960 as a flood control agency when severe flooding in west-central Florida, caused by a rainy season and Hurricane Donna, led the Florida legislature to mandate a district authority as a flood-control agency. However, when the District sponsored a plan by the U.S. Army Corps of Engineers to convert some of the Green Swamp lands into flood-detention areas, controversy arose about disturbing the natural ecosystem, and the District took a "non-structural approach to flood protection by leaving the Green Swamp in its natural state" ("Green Swamp Interactive"). As the state's population grew and its water needs and demands changed, the District's responsibilities also grew and changed.

Water Wars

One of the most notable controversies is the nearly 25 years of "water wars"—over piping water from wellfields in rural eastern parts of Pasco and Hillsborough counties, where ground water is abundant, to the urban western coastal regions of Pasco County and further south to Pinellas County and the city of St. Petersburg, the most densely populated area of the state, where the ground water has been contaminated by saltwater since the 1920s. The wars centered on decreased water levels in lakes and wetlands in the vicinity of four wellfields which were owned by the City of St. Petersburg, and a local water authority in Pasco and Hillsborough counties. Although these water wars centered in the Tampa Bay region, the issues "epitomized those of many areas in Florida" (Regan 141).

For years, residents near the wellfields complained about diminished amounts of water in lakes and wetlands because of the pumping at the wellfields. The situation festered and finally erupted into long-term litigation among these citizens, local governments, the local water authority, and SWFWMD. At the time of the dispute, the local water authority provided water for about 1.8 million people of SWFWMD's jurisdiction (Regan 143). In 1999, an administrative judge issued findings that, among other factors, said there had been environmental damage as a result of the pumping; the primary cause for the lower lake and wetlands water levels in the vicinity of the wellfield was the withdrawal from the wellfields; yet, he also recognized the critical importance of the wellfields to the public water supply (Regan 147-50). According to SWFWMD, an "historic" partnership agreement was signed and implemented that reorganized a local water supply authority and its member governments into the Tampa Bay Water authority (SWFWMD, Issue Papers, "Partnership Agreement") a regional wholesale water utility with a unitary rate for existing and new sources of supply. As part of the agreement, the pumping at the wellfields was to be reduced, and the Tampa Bay Water Authority and SWFWMD were to provide funding for new alternative sources of water (Hillsborough County) such as desalination facilities (Petrimoulx) as well as implementing measures to "mitigate the adverse environmental impacts that wellfields have caused in the past, [and] will continue to cause in the future" (Regan 160).

Wetlands Preservation and Restoration

The Tampa Bay water wars "ultimately illustrate that the communication and cooperation among regulatory agencies and permittees is necessary in order to achieve workable water management decisions" (Regan 185); they also demonstrate the vital part the wetlands play in the ecosystem and thus the well-being of natural water resources. Although wetlands once covered about half of Florida, today more than half of the wetlands have been drained or developed (Noss and Peters 15). Yet, "the state still has vast and diverse wetlands" (Purdum 49). Typically thought of as swamps or marshes, wetlands are areas where soil is saturated by water and where wildlife live and breed. Wetlands "improve water quality by trapping nutrients such as nitrogen and phosphorus, toxic substances and disease-causing microorganisms. They slow and intercept runoff, protect shorelines and banks from erosion, and protect upland areas from floods" (Purdum 61).

Throughout Florida efforts are underway to protect and restore the wetlands. SWFWMD's "Surface Water Improvement and Management" (SWIM) program brings together federal, state, and local governments as well as citizen volunteers to restore natural water systems like wetlands ("Water Quality"), including one such project in northwestern Manatee County, a county south of Tampa and north of Sarasota, stretching from the Gulf of Mexico to the middle of the state. The project calls for the kind of communication, cooperation, and coordination among agencies, stakeholders and interested individuals that is necessary for an extensive environmental undertaking. The SWIM plan for Tampa and Sarasota bays include restoring habitats and reducing pollution entering the bays. The project—"Robinson Preserve" involving the Manasota Basin Board of SWFWMD, the Manatee County Board of Commissioners, the Sarasota Bay and Tampa Bay National Estuary Programs, Florida Department of Environmental Protection (FDEP), the U.S. EPA, U.S. Fish and Wildlife Service, the Gulf of Mexico Program, and a private landowner—is the restoration and creation of approximately 150 acres of intertidal wetlands within a 465-acre parcel located along the lower southeastern portion of Tampa Bay, bordered on the north by the mouth of the Manatee River, Perico Bayou to the west, and Palma Sola Bay to the east (Florida Department of Environmental Protection). This parcel, which was slated for a housing development (Florida Department of Environmental Protection) prior to its acquisition by Manatee County, includes piney flatwoods (called "uplands"), mangrove areas, and salt barrens. Now called the Robinson Preserve after the landowner whose charitable donation helped establish the project, the project is one of several environmental restoration projects within the Tampa Bay and Sarasota National Estuary programs (Hunsicker). These wetlands are part of estuaries, where freshwater rivers intersect with incoming saltwater tides and form the important breeding ground and nurseries for sea life.

Activities and Assignments

Individual or Group Activity: *Document 1:* "Robinson Preserve Environmental Restoration" Ongoing Status Report

As you can imagine, documents created by governmental writers in environmental efforts range from highly technical to politically focused to everyday informational and somewhere in between. The "Robinson Preserve" document is in the genre of an ongoing status report because of what it does: although the applications for funding the project can be lengthy, this type of document provides a lot of information in a short amount of time for an update on the status of an ongoing project. (The photo with it was not part of the document but is included here to illustrate how the area looks.) Who are the stakeholders for this document? How does the formatting of it—the subheads, bolding of certain words, short paragraphs, and straightforward sentences serve the readers? Where do you think the writer got the information for this document? How might the information change with the next status report? What other category(s) might be included or excluded in the future? As pointed out throughout the textbook effective government writing today requires a cultural awareness and often social interaction among writers, stakeholders, within and outside of agencies. In what ways does this document demonstrate this principle?

Find an environmental project in your region and compare a brief status report about it with this one. How do they compare? Who are the stakeholders? Write a research paper about what you find to share with your classmates.

Project:	**Robinson Preserve Environmental Restoration**
Project #:	W393 1 Basin: 021,
Phase:	01 Project Status: Ongoing
Cooperator:	Manatee County
Coop. Contact:	Hunsicker, Charlie
Project Manager:	Powers, Stephanie
Task Manager:	
Project Type:	SWIM

DESCRIPTION: This project is in response to a request from Manatee County to restore and enhance habitats on approximately 150 acres of intertidal wetlands and uplands in northwestern Manatee County. The land purchase was made possible though funding provided by Manatee County, Florida Communities Trust, and a donation by the landowner. Partners for this project include Manatee County, the Manasota Basin Board, the SWIM Program, the Florida Department of Environmental Protection, the U.S. Environmental Protection Agency, and the Sarasota Bay Estuary Program. The design phase of this project is complete and the final permits are being secured by the County.

Benefits: The proposed restoration will target the creation and enhancement of open water, intertidal habitats, and coastal uplands. Exotic plants such as Australian Pine and Brazilian Pepper will be removed and replaced with both planted and naturally recruiting native species. Upon completion, the project will provide significant benefits to habitat and water quality. The County also plans to provide passive recreational and educational opportunities to the public. Because the project site drains to both Tampa Bay and to Sarasota Bay, this project will benefit both systems.

Costs: The total project cost is $4.5 million, with the County and the District each contributing 50 percent of the necessary funding. The FY2007 project cost is $1,230,000 with Manatee County contributing $615,000. The District's share is requested to be $615,000. The Manasota Basin Board is requested to fund 50% of the District's share ($307,500) and the remaining 50% ($307,500) will come from State Appropriation funds. District funds for FY2007 will be used for the construction of the project.

ADDITIONAL INFORMATION: Since 1950, approximately 50 percent of Tampa Bay's natural shoreline and approximately 40 percent of Sarasota Bay's intertidal wetland habitat has been lost due to development and reduction in water quality. This resulted in a decline in the aesthetic, recreational, and commercial value of the bay, as well as a loss of habitat for native plants and animals. The SWIM Plans for Tampa Bay and Sarasota Bay outline goals to restore habitat throughout the bay areas and reduce pollutant loads entering the bays. The objectives of this project are consistent with these goals.

Source	Prior Funding	FY 2006 Budget	FY 2007 Budget	Future Funding	Total Funding	Expended 2006
Manatee County	$0	$615,000	$615,000	$0	$1,230,000	$0
State SWIM	$0	$310,017	$9,136	$0	$319,153	$0
Manasota Basin	$0	$310,016	$309,152	$0	$619,168	$421
State Appropriation	$0	$600,000	$318,750	$0	$918,750	$0
TOTAL					$3,087,071	$421

Critical Project Milestones:	Projected:	Amended:	Actual:
District Recognition/Signage: YES			
Will be placed upon commencement of construction.	05/01/06		
County to release RFB	02/01/06		
County to Issue Notice to Proceed to Contractor	04/01/06		
Construction Commences	05/01/06		
Construction Completed	05/01/07		
Contract Expiration	12/31/07		

Status As Of: 04/20/2006 - Final design plans have been received from Manatee County. An agreement with the County has been drafted and forwarded to the County for review and signature. The County advertised the construction bid for the project and held a pre-bid meeting at the site on February 6, 2006. The County opened bids on March 15, 2005, and is in the process of approving the qualified, low bidder. Manatee County submitted an FY2007 cooperative funding request for additional funds for the construction phase of the project.

FIGURE CS2.4   Robinson Preserve Environmental Restoration Ongoing Status Report

FIGURE CS2.5 Source: Photo from FDEP: 2002 Flyover of Project Area

Find more lengthy reports about the environmental project in your area, and summarize one or more of them using the format for this report or create your own format. How did you decide what information to use? Did you find it difficult to pick and choose key information to be included?

Individual or Group Activity: *Document 2:* "SWFWMD Mission Statement"
What is a "mission statement"? Who is the audience for this Mission Statement for SWFWMD? What is its purpose? Why is it important? In Chapter 2, we discussed how "conservation ethics" are becoming increasingly important for government writers because of the interconnection of incidents, laws, and almost all human activities with the ecosystem. What kind of language does this document show that demonstrates an awareness of conservation ethics? For example, does the notion of "managing" a natural resource sound like an awareness of conservation? How about the notion of balancing water needs of current and future users? Does this language sound like they are planning for the needs of the future?

How do you think the Mission Statement came about? Who decides what the mission of the agency should be? What *ethos* of the agency does the statement present? Does the agency seem to be only for individuals with technical expertise or for the "average citizen"? Does the language in the statement come across as sincere about its mission or flippant? What specific words lead you to that conclusion?

Southwest Florida Water Management District

The mission of the Southwest Florida Water Management District is to manage water and related natural resources to ensure their continued availability while maximizing environmental, economic and recreational benefits. Central to the mission is maintaining the balance between the water needs of current and future users while protecting and maintaining water and related natural resources which provide the District with its existing and future water supply.

The Governing Board of the Southwest Florida Water Management District assumes its responsibilities as authorized in Chapter 373 and other chapters of the Florida Statutes by directing a wide-range of programs, initiatives, and actions. These programs include, but are not limited to, flood control, regulatory programs, water conservation, education, and supportive data collection and analysis efforts.

Water Supply

To ensure an adequate supply of the water resource for all reasonable and beneficial uses, now and in the future, while protecting and maintaining the water and water-related resources of the District.

Flood Protection

To minimize the potential for damage from floods by protecting and restoring the natural water storage and conveyance functions of floodprone areas. The District shall give preference whenever possible to non-structural surface water management methods.

Water Quality Management

To protect water quality by preventing further degradation of the water resource and enhancing water quality where appropriate.

Natural System Management

To preserve, protect and restore natural systems to support their natural hydrologic and ecologic functions.

Management Support

To ensure management support services effectively and efficiently contribute to realization of the District's mission to manage and protect water resources.

Find a mission statement for a local or regional water authority or environmental organization in your area, and compare it with the one for SWFWMD. How is the language and format of the statement the same or different?

Look for a mission statement for some other organization in which you are involved, such as your own university or college. How does it compare with the audience and stakeholders, purpose, and context of this one for the water management district? Research about how that mission statement came about and/or interview the people involved with the decision. Do you think it is a useful document—why or why not? What would you change, if anything, about the mission statement?

Check out the SWFWMD website to see if there is a new mission statement. If so, how does it compare with the one in this case study? Write a mission statement for SWFWMD for the year 2025. How might it be the same or different?

Individual or Group Activity: *Document 3:* Rules of the Southwest Florida Water Management District

Another outcome of the "water wars" was a more extensive evaluation of present and potential adverse affects of water withdrawal. Permits for large amounts of water withdrawal are part of the role of the water management districts. "Permits help quantify the amount of surface and underground water used and help [SWFWMD] protect associated environmental resources" ("About the Permitting Process"). The document comes from the SWFWMD manual *Rules of the Southwest Florida Water Management District Chapter 40D-2 Consumptive Use of Water.* The manual provides information such as the historical background of permitting authorization, what kinds of water withdrawals require permits, what exemptions are allowed, the content of the applications, and renewal requirements for permits.

40D-2.301 Conditions for Issuance of Permits

(1) In order to obtain a Water Use Permit, an Applicant must demonstrate that the water use is reasonable and beneficial, is in the public interest, and will not interfere with any existing legal use of water, by providing reasonable assurances, on both an individual and a cumulative basis, that the water use:

(a) Is necessary to fulfill a certain reasonable demand;

(b) Will not cause quantity or quality changes that adversely impact the water resources, including both surface and ground waters;

(c) Will not cause adverse environmental impacts to wetlands, lakes, streams, estuaries, fish and wildlife, or other natural resources;

(d) Will comply with the provisions of 4.3 of the Basis of Review described in 40D-2.091;

(e) Will utilize the lowest water quality the Applicant has the ability to use;

(f) Will not significantly induce saline water intrusion;

(g) Will not cause pollution of the aquifer;

(h) Will not adversely impact offsite land uses existing at the time of the application;

(i) Will not adversely impact an existing legal withdrawal;

(j) Will incorporate water conservation measures;

(k) Will incorporate reuse measures to the greatest extent practicable;

(l) Will not cause water to go to waste; and

(m) Will not otherwise be harmful to the water resources within the District (2-6-2-7).

The manual also describes when the SWFWMD's Governing Board may declare a water shortage as well as designate "Water Use Caution Areas." The second excerpt from this document shows such a designation:

(1) When the Governing Board determines that regional action is necessary to address cumulative water withdrawals which are causing or may cause adverse impacts to the water and related land resources or the public interest, it shall declare, delineate, or modify Water-Use Caution Areas. The Governing Board shall declare a Water-Use Caution Area by adopting a rule or issuing an order imposing special requirements for existing water users and permit Applicants to prevent or remedy site-specific problems.

(2) In determining whether an area should be declared a Water-Use Caution Area, the Governing Board shall consider the following factors:

(a) The quantity of water available for use from groundwater sources, surface water sources, or both;

(b) The quality of water available for use from groundwater sources, surface water sources, or both, including impacts such as saline water intrusion, mineralized water upcoming, or pollution;

(c) Environmental systems, such as wetlands, lakes, streams, estuaries, fish and wildlife, or other natural resources;

(d) Lake stages or surface water rates of flow;

(e) Offsite land uses; and

(f) Other resources as deemed appropriate by the Governing Board.

(2-15)

Chapters 3 and 4 of *Writing for the Government* are about rules and regulations and about manuals. Reflecting on these earlier chapters, who would be the key stakeholders for these rules from the SWFWMD manual? Would they be experts or nonexperts or both? What is the cultural context for this document? What historical, political, social, economic, ethical, and technological circumstances and constraints would the writers have had to consider in writing these rules? Which kinds of stakeholders would need to know about these rules and would want their input included in them? Why is the document written in such a formal format and language? How important is it that those people who want permits follow these "rules"? What might be the consequences of not following them? How might such language find its way into court cases? Collect your answers to these questions with evidence from your readings from the earlier chapters in the textbook and your own research; then write a paper about your findings to share with your classmates.

Create your own set of "rules" for some process that you are familiar with, which can be as simple as parking a car on campus or as complex as online course registration, or edit rules that are already in place. Have your classmates review your rules and make suggestions. If you want, share your rules with the appropriate department on campus.

Choose an environmental issue in your area and find documents related to it. Research the issue. If possible, interview someone who is familiar with the documents you have chosen to find out why they are written or presented in the way they have been presented. Compare the documents with the various genres in this textbook's chapters, and write a research paper about what you find.

Choose an environmental issue in your area, and write a document for the issue focusing on the various types of documents and genres presented in this textbook's earlier chapters.

Works Cited

Environmental Protection Agency. "Drinking Water." 23 July 2006 <http://www.epa.gov/ebtpages/waterdrinkingwater.html>.

Florida Department of Environmental Protection. "Preliminary Proposal for EPA Region 4 Wetlands Protection Program Grant: Estuary Preserve Manatee County, Florida." Spring 2003.

"Green Swamp Interactive." 11 June 2006 <http://www.swfwmd.state.fl.us/education/interactive/greenswamp/textonly.html>.

Hillsborough County Water Resources Team. "Legal Agreements." 02 July 2006 <http://www.hillsboroughcounty.org/waterresources/legal/>.

Hunsicker, Charlie. "Re: Wetlands." E-mail to Libby Allison. 19 July 2006.

Noss, Reed F. and Robert L. Peters. "Endangered Ecosystems: A Status Report of America's Vanishing Habitat and Wildlife." Washington, D.C.: Defenders of Wildlife, 1995.

Petrimoulx, John. "The $1-Billion Water Fix." *Creative Loafing: Weekly Planet Tampa.* 14 Aug. 2002. 02 July 2006 <http://www.weeklyplanet.com>.

Purdum, Elizabeth D. *Florida Waters: A Water Resources Manual from Florida's Water Management Districts.* Southwest Florida Water Management District, April 2002. 8 June 2007 <http://www.swfwmd.state.fl.us/publications/files/floridawaters.pdf>.

Regan, Kevin E. "Balancing Public Water Supply and Adverse Environmental Impacts under Florida Law: From Water Wars to Adaptive Management." *Journal of Land Use* 19.1 (Fall 2003): 123–85.

"Robinson Preserve Environmental Restoration." Ongoing Status Report. Charlie Hunsicker and Stephanie Powers. Manatee County and SWFWMD. 20 Apr. 2006.

Smith, Stanley K. "Florida Population Growth: Past, Present, and Future." Bureau of Economic and Business Research. University of Florida, June 2005. 8 June 2007 <http://www.bebr.ufl.edu/system/files/Floridapop2005.pdf>.

Southwest Florida Water Management District. (SWFWMD). <http://www.swfwmd.state.fl.us>.

—. *Strategic Plan.* "Meeting Present and Future Water Supply Needs." 10 July 2006 <http://www.swfwmd.state.fl.us/about/strategicplan/supply.html>.

—. "About the Permitting Process." 9 July 2006 <http://www.swfwmd.state.fl.us/permits/about/>.

—. Fiscal Year 2006 Budget in Brief Southwest Water Management District. 8 June 2007 <http://www.swfwmd.state.fl.us/business/budget/budget_in_brief_2006pdf>.

—. Issue Papers, "Basin Boards." 11 June 2006 <http://www.swfwmd.state.fl.us/about/isspapers/basinboards.html>.

—. Issue Papers, "Partnership Agreement." 11 June 2006 <http://www.swfwmd.state.fl.us/about/isspapers/partnershipagreement.html>.

—. Issue Papers, "A Sustainable Water Supply." 11 June 2006 <http://www.swfwmd.state.fl.us/about/isspapers/watersupply.html>.

"Water Quality." *WaterWeb: Watersheds* 2005. Southwest Florida Water Management District. modified. 24 Apr. 2006. 23 July 2006 <http://www.swfwmd.state.fl.us/publications/files/waterweb_watersheds.pdf>.

CASE STUDY 3: The Nonprofit Organization and Government Documents: The National Multiple Sclerosis Society

The nonprofit, voluntary, civic, or charitable sector in the United States comprises a vast and diverse set of organizations. From soup kitchens, daycare centers, environmental, advocacy, and civil rights groups; to hospitals, educational institutions, theatres, and faith based organizations, charitable organizations exist to serve and promote the common good. In most corners of the United States you will find hard working and committed individuals coming together to make their communities stronger, safer, and better for all.

Audrey R. Alvarado, Ph.D., Executive Director
National Council of Nonprofit Associations Report, 2003

At the National Multiple Sclerosis Society, "advocacy," encompasses the Society's efforts to influence the public and private sectors to obtain benefits and resources for people with MS and their families. Most of our advocacy is directed toward the public sector, where we work largely with the legislative branch of the federal, state, and local units of governments. Public sector advocacy also may require activity in the executive and judicial branches of government. All of the Society's public policy advocacy relates to medical research, health care, long-term care, health insurance and disability matters.

National MS Society, *Advocacy Training Manual*, Introduction

In Case Studies 1 and 2 in *Writing for the Government*, we looked at a wide assortment of government documents from local, state, and federal agencies. Case Study 3 focuses on the nonprofit (or "not-for-profit") organization and government documents. Many college graduates, especially students in English, Political Science, Psychology, Public Administration, Sociology, Technical Communication, and other humanities and social sciences fields begin their careers at nonprofits, where they build on the civic consciousness inspired by their college courses.

The nonprofit organization holds a unique legal and important social and cultural place in U.S. history and economy, and, "at some point, affect everyone's life" (U.S. Department of Labor). Although a nonprofit is not a governmental agency per se, its employees frequently are responsible for contributing to writing a wide range of government documents, from grant proposals to monthly government reports to legislative language for policymakers. When nonprofit employees are not participating in the writing of government documents, they are reading and interpreting them. Nonprofit employees and government employees often work closely together.

In 2004, these nonprofit—advocacy, grant making, and civic—organizations had some $1.2 million wage and salary jobs. "Employers [in this sector of the economy] need individuals with strong communication and fundraising skills, because organizations must constantly mobilize public support for their activities" (U.S. Department of Labor). Job opportunities are projected to be excellent in this sector, and although there may be relatively low wages in some nonprofits, many others, such as universities, hospitals, and large national charities, pay wages comparable to for-profit businesses (New York Times).

In the United States in 2003, there were nearly 1.4 million 501(c)3 organization, (National Council), an official designation given to nonprofits by the Internal Revenue Service, granting the organization tax exempt status and allowing individuals and businesses to receive tax deductions for contributions. The total assets of the more than 800,000 charitable nonprofits in the United States (excluding foundations and religious congregations) is more than $1.76 trillion (National Council). Nonprofits can range in size from small neighborhood groups with no revenue and no paid employees to the largest nonprofit in the United States, the Bill and Melinda Gates Foundation, which has an endowment of approximately $29.1 billion with 263 employees. Among the most recognizable nonprofits are the American Cancer Society, the American Red Cross, the Better Business Bureau, the Special Olympics, the Public Broadcasting Service, and the U.S. Humane Society.

Most nonprofits are incorporated, although some are not, but none are created or sustained to generate a profit for stockholders, trustees, or owners. Most focus on some charitable endeavor. Many receive donations from private individuals, which are tax deductible to donors; some, such as universities and colleges, charge fees for services, or sell products, but many depend on various government grants, and a number of nonprofits depend entirely on government grants to survive.

Nonprofits that either seek grant funding and/or give grants fall into two categories: private and public foundations. Private foundations are typically funded through one individual, a family, or corporation donations; public foundations are usually funded through numerous sources, including government agencies, private foundations, individual donations, and fees for service. In recent years, joint ventures or partnerships between nonprofits, government agencies, and private corporations have arisen to ensure continued funding for the important work of the nonprofit. For instance, corporations will sponsor fund-raising walks and sell products, with proceeds going to the nonprofit (U.S. Department of Labor).

In addition, new information technology is increasing the capacity for nonprofits to advance their causes and raise funds. From accepting online memberships and donations to collecting and reporting data quickly, to emailing legislative alerts to their constituency, to submitting online grant proposals, to access to interactive websites, email, and electronic databases, nonprofits communicate and interact electronically with their supporters, the public, donors, and policymakers. All of these activities—online or paper—require nonprofit employees to have communicative expertise.

The Role of Advocate and Government Writing

Writing for the Government underscores the fundamental principles of knowing an audience, having a clear purpose, and understanding the cultural context (the historical, political, social, economic, ethical, and technological possibilities and constraints) in which pieces are written and distributed, including those about advocacy work.

Although nonprofit advocacy takes many forms, from working with individual constituents to working with specific groups within constituencies, to working with the public at large, to working with policymakers, advocates must write and communicate matters that could eventually make their way into policies, laws, and other government documents. The many different written documents that nonprofit advocates create have many purposes—such as raising awareness by the public about an issue, encouraging constituents to vote for certain policies, instructing individuals how to negotiate bureaucratic problems, speaking before public meetings and giving public testimony, emailing constituents about upcoming issues of interest, researching for white papers, and scripting radio and TV interviews and appearances.

An example of how nonprofits focus on individual constituents' needs is the Tax Counseling for the Elderly (TCE) and the American Association of Retired Persons (AARP) that offer free help to people aged 60 and older with filling out income tax forms, which are complex and can change from year to year. The IRS provides grants for the service to nonprofits (IRS). On a larger scale, nonprofits, such as voluntary health organizations, raise funds for health-related research, disease awareness and prevention, and health education (U.S. Department of Labor), but they are also advocates for their constituency.

The National Multiple Sclerosis Society

One such health organization is the National Multiple Sclerosis (MS) Society. The National MS Society began in 1946 and has chapters in all 50 states. The Society's mission is "to end the devastating effects of MS." MS is a chronic, frequently progressive, and at times severely disabling disease. It is the most common neurologic disease leading to disability in young adults in the United States, and the cause of the disease is not known (Texas Department of State Health Services). It is usually diagnosed in people ages 20–50, but younger and older individuals can have it too. Similar to some other illnesses such as prostate cancer, AIDS, and mental illness, MS is also a widely misunderstood disease that can stigmatize the individual who has it. Two out of three people diagnosed are women, and although it appears to be more common in Caucasians, people of African, Asian, and Hispanic backgrounds have been diagnosed with it. The Society estimates that at least 400,000 Americans have the disease, but research is ongoing to determine a more exact number (National MS Society "Research/Clinical update"). "Few diseases have been studied so exhaustively by a variety of epidemiological methods without a cause being revealed" (Bashir and Whitaker 28).

Multiple Sclerosis (MS) is believed to be caused when the immune system, which is responsible for defending the body against viruses and bacteria, misidentifies the body's own tissue as being a foreign substance and begins attacking the myelin, a kind of protective sheath, surrounding the nerves in the brain, spinal cord, and/or optic nerve. The underlying nerve fibers are also damaged, which can lead to progressive disability. The name comes from myelin breaking down in multiple areas and being replaced by scar tissue called sclerosis. The resulting lesions can distort or even block messages between the brain and different parts of the body's motor and sensory system leading to a variety of unpredictable symptoms, which widely vary by individual or even within the same individual over time. Typical symptoms are debilitating fatigue, numbness and tingling, pain, tremors, poor coordination, difficulty walking, slurred speech, blurred or double vision or even blindness, forgetfulness, confusion, and in severe cases partial or complete paralysis (*Lone Star* Chapter "About MS").

Since MS is often difficult to diagnose, it can take several years for some individuals to get a definitive diagnosis. However, in recent years Magnetic Resonance Imaging (MRI) technology, with brain scans that reveal the MS lesions, have helped physicians make a more timely diagnosis, and since 1993, new medications have been developed that have shown promising results in modulating the immune system and impacting the underlying disease course by reducing the frequency and severity of MS attacks and slowing the disease process. This has helped thousands of individuals with the disease to maintain more independence and develop less disability. Many people with the disease do not show outward signs of MS, although they, for instance, may suffer from severe fatigue.

Policy Area	Jurisdiction
Research—Funding for MS-related biomedical and rehabilitative research, especially funding for the National Institutes of Health (NIH)	Federal & State
Health Insurance—coverage at an affordable price	Federal, State & Local
Health Care—protection and access to quality health care for public and private plans	Federal & State
Long-term Care—quality, affordable ways to keep patients in the community and functioning at the highest level	Federal, State & Local
Disability Rights—assuring physical accessibility for disabled, protecting their well-being, and preventing discrimination	Federal, State & Local

TABLE CS3.1 Source: MS Society, *Advocacy Training Manual*, 5.

In 2006, the MS Society invested more than $42 million in MS-related research (Nelson); some of the funding came from individual donors, some from foundations, and some from corporate giving. In addition to raising funds for MS research, services for people with MS, and professional education programs, the Society also raises funds to support advocacy efforts both on a state and federal level for people with MS. The National MS Society offers a 71-page *Advocacy Training Manual* to help volunteers, interested individuals, and local chapter officials learn how to be effective activists. The *Manual* begins by explaining the audience and role of an MS advocate: "to influence the public and private sectors to obtain benefits and resources for people with MS and their families" (3). The *Manual* lists the five most important public policy areas for people with MS and what jurisdiction they fall under—whether they are primarily national, state, or local matters. (See Table CS3.1.)

To decide whether an issue is a legislative matter, the *Manual* advises advocates to determine whether "the solution to a problem requires the creation of a new public program or a significant change to an existing program," then "legislation is required to authorize the proper department to establish a new program or amend an existing program" (35). When contemplating having a [legislative] member introduce legislation, an advocate must "develop a clear written description of your idea. The description should include a statement of purpose, describe who the bill will help and how, what it will cost/save and any other relevant information" (40). The following questions help determine when to propose legislation and what to address in advocacy materials:

- Can you present a compelling reason for having legislation introduced?
- What are the long-term implications of the legislation?
- Do you have the resources to follow this piece of legislation through?
- Does the legislation make good sense?
- Is there a broader audience for this legislation or is it self-serving?

Source: MS Society *Advocacy Training Manual*, 40.

Example of Advocacy Testimony

Included here is an excerpt from oral testimony that was then written and made available to the public. It is a statement by James C. Dickson, the vice president for Governmental Affairs of the American Association of People with Disabilities (AAPD), the largest organization that represents people with disabilities, including people with MS, in the country. Dickson gave this testimony to the U.S. Senate Committee on Rules and Administration, in which he argues that a federal proposal, the Voter Verified Paper Audit Trail (VVPAT) that calls for voting machines to have a paper method for manually counting votes to guard against fraud or malfunction of the machines has derailed progress of the Help America Vote Act (HAVA), which requires local polling places to make voting accessible to disabled individuals. The HAVA was one of a number of initiatives that arose out of the voting problems in the 2000 presidential election.

Dickson contends that the focus on the VVPAT by local voting offices circumvents the disability issue and delays the implementation of the needed accessibility aids that enable those who are disabled to participate in the voting process. We have annotated Dickson's written testimony to show how it meets the principles of writing and communicating, how he constructs an *ethos*—a presentation of credibility—for himself, how it is formatted to the conventions of legislative testimony, and how it fits into the argumentation genre of legislative testimony.

Personal Stories and Advocacy

Nonprofits that represent constituents with health-related problems normally use personal stories to put a human face on illness and adversity; personal stories draw the public and policymakers to the reality of the statistical and medical technical information, and, moreover, personal stories are memorable. Personal stories leave a lasting impression when other information fades from memory. Sandra Grance, State Public Policy Analyst for the National MS Society, says this about the use of personal stories and advocacy:

> The National MS Society values the use of personal stories when engaging in advocacy because of the powerful message that individual advocates can share. It is especially important to the MS community since each person's diagnosis and progression of the disease vary.
>
> Chapters actively recruit for volunteers who are interested in advocacy and are knowledgeable of the legislative process. We encourage chapters to use volunteers and clients in addition to staff when presenting testimony at legislative hearings and meetings with legislators. Many chapters also hold state lobby days and will take a delegation of 15–250 volunteers to their state capitol and spend the day meeting with legislators.
>
> By using these tactics, legislators and policymakers are able to learn about issues important to people with MS but also able to hear how the disease affects people on an everyday basis. . . .

The section of the *Manual* called "Advocacy Tactics: The Right Choice at the Right Time" says to use personal stories and anecdotes. "Your job is to persuade. A personal story will leave an image the legislator will remember when voting on the issue. Of course, it is important to make sure your story is directly related to the issue" (54).

Then in the section entitled "Tactic 3—How to Submit and Present Testimony," on "Writing Testimony," it gives this advice: "Use your personal statement to develop points in your testimony. . . . Use personal experience you or the chapter has had on the issue. . . . If you are giving oral testimony, submit your written remarks with all of the supporting documentation before the hearing." And, it says, "If you are not accepted [to testify], ask if you can submit written testimony" (55).

Format: heading with date, type of testimony, and committee members— the audience

Format: polite Intro, name, org. This creates an *ethos* for the speaker

Genre: national statistics, facts, background to back up argument

Genre: the premise of argument

Genre and *ethos*: added authority because of numbers; he knows history of problem

His personal story adds credibility. It contributes to *ethos*

June 21, 2005

Committee on Rules and Administration

Hearing Testimony: Voter Verification in the Federal Elections Process

Chairman Senator Trent Lott, Ranking Member Senator Christopher Dodd,
and Members of the Senate Committee on Rules and Administration:

Thank you for the opportunity to submit testimony and appear before you. I'm Jim Dickson, Vice President of Government Affairs for the American Association of People with Disabilities (AAPD). AAPD supports secure, accurate and independent voting for all Americans and full implementation of the Help America Vote Act (HAVA) as does every member of the Disability Vote Project Coalition.

People with disabilities make up approximately 20% of the population and there are approximately 37.5 million voting aged Americans with disabilities, less than half of whom actually vote. Most people with disabilities have invisible disabilities. For every noticeable blind person, there are 9 individuals whose vision is so poor that they are unable to read standard print. Most people with multiple sclerosis do not have to use a wheel chair all of the time. The disease does limit or prevent people from walking normal distances or climbing and descending stairs. The same is true for people who have hypertension and asthma.

The disability and civil rights communities oppose opening up HAVA for any amendments. The passage of the Help America Vote Act was a huge step forward for the nation's largest minority. For all Americans, the law made significant improvements to our voting system. Election officials are hard at work implementing HAVA's historic features. Changes to our voting system must come incrementally. We need data based on real life experiences before the law is amended. Amending HAVA would be like trying to change the tires on a car traveling while traveling on an interstate at 60 mph.

The Voter Verified Paper Audit Trail (VVPAT) is a theory. It has barely been tested in actual elections. It is dangerous to the health of our Republic to force into our already complex voting system a mandate that is unproven. All of HAVA's changes were based on actual voting place experience carried out in the states. Before Congress mandates a VVPAT, it must be proven to work at the local and state level. We need scientific and empirical proof that a VVPAT actually works and can be accessible before Congress acts.

The disability and civil rights communities supports safe, accurate, secure, and accessible voter verification systems. The only way to meet these four objectives for accessible voter verification systems is to test the system under actual election circumstances in a variety of settings, communities, and elections.

AAPD is the nation's largest cross-disability organization with over 100,000 members. I chair the Disability Vote Project Coalition with 38 national member organizations. . . .

Regarding HAVA's requirement for one accessible voting machine in every polling place by January 1, 2006, there is a misperception that states are rushing to purchase accessible touchscreen voting machines. This is not factually true. In a forthcoming report, Election Data Services and AAPD will document that 14% of voters had access to an accessible touchscreen in last year's presidential election. In fact, the overwhelming majority of states and counties are putting off the purchase of accessible equipment because of the Voter Verified Paper Audit Trail (VVPAT) hysteria. . . .

Supporters of a VVPAT claim to support access for voters with disabilities. In state after state, county after county, they have prevented jurisdictions from purchasing equipment that meets HAVA's January 1, 2006 deadline. . . .

In order for people with disabilities to be able to vote, we must run a gauntlet of physical and attitudinal barriers that often frustrate, humiliate and embarrass voters. I personally have had five experiences and my colleagues have had hundreds of thousands, if not millions of such negative experiences. Because I had to rely on third-party assistance to read the ballot, I had a pollworker say to me loud enough for everyone in the polling place to hear, "You want to vote for who?" I had a pollworker tell me, "Nobody understands these referenda. I'm really busy so we'll just end your voting now." Several of my blind colleagues also had the experience of a pollworker saying to them, as one did to me, "I can't read this small print, so let's stop here. That did not evoke much sympathy from me. . . .

In addition to painful experiences like these, millions of Americans who use wheelchairs, walkers, and while able to walk, cannot climb stairs, can't even get into the polling place. In 1984, Congress passed the Accessible Polling Place Act for the Elderly and Handicapped. 16 years later, during the 2000 election, the Government Accountability Office scientifically

---

FIGURE CS3.1   Excerpt from Cogressional Testimony. Source: Committee on Rules and Administration, United States Senate. 21 June 2005. http://rules.senate.gov/hearings/2005/062/05_hearings_htm

surveyed the nation's polling places for access on Election Day. Findings showed 84% of polling places were not accessible. For example, five years later, there has been some improvement, but not much. In Missouri, after finally surveying every polling place in 2004, 71% of polling places are not accessible. Ohio is one of several states that has not yet even begun to survey its polling places for physical accessibility.

. . . Last year, AAPD, with our grassroots colleagues across the nation, compared our member and client lists with the state voter registration files. More than 1.7 million individuals with disabilities were identified, and of the records compared, 55.7% were not registered to vote. Section 7 of the National Voter Registration Act (NVRA) requires that state funded agencies primarily providing services to people with disabilities must offer the opportunity to register to vote during intake and recertification procedures. Implementation of this requirement is uniformly infrequent, sloppy, and in some states and agencies, has never occurred. . . .

Recommendations:

• Complete access for people who have physical, mental, and sensory disabilities, to include voter registration, voting processes, and vote verification. Laws have been passed with the intention of facilitating the ability of voters with disabilities to cast a vote. These laws are often ignored and implementation has been consistently delayed. 21 years after the passage of the Accessible Polling Place Act, the majority of polling places are **not** accessible. 12 years after the passage of the National Voter Registration Act, poor people and voters with disabilities are **not** being offered the opportunity to register to vote in social service offices. The accessibility deadlines for HAVA have not yet arrived and we have organizations like the National Association of Secretaries of State and the National Association of County Organizations lobbying Congress to postpone HAVA's deadlines. If accessible voting is to become a reality, then the Election Assistance Commission must have the authority to withhold funds if a state or county is not accessible. The Department of Justice Disability Rights section needs additional funding to enforce compliance.

• Permanent and on-going federal funding for the administration of elections. Under HAVA, Congress allocated funds for elections research and development of new voting systems. To date, Congress has failed to appropriate any funds for research and development. The federal government must provide cash strapped counties and states with funds to conduct federal elections.

• Data collection and fact-based decision making regarding election administration and equipment. The federal government should support in every state a university based elections research and support center. In Georgia, Kennesaw State University has done an outstanding job with the statewide accessible touchscreen voting system. In addition to addressing the technology needs of elections, these centers could assist with other parts of our election process. The law school could provide assistance in writing contracts, using the expertise of professors who specialize in technology. The education department could provide assistance in developing public education programs, as well as pollworker training materials and procedures. The business school could analyze the election offices, their administrative procedures and personnel functions. Lastly, because each state has its own laws and procedures, there is need for a university elections center in each state.

The federal government, through our universities, supports just about every other aspect of American life. The federal government supports research and development for business and agriculture; for science and education, why not support the administration and conducting of elections?...

Thank you for this opportunity and I look forward to working with you as you prepare your report.

JAMES C. DICKSON

Jim Dickson is Vice President for Governmental Affairs of the American Association of People with Disabilities (AAPD). He leads the AAPD Disability Vote Project, a broad coalition of 38 national disability-related organizations to close the political participation gap for people with disabilities. The project focuses on election reform, polling place access, voter registration, education and get-out-the-vote drives. Jim has over 20 years' experience with voting and election administration issues.

FIGURE CS3.1   *(continued)*

Personal Stories: Celebrity and *Ethos*

The most recognized personal stories are those by celebrities. Celebrities can bring a heightened awareness about health-related issues because of their fame. They can create *ethos*—an appearance of credibility and respect—that helps generate support for the issue because they show that the disease can affect anyone in any circumstances. In addition, because they are celebrities, the media will be wherever they are to cover what they have to say, so policymakers will also pay more attention to them.

A recent noted example is entertainer Michael J. Fox's advocacy on behalf of individuals with Parkinson's disease, which is a chronic, progressive disorder of the central nervous system, leaving patients unable to direct or control their movements. In his thirties, Fox announced that he had been diagnosed with young-onset Parkinson's, a disease that usually affects individuals after their fifties. Fox has become a national spokesperson for the disease, citing his life and story as representative of Parkinson's patients' desires and needs. As we learn from the foundations website, "Fox wholeheartedly believes that if there is a concentrated effort from the Parkinson's community, elected representatives in Washington, DC, and (most importantly) the general public, researchers can pinpoint the cause of Parkinson's and uncover a cure within our lifetime."

The MS Society has "National Ambassadors," celebrities who have the disease and are willing to share their personal stories. Country music singer Clay Walker, actresses Teri Garr and Annette Funicello, actors David Lander and Jonathan Katz, and TV business host Neil Cavuto are National Ambassadors. Their health and professional schedules permitting, these celebrities tour the country to give speeches about MS, attend fund-raisers, and take opportunities to talk about their stories on local and national television shows. For instance, Walker has addressed Congressional members about new legislation affecting those living with MS; Garr is the first national chair of the Women Against MS Program, an education and fund-raising program, and David Lander, who played "Squiggy" on the TV sitcom *Laverne & Shirley* has both a print and audio book about his struggles with MS called *Fall Down Laughing*.

Furthermore, the writers of the fictional character President Josiah Bartlet on the hit show, *The West Wing*, heightened awareness about the misconceptions, stereotypes, and real-life challenges associated with an unpredictable disease such as MS. Bartlet, played by Martin Sheen, experienced the same type of MS symptoms, including fatigue, difficulty walking, vision issues, and memory problems, even the weighty burden of whether or not to publicly disclose the fact he had the disease that a person with MS suffers—whether he or she might be the "president" of the United States or a homemaker living in America's heartland. President Bartlet's story reinforced the many personal stories told by the Society's constituents and advocates. These diverse stories bring credibility—*ethos*—to the organization's goals.

Personal Stories and Technology

One of the factors in writing and presenting personal stories is the technological delivery of them. Included here are two different forms of delivery technologies.

The "Face of MS.org" is an interactive MS community sponsored by the National MS Society that encourages all those impacted by MS to share their stories so that visitors to the site better understand that there is no one face of MS but multi-thousands of faces (National MS Society "Face").

In addition to interactive website features and printed publications—such as *InsideMS*, magazines directed to teenagers and to children, and educational brochures—the Society also provides, on occasion with the help of unrestricted educational grants, booklets such as *MS: My Story, My Strength, My Success*. In the booklet are 17 personal stories by people

FIGURE CS3.2　Face of MS Website. Source: National MS Society

Come Face to Face with MS

How do you tell the story of multiple sclerosis?

How do you put a face on a disease that affects each person living with it so differently? With your story and your voice.

FaceofMS.org is an online community created by you. It is where people with MS and those in the fight against MS can go to share their experiences and hear the stories of others. It is where people who know little about MS can go to gain understanding from those closest to the disease. It is through collaboration that the National MS Society seeks to raise MS awareness. We want

everyone impacted by this disease to help build the Face of MS—a face that is as unique and diverse as the millions of people whose lives have been changed forever by Multiple Sclerosis. The project is dynamic. As new stories are added, the Face of MS will evolve to represent a growing number of people united in a common goal: To wipe the devastating effects of MS from the face of the earth.

Organized and produced by the National MS Society.

Designed and developed by Missing Pixel. (National MS Society "Face").

across the country with photos of the writers with their initials but without full names. This type of booklet is given out during MS chapter meetings and seminars. Participants then walk away from these events holding a booklet that can increase awareness of the fact that the disease affects people in all walks of life and demonstrates that people with MS and their families are not alone in the struggle.

The following is an example of one of the personal stories within the booklet. Cheryl C. says,

> I never dreamed living with a chronic disease could create such an opportunity. My MS changed my life, and for the better. Fourteen years ago my family was diagnosed with the disease. We are a military crew accustomed to tackling challenges head-on. So that is how we handled the diagnosis.

FIGURE CS3.3 *MS: My Story, My Strength, My Success*

FIGURE CS3.4 Photo of Cheryl C. in *MS: My Story, My Strength, My Success*

The writer then continues to explain how the diagnosis motivated her to help others. What kind of *ethos* does this presentation provide? Why is that important? How does that presentation inspire advocacy?

Ethical Issues in Advocacy Role and Personal Stories

Writing advocacy documents for nonprofits carries a host of ethical considerations as well as legal ones. Two of the hallmarks of effective advocacy are "a strong response network of individuals willing to testify, make phone calls, and generally react quickly and reliably to an advocacy call to action," and "a reputation as an independent source of unbiased information" (*Manual* 14). Advocates who provide policymakers with misleading or deceptive information jeopardize their effectiveness.

The *Manual* says that, "chapters [need] to use **extreme caution** [emphasis theirs] in working with someone who is running for office . . . as your activities and interactions with candidates can potentially cause election law violations and/or endanger the chapter's [nonprofit] status" (24). The following example from the *Manual* concerns ethical and legal issues in advocacy writing matters. In Figure CS3.5 Scenario it shows ethical and legal problems in writing and publishing an article.

> **Scenario #1:**
>
> A chapter has worked with State Senator Smith on many activities and writes an article about Senator Smith. The article outlines her devotion to MS research and her intent to strongly support Medicaid reforms that would benefit people with MS. The chapter publishes this interview and picture in its quarterly newsletter and Web site. State Senator Smith is up for election this year, and has declared her candidacy for office some time ago by setting up a reelection fund.
>
> **Potential Conflicts/Violations:**
>
> As a 501(c)(3) nonprofit organization, chapters should not endorse, contribute to, work for, or otherwise support a candidate for political office. The chapter has endangered its nonprofit status under IRS law by actions that could be viewed as an endorsement of State Senator Smith. Additionally, if the state's laws were similar to federal elections laws (as in many states) the chapter could be the subject of a campaign finance or elections law violation complaint and/or fines. Its newsletter could be considered a campaign contribution or expenditure under the law, and would bring the chapter's activities under political actions and disclosure laws.

FIGURE CS3.5   "Scenario." Source: National MS Society *Advocacy Training Manual*: 25

The anonymous entries in the *MS: My Story, My Strength, My Success* booklet demonstrate another important point of using personal stories. Although personal stories put a human face on illness and adversity, they also require a special kind of ethical prudence, especially with an illness that can stigmatize an individual. Reproduced here is a form from the National MS Society asking for individuals to provide written testimony for the legislative process, including their personal stories for policymakers; however, notice the authorization section of the form, which ensures that the Society can use the information.

Personal Stories, Facts, and Statistics

Personal stories alone however do not make for good public policy. Grance adds, "We found that it is best to combine personal stories with facts and statistics about the disease." Grance's point is echoed by others.

In "Do Good Stories Make for Good Policy?" David A. Hyman of the University of Maryland School of Law, says, "Health care policy is routinely influenced by stories. . . . Stories may be effective in mobilizing support for policy, but it is quite a different question whether sound policies will result" (1149). Hyman points out that narratives "help combat the psychological distancing that results from using statistical tools to address matters of life and death" (1154), but personal stories alone are problematic in that they can be atypical or unrepresentative of a group of people, and/or incomplete, and, therefore, "their selective focus precludes an appreciation of the reasons for existing institutional arrangements and the adverse consequences associated with proffered 'reforms' " (1150). Like Grance, Hyman contends that good policy comes from personal stories, facts, and statistics.

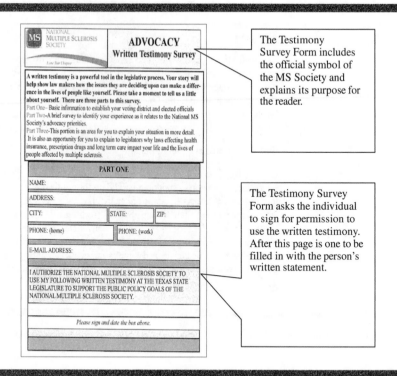

The Testimony Survey Form includes the official symbol of the MS Society and explains its purpose for the reader.

The Testimony Survey Form asks the individual to sign for permission to use the written testimony. After this page is one to be filled in with the person's written statement.

FIGURE CS3.6 Advocacy form. Source: Lone Star Chapter of the National MS Society

One of the most important research areas that the National MS Society watches intently is the development of new drugs for MS, investing over $42 million annually on its own to support over 350 research projects around the world. The Society actively pursues the goal of giving people with MS more choices for safe and effective treatments. Most recently, the Society worked to assist the Federal Drug Administration (FDA) in trying to determine whether the safety issues associated with a potentially promising therapy, Tysabri (pronounced *tie-sab-rae*), might be managed so that it could be brought back to market. Toward that end, the Society pursued avenues to assure that the FDA brought together the expertise required to evaluate all of the data in order to come to the best possible decision. In this effort, the Society submitted a recommended list of reviewers, who in its opinion, brought to the table a comprehensive and balanced understanding of the issues associated with the return of Tysabri to market. It also provided recommendations on clinical and scientific experts, as well as people with MS, to speak at the open public hearings. The Society also dedicated a month-long link from its website, which attracts over 14.5 million visits a year, to the FDA comment page and provided information on submitting testimony and participating in the hearings in person.

In addition, the Society commissioned an online survey of a random sample of over 800 people with MS, seeking their opinions on Tysabri with particular emphasis on determining the amount of risk that they would be willing to accept and still take the drug. The study was coordinated by International Communications Research with Harris Interactive Online. The results of the survey were provided to the FDA and after the FDA Advisory Panel made their recommendations, the full survey was also mounted on the Society's website. After having presented the best possible information and feedback to the FDA to support their review process, the Society supported the decision to bring Tysabri back to market with a safety monitoring program as it added yet one more option to the available treatment arsenal for people with MS.

The excerpt from Gary Sullivan's article in *InsideMS* briefly describes the history of the drug and subsequent testimony.

In November 2004, the Federal Drug Administration (FDA) accelerated the approval of the drug, Tysabri, for the treatment of relapsing MS, the least aggressive of the types of MS, as an option to other medications because early trials for the drug demonstrated remarkable reductions in the lesions of hundreds of those taking the drug rather than the placebo. However, after the drug was approved for release, three people developed another neurological disease that caused two of them to die and one to be seriously disabled.

Tysabri's sponsors Biogen Idec and Elan Pharmaceuticals immediately withdrew the drug from the market and began safety reviews of the 3,000 people involved in the Tysabri trials. In the intervening time, in March 2006, some 40 people, many of whom had MS, testified during a public discussion in a two-day FDA Advisory Committee meeting on their opinions of the drug, which ranged from very positive to very negative.

Barbara Crooks, testified: "Tysabri was easy to take, and it improved my walking and mobility. I am not afraid of dying; I'm afraid of living as a burden to those I love" (28).

Stan Croydon, who has had MS for 38 years and gone through a regimen of MS medications, said, "I've never taken Tysabri, but I want the option" (29). At the end of the

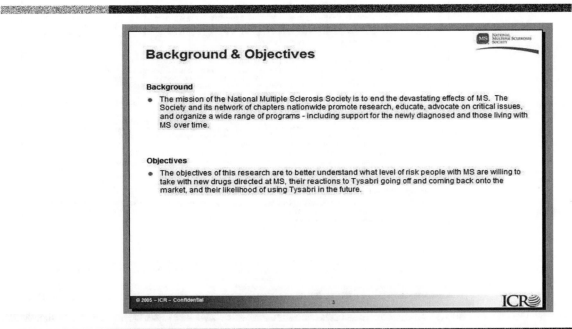

FIGURE CS3.7 Multiple Sclerosis Drug Study. Source: Nicholas G. La Rocca, International Communication Research February 2006

meeting, the FDA Advisory Committee unanimously voted to recommend to the FDA that the drug be returned to the market.

Figures CS3.7–3.9 demonstrate the objectives, methodology, and some key findings of the study. By combining personal stories with statistical information, the MS Society has provided the FDA the numbers and the faces to make a determination about whether a new drug should be allowed back on the market. What do you think about the comprehensiveness of the survey? How about the survey findings? How might the language of personal stories and survey information be alike or different? How might personal stories be part of surveys? What might further convince legislators? Why do you think that is the case?

Methodology

Methodology

- Interviews were completed among 810 people with Multiple Sclerosis randomly selected from Harris Interactive's Online MS panel of 4,351 people who personally have been diagnosed by a medical doctor or healthcare professional as having Multiple Sclerosis. All respondents were from the U.S. and were at least 18 years of age.
- This was an online survey, which took on average between 15 and 20 minutes to complete.
- Data collection was completed between December 13 and December 19, 2005. A follow-up survey was done in which 651 respondents were re-contacted to correct a programming issue with four risk-type (Standard Gamble) questions on the survey. This follow-up was conducted between December 28, 2005 and January 17, 2006.
- The initial survey had a response rate of 31.7% with 810 surveys completed. The follow-up survey had a response rate of 73.9% with 557 of the targeted 651 completing the follow-up survey.

Harrris Poll Online Panel Information

- Harris Poll Online℠ (HPOL) is a multimillion-member panel of online respondents. It is the largest database of individual double opt-in respondents in the world.
- All panelists recruited have completed a "confirmed" or "double" opt-in (COI/DOI) process.
  - This process requires that each registrant confirm his or her desire to join the panel by clicking on a link within an email that is sent to the registrant's email address upon registering. If the registrant clicks on the link within the email, he or she is added to the Harris Poll Online. If the registrant takes some other action or simply deletes the email, he or she is not added to the database.
- Panelists have joined the Harris Poll Online through over 100 different sources.
  - Many different diverse methods are leveraged to gain panelists, including co-registration offers on partners' websites, targeted emails sent by online partners to their audiences, graphical and text banner placement on partners' websites, trade show presentations, targeted postal mail invitations, TV advertisements, member referrals, and telephone recruitment of targeted populations.
- Many respondents with MS belong to the Chronic Illness panel, a specialty panel within the Harris Poll Online Panel.
  - These panelists participate in a variety of different surveys and have been screened into this panel by completing the Harris online health and wellness screener. This screener captures a variety of illnesses, which must be diagnosed by a physician and/or health care provider in order to qualify for the Chronic Illness panel. Members of the Chronic Illness panel typically respond between 30-40%.
- There are 8,172 respondents in this panel with MS (self and household). Of those, 7,469 are from the United States and are 18+ years old. 4,351 have MS themselves. The other 3,118 panel members have someone in their household that has MS.

Margin of Error

- Because this is a sample, and not an actual population, an associated margin of error applies. At a 95% level of confidence, the margin of error for this sample of 810 total is +/- 3.4% or better. This essentially means that we can be 95% certain that, for any percentage result for the total sample, the "true" percentage is within +/- 3.4 percentage points of that which is actually reported.

Significant Differences

- Within this report, significant differences are reported among analytic subgroups at the 95% level of confidence and are noted by **Bold** percentages. Those subgroups and associated percentages that are significantly lower than what is **Bold** are shown in *italics*.

© 2005 - ICR - Confidential

ICR

FIGURE CS3.8

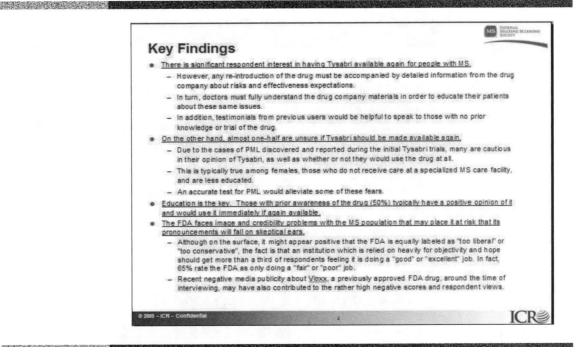

Key Findings

- There is significant respondent interest in having Tysabri available again for people with MS.
  - However, any re-introduction of the drug must be accompanied by detailed information from the drug company about risks and effectiveness expectations.
  - In turn, doctors must fully understand the drug company materials in order to educate their patients about these same issues.
  - In addition, testimonials from previous users would be helpful to speak to those with no prior knowledge or trial of the drug.
- On the other hand, almost one-half are unsure if Tysabri should be made available again.
  - Due to the cases of PML discovered and reported during the initial Tysabri trials, many are cautious in their opinion of Tysabri, as well as whether or not they would use the drug at all.
  - This is typically true among females, those who do not receive care at a specialized MS care facility, and are less educated.
  - An accurate test for PML would alleviate some of these fears.
- Education is the key. Those with prior awareness of the drug (50%) typically have a positive opinion of it and would use it immediately if again available.
- The FDA faces image and credibility problems with the MS population that may place it at risk that its pronouncements will fall on skeptical ears.
  - Although on the surface, it might appear positive that the FDA is equally labeled as "too liberal" or "too conservative", the fact is that an institution which is relied on heavily for objectivity and hope should get more than a third of respondents feeling it is doing a "good" or "excellent" job. In fact, 65% rate the FDA as only doing a "fair" or "poor" job.
  - Recent negative media publicity about Vioxx, a previously approved FDA drug, around the time of interviewing, may have also contributed to the rather high negative scores and respondent views.

© 2005 – ICR – Confidential

ICR

FIGURE CS3.9

Activities and Assignments

1. **Individual or Group Activity:** The screen shot of a MS website homepage is annotated to show ways the site addresses the principles of audience, purpose, and cultural context in the presentation of information about the organization. As individuals or in groups, create your own site with those characteristics, or find other websites for nonprofits and analyze their presentations; then determine whether they are addressing these key principles—and if not, suggest what they should do to change the site. Share with your classmates what you find. If you wish, contact the organization about your findings.

2. **Individual or Group Activity:** The case study in this chapter focuses on MS, an illness that stigmatizes the individuals who have it. In a similar way, breast cancer has been an illness that stigmatizes. Barbara F. Sharf writes, in the article, "Out of the Closet and Into the Legislature: Breast Cancer Stories":

   In living color twenty-three figures appear in photographs before and after breast cancer surgery in *Show Me*, a recent book in both print and online forms. The women display in stark details lumpectomies, mastectomies, and reconstructions, along with their reactions to these treatments. Clearly women have come a long way since the stigmatized silence of twenty years ago. . . .

Advocacy webpage

Advocacy Notice

Personal stories
Online

Celebrity
endorsement

Facts and
Statistics

Brochures

Personal story:
Celebrity Paper
magazine

Audience: Teenagers
and children

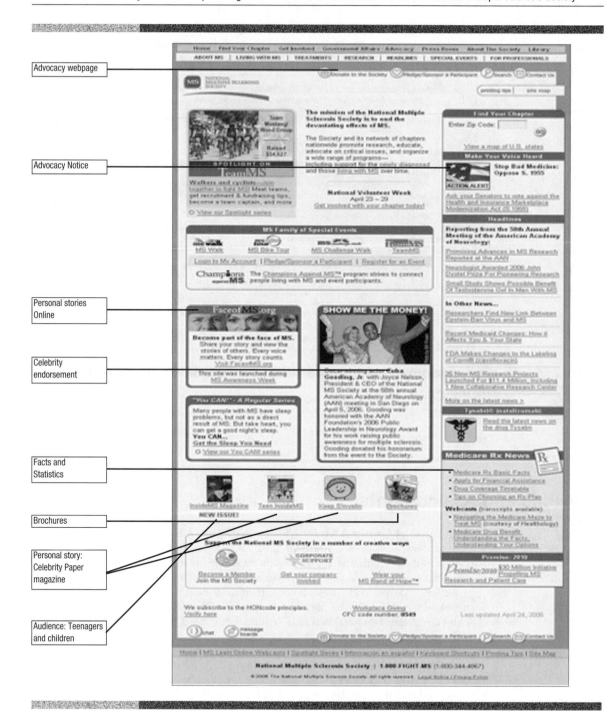

FIGURE CS3.10   Source: National MS Society, 27 April 2006. http://www.nmss.org.

Personal stories of breast cancer have raised social awareness, destigmatized the disease, and been key in creating significant changes in health policies. . . .

[Poet] Audre Lord wonders in *The Cancer Journals,* "What would happen if an army of one-breasted women descended upon Congress?". . . She alerted us to the idea that shared biographies are integral to advocacy, and advocacy, of course, can alter policy" (213–14).

Personal stories by women with breast cancer have opened a closeted door and changed how Americans think about the cancer and increased governmental funding for breast cancer research. Other illnesses such as prostate cancer, mental illness, and AIDS also stigmatize. Research other illnesses that have stigmatized individuals and write an essay about what kinds of governmental funding and advocacy are done by organizations for those individuals and causes. Share your findings with your classmates.

3. **Individual or Group Activity:** Michael J. Fox and the late Christopher Reeve are two of the most well-known entertainers to become advocates for specific health-related causes. Both have spoken before Congress about the controversial subject of stem cell research. Check out their foundation websites, and analyze what language and visuals are being used to create *ethos.* Why do you think it has been done this way? Research their testimonies and analyze the way they include personal stories with statistics and facts. Write a report and share it with your classmates.

4. **Individual or Group Activity:** Find other Congressional hearing testimony, and compare it with the "Hearing testimony: Vote Verification in the Federal Elections Process" in this chapter. How is it formatted? How is the argumentation approach of the genre apparent in the testimony you found? Write a report on your findings and share it with your classmates.

5. **Individual or Group Activity:** Draft your own argument for some legislative action that you would like to see changed. Pretend you are going to speak before Congress. Write up your argument; analyze whether you have addressed the writing and communicating principles and answered the questions about the importance of the legislation presented earlier in this case study. Share this with your classmates.

6. **Individual or Group Activity:** Find and research nonprofits in your own community. Analyze their documents and websites. Interview the officials of the nonprofit. Depending on what you find, you may want to offer to write a manual or some other kind of documents for the nonprofit.

7. **Individual or Group Activity:** Review a local nonprofit website. Then interview officials with the nonprofit to ask if you may get copies of their grant proposals. Review the chapter on writing proposals in this textbook, determine who the audience is for the nonprofit's proposal, what the purpose is for it, and its cultural context. If the nonprofit officials do not mind, share what you find with your classmates and with them.

Resources for Nonprofit Organizations and Legislative Advocacy

Federal Government	<http://www.USA.gov>
State Government	<http://www.loc.gov/rr/news/stategov/stategov.html>
Centers for Medicare and Medicaid (CMMS)	<http://www.cms.hhs.gov>
Health Privacy Project	<http://www.healthprivacy.org>
Hauser Center for Nonprofits	<http://www.ksghauser.harvard.edu/>
Idealist Organization: Action without Borders	<http://www.idealist.org/>

GuideStar, organization for nonprofits	<http://www.guidestar.org>
Independent Sector	<http://www.independentsector.org>
Internal Revenue Service	<http://irs.gov>
Kaiser Family Foundation	<http://www.kff.org>
National Conference of State Legislatures	<http://www.ncsl.org>
National Council of Nonprofit Associations	<http://www.ncna.org/>
National Institutes of Health	<http://www.nih.gov>
Social Security Administration (SSA)	<http://www.ssa.gov>
Society for Nonprofit Organizations	<http://www.snpo.org/>
State Health Facts Online	<http://www.statehealthfacts.kff.org>
Library of Congress Legislative Information	<http://thomas.loc.gov>
U.S. House of Representatives	<http://www.house.gov>
U.S. Senate	<http://www.senate.gov>
United Way of America	<http://national.unitedway.org/>
United We Ride	<http://www.unitedweride.gov>
The White House	<http://www.whitehouse.gov>

Works Cited

Alvarado, Audrey R. "The United States Nonprofit Sector Report 2003." National Council of Nonprofit Associations. 7 April 2006 <http://www.ncna.org/>.

American Association of Retired Person (AARP) "AARP Tax-Aide." 16 Aug. 2007 <http://aarp.org/money/taxaide/>.

Bashir, Khurram, and John N. Whitaker. *Handbook of Multiple Sclerosis*. Philadelphia, PA: Lippincott, Williams & Wilkins, 2002.

Christopher Reeve Foundation. 5 Sept. 2006 <http://www.christopherreeve.org>.

Dickson, James C. "Hearing Testimony: Voter Verification in the Federal Elections Process." U.S. Senate Committee on Rules and Regulations. 21 June 2005. 29 April 2006 <http://rules.senate.gov/hearings/2005/62105_hearing_html>.

Grance, Sandra. "Re: NMSS." Email to Libby Allison. 21 April 2006.

Hyman, David A. "Do Good Stories Make for Good Policy?" *Journal of Health Politics, Policy and Law*. 25.6 (Dec. 2000). Durham, N.C.: Duke UP: 1149–55.

Internal Revenue Service. "Tax Counseling for the Elderly (TCE)." 5 Sept. 2006 <http://www.irs.gov>.

La Rocca, Nicholas G. International Communication Research. "Multiple Sclerosis Drug Study." February 2006. Powerpoint Presentation. Email to Libby Allison. 28 April 2006.

Lone Star Chapter National Multiple Sclerosis Society "About MS." 7 April 2006. <txhenmss.org>.

Michael J. Fox Foundation. 5 Sept 2006 <http://www.michaeljfox.org>.

National Council of Nonprofit Associations. "The United States Nonprofit Society Report 2003." 7 Apr. 2006 <http://www.nona.org/>.

National Multiple Sclerosis Society. Angela M. Ostrom, Director Public policy Research & Advocacy Communications, National Society. Email to Libby Allison. 15 March 2006.

—. *Advocacy Training Manual*, revised March 2006.

—. "Face of MS. org." 26 April 2006 <http://www.nmss.org>.

—. *MS: My Story, My Strength, My Success*. Shared Solutions. April 2006.

—. "Research/Clinical Update" 30 Jan 2007 <http://www.nmss.org>.

Nelson, Joyce. National MS Society fundraising letter. 3 April 2006.

New York Times. "What is a Nonprofit?" About.com. New York Times, Co, 2006. 4 April
    2006 <http://nonprofit.about.com/od/nonprofitstartup/a/what_is_np.htm>.
Sharf, Barbara F. "Out of the Closet and Into the Legislature: Breast Cancer Stories." *Health
    Affairs* January/February 2001: 213–18.
Sullivan, Gary. "Voices of Hope and Determination: People with MS Impact Tysabri
    Recommendation." *InsideMS*. Special Report. April-May 2006: 27–30.
Texas Department of State Health Services. "Case Control of Environmental Exposures
    and Genetic Susceptibility in Individuals with Multiple Sclerosis in Three Geographic
    Areas." 18 Oct. 2005. 22 April 2006 <http://dshs.state.tx.us/epitox.casecontrol.shtm>.
U.S. Department of Labor, Bureau of Labor Statistics "Career Guide to Industries,"
    2006–07 Ed. Advocacy, Grantmaking, and Civic Organizations. 7 April 2006.
    <http://www.bls.gov/oco/cg/cgs054.htm>.

APPENDIX A: List of Federal Departments and Agencies

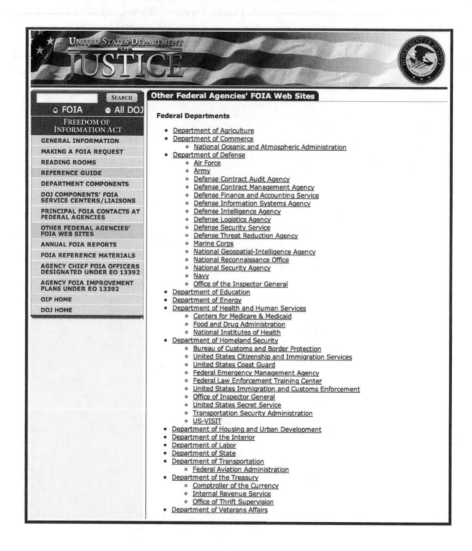

United States Department of Justice

Other Federal Agencies' FOIA Web Sites

SEARCH

○ FOIA   ● All DOJ

FREEDOM OF INFORMATION ACT

GENERAL INFORMATION

MAKING A FOIA REQUEST

READING ROOMS

REFERENCE GUIDE

DEPARTMENT COMPONENTS

DOJ COMPONENTS' FOIA SERVICE CENTERS/LIAISONS

PRINCIPAL FOIA CONTACTS AT FEDERAL AGENCIES

OTHER FEDERAL AGENCIES' FOIA WEB SITES

ANNUAL FOIA REPORTS

FOIA REFERENCE MATERIALS

AGENCY CHIEF FOIA OFFICERS DESIGNATED UNDER EO 13392

AGENCY FOIA IMPROVEMENT PLANS UNDER EO 13392

OIP HOME

DOJ HOME

Federal Departments

- Department of Agriculture
- Department of Commerce
  - National Oceanic and Atmospheric Administration
- Department of Defense
  - Air Force
  - Army
  - Defense Contract Audit Agency
  - Defense Contract Management Agency
  - Defense Finance and Accounting Service
  - Defense Information Systems Agency
  - Defense Intelligence Agency
  - Defense Logistics Agency
  - Defense Security Service
  - Defense Threat Reduction Agency
  - Marine Corps
  - National Geospatial-Intelligence Agency
  - National Reconnaissance Office
  - National Security Agency
  - Navy
  - Office of the Inspector General
- Department of Education
- Department of Energy
- Department of Health and Human Services
  - Centers for Medicare & Medicaid
  - Food and Drug Administration
  - National Institutes of Health
- Department of Homeland Security
  - Bureau of Customs and Border Protection
  - United States Citizenship and Immigration Services
  - United States Coast Guard
  - Federal Emergency Management Agency
  - Federal Law Enforcement Training Center
  - United States Immigration and Customs Enforcement
  - Office of Inspector General
  - United States Secret Service
  - Transportation Security Administration
  - US-VISIT
- Department of Housing and Urban Development
- Department of the Interior
- Department of Labor
- Department of State
- Department of Transportation
  - Federal Aviation Administration
- Department of the Treasury
  - Comptroller of the Currency
  - Internal Revenue Service
  - Office of Thrift Supervision
- Department of Veterans Affairs

Federal Agencies

- Agency for International Development
- American Battle Monuments Commission
- Amtrak (National Railroad Passenger Corporation)
- Broadcasting Board of Governors
- Central Intelligence Agency
- Chemical Safety and Hazard Investigation Board
- Commission on Civil Rights
- Committee for Purchase from People who Are Blind or Severely Disabled
- Commodity Futures Trading Commission
- Consumer Product Safety Commission
- Corporation for National Service
- Court Services and Offender Supervision Agency
- Defense Nuclear Facilities Safety Board
- Environmental Protection Agency
- Equal Employment Opportunity Commission
- Executive Office of the President
    - Council on Environmental Quality
    - Office of Administration
    - Office of Management and Budget
    - Office of National Drug Control Policy
    - Office of Science and Technology Policy
    - Office of the United States Trade Representative
    - Privacy and Civil Liberties Oversight Board
- Export-Import Bank
- Farm Credit Administration
- Farm Credit System Insurance Corporation
- Federal Communications Commission
- Federal Deposit Insurance Corporation
- Federal Election Commission
- Federal Energy Regulatory Commission
- Federal Housing Finance Board
- Federal Labor Relations Authority
- Federal Maritime Commission
- Federal Mediation and Conciliation Service
- Federal Mine Safety and Health Review Commission
- Federal Open Market Committee
- Federal Reserve System
- Federal Retirement Thrift Investment Board
- Federal Trade Commission
- General Services Administration
- Institute of Museum and Library Services
- Inter-American Foundation
- Legal Services Corporation
- Merit Systems Protection Board
- Millennium Challenge Corporation
- National Aeronautics and Space Administration
- National Archives and Records Administration
- National Capital Planning Commission
- National Credit Union Administration
- National Endowment for the Arts
- National Endowment for the Humanities
- National Indian Gaming Commission
- National Labor Relations Board
- National Mediation Board
- National Science Foundation
- National Transportation Safety Board
- Nuclear Regulatory Commission
- Occupational Safety and Health Review Commission
- Office of the Director of National Intelligence
- Office of Federal Housing Enterprise Oversight
- Office of Government Ethics
- Office of Personnel Management
- Office of Special Counsel
- Overseas Private Investment Corporation
- Peace Corps
- Pension Benefit Guaranty Corporation
- Postal Regulatory Commission
- Railroad Retirement Board
- Securities and Exchange Commission
- Selective Service System
- Small Business Administration
- Social Security Administration
- Surface Transportation Board
- Tennessee Valley Authority
- United States Copyright Office
- United States International Trade Commission
- United States Postal Service
- United States Trade and Development Agency

APPENDIX B: The Declaration of Independence, The U.S. Constitution, and Bill of Rights

Source: Engrossed copy of the Declaration of Independence, August 2, 1776; Miscellaneous Papers of the Continental Congress, 1774–1789; Records of the Continental and Confederation Congresses and the Constitutional Convention, 1774–1789, Record Group 360; National Archives.

In CONGRESS, July 4, 1776.

A DECLARATION

By the REPRESENTATIVES of the

UNITED STATES OF AMERICA,

In GENERAL CONGRESS Assembled.

WHEN in the Course of human Events, it becomes necessary for one People to dissolve the Political Bands which have connected them with another, and to assume among the Powers of the Earth, the separate and equal Station to which the Laws of Nature and of Nature's God entitle them, a decent Respect to the Opinions of Mankind requires that they should declare the causes which impel them to the Separation.

We hold these Truths to be self-evident, that all Men are created equal, that they are endowed by their Creator with certain unalienable Rights, that among these are Life, Liberty, and the Pursuit of Happiness—That to secure these Rights, Governments are instituted among Men, deriving their just Powers from the Consent of the Governed, that whenever any Form of Government becomes destructive of these Ends, it is the Right of the People to alter or to abolish it, and to institute new Government, laying its Foundation on such Principles, and organizing its Powers in such Form, as to them shall seem most likely to effect their Safety and Happiness. Prudence, indeed, will dictate that Governments long established should not be changed for light and transient Causes; and accordingly all Experience hath shewn, that Mankind are more disposed to suffer, while Evils are sufferable, than to right themselves by abolishing the Forms to which they are accustomed. But when a long Train of Abuses and Usurpations, pursuing invariably the same Object, evinces a Design to reduce them under absolute Despotism, it is their Right, it is their Duty, to throw off such Government, and to provide new Guards for their future Security. Such has been the patient Sufferance of these Colonies; and such is now the Necessity which constrains them to alter their former Systems of Government. The History of the present King of Great-Britain is a History of repeated Injuries and Usurpations, all having in direct Object the Establishment of an absolute Tyranny over these States. To prove this, let Facts be submitted to a candid World.

He has refused his Assent to Laws, the most wholesome and necessary for the public Good.

He has forbidden his Governors to pass Laws of immediate and pressing Importance, unless suspended in their Operation till his Assent should be obtained; and when so suspended, he has utterly neglected to attend to them.

He has refused to pass other Laws for the Accommodation of large Districts of People, unless those People would relinquish the Right of Representation in the Legislature, a Right inestimable to them, and formidable to Tyrants only.

He has called together Legislative Bodies at Places unusual, uncomfortable, and distant from the Depository of their public Records, for the sole Purpose of fatiguing them into Compliance with his Measures.

He has dissolved Representative Houses repeatedly, for opposing with manly Firmness his Invasions on the Rights of the People.

He has refused for a long Time, after such Dissolutions, to cause others to be elected; whereby the Legislative Powers, incapable of Annihilation, have returned to the People at large for their exercise; the State remaining in the mean time exposed to all the Dangers of Invasion from without, and Convulsions within.

He has endeavoured to prevent the Population of these States; for that Purpose obstructing the Laws for Naturalization of Foreigners; refusing to pass others to encourage their Migrations hither, and raising the Conditions of new Appropriations of Lands.

He has obstructed the Administration of Justice, by refusing his Assent to Laws for establishing Judiciary Powers.

He has made Judges dependent on his Will alone, for the Tenure of their Offices, and the Amount and Payment of their Salaries.

He has erected a Multitude of new Offices, and sent hither Swarms of Officers to harrass our People, and eat out their Substance.

He has kept among us, in Times of Peace, Standing Armies, without the consent of our Legislatures.

He has affected to render the Military independent of and superior to the Civil Power.

He has combined with others to subject us to a Jurisdiction foreign to our Constitution, and unacknowledged by our Laws; giving his Assent to their Acts of pretended Legislation:

For quartering large Bodies of Armed Troops among us:

For protecting them, by a mock Trial, from Punishment for any Murders which they should commit on the Inhabitants of these States:

For cutting off our Trade with all Parts of the World:

For imposing Taxes on us without our Consent:

For depriving us, in many Cases, of the Benefits of Trial by Jury:

For transporting us beyond Seas to be tried for pretended Offences:

For abolishing the free System of English Laws in a neighbouring Province, establishing therein an arbitrary Government, and enlarging its Boundaries, so as to render it at once an Example and fit Instrument for introducing the same absolute Rule into these Colonies:

For taking away our Charters, abolishing our most valuable Laws, and altering fundamentally the Forms of our Governments:

For suspending our own Legislatures, and declaring themselves invested with Power to legislate for us in all Cases whatsoever.

He has abdicated Government here, by declaring us out of his Protection and waging War against us.

He has plundered our Seas, ravaged our Coasts, burnt our Towns, and destroyed the Lives of our People.

He is, at this Time, transporting large Armies of foreign Mercenaries to compleat the Works of Death, Desolation, and Tyranny, already begun with circumstances of Cruelty and Perfidy, scarcely paralleled in the most barbarous Ages, and totally unworthy the Head of a civilized Nation.

He has constrained our fellow Citizens taken Captive on the high Seas to bear Arms against their Country, to become the Executioners of their Friends and Brethren, or to fall themselves by their Hands.

He has excited domestic Insurrections amongst us, and has endeavoured to bring on the Inhabitants of our Frontiers, the merciless Indian Savages, whose known Rule of Warfare, is an undistinguished Destruction, of all Ages, Sexes and Conditions.

In every stage of these Oppressions we have Petitioned for Redress in the most humble Terms: Our repeated Petitions have been answered only by repeated Injury. A Prince, whose Character is thus marked by every act which may define a Tyrant, is unfit to be the Ruler of a free People.

Nor have we been wanting in Attentions to our British Brethren. We have warned them from Time to Time of Attempts by their Legislature to extend an unwarrantable Jurisdiction over us. We have reminded them of the Circumstances of our Emigration and Settlement here. We have appealed to their native Justice and Magnanimity, and we have conjured them by the Ties of our common Kindred to disavow these Usurpations, which, would inevitably interrupt our Connections and Correspondence. They too have been deaf to the Voice of Justice and of Consanguinity. We must, therefore, acquiesce in the Necessity, which denounces our Separation, and hold them, as we hold the rest of Mankind, Enemies in War, in Peace, Friends.

We, therefore, the Representatives of the UNITED STATES OF AMERICA, in General Congress, Assembled, appealing to the Supreme Judge of the World for the Rectitude of our Intentions, do, in the Name, and by Authority of the good People of these Colonies, solemnly Publish and Declare, That these United Colonies are, and of Right ought to be, Free and Independent States; that they are absolved from all Allegiance to the British Crown, and that all political Connection between them and the State of Great-Britain, is and ought to be totally dissolved; and that as Free and Independent States, they have full Power to levy War, conclude Peace, contract Alliances, establish Commerce, and to do all other Acts and Things which Independent States may of right do. And for the support of this Declaration, with a firm Reliance on the Protection of divine Providence, we mutually pledge to each other our Lives, our Fortunes, and our sacred Honor.

Signed by Order *and in* Behalf *of the* Congress,

JOHN HANCOCK, President.

Attest.
CHARLES THOMSON, Secretary.

PHILADELPHIA: PRINTED BY JOHN DUNLAP.

Source: Signed Copy of the Constitution of the United States; Miscellaneous Papers of the Continental Congress, 1774–1789; Records of the Continental and Confederation Congresses and the Constitutional Convention, 1774–1789, Record Group 360; National Archives.

Source: Engrossed Bill of Rights, September 25, 1789; General Records of the United States Government; Record Group 11; National Archives.

Congress may by general Laws prescribe the Manner in which such Acts, Records and Proceedings shall be proved, and the Effect thereof.

Section. 2. The Citizens of each State shall be entitled to all Privileges and Immunities of Citizens in the several States.

A Person charged in any State with Treason, Felony, or other Crime, who shall flee from Justice, and be found in another State, shall on Demand of the executive Authority of the State from which he fled, be delivered up, to be removed to the State having Jurisdiction of the Crime.

No Person held to Service or Labour in one State, under the Laws thereof, escaping into another, shall, in Consequence of any Law or Regulation therein, be discharged from such Service or Labour, but shall be delivered up on Claim of the Party to whom such Service or Labour may be due.

Section. 3. New States may be admitted by the Congress into this Union; but no new State shall be formed or erected within the Jurisdiction of any other State; nor any State be formed by the Junction of two or more States, or Parts of States, without the Consent of the Legislatures of the States concerned as well as of the Congress.

The Congress shall have Power to dispose of and make all needful Rules and Regulations respecting the Territory or other Property belonging to the United States; and nothing in this Constitution shall be so construed as to Prejudice any Claims of the United States, or of any particular State.

Section. 4. The United States shall guarantee to every State in this Union a Republican Form of Government, and shall protect each of them against Invasion; and on Application of the Legislature, or of the Executive (when the Legislature cannot be convened) against domestic Violence.

Article. V.

The Congress, whenever two thirds of both Houses shall deem it necessary, shall propose Amendments to this Constitution, or, on the Application of the Legislatures of two thirds of the several States, shall call a Convention for proposing Amendments, which, in either Case, shall be valid to all Intents and Purposes, as Part of this Constitution, when ratified by the Legislatures of three fourths of the several States, or by Conventions in three fourths thereof, as the one or the other Mode of Ratification may be proposed by the Congress; Provided that no Amendment which may be made prior to the Year One thousand eight hundred and eight shall in any Manner affect the first and fourth Clauses in the Ninth Section of the first Article; and that no State, without its Consent, shall be deprived of its equal Suffrage in the Senate.

Article. VI.

All Debts contracted and Engagements entered into, before the Adoption of this Constitution, shall be as valid against the United States under this Constitution, as under the Confederation.

This Constitution, and the Laws of the United States which shall be made in Pursuance thereof; and all Treaties made, or which shall be made, under the Authority of the United States, shall be the supreme Law of the Land; and the Judges in every State shall be bound thereby, any Thing in the Constitution or Laws of any State to the Contrary notwithstanding.

The Senators and Representatives before mentioned, and the Members of the several State Legislatures, and all executive and judicial Officers, both of the United States and of the several States, shall be bound by Oath or Affirmation, to support this Constitution; but no religious Test shall ever be required as a Qualification to any Office or public Trust under the United States.

Article. VII.

The Ratification of the Conventions of nine States, shall be sufficient for the Establishment of this Constitution between the States so ratifying the Same.

done in Convention by the Unanimous Consent of the States present the Seventeenth Day of September in the Year of our Lord one thousand seven hundred and Eighty seven and of the Independance of the United States of America the Twelfth In witness whereof We have hereunto subscribed our Names,

Attest William Jackson Secretary

Go. Washington
Presidt and deputy from Virginia

Delaware
Geo: Read
Gunning Bedford jun
John Dickinson
Richard Bassett
Jaco: Broom

Maryland
James McHenry
Dan of St Thos. Jenifer
Danl. Carroll

Virginia
John Blair —
James Madison Jr.

North Carolina
Wm. Blount
Richd. Dobbs Spaight
Hu Williamson

South Carolina
J. Rutledge
Charles Cotesworth Pinckney
Charles Pinckney
Pierce Butler

Georgia
William Few

New Hampshire
John Langdon
Nicholas Gilman

Massachusetts
Nathaniel Gorham
Rufus King

Connecticut
Wm. Saml. Johnson
Roger Sherman

New York
Alexander Hamilton

New Jersey
Wil: Livingston
David Brearley
Wm. Paterson
Jona: Dayton

Pennsylvania
B Franklin
Thomas Mifflin
Robt. Morris
Geo. Clymer
Thos. FitzSimons
Jared Ingersoll
James Wilson
Gouv Morris

GLOSSARY

Accessibility   Federal government websites are mandated to be accessible to the disabled by amendments to Section 508 of the Rehabilitation Act of 1973. For example, webpages need to have "text equivalents" for images so individuals with limited sight who use software readers that read aloud content of webpages can also hear a description of what an image presents. More information can be found at http://www.section508.gov.

Active voice   In active voice sentences, the subject of the sentence does the action; while, in passive voice sentences, the subject of the sentence is acted on by the verb. (See **Passive Voice**). Active voice sentences are preferable for reading comprehension.

Bandwidth   the capacity and speed a communications channel can send data.

Best Practices   strategies, approaches, techniques, and activities that have proven over time and through practice to be the most successful.

Broadband   communication technologies that allow high-speed Internet access.

Browser   software on computers that displays webpages. The most common are Internet Explorer, Firefox, and Netscape Navigator.

Cascading Style Sheets (CSS)   file with the formatting characteristics for page elements such as text, objects, and tables.

Chunking   the grouping of text into sentences, paragraphs, sections, and/or topics and/or visuals that relate to each other. These chunks may pertain to one webpage, spread out through different webpages, or used for deciding where links will be placed within the website. The groups or "chunks" can be sorted according to priority to determine where on a website hierarchy the information will appear.

Classified   when a government agency or official has restricted a document from the public.

Code   the instructions in a computer program.

Code of Federal Regulations (CFR)   the set of volumes that contains all federal regulations.

Code or Source View   the "view" feature on many browser windows that uncovers the code within a webpage. In many browser windows, the code can be seen by clicking on the "view" feature on the top menu bar and dragging down to "source."

Codify   to place adopted rules or laws into a body of law, like the *Code of Federal Regulations,* to make it enforceable.

Collaborate   to work together on a common endeavor toward a common end.

Content Inventory   a listing or database of types of information that will be on a website. The Content Inventory can include a **Design Inventory** of graphics, video, multimedia, and audio, as well as a **Technology Inventory** of important technology considerations for the users and the web developers.

Content Management Systems (CMS)   applications that allow a website manager to create, modify, or update content without needing to know programming language or code.

Contextual interviews   informal interviews that take place within the natural setting or situation in which a user does his or her own work.

Copyright   legal protection for creators or owners of literary, dramatic, musical, artistic, and other types of intellectual property, published or unpublished, or online. Government documents and websites are not eligible for copyright protection, although there may be information in them that is eligible for copyright protection.

Cross-computer platform   software that can run on different types of computers. Although browsers tend to display webpages in the same way, there can be display differences that web designers should know such as type faces and colors on different types of computers.

Cultural Context   the historical, political, social, economic, and ethical as well as technological possibilities and constraints in which a paper document, online document, or website is written, edited, designed, and delivered.

Data file   a file of text, webpages, or other information that is created using a software program.

Declassified   a document that was once confidential that has been approved for review by the public.

Discourse community   the members of a group who engage in discourse conventions.

Discourse conventions   the way a group organizes experience, knowledge, or ideas by social interaction and exchange.

Ethics   standards by which human behavior is judged as right or wrong. The word ethics comes from the Greek word **ethos**, which means character.

Ethos   the appearance of credibility by an individual, group, or institution. Credibility is key to whether a message is accepted by an audience.

Executive departments   federal departments that help make up the executive branch: Agriculture, Commerce, Defense, Education, Energy, Health and Human Services, Homeland Security, Housing and Urban Development, Interior, Justice, Labor, State, Transportation, the Treasury, and Veterans Affairs.

Expert audiences   people who are experienced with the subject matters and language used in various genres of technical communication. These audiences require less explanatory information than nonexpert audiences.

External handbooks users   people who use government handbooks to interact with government agencies or to follow government laws or rules.

FAQ   an acronym for frequently asked questions. This is a feature on websites that have become part of their conventional format.

Federal Register   a publication published by the federal government that notifies the public of proposed and adopted rules, grant and contract announcements and awards, and other notices.

File formats   the type of program language or code a file was created or saved in.

File extensions   the last letters at the end of a file name after the dot. Some of the typical file extensions are .doc for documents, .html for webpages, .jpeg, .gif, and .png for images, and .mp3, .wav for audio, .rm for Real Media, .mwv for Windows Media, and .mov for movies.

Format   the general makeup of something printed or of a website.

Genre   the writing and design conventions of documents and websites. Genres are categories or forms into which documents and websites are grouped together based on written and visual characteristics they have in common. Genres' predictable forms and consistency aid in reading comprehension and efficiency, but genres can change over time.

Government contractors   individuals or organizations who make legal agreements or contracts with government organizations for goods or services.

Government grants   sums of money provided to beneficiaries, including other government entities, private businesses, researchers and students, nonprofit organizations, and other organizations and individuals willing to provide goods and services to the public on behalf of government agencies.

Government handbooks   documents that advise the public about how to abide by government rules and laws and how to take part in services provided by the government agencies.

Grants-in-aid   grants transferred from one government agency to another government agency.

Grant proposals   the genre of technical communication used to convince funding sources (both government agencies and private donors) that a project can be implemented and meets the objectives of the funding organizations.

Headings   text styles that can be applied from largest to smallest point or inch sizes. In style sheets, heading designations create consistency in document and/or website design.

Homepage   the first page of a website and the one most users reach first.

Human-computer interface   the field that focuses on how humans beings interact with computer technology.

HTML (hypertext markup language)   the series of tags or code used on the Internet to link between webpages and websites and to structure text, multimedia, and graphic elements within webpages.

Information architecture   the structuring of information and data for websites. Ideas about the way information and data should connect together by webpages go from the conceptual into hierarchical diagrams and then into prototypes.

Internal handbooks users   people employed or contracted by the government agencies who use government handbooks to do government work.

Intellectual property   the concepts and ideas of the human mind that become tangible in shapes such as literary works, music, performance, distinctive designs, paintings, and much more. Laws about intellectual property cover protection such as copyrights, patents, trademarks, and trade secrets, as well as other areas.

Java   a programming language that incorporates interactive features to webpages.

Jpeg (Joint Photographic Experts Group)   the file format for saving images and commonly used for images on websites.

Keywords   words that refer to the content of a website. They are in the head section of the site and are the ones that many search engines match for users' inquiries.

Laws   legally binding standards enacted by city councils, state legislatures, and Congress.

Layout   the plan, arrangement, or organization of text and design features of a document or websites.

Legal and ethical inventory   a list of important legal matters and ethical considerations regarding the writing, editing, designing, and distribution of document or development and maintenance of a website. The legal and ethical inventory can be part of the agency or organization's style guide.

Links   the paths by which webpages are connected, and the origin of the link is where users click to move to the next page.

Memorandums of understanding   memorandums drafted to confirm an agreement or collaboration between different government agencies.

Meta tags   codes that are in the head section of a webpage and include keywords and descriptions. Users cannot see the meta tags on webpages, but search engines look for them to answer users' inquiries.

Nodes   chunks of content that generally form the basis for webpages. Nodes can be pages that open sections of websites.

Node-link diagrams   representations of how webpages are linked.

Non-expert audiences   people who are inexperienced with the subject matters and language used in various genres of technical communication. These audiences require more explanatory information than expert audiences.

Nonprofit organizations   groups, institutions, or corporations in which no individual or owner can share in the profits of the organization. The goal of a nonprofit organization is not to make a profit but rather to assist individuals or promote causes. These organizations are typically exempt from taxes. Nonprofit organizations are a wide, diverse group from advocacy to charity to church to recreational groups.

Ordered list   a group of items that need to be placed in a specific order. The opposite is unordered list.

Passive voice   one of the two "voices" of verbs—active and passive.

Passive voice sentence   construction of a sentence that is useful when the receiver of the action is the more important than the doer of the action or when the doer of the action is unknown or the writer wishes to keep the doer from being revealed. (See **Active Voice**.)

Personas   fictional characters whose personal characteristics, demographic information, and professional needs represent users of a government website.

Plain Language   communication an audience can understand the first time they read or hear it, according to the government Plain Language website. Written material is in plain language if an audience can find what they need, understand what they find, and use what they find to meet their needs (http://www.plainlanguage.gov/whatisPL/index.cfm).

Plagiarism   when someone uses the ideas, words, music, design, and any other intellectual property of someone else and passes it off as his or her own work.

Although plagiarism is not a legal matter, per se, acts of plagiarism are used in court cases regarding copyright violations.

Policies various types of government mandated and agreed-upon requirements, including federal, state, county, and local rules and laws.

Policy memorandums government-initiated documents used to inform policy development, policy evaluation, and policy implementation at the local, state, and federal levels. Policy memorandums are written by government agency staff and officials within and across government agencies.

Policy reports government-initiated reports that explain what happens to policy initiatives, why policy issues occur, if and how policy should be changed, and how to implement new policy to prevent problems.

Portable Document Format (PDF) a file format developed by the Adobe Corporation and used for documents that are electronically distributed. PDFs go across computer platforms.

Program file the file within software programs that allows users to create documents, webpages, etc.

Proposal Guidelines the specific instructions and criteria in request for applications and request for proposals that aid proposal writers in their efforts and define the scope of the proposal.

Public comments any written or oral feedback the public provides to government agencies regarding any proposed rule changes.

Public comment periods dates published in the *Federal Register* or state registers to inform the public of how much time is available to give agencies feedback on proposed rule changes.

Regulations See **Rules**.

Request for Applications (RFAs) documents written by government employees to solicit grant proposals and to present potential grant applicants with the guidelines for the written proposal.

Request for Proposals (RFPs) See **RFA**.

Repeal to remove or rescind a rule so that it is no longer enforceable.

Rule Preamble the explanatory information published in the *Federal Register* or state registers that precedes the text of the proposed, adopted, or repealed rule. The rule preamble includes a rationale for the rule changes and discussion of the legal, fiscal, and technological impacts of these changes. Rule preambles also include public comments and the appropriate agency's response to public comments.

Rules local, state, and federal policies written and approved by governmental and administrative agencies to protect the various interests of citizens of their constiuents.

Sans-serif fonts characters of typefaces that do not have the small strokes (also called "feet") at the bottom of them. Most text today on websites is in sans-serif fonts. Common sans-serif fonts are Arial and Verdana.

Serif fonts characters of typefaces that do have the small strokes (also called "feet") at the bottom of them. Most text today on websites is in sans-serif fonts, while text in larger groups like on documents is in serif fonts. Common serif fonts are Times Roman and Century Schoolbook.

Single source publishing   the production of a single file for use in a variety of formats. Single-source publishing increases efficiency by decreasing the duplication of work required to produce the same document in different formats.

Site index   an alphabetical list of keywords on a website that often are linked to the part of the website to which the words refer.

Site map   the diagrammatic presentation of how webpages relate to each other. However, "site map" features can also be found on websites, typically the homepage, for users to see what content sections are available on the site.

Site Specifications   lists or defines the scope of the content, schedule, budget, and technical aspects of the website.

Stakeholders   individuals and/or groups affected by a government communication, who thus have a "stake" or vested interest in what happens or what could happen as a result of the communication.

Style   the unique and personal way a writer puts together words that create his or her particular writing voice.

Style guides   handbooks that contain agreed-upon writing standards and formatting for writing, document design, and websites.

Style sheets   documents showing the collection of choices made about the mechanics of spelling, abbreviations, numbers, etc., for a document or website.

Subject matter expert (SME)   a type of stakeholder employed by federal and state agencies to write rules because of their knowledge of issues addressed in a rule. In both the disciplines of technical communication and public policy, the person with content-area expertise is referred to as a subject matter expert.

Tables   graphic grids with rows and columns that can be used to present tabular data or used as a basic design tool for webpage layout.

Technology Inventory   a comprehensive as possible list of the potential and limits of your own software and hardware, and that of your users.

Template   a predetermined design or pattern used as a guide for document or website creation. Users can create their own templates or use those commercial software programs often offer.

Tone   the way words are put together to create an impression by readers of the writer's attitude toward them or others.

Universal Resource Locator (URL)   an official website or webpage address on the Internet.

Usability testing   a study of how well people are able to use some human-made object, such as a computer, device, and/or able to comprehend text, information, and messages within a document or website.

Web content   generally refers to all the text, images, graphics, multimedia on a website or webpage.

Webpage   the name of a collection of text and images in html format that constitutes a page of a website.

Website   a group of webpages connected to the Internet that users can view online.

White space   the area of a document or webpage in which there are no graphics or text. Good design includes appropriate use of white space.

Wireframe   the visual representation of all the elements of one webpage from a website.

Wizards   help features in software programs that assist users through a process that would otherwise be complex. Users typically click through a series of steps in which they answer questions to complete a task.

World Wide Web Consortium (W3C)   a group of technical staff and volunteers over the world who establish standards, create guidelines, and make recommendations about web technologies so they are compatible with each other. The consortium has best practices for websites that include voluntary standards and guidelines for accessibility. The consortium website is http://www.w3.org/Consortium/.

WYSIWYG   an acronym for What You See is What You Get, meaning that as you are designing a webpage, it will appear the same in a browser window.

NAME INDEX

SUBJECT INDEX